Clifford Stoessel
Technical I.A.

MATHEMATICAL TEXTS

FOR COLLEGES

EDITED BY

PERCEY F. SMITH, Ph. D.

PROFESSOR OF MATHEMATICS IN THE SHEFFIELD
SCIENTIFIC SCHOOL OF YALE UNIVERSITY

PLANE AND SPHERICAL TRIGONOMETRY

AND FOUR-PLACE TABLES

BY WILLIAM ANTHONY GRANVILLE, Ph.D., LL.D.
FORMERLY PRESIDENT OF GETTYSBURG COLLEGE

REVISED BY

PERCEY F. SMITH, Ph.D.
Professor of Mathematics in Yale University

AND

JAMES S. MIKESH, B. A.
Master in Mathematics in Lawrenceville School

GINN AND COMPANY
BOSTON · NEW YORK · CHICAGO · LONDON · ATLANTA · DALLAS · COLUMBUS · SAN FRANCISCO

The Athenæum Press
GINN AND COMPANY · PRO-
PRIETORS · BOSTON · U.S.A.

8

PREFACE

In revising Granville's *Plane and Spherical Trigonometry* the authors have kept in mind the features which have made the Granville textbooks popular with teachers and students, namely, simplicity and clearness of exposition, an abundance of examples worked out in the text, and a large variety of problems covering a wide range of applications. Such changes as have been made in the text are mainly for the purpose of change in emphasis. In the revision this emphasis is placed more on the trigonometric functions as such, dissociated from a right triangle. Every effort has been made to present this functional aspect in a clear and simple manner. Following this exposition there will be found in Chapters IV and V applications both with and without logarithms. Then follows a chapter on trigonometric analysis, in which the treatment of trigonometric identities and equations has been revised.

The references in the text, as in the original edition, are to *Four-Place Tables*, by the same authors. These tables differ from Granville's *Four-Place Tables* in two respects. The table of natural values of trigonometric functions, originally a one-page table giving values of the functions for angles at intervals of one degree, has been replaced by two tables (IV and V) which give the values of the sine, cosine, tangent, and cotangent for angles at intervals of ten minutes. In the revised tables, also, there is included some explanation of the use of the tables.

These tables as originally published were unique in making possible uniform four-figure accuracy in calculations. Emphasis is again placed on this feature, and in the new tables (IV and V) either the values are given to four significant figures or methods by which four significant figures can be obtained are explained.

As in the original edition, problems are given in which angles are expressed in degrees and minutes as well as in degrees and decimal parts of a degree. The choice between the methods of angular measurement is left to the teacher. The tables provide for either set of problems.

In the section on spherical trigonometry only slight changes have been made. The authors see no reason for departing from the simple and direct presentation which appeared in the first edition.

s

CONTENTS

PLANE TRIGONOMETRY

CHAPTER I. THE TRIGONOMETRIC FUNCTIONS

CHAPTER II. FUNDAMENTAL RELATIONS; REDUCTION FORMULAS

CHAPTER VI. TRIGONOMETRIC ANALYSIS

CHAPTER VII. ACUTE ANGLES NEAR 0° OR 90°

s

SPHERICAL TRIGONOMETRY

CHAPTER I. RIGHT SPHERICAL TRIANGLES

CHAPTER II. OBLIQUE SPHERICAL TRIANGLES

s

CONTENTS

FOUR–PLACE TABLES

TABLE I

TABLE II

TABLE III

TABLE IV

TABLE V

PLANE TRIGONOMETRY

CHAPTER I

THE TRIGONOMETRIC FUNCTIONS

1. Trigonometry. In trigonometry we are concerned with the study of certain magnitudes, called the *trigonometric functions*. To define these functions, and to make elementary applications of them, is the objective of this chapter.

2. Variables; constants. The magnitudes involved in a problem are either variables or constants. The distinction between them must be made precise. A *variable* is a quantity to which an unlimited number of values can be assigned in a problem. Variables are usually denoted by the later letters of the alphabet, as x, y, z.

A *constant* is a quantity whose value remains unchanged in a problem. *Numerical* or *absolute constants* retain the same values in all problems, as 2, 5, $\sqrt{7}$, π, etc. *Arbitrary constants* are constants whose values are arbitrary, but fixed in any particular problem. These are usually denoted by the earlier letters of the alphabet, as a, b, c, etc.

3. Functions. A *function of a variable* is a magnitude whose value is always determined when a suitable value of the variable is given. The *area* of a square is a function of the *length* of a side, and the *volume* of a sphere is a function of its *diameter*. Similarly, the trinomial $x^2 - 7x - 6$ is a *function of* x because its value is determined when a value of x is given. In the trigonometric functions the variable is the measure of an angle, and the values of these functions are always determined when the measure of the angle is given. For the present we are to think of angle measurement as expressed in degrees. Later we shall consider a second method of measuring angles.

4. Trigonometric functions of an acute angle. It is assumed that the student is familiar with the notion of the *angle between two lines* as presented in elementary plane geometry. In this article, we confine ourselves to the consideration of acute angles.

1

Let EAD be an angle less than 90°, that is an acute angle. From B, any point in one of the sides of the angle, draw a perpendicular to the other side, thus forming a right triangle, as ABC. Let the capital letters A, B, C denote the measures of the angles and the small letters a, b, c the lengths of the corresponding opposite sides in the right triangle.* We know in a general way from geometry that the sides and angles of this triangle are mutually dependent. Trigonometry begins by showing the exact nature of this dependence, and for this purpose

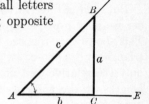

employs the *ratios of the sides*. These ratios are called *trigonometric functions*. The six trigonometric functions of any acute angle, as A, are denoted as follows:

$\sin A$,   read   "sine of A";

$\cos A$,   read   "cosine of A";

$\tan A$,   read   "tangent of A";

$\csc A$,   read   "cosecant of A";

$\sec A$,   read   "secant of A";

$\cot A$,   read   "cotangent of A."

These trigonometric functions (ratios) are defined as follows (see figure):

(1) $\sin A = \dfrac{\text{opposite side}}{\text{hypotenuse}}\left(=\dfrac{a}{c}\right);$ (4) $\csc A = \dfrac{\text{hypotenuse}}{\text{opposite side}}\left(=\dfrac{c}{a}\right);$

(2) $\cos A = \dfrac{\text{adjacent side}}{\text{hypotenuse}}\left(=\dfrac{b}{c}\right);$ (5) $\sec A = \dfrac{\text{hypotenuse}}{\text{adjacent side}}\left(=\dfrac{c}{b}\right);$

(3) $\tan A = \dfrac{\text{opposite side}}{\text{adjacent side}}\left(=\dfrac{a}{b}\right);$ (6) $\cot A = \dfrac{\text{adjacent side}}{\text{opposite side}}\left(=\dfrac{b}{a}\right).$

The essential fact that the numerical value of any one of these functions depends upon the *magnitude* only of the angle A, that is, is independent of the point B from which the perpendicular upon the other side is let fall, is easily established.

For, let B' be any other point in AD, and B'' any point in AE. Draw the perpendiculars $B'C'$ and $B''C''$ to AE and AD respectively. The three triangles ABC, $AB'C'$, $AB''C''$ are mutually equi-

---

* Unless otherwise stated the hypotenuse of a right triangle will always be denoted by c and the right angle by C.

angular since they are right-angled and have a common angle A. Therefore they are similar, and we have

$$\frac{BC}{AB} = \frac{B'C'}{AB'} = \frac{B''C''}{AB''}.$$

But each of these ratios defines the *sine of A*. In the same manner we may prove this property for each of the other functions. This shows that the size of the right triangle we choose is immaterial; only the relative and not the actual lengths of the sides of the triangle are of importance.

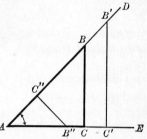

The student should also note that every one of the six ratios on page 2 will change in value when the angle A changes in magnitude.

These functions (ratios) are of fundamental importance in the study of trigonometry. In fact, no progress in the subject is possible without a thorough knowledge of the above six definitions. They are easy to memorize if the student will notice that the three in the first column are reciprocals, respectively, of those directly opposite in the second column. For

$$\text{(1)}\quad \sin A = \frac{a}{c} = \frac{1}{\frac{c}{a}} = \frac{1}{\csc A};$$
$$\text{(4)}\quad \csc A = \frac{c}{a} = \frac{1}{\frac{a}{c}} = \frac{1}{\sin A};$$

$$\text{(2)}\quad \cos A = \frac{b}{c} = \frac{1}{\frac{c}{b}} = \frac{1}{\sec A};$$
$$\text{(5)}\quad \sec A = \frac{c}{b} = \frac{1}{\frac{b}{c}} = \frac{1}{\cos A};$$

$$\text{(3)}\quad \tan A = \frac{a}{b} = \frac{1}{\frac{b}{a}} = \frac{1}{\cot A};$$
$$\text{(6)}\quad \cot A = \frac{b}{a} = \frac{1}{\frac{a}{b}} = \frac{1}{\tan A}.$$

Let us apply the definitions (1) to (6) inclusive to the acute angle B in the figure on page 2. Then opposite side $= AC = b$, adjacent side $= BC = a$. Hence

$$\text{(7)}\quad \sin B = \frac{b}{c};$$
$$\text{(10)}\quad \csc B = \frac{c}{b};$$

$$\text{(8)}\quad \cos B = \frac{a}{c};$$
$$\text{(11)}\quad \sec B = \frac{c}{a};$$

$$\text{(9)}\quad \tan B = \frac{b}{a};$$
$$\text{(12)}\quad \cot B = \frac{a}{b}.$$

Comparing these with the functions of the angle A, we see that

$$\sin A = \cos B; \qquad\qquad \csc A = \sec B;$$
$$\cos A = \sin B; \qquad\qquad \sec A = \csc B;$$
$$\tan A = \cot B; \qquad\qquad \cot A = \tan B.$$

Since $A + B = 90°$ (that is, A and B are complementary), the above results may be stated in compact form as follows:

Theorem. *A function of an acute angle is equal to the co-function* of its complementary acute angle.*

The statement of the theorem may be written

$$\sin A = \cos (90° - A); \qquad\qquad \csc A = \sec (90° - A);$$
$$\cos A = \sin (90° - A); \qquad\qquad \sec A = \csc (90° - A);$$
$$\tan A = \cot (90° - A); \qquad\qquad \cot A = \tan (90° - A).$$

EXAMPLE 1. Calculate the functions of the angle A in the right triangle where $a = 3$, $b = 4$.

Solution. $c = \sqrt{a^2 + b^2} = \sqrt{9 + 16} = \sqrt{25} = 5.$
Applying (1) to (6) inclusive, p. 2,

$$\sin A = \tfrac{3}{5}; \qquad \csc A = \tfrac{5}{3};$$
$$\cos A = \tfrac{4}{5}; \qquad \sec A = \tfrac{5}{4};$$
$$\tan A = \tfrac{3}{4}; \qquad \cot A = \tfrac{4}{3}.$$

Also find all functions of the angle B, and compare results.

EXAMPLE 2. Calculate the functions of the angle B in the right triangle where $a = 3$, $c = 4$.

Solution. $b = \sqrt{c^2 - a^2} = \sqrt{16 - 9} = \sqrt{7}.$

$$\sin B = \frac{\sqrt{7}}{4} = 0.66; \qquad \csc B = \frac{4}{\sqrt{7}} = \frac{4\sqrt{7}}{7} = 1.51;$$

$$\cos B = \frac{3}{4} = 0.75; \qquad \sec B = \frac{4}{3} = 1.33;$$

$$\tan B = \frac{\sqrt{7}}{3} = 0.88; \qquad \cot B = \frac{3}{\sqrt{7}} = \frac{3\sqrt{7}}{7} = 1.14.$$

Also find all functions of the angle A, and compare results.

---

* Sine and cosine are called co-functions of each other. Similarly tangent and cotangent, also secant and cosecant, are co-functions.

EXAMPLE 3. Calculate the functions of the angle A in the right triangle where $a = 2\,mn$, $b = m^2 - n^2$.

Solution.

$$c = \sqrt{a^2 + b^2} = \sqrt{4\,m^2n^2 + m^4 - 2\,m^2n^2 + n^4}$$
$$= \sqrt{m^4 + 2\,m^2n^2 + n^4} = m^2 + n^2.$$

$$\sin A = \frac{2\,mn}{m^2 + n^2}; \qquad \csc A = \frac{m^2 + n^2}{2\,mn};$$

$$\cos A = \frac{m^2 - n^2}{m^2 + n^2}; \qquad \sec A = \frac{m^2 + n^2}{m^2 - n^2};$$

$$\tan A = \frac{2\,mn}{m^2 - n^2}; \qquad \cot A = \frac{m^2 - n^2}{2\,mn}.$$

EXAMPLE 4. In a right triangle we have given $\sin A = \frac{4}{5}$ and $a = 80$; find c.

Solution. From (1), p. 2, we have

$$\sin A = \frac{a}{c}.$$

Substituting the values of $\sin A$ and a that are given, there results

$$\frac{4}{5} = \frac{80}{c};$$

and solving, $\qquad\qquad c = 100. \ Ans.$

5. Functions of 45°, 30°, 60°. These angles occur very frequently in problems that are usually solved by trigonometric methods. It is therefore important to find the values of the trigonometric functions of these angles and to memorize the results.

a. To find the functions of 45°. Draw an isosceles right triangle, as ABC. Then

$$\text{angle } A = \text{angle } B = 45°.$$

Since the relative and not the actual lengths of the sides are of importance, we may assign to the sides any lengths we please satisfying the condition that the right triangle shall be isosceles.

Let us choose the lengths of the short sides as unity, that is, let $a = 1$ and $b = 1$.

Then $c = \sqrt{a^2 + b^2} = \sqrt{2}$, and we get

$$\sin 45° = \frac{1}{\sqrt{2}} = \frac{\sqrt{2}}{2}; \qquad\qquad \csc 45° = \sqrt{2};$$

$$\cos 45° = \frac{1}{\sqrt{2}} = \frac{\sqrt{2}}{2}; \qquad\qquad \sec 45° = \sqrt{2};$$

$$\tan 45° = 1; \qquad\qquad\qquad \cot 45° = 1,$$

b. To find the functions of 30° and 60°. Draw an equilateral triangle, as ABD. Drop the perpendicular BC from B to AD, and consider the triangle ABC, where

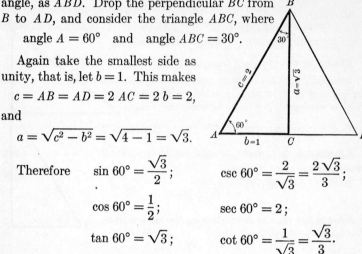

angle $A = 60°$ and angle $ABC = 30°$.

Again take the smallest side as unity, that is, let $b = 1$. This makes

$$c = AB = AD = 2\,AC = 2\,b = 2,$$

and

$$a = \sqrt{c^2 - b^2} = \sqrt{4 - 1} = \sqrt{3}.$$

Therefore
$$\sin 60° = \frac{\sqrt{3}}{2}; \qquad \csc 60° = \frac{2}{\sqrt{3}} = \frac{2\sqrt{3}}{3};$$

$$\cos 60° = \frac{1}{2}; \qquad \sec 60° = 2;$$

$$\tan 60° = \sqrt{3}; \qquad \cot 60° = \frac{1}{\sqrt{3}} = \frac{\sqrt{3}}{3}.$$

Similarly, from the same triangle,

$$\sin 30° = \frac{1}{2}; \qquad \csc 30° = 2;$$

$$\cos 30° = \frac{\sqrt{3}}{2}; \qquad \sec 30° = \frac{2}{\sqrt{3}} = \frac{2\sqrt{3}}{3};$$

$$\tan 30° = \frac{1}{\sqrt{3}} = \frac{\sqrt{3}}{3}; \qquad \cot 30° = \sqrt{3}.$$

Writing these results in tabulated form,* we have

Angle	sin	cos	tan	cot	sec	csc
30°	$\frac{1}{2}$	$\frac{\sqrt{3}}{2}$	$\frac{\sqrt{3}}{3}$	$\sqrt{3}$	$\frac{2\sqrt{3}}{3}$	2
45°	$\frac{\sqrt{2}}{2}$	$\frac{\sqrt{2}}{2}$	1	1	$\sqrt{2}$	$\sqrt{2}$
60°	$\frac{\sqrt{3}}{2}$	$\frac{1}{2}$	$\sqrt{3}$	$\frac{\sqrt{3}}{3}$	2	$\frac{2\sqrt{3}}{3}$

* To aid the memory we observe that the numbers in the first (or sine) column are respectively $\sqrt{1}$, $\sqrt{2}$, $\sqrt{3}$, each divided by 2.

The second (or cosine) column is formed by reversing the order in the first column.

The third (or tangent) column is formed by dividing the numbers in the first column by the respective numbers in the second column.

The student should become very familiar with the **45° right triangle** and the 30°, 60° right triangle. Instead of memorizing the above table we may then get the values of the functions directly from a mental picture of these right triangles.

EXAMPLE. Given a right triangle where $A = 60°$, $a = 100$; find c.

Solution. Since we know A (and therefore also any function of A), and the cosecant of A involves a, which is known, and c, which is wanted, we can find c by using the formula

$$\csc A = \frac{c}{a}. \qquad \text{By (4), p. 2}$$

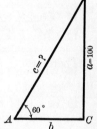

Substituting $a = 100$ and $\csc A = \csc 60° = \dfrac{2\sqrt{3}}{3}$ from the above table, we have

$$c = \frac{200\sqrt{3}}{3} = 115.5. \quad Ans.$$

What is the value of B? Following the method illustrated above, show that $b = 57.7$.

PROBLEMS

Only right triangles are referred to in the following problems. Answers are given in the order sine, cosine, tangent.

1. Find the functions of the angle A, having given $a = 8$, $b = 15$.
   Ans. $\sin A = \frac{8}{17}$, $\cos A = \frac{15}{17}$, $\tan A = \frac{8}{15}$, etc.

2. Find the functions of the angle B, having given $b = 5$, $c = 13$.

3. Find the functions of the angle B, having given $a = 0.6$, $b = 0.8$.
   Ans. $\sin B = 0.8$, $\cos B = 0.6$, $\tan B = 1.3$, etc.

4. Find the functions of the angle A, having given $b = 2$, $c = \sqrt{11}$.

5. Find the functions of the angle B, having given $a = 5$, $c = 7$.
   Ans. $\dfrac{2\sqrt{6}}{7}, \dfrac{5}{7}, \dfrac{2\sqrt{6}}{5}$, etc.

6. Find the functions of the angle A, having given $a = p$, $b = q$.

7. Find the functions of the angle A, having given $a = \sqrt{m^2 + mn}$, $c = m + n$.
   Ans. $\dfrac{\sqrt{m^2 + mn}}{m + n}, \dfrac{\sqrt{mn + n^2}}{m + n}, \dfrac{1}{n}\sqrt{mn}$, etc.

8. Given $\sin A = \frac{3}{5}$, $c = 200.5$; find a.

9. Given $\cos A = 0.44$, $c = 30.5$; find b. *Ans.* 13.42.

10. Given $\tan A = \frac{11}{3}$, $b = \frac{27}{11}$; find c.

11. Given $\tan B = k$, $a = r$; find c. *Ans.* $r\sqrt{k^2 + 1}$.

12. If $b = 2a$, find the functions of A. Why does neither a nor b appear in the answers?

13. The hypotenuse of a right triangle is three times as long as one of its legs. Find the functions of the angle opposite this leg. Why do the answers not depend on the length of this leg?   *Ans.* $\frac{1}{3}, \frac{2\sqrt{2}}{3}, \frac{\sqrt{2}}{4}$, etc.

14. If one leg of a right triangle is 16 and the cotangent of the opposite angle is $\frac{3}{4}$, how long is the other leg?

15. Given $A = 30°$, $a = 25$; find c, B, and b.
     Ans. $c = 50$, $B = 60°$, $b = 25\sqrt{3}$.

16. Given $B = 30°$, $c = 48$; find b, A, and a.

17. Given $B = 45°$, $b = 20$; find c, A, and a.
     Ans. $c = 20\sqrt{2}$, $A = 45°$, $a = 20$.

18. What are the acute angles of a right triangle if one leg is $\sqrt{3}$ times the other leg?

19. In a right triangle the hypotenuse is $\sqrt{2}$ times as long as a leg. What are the acute angles of the triangle?   *Ans.* $45°$, $45°$.

20. If $\sec B = \frac{2}{3}\sqrt{3}$ and $c = 480$, find B, A, a, and b.

21. Find the value of $\sin^2 A + \cos^2 A$ for $A = 30°$; $45°$; $60°$. *Ans.* 1.

22. Prove that $\cos 60° = 2\cos^2 30° - 1$.

23. Prove that $\tan 30° = \dfrac{\sec 60°}{(\sec 60° + 1)\csc 60°}$.

24. Express each of the following functions as a function of the complementary angle:

a. $\tan 30°$.   *d.* $\sin 33° \, 33'$.
b. $\cos 20°$.   *e.* $\csc 72° \, 17.4'$.
c. $\sec 81°$.

25. Prove that
a. $\sin 32° - \cos 58° = 0$.
b. $\csc 12° + \sec 78° = 2\csc 12° = 2\sec 78°$.

26. Find the acute angles, A and B, of a right triangle if $\sin 2A = \cos 3A$.

27. For what acute angle x does $\tan (30° - x)$ equal $\cot (30° + 3x)$?
     Ans. $15°$.

6. Construction of figures; the protractor. When beginning the study of trigonometry it is important that the student should draw the figures connected with the problems as accurately as possible. This not only leads to a better understanding of the problems themselves, but also gives a clearer insight into the meaning of the trigonometric functions and makes it possible to test roughly the accuracy of the results obtained. For this purpose the only instruments necessary are a graduated ruler and a protractor. A protractor is an instrument for measuring and constructing angles. On the inside of the back cover of this book will be found a Granville's Transparent Combined Ruler and Protractor, with directions for use. The ruler is graduated to inches and centimeters and the protractor to degrees. The student is advised to make free use of this instrument.

7. Table of values of the trigonometric functions. In Art. 5 the functions of 30°, 45°, and 60° were found. In more advanced treatises it is shown how to calculate the functions of any acute angle.

We shall now explain how to use the table on page 10, where the values of the trigonometric functions for each degree from 0° to 90° inclusive are correctly given to four (or five) significant figures. These values are called the *natural values* of the trigonometric functions in contradistinction to their logarithms.

In looking up the function of an angle between 0° and 45° inclusive, we look for the angle in the extreme left-hand vertical column. The required value of the function will be found on the same horizontal line with the angle, and in the vertical column having that function for a caption at the top. Thus,

$$\sin 15° = 0.2588,$$

$$\cot 41° = 1.1504, \text{ etc.}$$

Similarly, when looking up the function of an angle between 45° and 90° inclusive we look in the extreme right-hand vertical column. The required value of the function will be found on the same horizontal line with the angle as before, but in the vertical column having that function for a caption at the bottom. Thus,

$$\cos 64° = 0.4384,$$

$$\sec 85° = 11.474, \text{ etc.}$$

PROBLEMS

Using Table A on page 10, find the values of the following functions:

1. sin 28°. *Ans.* 0.4695.		2. tan 42°.
3. cos 67°. *Ans.* 0.3907.		4. cot 81°.
5. sec 3°. *Ans.* 1.0014.		6. tan 73°.
7. csc 46°. *Ans.* 1.3902.		8. cos 46°.

Table A. Natural Values of the Trigonometric Functions

Angle	sin	cos	tan	cot	sec	csc	
0°	.0000	1.0000	.0000	∞	1.0000	∞	90°
1°	.0175	.9998	.0175	57.290	1.0002	57.299	89°
2°	.0349	.9994	.0349	28.636	1.0006	28.654	88°
3°	.0523	.9986	.0524	19.081	1.0014	19.107	87°
4°	.0698	.9976	.0699	14.301	1.0024	14.336	86°
5°	.0872	.9962	.0875	11.430	1.0038	11.474	85°
6°	.1045	.9945	.1051	9.5144	1.0055	9.5668	84°
7°	.1219	.9925	.1228	8.1443	1.0075	8.2055	83°
8°	.1392	.9903	.1405	7.1154	1.0098	7.1853	82°
9°	.1564	.9877	.1584	6.3138	1.0125	6.3925	81°
10°	.1736	.9848	.1763	5.6713	1.0154	5.7588	80°
11°	.1908	.9816	.1944	5.1446	1.0187	5.2408	79°
12°	.2079	.9781	.2126	4.7046	1.0223	4.8097	78°
13°	.2250	.9744	.2309	4.3315	1.0263	4.4454	77°
14°	.2419	.9703	.2493	4.0108	1.0306	4.1336	76°
15°	.2588	.9659	.2679	3.7321	1.0353	3.8637	75°
16°	.2756	.9613	.2867	3.4874	1.0403	3.6280	74°
17°	.2924	.9563	.3057	3.2709	1.0457	3.4203	73°
18°	.3090	.9511	.3249	3.0777	1.0515	3.2361	72°
19°	.3256	.9455	.3443	2.9042	1.0576	3.0716	71°
20°	.3420	.9397	.3640	2.7475	1.0642	2.9238	70°
21°	.3584	.9336	.3839	2.6051	1.0711	2.7904	69°
22°	.3746	.9272	.4040	2.4751	1.0785	2.6695	68°
23°	.3907	.9205	.4245	2.3559	1.0864	2.5593	67°
24°	.4067	.9135	.4452	2.2460	1.0946	2.4586	66°
25°	.4226	.9063	.4663	2.1445	1.1034	2.3662	65°
26°	.4384	.8988	.4877	2.0503	1.1126	2.2812	64°
27°	.4540	.8910	.5095	1.9626	1.1223	2.2027	63°
28°	.4695	.8829	.5317	1.8807	1.1326	2.1301	62°
29°	.4848	.8746	.5543	1.8040	1.1434	2.0627	61°
30°	.5000	.8660	.5774	1.7321	1.1547	2.0000	60°
31°	.5150	.8572	.6009	1.6643	1.1666	1.9416	59°
32°	.5299	.8480	.6249	1.6003	1.1792	1.8871	58°
33°	.5446	.8387	.6494	1.5399	1.1924	1.8361	57°
34°	.5592	.8290	.6745	1.4826	1.2062	1.7883	56°
35°	.5736	.8192	.7002	1.4281	1.2208	1.7434	55°
36°	.5878	.8090	.7265	1.3764	1.2361	1.7013	54°
37°	.6018	.7986	.7536	1.3270	1.2521	1.6616	53°
38°	.6157	.7880	.7813	1.2799	1.2690	1.6243	52°
39°	.6293	.7771	.8098	1.2349	1.2868	1.5890	51°
40°	.6428	.7660	.8391	1.1918	1.3054	1.5557	50°
41°	.6561	.7547	.8693	1.1504	1.3250	1.5243	49°
42°	.6691	.7431	.9004	1.1106	1.3456	1.4945	48°
43°	.6820	.7314	.9325	1.0724	1.3673	1.4663	47°
44°	.6947	.7193	.9657	1.0355	1.3902	1.4396	46°
45°	.7071	.7071	1.0000	1.0000	1.4142	1.4142	45°
	cos	sin	cot	tan	csc	sec	Angle

9. By observing Table A, verify the theorem on page 4.

10. The hypotenuse of a right triangle is greater than either leg. By noting this fact in the definition of the trigonometric functions, tell which functions are always less than 1. Which functions are always greater than 1? Which functions may be either less than or greater than 1? Verify your answers by observing Table A.

11. By observing Table A, tell which of the functions increase in value as the angle increases from 0° to 90°. Which functions decrease?

12. Construct with a protractor the following angles: 10°; 60°; 90°; 35°; 57°; 135°; 111°; 162°.

13. Draw a triangle and measure with a protractor its three angles. Check your measurement by adding the angles.

14. Express in decimal form, to four places, the values of the functions of 30°, 45°, and 60°, and check your results with Table A.

15. With a protractor construct a right triangle in which angle $A = 35°$ and $b = 3.5$ in. Measure a and compute the value of $\dfrac{a}{b}$ to the nearest tenth. Check your result with Table A.

8. Generation of angles. After the preceding discussion of the trigonometric functions of an acute angle, we proceed to the study of trigonometric functions of any angle.

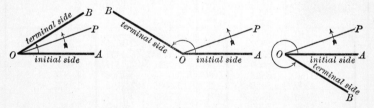

The notion of an angle as usually presented in elementary geometry is not general enough for the purposes of trigonometry. We shall have to deal with positive and negative angles of any magnitude. Such a conception of an angle may be formed as follows:

An angle may be considered as generated by a line which first coincides with one side of the angle, then revolves about the vertex, and finally coincides with the other side.

This line is called the *generating line* of the angle. In its first position it is said to coincide with the *initial side* of the angle, and in its final position with the *terminal side* of the angle.

Thus, the angle *AOB* is generated by the line *OP* revolving about *O* in the direction indicated from the initial side *OA* to the terminal side *OB*.

9. Positive and negative angles. In the figures on page 11 the angles were generated by revolving the generating line *counter-clockwise*; mathematicians have agreed to call such angles *positive*. Below are angles having the same initial and terminal sides as

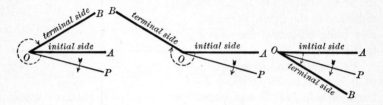

those on page 11, but the *angles are different* since they have been generated by revolving the generating line *clockwise*; such angles are said to be *negative*.

The arcs with arrowheads will be drawn full when indicating a positive angle, and dotted when indicating a negative angle.

10. Angles of any magnitude. Even if two angles have the same initial and the same terminal sides, and have been generated by rotation in the same direction, they may be different in magnitude. Thus, to generate one right angle, the generating line rotates into the position *OB*, as shown in Fig. *a*. If, however, the generating

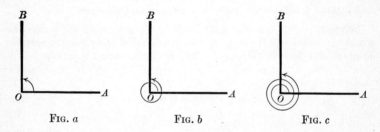

Fig. *a*   Fig. *b*   Fig. *c*

line stops in the position *OB* after making one complete revolution from *OB*, as shown in Fig. *b*, then we have generated an angle of magnitude five right angles; or, if two complete revolutions were first made, as shown in Fig. *c*, then we have generated an angle of magnitude nine right angles; and so on indefinitely. This also shows that positive angles may have any magnitude whatever. Similarly, by making complete revolutions clockwise, it is seen that negative angles may have any magnitude.

Thus, the minute hand of a clock generates − 4 right angles every hour, that is, − 96 right angles every day.

11. The four quadrants. It is customary to divide the plane about the vertex of an angle into four parts called *quadrants*, by passing two mutually perpendicular lines through the vertex. Thus, if O is the vertex, the different quadrants are named as indicated in the figure, **the initial side being horizontal and drawn to the right.**

Second Quadrant	*First Quadrant*
Third Quadrant	*Fourth Quadrant*

O *initial side* A

An angle is said to be (or lie) in a certain quadrant when its terminal side lies in that quadrant.

In the figures of Arts. 8 and 9, only the least positive and negative angles having the given initial and terminal sides are indicated by the arcs. As a matter of fact the number of positive and negative angles which have the same initial and terminal sides is unlimited. The following examples will illustrate this statement.

EXAMPLE 1. Show that $1000°$ lies in the fourth quadrant.

Solution. $1000° = 720° + 280° = 2 \times 360° + 280°$. Hence the generating line makes two complete revolutions in the positive direction and $280°$ beyond, and the terminal side of $280°$ lies in the fourth quadrant.

EXAMPLE 2. Show that $-568°$ lies in the second quadrant.

Solution. $-568° = -360° - 208°$. Hence the generating line makes one complete revolution in the negative direction and $208°$ beyond in the negative direction, and the terminal side of $-208°$ lies in the second quadrant.

PROBLEMS

In what quadrant is each of the following angles:

1. $225°$.   *Ans.* III.   **2.** $120°$.

3. $-315°$.   *Ans.* I.   **4.** $-240°$.

5. $651°$.   *Ans.* IV.   **6.** $-150°$.

7. $-75°$.   *Ans.* IV.   **8.** $-1200°$.

9. $540°$.   *Ans.* Between II and III.   **10.** $420°$.

11. $-910°$.   *Ans.* II.   **12.** $-300°$.

13. $1500°$.   *Ans.* I.   **14.** $810°$.

15. $-540°$.   *Ans.* Between II and III.   **16.** $537°$.

Give one positive and one negative angle each of which shall have the same initial side and same terminal side as each of the following angles:

17. 45°. *Ans.* 405°, − 315°.   **18.** − 30°.

19. 120°. *Ans.* 480°, − 240°.   **20.** − 200°.

21. − 390°. *Ans.* 330°, − 30°.   **22.** 340°.

12. Rectangular coördinates of a point in a plane. In order to define the functions of angles not acute, it is convenient to introduce the notion of *coördinates.* Let $X'X$ be a horizontal line and $Y'Y$ a line perpendicular to it at the point O. Any point in the plane of these lines (as P) is determined by its *distance* and *direction* from each of the perpendiculars $X'X$ and $Y'Y$. Its distance from $Y'Y$ (as $NP = a$) is called the *abscissa* of the point, and its distance from $X'X$ (as $MP = b$) is called the *ordinate* of the point.

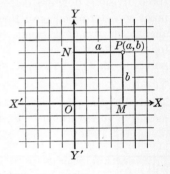

Abscissas measured to the *right* of $Y'Y$ are *positive.*

Abscissas measured to the *left* of $Y'Y$ are *negative.*

Ordinates measured *above* $X'X$ are *positive.*

Ordinates measured *below* $X'X$ are *negative.*

The abscissa and ordinate taken together are called the *coördinates* of the point and are denoted by the symbol (a, b).

The lines $X'X$ and $Y'Y$ are called the *axes of coördinates,* $X'X$ being the *axis of abscissas* or the *axis of X,* and $Y'Y$ the *axis of ordinates* or the *axis of Y*; and the point O is called the *origin of coördinates.*

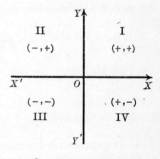

The axes of coördinates divide the plane into four parts called quadrants (just as in the preceding section), the figure indicating the proper signs of the coördinates in the different quadrants.

To *plot a point* is to locate its position from its coördinates. The most convenient way to do this is to first count off from O along $X'X$ a number of divisions equal to the abscissa, to the right or left according as the abscissa is positive or negative. Then from the point so determined count off a number of divisions equal to the ordinate, upward or downward according as the ordinate is positive or negative. The work of plotting points is much simplified by the use of *coördinate* or *plotting paper*, constructed by ruling off the plane into equal squares, the sides being parallel to the axes. Thus, to plot the point $(4, -3)$, count off four divisions from O on the axis of X to the right, and then three divisions downward from the point so determined on a line parallel to the axis of Y. Similarly, the following figures show the plotted points $(-2, 3)$, $(-3, -4)$, $(0, 3)$.

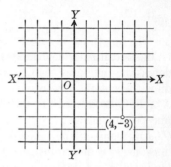

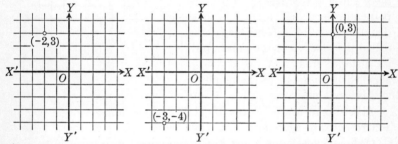

PROBLEMS

1. a. Plot accurately the points $(5, 4)$, $(-3, 4)$, $(-2, -4)$, $(5, -1)$, $(6, 0)$, $(-5, 0)$, $(0, 4)$, $(0, -3)$.

b. What is the distance of each point from the origin?

Ans. $\sqrt{41}$, 5, $2\sqrt{5}$, etc.

2. Plot accurately the points $(1, 1)$, $(-1, -1)$, $(-1, 1)$, $(\sqrt{3}, 1)$, $(\sqrt{3}, -1)$, $(-\sqrt{3}, -1)$, and find the distance of each one from the origin.

3. Plot accurately the points $(\sqrt{2}, 0)$, $(-5, -10)$, $(3, -2\sqrt{2})$, $(10, 3)$, $(0, 0)$, $(0, -\sqrt{5})$, $(3, -5)$, $(-4, 5)$.

13. Trigonometric functions of any angle defined. In Art. 4 the six trigonometric functions were defined for acute angles. Now, however, we shall give definitions which will apply to any angle whatever, and which agree with the definitions already given for acute angles.

Take the origin of coördinates as the vertex of the angle and the initial side as the axis of X. Draw an angle XOB in each quadrant,

Let P be any point on the terminal side OB of the angle and let its coördinates be (x, y). In all the figures,

$$OQ = x, \quad QP = y, \quad OP = r,$$

and $$\overline{OP}^2 = \overline{OQ}^2 + \overline{QP}^2.$$

The length OP is called the *distance*.

Substituting and extracting the square root, we get

(1) $$r = + \sqrt{x^2 + y^2}.$$

As indicated in (1), r is always a positive number.

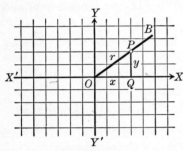

Angle in first quadrant

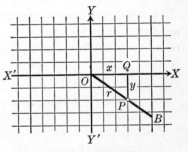

Angle in second quadrant

Angle in third quadrant   Angle in fourth quadrant

Denoting the angle in each figure by XOB, the definitions of the functions are as follows:

(7) $\sin XOB = \dfrac{\text{ordinate}}{\text{distance}} = \dfrac{y}{r}$;   (10) $\cot XOB = \dfrac{\text{abscissa}}{\text{ordinate}} = \dfrac{x}{y}$;

(8) $\cos XOB = \dfrac{\text{abscissa}}{\text{distance}} = \dfrac{x}{r}$;   (11) $\sec XOB = \dfrac{\text{distance}}{\text{abscissa}} = \dfrac{r}{x}$;

(9) $\tan XOB = \dfrac{\text{ordinate}}{\text{abscissa}} = \dfrac{y}{x}$;   (12) $\csc XOB = \dfrac{\text{distance}}{\text{ordinate}} = \dfrac{r}{y}$.

These definitions as applied to an angle XOB in the first quadrant agree with those in Art. 4. Two facts must be noted in the above definitions:

1. The value of each of the above ratios is *independent of the position* of P on OB. (Proof as in Art. 4.)

2. The values of the above functions depend in any case *only upon the position of the terminal side OB (the initial side OX being fixed).* That is, taking OX as the common initial side, for all angles with the same terminal side OB the functions will have the same values. Thus, for example, the angles $40°$, $400°$, $-320°$, have the same functions. The definitions (**7**) to (**12**) are fundamental and should be memorized.

Three other functions used are the versed sine (vers), coversed sine (covers), and haver sine (hav). These are defined by the equations vers $XOB = 1 - \cos XOB$; covers $XOB = 1 - \sin XOB$; hav $XOB = \frac{1}{2}(1 - \cos XOB) = \frac{1}{2}$ vers XOB.

From the definitions (**7**) to (**12**), it follows, as in Art. 4, that

the sine is the reciprocal of the cosecant;

the tangent is the reciprocal of the cotangent;

the cosine is the reciprocal of the secant.

14. Algebraic signs of the trigonometric functions. Bearing in mind the rule for the algebraic signs of the abscissas and ordinates of points given in Art. 12, and remembering that the distance OP $(= r)$ is always positive, we see at once, from the definitions of the trigonometric functions given in the last article, that

*In **Quadrant I all the functions** are positive.*
*In **Quadrant II sin** and **csc** are positive; all the rest are negative.*
*In **Quadrant III tan** and **cot** are positive; all the rest are negative.*
*In **Quadrant IV cos** and **sec** are positive; all the rest are negative.*

These results are also exhibited in the following table, which should be memorized:

Function	Quadrant I	Quadrant II	Quadrant III	Quadrant IV
Sine Cosecant $\Big\}\cdots$	+	+	−	−
Cosine Secant $\Big\}\cdots\cdots$	+	−	−	+
Tangent Cotangent $\Big\}\cdots$	+	−	+	−

15. Applications. In Art. 5 the functions of 30°, 45°, and 60° were found. From these values the functions of many angles may be derived.

EXAMPLE 1. Find the functions of 150°, 210°, and 330°.

Solution. We note that (see figure)

$$\angle XOB_2 = 150° = 180° - 30° = 180° - \angle XOB_1,$$
$$\angle XOB_3 = 210° = 180° + 30° = 180° + \angle XOB_1,$$
$$\angle XOB_4 = 330° = 360° - 30° = 360° - \angle XOB_1.$$

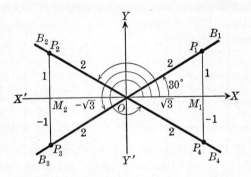

Take $OP_1 = OP_2 = OP_3 = OP_4 = 2$. Then the rt. $\triangle OM_1P_1$, OM_2P_2, OM_2P_3, OM_1P_4 are congruent. (Why?)

By Art. 5, the coördinates of P_1, P_2, P_3, P_4 are

$$P_1(\sqrt{3}, 1), \ P_2(-\sqrt{3}, 1), \ P_3(-\sqrt{3}, -1), \ P_4(\sqrt{3}, -1).$$

Then by (7) to (12), Art. 13, we find the table below.

Angle	sin	cos	tan	cot	sec	csc
30°	$\dfrac{1}{2}$	$\dfrac{\sqrt{3}}{2}$	$\dfrac{\sqrt{3}}{3}$	$\sqrt{3}$	$\dfrac{2\sqrt{3}}{3}$	2
150°	$\dfrac{1}{2}$	$-\dfrac{\sqrt{3}}{2}$	$-\dfrac{\sqrt{3}}{3}$	$-\sqrt{3}$	$-\dfrac{2\sqrt{3}}{3}$	2
210°	$-\dfrac{1}{2}$	$-\dfrac{\sqrt{3}}{2}$	$\dfrac{\sqrt{3}}{3}$	$\sqrt{3}$	$-\dfrac{2\sqrt{3}}{3}$	-2
330°	$-\dfrac{1}{2}$	$\dfrac{\sqrt{3}}{2}$	$-\dfrac{\sqrt{3}}{3}$	$-\sqrt{3}$	$\dfrac{2\sqrt{3}}{3}$	-2

The values in a column differ only in sign, and this sign is determined by the quadrant in which the angle is placed (Art. 14).

Another type of problem is the following:

Given one function; to construct the terminal sides of all corresponding angles, and to find the values of the other functions.

EXAMPLE 2. Given $\tan A = \frac{2}{3}$.

a. To construct the terminal sides of all the corresponding angles.

Solution. By Art. 14, the angle A lies in the first quadrant or in the third quadrant. By (9), Art. 13, we may write

$$\tan A = \frac{y}{x} = \frac{2}{3} = \frac{-2}{-3}.$$

Hence the terminal side of A in the first quadrant passes through $x = 3$, $y = 2$, as in Fig. *a.*

The terminal side of A in the third quadrant passes through $x = -3$, $y = -2$, as in Fig. *b.*

The corresponding angles are XOB in Fig. *a* and XOB' in Fig. *b.*

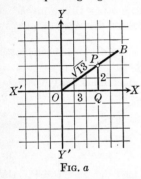
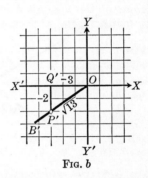

FIG. *a*   FIG. *b*

It is evident that, corresponding to each figure, there are an infinite number of both positive and negative angles differing by multiples of 360° which satisfy the given condition.

b. Find the other functions of A.

Solution. The distance in both figures is

$$r = +\sqrt{13}.$$

Hence we have the following cases:

When A lies in the first quadrant (Fig. *a*),

$$\sin XOB = \frac{2}{\sqrt{13}} = \frac{2\sqrt{13}}{13}; \qquad\qquad \csc XOB = \frac{\sqrt{13}}{2};$$

$$\cos XOB = \frac{3}{\sqrt{13}} = \frac{3\sqrt{13}}{13}; \qquad\qquad \sec XOB = \frac{\sqrt{13}}{3};$$

$$\tan XOB = \frac{2}{3}; \qquad\qquad \cot XOB = \frac{3}{2}.$$

When A lies in the third quadrant (Fig. *b*),

$$\sin XOB' = -\frac{2}{\sqrt{13}} = -\frac{2\sqrt{13}}{13}; \qquad\qquad \csc XOB' = -\frac{\sqrt{13}}{2};$$

$$\cos XOB' = -\frac{3}{\sqrt{13}} = -\frac{3\sqrt{13}}{13}; \qquad\qquad \sec XOB' = -\frac{\sqrt{13}}{3};$$

$$\tan XOB' = \frac{2}{3}; \qquad\qquad \cot XOB' = \frac{3}{2}.$$

Or, denoting by A an angle which satisfies the given condition, we may write down the results in more compact form as follows:

$$\sin A = \pm \frac{2}{\sqrt{13}} = \pm \frac{2\sqrt{13}}{13};\qquad \csc A = \pm \frac{\sqrt{13}}{2};$$

$$\cos A = \pm \frac{3}{\sqrt{13}} = \pm \frac{3\sqrt{13}}{13};\qquad \sec A = \pm \frac{\sqrt{13}}{3};$$

$$\tan A = \frac{2}{3};\qquad \cot A = \frac{3}{2}.$$

The terminal side of an angle is completely determined if the quadrant in which the angle falls is given and if also one of the functions of the angle is known. The other functions are then easily found. Example 2 above illustrates this statement.

EXAMPLE 3. Given $\sin A = -\frac{1}{3}$; construct the terminal sides of all corresponding angles, and find the other functions.

Solution. By Art. 14, the angle A lies in the third or fourth quadrant. By (7), Art. 13, we may write

$$\sin A = \frac{y}{r} = \frac{-1}{3}.$$

Take $y = -1$, $r = 3$. Now $x^2 = r^2 - y^2$. Hence

$$x^2 = 9 - 1 = 8, \quad \text{and} \quad x = \pm 2\sqrt{2}.$$

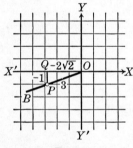

FIG. c

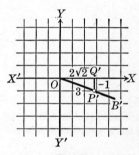

FIG. d

The terminal side of A in the third quadrant passes through $x = -2\sqrt{2}$, $y = -1$, as in Fig. c. The terminal side of A in the fourth quadrant passes through $x = 2\sqrt{2}$, $y = -1$, as in Fig. d.

Then we have

$$\sin A = -\frac{1}{3};\qquad \csc A = -3;$$

$$\cos A = \pm \frac{2\sqrt{2}}{3};\qquad \sec A = \pm \frac{3}{2\sqrt{2}} = \pm \frac{3\sqrt{2}}{4};$$

$$\tan A = \pm \frac{1}{2\sqrt{2}} = \pm \frac{\sqrt{2}}{4};\qquad \cot A = \pm 2\sqrt{2}.$$

EXAMPLE 4. Having given $\cot x = \dfrac{m}{n}$, find all the other functions of x.

Solution. Here we may write, by (10), Art. 13,

$$\cot x = \frac{m}{n} = \frac{-m}{-n} = \frac{\text{abscissa}}{\text{ordinate}},$$

and $\text{distance} = \sqrt{m^2 + n^2}.$

Hence one terminal side is determined by the origin and (m, n), and the other terminal side by the origin and $(-m, -n)$. Therefore

$$\sin x = \pm \frac{n}{\sqrt{m^2 + n^2}}; \qquad\qquad \csc x = \pm \frac{\sqrt{m^2 + n^2}}{n};$$

$$\cos x = \pm \frac{m}{\sqrt{m^2 + n^2}}; \qquad\qquad \sec x = \pm \frac{\sqrt{m^2 + n^2}}{m};$$

$$\tan x = \frac{n}{m}; \qquad\qquad\qquad \cot x = \frac{m}{n}.$$

PROBLEMS

Find the functions of the angle XOP for the following positions of P (OX being the initial side in each case). Express the answers as common fractions in simplest form. Answers are given in the order sine, cosine, tangent.

1. $(-4, 3)$.   *Ans.* $\frac{3}{5}, -\frac{4}{5}, -\frac{3}{4}$, etc.   **2.** $(-12, 9)$.

3. $(-1, -2)$.   *Ans.* $-\dfrac{2\sqrt{5}}{5}, -\dfrac{\sqrt{5}}{5}, 2$, etc.   **4.** $(12, -5)$.

5. $(1, 1)$.   *Ans.* $\dfrac{\sqrt{2}}{2}, \dfrac{\sqrt{2}}{2}, 1$, etc.   **6.** $(-15, 8)$.

7. $(-1, -1)$.   *Ans.* $-\dfrac{\sqrt{2}}{2}, -\dfrac{\sqrt{2}}{2}, 1$, etc.   **8.** $(-8, -6)$.

9. $(-6, 8)$.   *Ans.* $\frac{4}{5}, -\frac{3}{5}, -\frac{4}{3}$, etc.   **10.** $(3, -5)$.

11. What function has for all values of A the same sign (a) as $\sin A$; (b) as $\tan A$; (c) as $\sec A$?

In what quadrant is A for each of the following conditions?

12. $\sin A$ and $\tan A$ both positive.

13. $\sin A$ positive, $\cos A$ negative.   *Ans.* II.

14. $\tan A$ positive, $\sec A$ negative.

15. $\cos A$ negative, $\cot A$ negative.   *Ans.* II.

16. $\cos A$ positive, $\sin A$ negative.

Determine the sign of each of the following:

17. $\sin 160°$.   **19.** $\tan 200°$.   **21.** $\cot 460°$.

18. $\cos (-20°)$.   **20.** $\sec (-110°)$.   **22.** $\csc (-320°)$.

23. Following the method of Example 1, p. 18, obtain a table of values of the functions of 60°, 120°, 240°, and 300°. What do you observe about certain values appearing in any particular column?

Ans.

Angle	sin	cos	tan	cot	sec	csc
60°	$\dfrac{\sqrt{3}}{2}$	$\dfrac{1}{2}$	$\sqrt{3}$	$\dfrac{\sqrt{3}}{3}$	2	$\dfrac{2\sqrt{3}}{3}$
120°	$\dfrac{\sqrt{3}}{2}$	$-\dfrac{1}{2}$	$-\sqrt{3}$	$-\dfrac{\sqrt{3}}{3}$	-2	$\dfrac{2\sqrt{3}}{3}$
240°	$-\dfrac{\sqrt{3}}{2}$	$-\dfrac{1}{2}$	$\sqrt{3}$	$\dfrac{\sqrt{3}}{3}$	-2	$-\dfrac{2\sqrt{3}}{3}$
300°	$-\dfrac{\sqrt{3}}{2}$	$\dfrac{1}{2}$	$-\sqrt{3}$	$-\dfrac{\sqrt{3}}{3}$	2	$-\dfrac{2\sqrt{3}}{3}$

24. Obtain a table of values of the functions of 45°, 135°, 225°, and 315°.

25. What positive angle less than 360° has the same terminal side as − 30°? What are the values of the functions of − 30°?

$$\text{\textit{Ans.} } 330°\,; \;-\frac{1}{2},\; \frac{\sqrt{3}}{2},\; -\frac{\sqrt{3}}{3},\text{ etc.}$$

26. Give the values of the functions of − 45°.

Find the values of the functions of the following angles. In each case draw a figure indicating on it by an arrow the magnitude and direction of the angle, and by numbers the values of x, y, and r.

27. − 60°. *Ans.* $-\dfrac{\sqrt{3}}{2}, \dfrac{1}{2}, -\sqrt{3}$, etc. **28.** − 210°.

29. − 135°. *Ans.* $-\dfrac{\sqrt{2}}{2}, -\dfrac{\sqrt{2}}{2}, 1$, etc. **30.** 420°.

31. − 390°. *Ans.* $-\dfrac{1}{2}, \dfrac{\sqrt{3}}{2}, -\dfrac{\sqrt{3}}{3}$, etc. **32.** 585°.

Find the value of $\sin^2 A + \cos^2 A$ for each of the following values of A:

33. 120°. *Ans.* 1. **34.** 225°.

35. 210°. *Ans.* 1. **36.** − 45°.

37. Show that $\sin 150° \cos 240° + \cos 150° \sin 240° = \frac{1}{2}$.

38. Show that $\cos(-135°)\cos(-225°) - \sin(-135°)\sin(-225°) = 1$.

Find the value of each of the following expressions:

39. $4\sin^2 210° + 3\sec^2 135° - 2\cot^2 150°$. *Ans.* 1

40. $2\csc^2 30° + 2\cot^2 240° - 6\sin^2(-225°)$.

41. $\dfrac{\tan 120° + \tan(-150°)}{1 - \tan 120° \tan(-150°)}$. *Ans.* $-\dfrac{\sqrt{3}}{3}$.

42. $\dfrac{\cot^2(-120°) - 1}{2\cot(-120°)}$.

Give the values of A between $0°$ and $360°$ which satisfy each of the following equations:

43. $\sin A = \frac{1}{2}$.   *Ans.* $30°, 150°$.   **44.** $\cos A = -\frac{1}{2}$.

45. $\tan A = 1$.   *Ans.* $45°, 225°$.   **46.** $\cot A = -\sqrt{3}$.

47. $\sec A = 2$.   *Ans.* $60°, 300°$.   **48.** $\csc A = -2$.

49. $\sin A = -\dfrac{\sqrt{3}}{2}$.   *Ans.* $240°, 300°$.   **50.** $\cot A = -1$.

51. $\csc A = -\dfrac{2\sqrt{3}}{3}$.   *Ans.* $240°, 300°$.   **52.** $\cot A = \dfrac{\sqrt{3}}{3}$.

53. $2 \sin A + 1 = 0$.   *Ans.* $210°, 330°$.   **54.** $\sqrt{2} \cos A - 1 = 0$.

In each of the following construct all the possible terminal sides of the angle A, and find the values of the other functions. Answers are given in the order $\sin A$, $\cos A$, $\tan A$, $\cot A$, $\sec A$, $\csc A$.

55. $\sin A = \frac{3}{5}$.   *Ans.* $\frac{3}{5}, \pm \frac{4}{5}, \pm \frac{3}{4}$, etc.

56. $\cos A = -\frac{1}{3}$.

57. $\cot A = -3$.   *Ans.* $\pm \dfrac{\sqrt{10}}{10}, \pm \dfrac{3\sqrt{10}}{10}, -\dfrac{1}{3}$, etc.

58. $\sec A = -\frac{5}{3}$.

59. $\csc A = \frac{13}{5}$.   *Ans.* $\frac{5}{13}, \pm \frac{12}{13}, \pm \frac{5}{12}$, etc.

60. $\tan A = \dfrac{a}{b}$.

61. $\sin A = c$.   *Ans.* $c, \pm \sqrt{1 - c^2}, \pm \dfrac{c}{\sqrt{1 - c^2}}$, etc.

62. $\cos A = \dfrac{a^2 - b^2}{a^2 + b^2}$.

63. $\csc A = -\sqrt{3}$.   *Ans.* $-\dfrac{\sqrt{3}}{3}, \pm \dfrac{\sqrt{6}}{3}, \pm \dfrac{\sqrt{2}}{2}$, etc.

64. $\cos A = \dfrac{m}{c}$.

65. $\tan A = -\sqrt{7}$.   *Ans.* $\pm \dfrac{\sqrt{14}}{4}, \pm \dfrac{\sqrt{2}}{4}, -\sqrt{7}$, etc.

66. $\sin A = -\frac{2}{3}$.

67. $\tan A = 2.5$.   *Ans.* $\pm \dfrac{5\sqrt{29}}{29}, \pm \dfrac{2\sqrt{29}}{29}, \dfrac{5}{2}$, etc.

68. $\sec A = p$.

In each of the following find the functions of A from the given data:

69. $\sin A = \frac{3}{5}$, A in the first quadrant.   *Ans.* $\frac{3}{5}, \frac{4}{5}, \frac{3}{4}$, etc.

70. $\cos A = -\frac{3}{4}$, A in the second quadrant.

71. $\tan A = \frac{3}{4}$, A in the third quadrant.   *Ans.* $-\frac{3}{5}, -\frac{4}{5}, \frac{3}{4}$, etc.

72. $\cot A = -\frac{12}{5}$, $\sin A$ positive.

73. $\sec A = \frac{3}{2}$, $\tan A$ negative.   *Ans.* $-\dfrac{\sqrt{5}}{3}, \dfrac{2}{3}, -\dfrac{\sqrt{5}}{2}$, etc.

74. $\csc A = -3$, $\cot A$ positive.

75. $\tan A = 2$, $\sin A$ negative.   *Ans.* $-\dfrac{2\sqrt{5}}{5}, -\dfrac{\sqrt{5}}{5}, 2$, etc.

76. $\cos A = -\frac{8}{17}$, $\cot A$ negative.

16. To express five of the trigonometric functions in terms of the sixth. The method explained in this article is convenient and direct.

EXAMPLE 1. Express in terms of $\sin A$ each of the other five functions of A.

Solution. Using (7), Art. 13, we write

$$\sin A = \frac{\sin A}{1} = \frac{y}{r}.$$

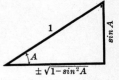

Take $r = 1$. Then $y = \sin A$. Now find x. We have

$$x = \pm\sqrt{r^2 - y^2} = \pm\sqrt{1 - \sin^2 A}.$$

Then by the definitions of Art. 13, we find

$$\sin A = \sin A; \qquad\qquad \csc A = \frac{1}{\sin A};$$

$$\cos A = \pm\sqrt{1 - \sin^2 A}; \qquad \sec A = \pm\frac{1}{\sqrt{1 - \sin^2 A}};$$

$$\tan A = \pm\frac{\sin A}{\sqrt{1 - \sin^2 A}}; \qquad \cot A = \pm\frac{\sqrt{1 - \sin^2 A}}{\sin A}.$$

It is convenient to draw as a check a right triangle in which $x =$ horizontal side, $y =$ vertical side, and $r =$ hypotenuse (see the accompanying figure).

EXAMPLE 2. Express in terms of $\tan A$ each of the other five functions of A.

Solution. Using (9), Art. 13, we may write

$$\tan A = \frac{\tan A}{1} = \frac{y}{x}.$$

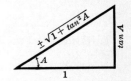

Take $x = 1$. Then $y = \tan A$. Now

$$r = \pm\sqrt{1 + \tan^2 A}.$$

Hence

$$\sin A = \pm\frac{\tan A}{\sqrt{1 + \tan^2 A}}; \qquad \csc A = \pm\frac{\sqrt{1 + \tan^2 A}}{\tan A};$$

$$\cos A = \pm\frac{1}{\sqrt{1 + \tan^2 A}}; \qquad \sec A = \pm\sqrt{1 + \tan^2 A};$$

$$\tan A = \tan A; \qquad\qquad \cot A = \frac{1}{\tan A}.$$

EXAMPLE 3. Given $\sec A = \frac{5}{4}$; find the other functions.

Solution. By (11), Art. 13, we have

$$\sec A = \frac{5}{4} = \frac{r}{x}.$$

Take $r = 5$. Then $x = 4$. Hence

$$y = \pm\sqrt{r^2 - x^2} = \pm 3.$$

Thus we have

$$\sin A = \pm\tfrac{3}{5}; \qquad\qquad \csc A = \pm\tfrac{5}{3};$$

$$\cos A = \tfrac{4}{5}; \qquad\qquad \sec A = \tfrac{5}{4};$$

$$\tan A = \pm\tfrac{3}{4}; \qquad\qquad \cot A = \pm\tfrac{4}{3}.$$

PROBLEMS

1. Express in terms of cos A each of the other five functions of A.

$$Ans. \quad \sin A = \pm\sqrt{1 - \cos^2 A}\,; \quad \csc A = \pm\frac{1}{\sqrt{1 - \cos^2 A}}\,;$$

$$\cos A = \cos A\,; \qquad\qquad \sec A = \frac{1}{\cos A}\,;$$

$$\tan A = \pm\frac{\sqrt{1 - \cos^2 A}}{\cos A}\,; \quad \cot A = \pm\frac{\cos A}{\sqrt{1 - \cos^2 A}}\,.$$

2. Express in terms of cot A each of the other five functions of A.

3. Express in terms of sec A each of the other five functions of A.

$$Ans. \quad \sin A = \pm\frac{\sqrt{\sec^2 A - 1}}{\sec A}\,; \quad \csc A = \pm\frac{\sec A}{\sqrt{\sec^2 A - 1}}\,;$$

$$\cos A = \frac{1}{\sec A}\,; \qquad\qquad \sec A = \sec A\,;$$

$$\tan A = \pm\sqrt{\sec^2 A - 1}\,; \quad \cot A = \pm\frac{1}{\sqrt{\sec^2 A - 1}}\,.$$

4. Express in terms of csc A each of the other five functions of A.

5. Having given sec $A = -\frac{17}{8}$, find the values of each of the other five functions of A. $\quad Ans. \quad \sin A = \pm\frac{15}{17}\,; \quad \csc A = \pm\frac{17}{15}\,;$

$$\cos A = -\frac{8}{17}\,; \quad \sec A = -\frac{17}{8}\,;$$

$$\tan A = \mp\frac{15}{8}\,; \quad \cot A = \mp\frac{8}{15}.$$

6. Having given sin $A = a$, find the values of each of the other functions of A.

CHAPTER II

FUNDAMENTAL RELATIONS; REDUCTION FORMULAS

17. Fundamental relations. In (**7**) to (**12**), Art. 13, let angle $XOB = A$. Then we have, for any angle A,

(1) $\sin A = \dfrac{y}{r}$; \qquad\qquad (4) $\csc A = \dfrac{r}{y}$;

(2) $\cos A = \dfrac{x}{r}$; \qquad\qquad (5) $\sec A = \dfrac{r}{x}$;

(3) $\tan A = \dfrac{y}{x}$; \qquad\qquad (6) $\cot A = \dfrac{x}{y}$.

We now prove the

Theorem. *The six trigonometric functions of an angle A satisfy the relations*

(13) $\sin A \csc A = 1.$ \qquad\qquad (17) $\cot A = \dfrac{\cos A}{\sin A}.$

(14) $\cos A \sec A = 1.$ \qquad\qquad (18) $\sin^2 A + \cos^2 A = 1.$

(15) $\tan A \cot A = 1.$ \qquad\qquad (19) $\sec^2 A = 1 + \tan^2 A.$

(16) $\tan A = \dfrac{\sin A}{\cos A}.$ \qquad\qquad (20) $\csc^2 A = 1 + \cot^2 A.$

Proof of (13). Using (1) and (4), we have

$$\sin A \csc A = \frac{y}{r} \times \frac{r}{y} = 1.$$

Formulas (**14**) and (**15**) are proved in a similar manner. From (**13**), we find

$$\sin A = \frac{1}{\csc A}, \quad \csc A = \frac{1}{\sin A},$$

as in Art. 13.

Proof of (16). Dividing numerator and denominator of the right-hand member of (3) by r, we find

$$\tan A = \frac{\dfrac{y}{r}}{\dfrac{x}{r}} = \frac{\sin A}{\cos A}. \qquad\qquad \text{By (1) and (2)}$$

26

Formula (**17**) is proved in a similar manner.

Proofs of (18) to (20). From (1), Art. 13, squaring both members, we get

(7) $$r^2 = x^2 + y^2.$$

Dividing each term by r^2, we find

(8) $$1 = \left(\frac{x}{r}\right)^2 + \left(\frac{y}{r}\right)^2.$$

Dividing each term by x^2, the result is

(9) $$\left(\frac{r}{x}\right)^2 = 1 + \left(\frac{y}{x}\right)^2.$$

Dividing each term by y^2, we get

(10) $$\left(\frac{r}{y}\right)^2 = \left(\frac{x}{y}\right)^2 + 1.$$

Consider (8). From (1) and (2), we find

$$\frac{x}{r} = \cos A, \quad \frac{y}{r} = \sin A.$$

Substituting in the right-hand member of (8), we get (**18**).

Similarly, from (9), using (5) and (3), we may prove (**19**), and from (10), using (4) and (6), we prove (**20**).

It is of the utmost importance to memorize formulas (**13**) to (**20**), p. 26. The student should also learn the following formulas derived from them :

(21) $\sin A = \dfrac{1}{\csc A}.$ From (**13**), p. 26

(22) $\sin A = \pm \sqrt{1 - \cos^2 A}.$*   Solving (**18**), p. 26, for $\sin A$

(23) $\cos A = \dfrac{1}{\sec A}.$ From (**14**), p. 26

(24) $\cos A = \pm \sqrt{1 - \sin^2 A}.$ Solving (**18**), p. 26, for $\cos A$

(25) $\tan A = \dfrac{1}{\cot A}.$ From (**15**), p. 26

(26) $\tan A = \pm \sqrt{\sec^2 A - 1}.$ Solving (**19**), p. 26, for $\tan A$

---

* The double sign means that we get two values for some of the functions unless a condition is given which determines whether to choose the plus or minus sign. The reason for this is that there are two angles less than 360° for which a function has a given value.

$$(27) \quad \tan A = \frac{\sin A}{\cos A} = \frac{\sin A}{\pm \sqrt{1 - \sin^2 A}} = \frac{\pm \sqrt{1 - \cos^2 A}}{\cos A}.$$

[From (16), p. 26; also (24) and (22).]

$(28) \quad \csc A = \dfrac{1}{\sin A}.$ \hfill From (13), p. 26

$(29) \quad \csc A = \pm \sqrt{1 + \cot^2 A}.$ \hfill Solving (20), p. 26, for csc A

$(30) \quad \sec A = \dfrac{1}{\cos A}.$ \hfill From (14), p. 26

$(31) \quad \sec A = \pm \sqrt{1 + \tan^2 A}.$ \hfill Solving (19), p. 26, for sec A

$(32) \quad \cot A = \dfrac{1}{\tan A}.$ \hfill From (15), p. 26

$(33) \quad \cot A = \pm \sqrt{\csc^2 A - 1}.$ \hfill Solving (20), p. 26, for cot A

$$(34) \quad \cot A = \frac{\cos A}{\sin A} = \frac{\cos A}{\pm \sqrt{1 - \cos^2 A}} = \frac{\pm \sqrt{1 - \sin^2 A}}{\sin A}.$$

[From (17), p. 26; also (22) and (24).]

18. Any function expressed in terms of each of the other five functions. By means of the above formulas we may easily find any function in terms of each one of the other five functions as follows:

EXAMPLE 1. Find sin A in terms of each of the other five functions of A.

$a.$ $\sin A = \dfrac{1}{\csc A},$ \hfill from (21)

$b.$ $\sin A = \pm \sqrt{1 - \cos^2 A},$ \hfill from (22)

$c.$ $\sin A = \dfrac{1}{\pm \sqrt{1 + \cot^2 A}},$ \hfill substituting (29) in a

$d.$ $\sin A = \pm \sqrt{1 - \dfrac{1}{\sec^2 A}} = \dfrac{\pm \sqrt{\sec^2 A - 1}}{\sec A},$ \hfill substituting (23) in b

$e.$ $\sin A = \dfrac{1}{\pm \sqrt{1 + \dfrac{1}{\tan^2 A}}} = \dfrac{\tan A}{\pm \sqrt{\tan^2 A + 1}}.$ \hfill Substituting (32) in c

EXAMPLE 2. Find cos A in terms of each of the other five functions.

$a.$ $\cos A = \dfrac{1}{\sec A},$ \hfill from (23)

$b.$ $\cos A = \pm \sqrt{1 - \sin^2 A},$ \hfill from (24)

$c.$ $\cos A = \dfrac{1}{\pm \sqrt{1 + \tan^2 A}},$ \hfill substituting (31) in c

$d.$ $\cos A = \pm \sqrt{1 - \dfrac{1}{\csc^2 A}} = \dfrac{\pm \sqrt{\csc^2 A - 1}}{\csc A},$ \hfill substituting (21) in b

$e.$ $\cos A = \dfrac{1}{\pm \sqrt{1 + \dfrac{1}{\cot^2 A}}} = \dfrac{\cot A}{\pm \sqrt{\cot^2 A + 1}}.$ \hfill Substituting (25) in c

EXAMPLE 3. Find $\tan A$ in terms of each of the other five functions.

a. $\tan A = \dfrac{1}{\cot A}$,   from **(25)**

b. $\tan A = \pm \sqrt{\sec^2 A - 1}$,   from **(26)**

c. $\tan A = \dfrac{\sin A}{\pm \sqrt{1 - \sin^2 A}}$,   from **(27)**

d. $\tan A = \dfrac{\pm \sqrt{1 - \cos^2 A}}{\cos A}$,   from **(27)**

e. $\tan A = \dfrac{1}{\pm \sqrt{\csc^2 A - 1}}$.   Substituting **(33)** in *a*

EXAMPLE 4. Prove that $\sec A - \tan A \cdot \sin A = \cos A$.

Solution. Let us take the first member and reduce it by means of the formulas **(21)** to **(34)**, pp. 27–28, until it becomes identical with the second member.

Thus $\sec A - \tan A \cdot \sin A = \dfrac{1}{\cos A} - \dfrac{\sin A}{\cos A} \cdot \sin A$

$$\left[\text{Since } \sec A = \frac{1}{\cos A} \text{ and } \tan A = \frac{\sin A}{\cos A}.^* \right]$$

$$= \frac{1 - \sin^2 A}{\cos A} = \frac{\cos^2 A}{\cos A} \quad \textbf{(18)}, \text{ p. 26}$$

$$= \cos A. \; Ans.$$

EXAMPLE 5. Prove that

$$\sin x \,(\sec x + \csc x) - \cos x \,(\sec x - \csc x) = \sec x \csc x.$$

Solution. $\sin x \,(\sec x + \csc x) - \cos x \,(\sec x - \csc x)$

$$= \sin x \left(\frac{1}{\cos x} + \frac{1}{\sin x} \right) - \cos x \left(\frac{1}{\cos x} - \frac{1}{\sin x} \right)$$

$$\left[\text{Since } \sec x = \frac{1}{\cos x} \text{ and } \csc x = \frac{1}{\sin x}. \right]$$

$$= \frac{\sin x}{\cos x} + 1 - 1 + \frac{\cos x}{\sin x}$$

$$= \frac{\sin x}{\cos x} + \frac{\cos x}{\sin x}$$

$$= \frac{\sin^2 x + \cos^2 x}{\cos x \sin x} = \frac{1}{\cos x \sin x} \quad \textbf{(18)}, \text{ p. 26}$$

$$= \frac{1}{\cos x} \cdot \frac{1}{\sin x} = \sec x \csc x. \; Ans.$$

---

* Usually it is best to change the given expression into one containing sines and cosines only, and then change this into the required form. Any operation is admissible that does not change the value of the expression. Use radicals only when unavoidable.

PROBLEMS

1. Find sec x in terms of each of the other five functions of x.

Ans. $\dfrac{1}{\cos x}$, $\pm\sqrt{1+\tan^2 x}$, $\dfrac{1}{\pm\sqrt{1-\sin^2 x}}$, $\dfrac{\pm\sqrt{\cot^2 x+1}}{\cot x}$, $\dfrac{\csc x}{\pm\sqrt{\csc^2 x-1}}$.

2. Find cot x in terms of each of the other five functions of x.

3. Find csc x in terms of each of the other five functions of x.

Ans. $\dfrac{1}{\sin x}$, $\pm\sqrt{1+\cot^2 x}$, $\dfrac{1}{\pm\sqrt{1-\cos^2 x}}$, $\dfrac{\pm\sqrt{\tan^2 x+1}}{\tan x}$, $\dfrac{\sec x}{\pm\sqrt{\sec^2 x-1}}$.

4. Prove the following:

a. $\cos x \tan x = \sin x$.

b. $\sin x \sec x = \tan x$.

c. $\sin y \cot y = \cos y$.

d. $(1 + \tan^2 y)\cos^2 y = 1$.

e. $\sin^2 A + \sin^2 A \tan^2 A = \tan^2 A$.

f. $\cot^2 A - \cos^2 A = \cot^2 A \cos^2 A$.

g. $\tan A + \cot A = \sec A \csc A$.

h. $\cos A \csc A = \cot A$.

i. $\cos^2 A - \sin^2 A = 1 - 2 \sin^2 A$.

j. $\cos^2 A - \sin^2 A = 2 \cos^2 A - 1$.

k. $(1 + \cot^2 B)\sin^2 B = 1$.

l. $(\csc^2 A - 1)\sin^2 A = \cos^2 A$.

m. $\sec^2 A + \csc^2 A = \sec^2 A \csc^2 A$.

n. $\cos^4 C - \sin^4 C + 1 = 2 \cos^2 C$.

o. $(\sin x + \cos x)^2 + (\sin x - \cos x)^2 = 2$.

p. $\sin^3 x \cos x + \cos^3 x \sin x = \sin x \cos x$.

q. $\sin^2 B + \tan^2 B = \sec^2 B - \cos^2 B$.

r. $\cot y + \dfrac{\sin y}{1 + \cos y} = \csc y$.

s. $\cos B \tan B + \sin B \cot B = \sin B + \cos B$.

t. $\sec x \csc x (\cos^2 x - \sin^2 x) = \cot x - \tan x$.

u. $\dfrac{\cos C}{1 - \tan C} + \dfrac{\sin C}{1 - \cot C} = \sin C + \cos C$.

v. $\dfrac{\sin z}{1 + \cos z} + \dfrac{1 + \cos z}{\sin z} = 2 \csc z$.

Use the fundamental relations **(13)** to **(20)** to find the values of all the functions from the following data:

5. $\cos A = -\frac{4}{5}$, A in the second quadrant.   *Ans.* $\frac{3}{5}$, $-\frac{4}{5}$, $-\frac{3}{4}$, etc.

6. $\tan A = \frac{3}{2}$, A in the third quadrant.

7. $\csc A = -3$, A in the fourth quadrant. *Ans.* $-\frac{1}{3}$, $\dfrac{2\sqrt{2}}{3}$, $-\dfrac{\sqrt{2}}{4}$, etc.

8. $\cot A = -2$, A in the second quadrant.

9. $\sin A = 0.25$, A in the second quadrant. *Ans.* 0.25, -0.97, -0.26, etc.

10. $\csc A = m$, A in the first quadrant.

Compute algebraically the value of each of the following expressions from the given data. In each case consider the angle as acute.

11. $(\cos^2 A - \sin^2 A)\tan^2 A$, given $\sin A = \frac{1}{2}$.   *Ans.* $\frac{1}{6}$.

12. $\left(\dfrac{\sin B - \cos B}{\sin B + \cos B}\right)^2$, given $\cot B = 2$.

13. $\sin^3 z \cos z + \cos^3 z \sin z$, given $\tan z = \frac{2}{5}$.   *Ans.* $\frac{10}{29}$.

14. $\dfrac{\sin z}{1 + \cos z} + \dfrac{1 + \cos z}{\sin z}$, given $\sec z = \dfrac{5}{4}$.

15. $\sec^4 \alpha - \sec^2 \alpha - \tan^4 \alpha - \tan^2 \alpha$, given $\csc \alpha = 3\sqrt{3}$. (α is the Greek letter "alpha.")   *Ans.* 0.

16. $\sec^2 \beta \, (1 + \cos \beta \tan \beta)$, given $\csc \beta = 2$. (β is the Greek letter "beta.")

17. Transform the following expressions into expressions containing no other functions than the sine and simplify your results. Consider the given angle as acute in each case.

 a. $\dfrac{\csc A}{\cot A}$.   *Ans.* $\dfrac{1}{\sqrt{1 - \sin^2 A}}$.

 b. $\sec y - \cos y$.   *Ans.* $\dfrac{\sin^2 y}{\sqrt{1 - \sin^2 y}}$.

 c. $\cot z \cos z - \csc z \, (1 - 2 \sin^2 z)$.   *Ans.* $\sin z$.

18. Transform the following into equivalent expressions containing only $\tan A$:

 a. $\sec^2 A - \csc^2 A$.

 b. $\sec A \csc A \, (\cos^2 A - \sin^2 A)$.

 c. $\dfrac{\sin^2 A}{\cot^2 A} - \dfrac{\cos^2 A}{1 - \sec^2 A}$.

Transform the following into equivalent expressions involving only sines and cosines. Simplify the results.

19. $\tan z + \cot z$.   *Ans.* $\dfrac{1}{\sin z \cos z}$.

20. $\csc A - \sin A \cot^2 A$.

21. $\dfrac{1 + \tan \alpha}{\sec \alpha}$.   *Ans.* $\sin \alpha + \cos \alpha$.

22. $\dfrac{\tan A + \tan B}{1 - \tan A \tan B}$.

19. Division by zero; infinity. A difficulty presented in the next article must be discussed here. If a and b are two numbers, and b is not zero, then there is always a unique third number x, satisfying

 (1) $a = bx,$

and

 (2) $x = \dfrac{a}{b}.$

If $b = 0$, equation (1) does not hold unless a also is zero, and it is then true for *every* number x.

This argument is given to set forth with emphasis the fact that the expression

(3) $\dfrac{a}{0}$ ("a divided by zero")

is meaningless. *Division by zero* is not an operation of arithmetic.
Consider the functional relation

(4) $y = \dfrac{1}{x}.$

The value of y will be determined when any value is given to x *except* zero. Consider now the values of y when positive values are given to x which *decrease* constantly and approach zero. Then the values of y will increase constantly and eventually exceed any positive number. If negative values are given to x which decrease constantly in numerical value, the values of y will be negative and will increase constantly in numerical value. This fact is expressed thus: *When the values of x decrease constantly in numerical value and approach zero, the function*

$$\dfrac{1}{x}$$

becomes infinite. When a variable y becomes infinite, we write, briefly, $y = \infty$.

20. Functions of 0°, 90°, 180°, 270°. Take a point on each of the terminal sides of these angles at unit distance from the origin. Then the coördinates are as follows:

0° : for P_0 we have $x = 1$, $y = 0$;
90° : for P_1 we have $x = 0$, $y = 1$;
180° : for P_2 we have $x = -1$, $y = 0$;
270° : for P_3 we have $x = 0$, $y = -1$.

In each case $r = 1$.

The above values may be used in (7) to (12), Art. 13, unless the value zero appears in a denominator. For example, for 0° we have

$$\sin 0° = \dfrac{0}{1} = 0 ; \quad \cos 0° = \dfrac{1}{1} = 1 ;$$

$$\tan 0° = \dfrac{0}{1} = 0 ; \quad \sec 0° = \dfrac{1}{1} = 1.$$

But (10) and (12), Art. 13, are meaningless, since "division by zero" is indicated.

We find cot 0° as follows: From (**32**), Art. 17, we get

$$\cot A = \frac{1}{\tan A}.$$

As A decreases and approaches 0°, tan A decreases and approaches zero (tan 0° = 0), and hence cot A becomes infinite. That is (Art. 19),

$$\cot 0° = \infty.$$

The argument is the same in every case when the denominator in (**7**) to (**12**), Art. 13, is zero, that is, when the corresponding reciprocal function becomes infinite.

In fact, for a second illustration, consider sec A when $A = 90°$. Then (**11**), Art. 13, is meaningless, since $x = 0$. Now

$$\sec A = \frac{1}{\cos A}. \qquad \text{(30), Art. 17}$$

Also cos 90° = 0. Then as A increases and approaches 90°, sec A becomes infinite.

The following table is readily verified:

Angle	sin	cos	tan	cot	sec	csc
0	0	1	0	∞	1	∞
90°	1	0	∞	0	∞	1
180°	0	-1	0	∞	-1	∞
270°	-1	0	∞	0	∞	-1

The functions of 360° are the same as those of 0°, since these angles have the same terminal side.

PROBLEMS

Prove that

1. $\sin 0° + \cos 90° = 0$.

2. $\sin 180° + \cos 270° = 0$.

3. $\cos 0° + \tan 0° = 1$.

4. $\tan 180° + \cot 90° = 0$.

5. $\sin 270° - \sin 90° = -2$.

6. $\cos 0° + \sin 90° = 2$.

7. $\sec 0° + \csc 90° = 2$.

8. $\sin 90° + \cos 90° + \csc 90° + \cot 90° = 2$.

9. $\cos 180° + \sec 180° + \sin 180° + \tan 180° = -2$.

10. $(a^2 - b^2)\cos 360° - 4\,ab \sin 270° = a^2 + 4\,ab - b^2$.

Prove that

11. $\cos 30° \cos 60° - \sin 30° \sin 60° = \cos 90°$.

12. $\sin 180° + \sin 90° = 2 \sin 135° \cos 45°$.

13. $\sin 90° = \sin 180° \cos (- 90°) + \cos 180° \sin (- 90°)$.

14. $4 \cos^3 60° - 3 \cos 60° = \cos 180°$.

15. Compare the value of $\sin (90° + 60°)$ with the value of $\sin 90° + \sin 60°$.

16. Compare the value of $\tan (120° + 60°)$ with the value of $\tan 120° + \tan 60°$.

17. Compare the value of $2 \sin 45°$ with the value of $\sin (2 \times 45°)$.

18. Find the value of

$\cos A + \cos 2 A + \cos 3 A + \cos 4 A + \cos 5 A + \cos 6 A$ if $A = 60°$.

21. Measurement of angles. There are two systems in general use for the measurement of angles. For elementary work in mathematics and for engineering purposes the system most employed is

*Degree measure, or the sexagesimal system.** The unit angle is one degree, being the angle subtended at the center of a circle by an arc whose length equals* $\frac{1}{360}$ *of the circumference of the circle.* The degree is subdivided into 60 *minutes,* and the minute into 60 *seconds.* Degrees, minutes, and seconds are denoted by symbols. Thus 63 degrees 15 minutes 36 seconds is written $63° 15' 36''$. Reducing the seconds to the decimal part of a minute, the angle may be written $63° 15.6'$. Reducing the minutes to the decimal part of a degree, the angle may also be written $63.26°$.† It has been assumed that the student is already familiar with this system of measuring angles, and the only reason for referring to it here is to compare it with the following system.

22. Circular measure. *The unit angle is* **one radian,** *and is the angle subtended at the center of a circle by an arc whose length equals the length of the radius of the circle.*

Thus, in the figure at the top of the next page, if the length of the arc AB equals the radius of the circle, then

angle $AOB = 1$ radian.

---

* Invented by the early Babylonians, whose tables of weights and measures were based on a scale of 60. This was probably due to the fact that they reckoned the year at 360 days. This led to the division of the circumference of a circle into 360 degrees. A radius laid off as a chord would then cut off 60 degrees.

† To reduce seconds to the decimal part of a minute we divide the number of seconds by 60. Similarly, we reduce minutes to the decimal part of a degree. See Conversion Tables of *Four-Place Tables* by Granville, Smith, and Mikesh (Ginn and Company).

The *circular measure* of an angle is its magnitude expressed in terms of radians. This system was introduced early in the last century. It is now used to a certain extent in practical work, and is universally used in the higher branches of mathematics.

Both of the above systems will be used in this book.

Now let us find the relation between the old and new units. From geometry we know that the circumference of a circle equals $2\pi R$; and this means that the ratio of the circumference to the radius is 2π. But a circumference subtends a central angle of 360°. Therefore

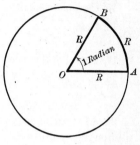

$$2\pi \text{ radians} = 360°,$$

$$\pi \text{ radians} = 180°,$$

$$1 \text{ radian} = \frac{180°}{\pi} = \frac{180°}{3.1416}, \text{ or}$$

(35) $1 \text{ radian} = 57.2958° = 57°\ 17'\ 44.8''.$

It therefore follows at once that

To reduce radians to degrees, *multiply the number of radians by* $57.2958 \left(= \dfrac{180}{\pi}\right).$

Since $360° = 2\pi$ radians,

$$1° = \frac{\pi}{180} \text{ radian} = \frac{3.1416}{180} \text{ radian, or}$$

(36) $1° = 0.017453 \text{ radian.}$

Hence

To reduce degrees to radians, *multiply the number of degrees by* $0.017453 \left(= \dfrac{\pi}{180}\right).$

The student should now become accustomed to expressing angles in circular measure, thus:

$$360° = 2\pi \text{ radians,} \qquad\qquad 60° = \frac{\pi}{3} \text{ radians,}$$

$$180° = \pi \text{ radians,} \qquad\qquad 30° = \frac{\pi}{6} \text{ radians,}$$

$$90° = \frac{\pi}{2} \text{ radians,} \qquad\qquad 45° = \frac{\pi}{4} \text{ radians,}$$

$$270° = \frac{3\pi}{2} \text{ radians,} \qquad\qquad 15° = \frac{\pi}{12} \text{ radians, etc.}$$

When writing the trigonometric functions of angles expressed in circular measure it is customary to omit the word "radians," thus:

$\sin$ (π radians) is written simply $\sin \pi$ and $= \sin 180°$;

$\tan \left(\dfrac{\pi}{2} \text{ radians}\right)$ is written simply $\tan \dfrac{\pi}{2}$ and $= \tan 90°$;

$\cot \left(\dfrac{3\,\pi}{4} \text{ radians}\right)$ is written simply $\cot \dfrac{3\,\pi}{4}$ and $= \cot 135°$;

$\cos \left(\dfrac{5\,\pi}{6} \text{ radians}\right)$ is written simply $\cos \dfrac{5\,\pi}{6}$ and $= \cos 150°$;

$\csc$ (1 radian) is written simply $\csc 1$ and $= \csc 57.30°$;

$\sec$ ($\frac{1}{2}$ radian) is written simply $\sec \frac{1}{2}$ and $= \sec 28.65°$, etc.

Since the number of times that the radius of a circle can be measured off on an arc of the same circle determines the number of radians in the angle subtended at the center by that arc, we have

$$(37) \quad \textbf{measure of an angle in radians} = \frac{\textbf{length of subtending arc}}{\textbf{length of radius}}.$$

Hence, knowing any two of the three quantities involved, the third may easily be found.

EXAMPLE 1. Reduce $\dfrac{3\,\pi}{5}$ radians to degrees.

Solution. Since 1 radian $= \dfrac{180°}{\pi}$,

$$\frac{3\,\pi}{5} \text{ radians} = \frac{3\,\pi}{5} \left(\frac{180°}{\pi}\right),$$
$$= 108°. \quad Ans.$$

EXAMPLE 2. Reduce 1.27 radians to degrees.

Solution. Since 1 radian $= \dfrac{180°}{\pi} = 57.2958°$,

$$1.27 \text{ radians} = 1.27(57.2958)°$$
$$= 72.7657°$$
$$= 72° \; 45' \; 56''. \quad Ans.$$

EXAMPLE 3. Reduce 205° to radians.

Solution. Since $1° = 0.017453 \left(= \dfrac{\pi}{180}\right)$ radian,

$$205° = 205(0.017453) \text{ radians},$$
$$= 3.5779 \text{ radians}. \quad Ans.$$

EXAMPLE 4. Reduce 25° 13′ 16″ to radians.

Solution. We first reduce the minutes and seconds to a decimal part of a degree and obtain

$$25° 13′ 16″ = 25.2214°.$$

Hence $\qquad 25.2214° = 25.2214(0.017453)$ radian,

$$= 0.44019 \text{ radian. } Ans.$$

EXAMPLE 5. What is the circular measure of the angle subtended by an arc of length 3.7 in. if the radius of the circle is 2 in.? Also express the angle in degrees.

Solution. Substituting in (37), we have

$$\text{measurement in radians} = \frac{3.7}{2} = 1.85. \text{ } Ans.$$

To reduce this angle to degrees, we have, from (35),

$$1.85 \times 57.2958° = 105.997°. \text{ } Ans.$$

EXAMPLE 6. What is the radius of a circle in which an arc of length 64 in. subtends an angle of 2.5 radians?

Solution. Substituting in (37), $\qquad 2.5 = \dfrac{64}{R}$,

$$R = 25.6 \text{ in. } Ans.$$

PROBLEMS

The following angles are given in circular measure. Express them in degrees.

1. $\dfrac{\pi}{3}$. $\qquad$ *Ans.* 60°. $\qquad\qquad$ 2. $\dfrac{\pi}{4}$.

3. $-\dfrac{\pi}{2}$. $\qquad$ *Ans.* − 90°. $\qquad\qquad$ 4. $\dfrac{4\pi}{3}$.

5. $-\dfrac{7\pi}{5}$. $\qquad$ *Ans.* − 252°. $\qquad\qquad$ 6. $-\dfrac{5\pi}{6}$.

7. 1.3. $\qquad$ *Ans.* 74° 29′ 4″. $\qquad\qquad$ 8. $\frac{1}{2}$.

9. − 2.5. $\qquad$ *Ans.* − 143° 14′ 22″. $\qquad$ 10. − 3.

11. $\dfrac{\pi+1}{6}$. $\qquad$ *Ans.* 39° 32′ 57″. $\qquad$ 12. $\dfrac{3\pi+2}{5}$.

Express the following angles in radians:

13. 22½°. $\qquad$ *Ans.* $\dfrac{\pi}{8}$. $\qquad\qquad$ 14. 60°.

15. 135°. $\qquad$ *Ans.* $\dfrac{3\pi}{4}$. $\qquad\qquad$ 16. − 720°.

17. 990°. $\qquad$ *Ans.* $\dfrac{11\pi}{2}$. $\qquad\qquad$ 18. − 120°.

19. − 100.28°. $\qquad$ *Ans.* − 1.7502. $\qquad$ 20. 45.6°.

21. 142° 43.2′. $\qquad$ *Ans.* 2.4909. $\qquad$ 22. − 243.87°.

23. 125° 23′ 19″. $\qquad$ *Ans.* 2.1884. $\qquad$ 24. 205° 35.4′.

Give the values of the following functions:

25. $\sin \dfrac{\pi}{3}$.   *Ans.* $\dfrac{\sqrt{3}}{2}$.   **26.** $\cos \dfrac{\pi}{4}$.

27. $\tan \left(-\dfrac{5\pi}{6}\right)$.   *Ans.* $\dfrac{\sqrt{3}}{3}$.   **28.** $\cot \left(-\dfrac{\pi}{2}\right)$.

29. $\sec \dfrac{5\pi}{4}$.   *Ans.* $-\sqrt{2}$.   **30.** $\sin \left(-\dfrac{11\pi}{2}\right)$.

Find the values of θ between 0 and 2π which satisfy each of the following equations (θ is the Greek letter "theta"):

31. $\sin \theta = \frac{1}{2}$.   *Ans.* $\dfrac{\pi}{6}, \dfrac{5\pi}{6}$.   **32.** $\cos \theta = -\frac{1}{2}$.

33. $\tan \theta = -1$.   *Ans.* $\dfrac{3\pi}{4}, \dfrac{7\pi}{4}$.   **34.** $\csc \theta = \dfrac{2\sqrt{3}}{3}$.

35. $\sin \theta = -\dfrac{\sqrt{2}}{2}$.   *Ans.* $\dfrac{5\pi}{4}, \dfrac{7\pi}{4}$.   **36.** $\tan \theta = \sqrt{3}$.

37. $\cot \theta + \sqrt{3} = 0$.   *Ans.* $\dfrac{5\pi}{6}, \dfrac{11\pi}{6}$.   **38.** $\sqrt{3} \sec \theta + 2 = 0$.

39. Express in degrees and in radians:
   a. Seven tenths of four right angles.
   b. Five fourths of two right angles.
   c. Two thirds of one right angle.

   Ans. (a) $252°, \dfrac{7\pi}{5}$; (b) $225°, \dfrac{5\pi}{4}$; (c) $60°, \dfrac{\pi}{3}$.

40. Find the number of radians in an angle at the center of a circle of radius 25 ft. which intercepts an arc of $37\frac{1}{2}$ ft.

41. Find the length of the arc subtending an angle of $4\frac{1}{2}$ radians at the center of a circle whose radius is 25 ft.   *Ans.* $112\frac{1}{2}$ ft.

42. Find the length of the radius of a circle at whose center an angle of 1.2 radians is subtended by an arc whose length is 9.6 ft.

43. Find the length of an arc of 80° on a circle of 4 ft. radius.

   Ans. 5.6 ft.

44. Find the number of degrees in an angle at the center of a circle of radius 10 ft. which intercepts an arc of 5π ft.

45. Find the number of radians in an angle at the center of a circle of radius $3\frac{2}{11}$ in. which intercepts an arc of 2 ft.   *Ans.* 7.54.

46. How long does it take the minute hand of a clock to turn through $-1\frac{2}{3}$ radians?

47. What angle in circular measure does the hour hand of a clock describe in 39 min. $22\frac{1}{2}$ sec.?   *Ans.* $-\dfrac{7\pi}{64}$ rad.

48. A wheel makes 10 revolutions per second. How long does it take to turn through 2 radians, taking $\pi = \frac{22}{7}$?

49. A railway train is traveling on a curve of half a mile radius at the rate of 20 mi. per hour. Through what angle has it turned in 10 sec.?

Ans. $6\frac{4}{11}°$.

50. The radius of a wagon wheel is 1.5 ft. Through what angle does the wheel turn when the wagon moves a distance of 3 ft.?

51. The angle subtended by the sun at the eye of an observer is about half a degree. Find approximately the diameter of the sun if its distance from the observer is 90,000,000 mi. *Ans.* 785,400 mi.

23. Reduction of trigonometric functions to functions of acute angles. The values of the functions of different angles are given in trigonometric tables, such, for instance, as the one on page 10. These tables, however, give the trigonometric functions of angles between 0° and 90° only, while in practice we sometimes have to deal with positive angles greater than 90° and also with negative angles. We shall now show that the trigonometric functions of an angle of any magnitude whatever, positive or negative, can be expressed in terms of the trigonometric functions of a positive angle less than 90°, that is, of an acute angle. In fact, we shall show, although this is of less importance, that the functions of any angle can be found in terms of the functions of a positive angle not greater than 45°.

24. Functions of complementary angles. To make our discussion complete we repeat the following from page 4 :

Theorem. *A function of an acute angle is equal to the co-function of its complementary acute angle.*

EXAMPLE. Express sin 72° as the function of a positive angle less than 45°.

Solution. Since $90° - 72° = 18°$, 72° and 18° are complementary, and we get $\sin 72° = \cos 18°$. *Ans.*

PROBLEMS

1. Express the following as functions of the complementary angle :

a. cos 68°.

b. tan 48.6°.

c. sec 81° 16′.

d. $\sin \dfrac{\pi}{3}$.

e. cot 9.167°.

f. sin 72° 51′ 43″.

g. $\cos \dfrac{\pi}{6}$.

h. sec 19° 29.8′.

i. csc 52° 18′.

j. $\cot \dfrac{2\pi}{5}$.

k. sin 1.2.

l. tan 66° 22.3′.

2. Show that in a right triangle any function of one of the acute angles equals the co-function of the other acute angle.

3. If A, B, C are the angles of any triangle, prove that

$$\sin \tfrac{1}{2} A = \cos \tfrac{1}{2}(B + C).$$

25. Reduction formulas for angles lying in the second quadrant. First method. In the figure, let OB_2 be the terminal side of any angle lying in the second quadrant. The functions of this angle are the same as the corresponding functions of the positive angle XOB_2, and

(1) $\qquad$ angle $XOB_2 = 180° -$ angle B_2OX'.

Let A be the measure of the acute angle B_2OX'. Then, from (1), we have

(2) $\qquad$ angle $XOB_2 = 180° - A$.

In the first quadrant construct angle $XOB_1 =$ angle $B_2OX' = A$. Take $OP_1 = OP_2 = r$, and draw the ordinates M_1P_1 and M_2P_2. Then the right triangles OM_1P_1 and OM_2P_2 are congruent.

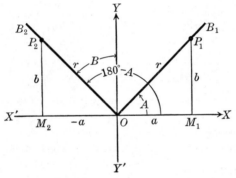

We wish to compare the values of the functions of the supplemental angles A and $180° - A$. As shown in the figure,

for P_1, $\quad x = OM_1 = a$, $\quad y = M_1P_1 = b$;

for P_2, $\quad x = OM_2 = -a$, $\quad y = M_2P_2 = b$.

Hence, by (7) to (12), Art. 13,

(3)
$$
\begin{cases}
\sin (180° - A) = \dfrac{b}{r}, & \sin A = \dfrac{b}{r}; \\[2mm]
\cos (180° - A) = -\dfrac{a}{r}, & \cos A = \dfrac{a}{r}; \\[2mm]
\tan (180° - A) = -\dfrac{b}{a}, & \tan A = \dfrac{b}{a}; \\[2mm]
\cot (180° - A) = -\dfrac{a}{b}, & \cot A = \dfrac{a}{b}; \\[2mm]
\sec (180° - A) = -\dfrac{r}{a}, & \sec A = \dfrac{r}{a}; \\[2mm]
\csc (180° - A) = \dfrac{r}{b}, & \csc A = \dfrac{r}{b}.
\end{cases}
$$

Thus, by comparison, we find

$$(4) \begin{cases} \sin (180^\circ - A) = \sin A ; & \csc (180^\circ - A) = \csc A ; \\ \cos (180^\circ - A) = -\cos A ; & \sec (180^\circ - A) = -\sec A ; \\ \tan (180^\circ - A) = -\tan A ; & \cot (180^\circ - A) = -\cot A. \end{cases}$$

Hence we have the

Theorem. *The functions of an angle in the second quadrant equal numerically the same-named functions of the acute angle between its terminal side and the terminal side of 180°. The algebraic signs, however, are those for an angle in the second quadrant.*

The student will see that it was hardly necessary to write out the equations (3). For the points P_1 and P_2 have equal distances and equal ordinates, and their abscissas differ only in sign. Hence their corresponding functions can, at the most, differ only in sign, and equations (4) and the theorem are obvious.

The "acute angle" referred to in this theorem is called the *related angle*. For example, the related angle for 165° is 15°.

EXAMPLE 1. Express sin 123° as a function of an acute angle, and find its value.

Solution. Since $180^\circ - 123^\circ = 57^\circ$, the related angle is 57°.

$$\sin 123^\circ = \sin (180^\circ - 57^\circ) = \sin 57^\circ = 0.8387. \ Ans.$$

EXAMPLE 2. Find the value of $\sec \dfrac{5\pi}{6}$.

Solution. $\sec \dfrac{5\pi}{6} = \sec 150^\circ = \sec (180^\circ - 30^\circ) = -\sec 30^\circ = -\dfrac{2}{\sqrt{3}}. \ Ans.$

EXAMPLE 3. Find tan 516°.

Solution. 516° is an angle in the second quadrant, for $516^\circ - 360^\circ = 156^\circ$. Hence $\tan 516^\circ = \tan 156^\circ{}^* = \tan (180^\circ - 24^\circ) = -\tan 24^\circ = -0.4452. \ Ans.$

Second method. The angle XOB_2 may also be written $90^\circ + B$, where B measures the acute angle YOB_2. Since the angles YOB_2 and B_2OX' are complementary, we have, from the theorem of Art. 24,

$$\sin A = \cos B ; \qquad \csc A = \sec B ;$$
$$\cos A = \sin B ; \qquad \sec A = \csc B ;$$
$$\tan A = \cot B ; \qquad \cot A = \tan B.$$

---

* The above theorem was proved for an angle of any magnitude whatever whose terminal side lies in the second quadrant. The generating line of the angle may have made one or more complete revolutions before assuming the position of the terminal side. In that case we should first (if the revolutions have been counterclockwise, that is, in the positive direction) subtract such a multiple of 360° from the angle that the remainder will be a positive angle less than 360°.

Since $180° - A = 90° + B$, we get, combining these results with the results at the top of page 41,

$$(5) \begin{cases} \sin (90° + B) = \cos B; & \csc (90° + B) = \sec B; \\ \cos (90° + B) = -\sin B; & \sec (90° + B) = -\csc B; \\ \tan (90° + B) = -\cot B; & \cot (90° + B) = -\tan B. \end{cases}$$

Hence we have the

Theorem. *The functions of an angle in the second quadrant equal numerically the co-named functions of the acute angle between its terminal side and the terminal side of 90°. The algebraic signs, however, are those for an angle in the second quadrant.*

EXAMPLE 4. Find the value of cos 109° by the second method.

Solution. Since $109° = 90° + 19°$,

$$\cos 109° = \cos (90° + 19°) = -\sin 19° = -0.3256. \ \textit{Ans.}$$

EXAMPLE 5. Find the value of $\cos \dfrac{19\,\pi}{4}$ by the second method.

Solution. $\dfrac{19\,\pi}{4} = 855° = 720° + 135°$. Therefore

$$\cos \frac{19\,\pi}{4} = \cos 855° = \cos 135° = \cos (90° + 45°) = -\sin 45° = -\frac{1}{\sqrt{2}}. \ \textit{Ans.}$$

The above two methods teach us how to do the same thing, namely, *how to find the functions of an angle in the second quadrant in terms of functions of an acute angle.* The first method is generally to be preferred, however, as the name of the function does not change, and hence we are less likely to make a mistake.

PROBLEMS

1. Using formulas (4), p. 41, construct a table of sines, cosines, and tangents of all angles from 0° to 180° at intervals of 30°.

Ans.

	0°	30°	60°	90°	120°	150°	180°
sin	0	$\dfrac{1}{2}$	$\dfrac{\sqrt{3}}{2}$	1	$\dfrac{\sqrt{3}}{2}$	$\dfrac{1}{2}$	0
cos	1	$\dfrac{\sqrt{3}}{2}$	$\dfrac{1}{2}$	0	$-\dfrac{1}{2}$	$-\dfrac{\sqrt{3}}{2}$	-1
tan	0	$\dfrac{1}{\sqrt{3}}$	$\sqrt{3}$	∞	$-\sqrt{3}$	$-\dfrac{1}{\sqrt{3}}$	0

2. Using the table on page 10 and formulas (4), p. 41, construct a table of sines, cosines, and tangents of all angles from 90° to 180° at intervals of 15°.

Express the following as functions of an acute angle:

3. $\sin 111°$.   *Ans.* $\sin 69°$, or   4. $\cos 165° 20'$.
                $\cos 21°$.

5. $\cos 165° 20'$. *Ans.* $-\sin 75° 20'$, or   6. $\tan 170.48°$.
                $-\cos 14° 40'$.

7. $\tan \dfrac{4\pi}{5}$. *Ans.* $-\tan \dfrac{\pi}{5}$, or   8. $\cot \dfrac{13\pi}{5}$.

                $-\cot \dfrac{3\pi}{10}$.

9. $\sec 883°$.   *Ans.* $-\sec 17°$, or   10. $\csc 758°$.
                $-\csc 73°$.

11. $\csc 2$.   *Ans.* $\csc 1.1$, or   12. $\sec 2.2$.
                $\sec 0.5$.

Find the values of the following functions:

13. $\sin 133°$.   *Ans.* 0.7314.   14. $\cos 175°$.

15. $\cos 160°$.   *Ans.* -0.9397.   16. $\tan 131°$.

17. $\tan \dfrac{3\pi}{4}$.   *Ans.* -1.   18. $\cot \dfrac{11\pi}{4}$.

19. $\csc 870°$.   *Ans.* 2.   20. $\sin 1200°$.

21. $\sec 135°$.   *Ans.* $-\sqrt{2}$.   22. $\sec 131°$.

23. $\cot 852°$.   *Ans.* -0.9004.   24. $\csc 491°$.

Express the following as functions of an acute angle less than $45°$:

25. $\sin 106°$.   *Ans.* $\cos 16°$.   26. $\tan 862°$.

27. $\cos 148.3°$. *Ans.* $-\cos 31.7°$.   28. $\cot \dfrac{11\pi}{12}$.

29. $\sec 794° 52'$. *Ans.* $\csc 15° 8'$.   30. $\csc \dfrac{23\pi}{9}$.

26. Reduction formulas for angles lying in the third quadrant.
First method. The functions of any angle in the third quadrant whose terminal side is OB_3 (see figure on following page) are the same as the corresponding functions of the positive angle XOB_3, and

(1)   angle $XOB_3 = 180° +$ angle $X'OB_3$.

Let the measure of the acute angle $X'OB_3$ equal A, and construct, in the first quadrant,

        angle $XOB_1 =$ angle $X'OB_3 = A$.

Complete the figure as shown. The coördinates of P_1 are (a, b). The coördinates of P_3 are $(-a, -b)$, and

          $OP_1 = OP_3 = r$.

Hence for the angles $180° + A (\angle XOB_3)$ and $A (\angle XOB_1)$,

$\sin (180° + A) = -\sin A$; $\csc (180° + A) = -\csc A$;

$\cos (180° + A) = -\cos A$; $\sec (180° + A) = -\sec A$;

$\tan (180° + A) = \tan A$; $\cot (180° + A) = \cot A$.

Thus we have the

Theorem. *The functions of an angle in the third quadrant equal numerically the same-named functions of the acute angle between its terminal side and the terminal side of 180°. The algebraic signs, however, are those for an angle in the third quadrant.*

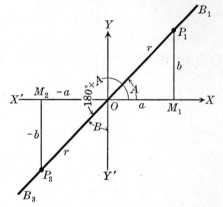

The "acute angle" referred to in this theorem is called the *related angle*. Thus, for example, the related angle for 215° is 35°.

EXAMPLE 1. Express $\cos 217°$ as the function of an acute angle, and find its value.

Solution. Since $217° - 180° = 37°$, the related angle is 37°.

$$\cos 217° = \cos (180° + 37°) = -\cos 37° = -0.7986. \quad Ans.$$

EXAMPLE 2. Find the value of $\csc 225°$.

Solution. $\csc 225° = \csc (180° + 45°) = -\csc 45° = -\sqrt{2}. \quad Ans.$

EXAMPLE 3. Find the value of $\sin 600°$.

Solution. 600° is an angle in the third quadrant, for $600° - 360° = 240°$.

Hence $\sin 600° = \sin 240° = \sin (180° + 60°) = -\sin 60° = -\dfrac{\sqrt{3}}{2}. \quad Ans.$

Second method. The angle XOB_3 may also be written $270° - B$, where B measures the acute angle B_3OY'. Since the angles B_3OY' and $X'OB_3 (= \angle XOB_1)$ are complementary, we have, from the theorem of Art. 24, combined with the above results, remembering that $180° + A = 270° - B$,

$\sin (270° - B) = -\cos B$; $\csc (270° - B) = -\sec B$;

$\cos (270° - B) = -\sin B$; $\sec (270° - B) = -\csc B$;

$\tan (270° - B) = \cot B$; $\cot (270° - B) = \tan B$.

Hence we have the

Theorem. *The functions of an angle in the third quadrant equal numerically the co-named functions of the acute angle between its terminal side and the terminal side of 270°. The algebraic signs, however, are those of an angle in the third quadrant.*

EXAMPLE 4. Find sin 259° by the second method.

Solution. sin 259° = sin (270° − 11°) = − cos 11° = − 0.9816. *Ans.*

As in the last case, the first method is generally to be preferred.

PROBLEMS

1. Construct a table of sines, cosines, and tangents of all angles from 0° to 270° at intervals of 45°.

Ans.

	0°	45°	90°	135°	180°	225°	270°
sin	0	$\dfrac{1}{\sqrt{2}}$	1	$\dfrac{1}{\sqrt{2}}$	0	$-\dfrac{1}{\sqrt{2}}$	− 1
cos	1	$\dfrac{1}{\sqrt{2}}$	0	$-\dfrac{1}{\sqrt{2}}$	− 1	$-\dfrac{1}{\sqrt{2}}$	0
tan	0	1	∞	− 1	0	1	∞

2. Construct a table of sines, cosines, and tangents of all angles from 180° to 270° at intervals of 15°, using the table on page 10.

Express the following as functions of an acute angle:

3. cos 212°.   *Ans.* − cos 32°, or − sin 58°.

4. sin 263°.

5. sin 582°.   *Ans.* − sin 42°, or − cos 48°.

6. cot 570°.

7. $\tan \dfrac{6\pi}{5}$.   *Ans.* $\tan \dfrac{\pi}{5}$, or $\cot \dfrac{3\pi}{10}$.

8. $\cos \dfrac{8\pi}{7}$.

9. sec 255°.   *Ans.* − sec 75°, or − csc 15°.

10. csc 607°.

11. csc 910°.   *Ans.* − csc 10°, or − sec 80°.

12. $\tan \dfrac{10\pi}{9}$.

Express the following as functions of an acute angle less than 45°:

13. $\cos \dfrac{17\pi}{12}$.   *Ans.* $-\sin \dfrac{\pi}{12}$.

14. $\sec \dfrac{5\pi}{4}$.

15. tan 236.5°.   *Ans.* cot 33.5°.

16. $\sin \dfrac{23\pi}{7}$.

17. sin 594°.   *Ans.* − cos 36°.

18. cos 260° 53.4′.

Find the values of the following functions:

19. $\sin 216°$.   *Ans.* -0.5878.   20. $\cos 193°$.

21. $\cot 572°$.   *Ans.* 1.600.   22. $\tan 622°$.

23. $\tan \dfrac{6\pi}{5}$.   *Ans.* 0.7265.   24. $\csc \dfrac{8\pi}{7}$.

25. $\sec 930°$.   *Ans.* $-\dfrac{2\sqrt{3}}{3}$.   26. $\sin \dfrac{7\pi}{5}$.

27. Reduction formulas for angles lying in the fourth quadrant.
First method. The functions of an angle in the fourth quadrant whose terminal side is OB_4 (see figure) are the same as the corresponding functions of the positive angle XOB_4, and

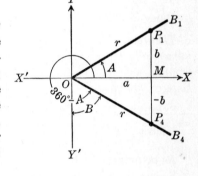

(1)   angle $XOB_4 = 360° - A$,

when A is the measure of the acute angle B_4OX. In the figure, the right triangles OMP_1 and OMP_4 are congruent. The coördinates of P_1 are (a, b). The coördinates of P_4 are $(a, -b)$, and $OP_1 = OP_4 = r$. Hence for the angles $360° - A (= \angle XOB_4)$ and $A (= \angle XOB_1)$

$$\sin (360° - A) = -\sin A; \qquad \csc (360° - A) = -\csc A;$$
$$\cos (360° - A) = \cos A; \qquad \sec (360° - A) = \sec A;$$
$$\tan (360° - A) = -\tan A; \qquad \cot (360° - A) = -\cot A.$$

Thus we have the

Theorem. *The functions of an angle in the fourth quadrant equal numerically the same-named functions of the acute angle between its terminal side and the terminal side of $360°$. The algebraic signs, however, are those for an angle in the fourth quadrant.*

The "acute angle" referred to in this theorem is called the *related angle*.

EXAMPLE 1. Express $\sin 327°$ as the function of an acute angle, and find its value.

Solution. Since $360° - 327° = 33°$, the related angle is $33°$.

$$\sin 327° = \sin (360° - 33°) = -\sin 33° = -0.5446. \quad Ans.$$

EXAMPLE 2. Find the value of $\cot \dfrac{5\pi}{3}$.

Solution. $\cot \dfrac{5\pi}{3} = \cot 300° = \cot (360° - 60°) = -\cot 60° = -\dfrac{1}{\sqrt{3}}. \quad Ans.$

EXAMPLE 3. Find the value of cos 1000°.

Solution. This is an angle in the fourth quadrant, for $1000° - 720° = 280°$. Hence $\cos 1000° = \cos 280° = \cos (360° - 80°) = \cos 80° = 0.1736$. *Ans.*

Second method. The positive angle XOB_4 may also be written $270° + B$, where B measures the acute angle $Y'OB_4$. Since the angles $Y'OB_4$ and B_4OX are complementary, we have, from the theorem of Art. 24, combined with the above results, remembering that $360° - A = 270° + B$,

$$\sin (270° + B) = - \cos B; \qquad \csc (270° + B) = - \sec B;$$
$$\cos (270° + B) = \sin B; \qquad \sec (270° + B) = \csc B;$$
$$\tan (270° + B) = - \cot B; \qquad \cot (270° + B) = - \tan B.$$

Hence we have the

Theorem. *The functions of an angle in the fourth quadrant equal numerically the co-named functions of the acute angle between its terminal side and the terminal side of 270°. The algebraic signs, however, are those of an angle in the fourth quadrant.*

EXAMPLE 4. Find the value of $\cos \dfrac{11\,\pi}{6}$ by the second method.

Solution. $\cos \dfrac{11\,\pi}{6} = \cos 330° = \cos (270° + 60°) = \sin 60° = \dfrac{\sqrt{3}}{2}$. *Ans.*

As before, the first method is generally to be preferred.

PROBLEMS

1. Construct a table of sines, cosines, and tangents of all angles from 180° to 360° at intervals of 30°.

Ans.

	180°	210°	240°	270°	300°	330°	360°
sin	0	$-\dfrac{1}{2}$	$-\dfrac{\sqrt{3}}{2}$	-1	$-\dfrac{\sqrt{3}}{2}$	$-\dfrac{1}{2}$	0
cos	-1	$-\dfrac{\sqrt{3}}{2}$	$-\dfrac{1}{2}$	0	$\dfrac{1}{2}$	$\dfrac{\sqrt{3}}{2}$	1
tan	0	$\dfrac{1}{\sqrt{3}}$	$\sqrt{3}$	∞	$-\sqrt{3}$	$-\dfrac{1}{\sqrt{3}}$	0

2. Construct a table of sines, cosines, and tangents of all angles from 270° to 360° at intervals of 15°, using the table on page 10.

Express the following as functions of an acute angle:

3. sin 291°. *Ans.* $-\sin 69°$, or $-\cos 21°$.

4. cos 316°.

5. cos 333.3°.   *Ans.* cos 26.7°, or
                        sin 63.3°.

6. cot 669.3°.

7. tan 700°.   *Ans.* − tan 20°, or
                      − cot 70°.

8. sin 289° 16′.

9. csc $\dfrac{9\,\pi}{5}$.   *Ans.* − csc $\dfrac{\pi}{5}$, or

                      − sec $\dfrac{3\,\pi}{10}$.

10. sec $\dfrac{35\,\pi}{9}$.

11. cot 5.2.   *Ans.* − cot 1.1, or
                     − tan 0.5.

12. tan 275.5°.

Find the values of the following functions:

13. sin 301°.   *Ans.* − 0.8572.

14. cos 342°.

15. cos 353°.   *Ans.* 0.9925.

16. sin 317°.

17. tan 703°.   *Ans.* − 0.3057.

18. cot 659°.

19. cot $\dfrac{7\,\pi}{4}$.   *Ans.* − 1.

20. tan $\dfrac{9\,\pi}{5}$.

21. sec $\dfrac{23\,\pi}{6}$.   *Ans.* $\dfrac{2\sqrt{3}}{3}$.

22. csc $\dfrac{17\,\pi}{9}$.

23. csc 675°.   *Ans.* − $\sqrt{2}$.

24. sec 701°.

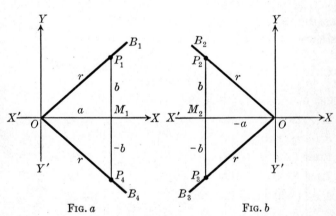

FIG. *a*   FIG. *b*

28. Reduction of functions of negative angles. Simple relations
exist between the functions of the angles A and $-A$ where A is any
angle whatever. It is evident that A and $-A$ will lie, one in the
first quadrant and the other in the fourth quadrant, as angles
XOB_1 and XOB_4 in Fig. *a*, above; or one will lie in the second
quadrant and the other in the third quadrant, as the angles XOB_2
and XOB_3 in Fig. *b*.

In either figure, the points chosen on the terminal sides have the same abscissa and equal distances, and their ordinates differ only in sign. Then for the values of the functions of angles XOB_1 and XOB_4 in Fig. a, and also of angles XOB_2 and XOB_3 in Fig. b, we find

$$\sin(-A) = -\sin A; \qquad \csc(-A) = -\csc A;$$
$$\cos(-A) = \cos A; \qquad \sec(-A) = \sec A;$$
$$\tan(-A) = -\tan A; \qquad \cot(-A) = -\cot A.$$

Hence we have the

Theorem. *The functions of $-A$ equal numerically the same-named functions of A. The algebraic sign, however, will change for all functions except the cosine and secant.**

EXAMPLE 1. Express $\tan(-29°)$ as a function of an acute angle, and find its value.

Solution. $\tan(-29°) = -\tan 29° = -0.5543$. *Ans.*

EXAMPLE 2. Find the value of $\sec(-135°)$.

Solution. $\sec(-135°) = \sec 135° = \sec(180° - 45°) = -\sec 45°$
$$= -\sqrt{2}. \; Ans.$$

EXAMPLE 3. Find the value of $\sin(-540°)$.

Solution. $\sin(-540°) = -\sin 540° = -\sin(360° + 180°)$
$$= -\sin 180° = 0. \; Ans.$$

PROBLEMS

Find the values of the following functions:

1. $\sin(-67°)$.   *Ans.* -0.9205.   2. $\cos(-292°)$.

3. $\cos(-138°)$.   *Ans.* -0.7431.   4. $\sin(-400°)$.

5. $\tan(-33°)$.   *Ans.* -0.6494.   6. $\cot(-117°)$.

7. $\cot(-211°)$.   *Ans.* -1.664.   8. $\tan(-842°)$.

9. $\sec(-315°)$.   *Ans.* $\sqrt{2}$.   10. $\csc\left(-\dfrac{8\pi}{9}\right)$.

11. $\csc\left(-\dfrac{17\pi}{6}\right)$.   *Ans.* -2.   12. $\sec(-700°)$.

* Another method for reducing the functions of a negative angle consists in adding such a multiple of $+360°$ to the negative angle that the sum becomes a positive angle less than $360°$. The functions of this positive angle will be the same as the functions of the given negative angle, since their terminal sides will coincide. To illustrate:

EXAMPLE. Find the value of $\cos(-240°)$.

Solution. Adding $+360°$ to $-240°$ gives $+120°$.

Hence $\cos(-240°) = \cos 120° = \cos(180° - 60°) = -\cos 60° = -\frac{1}{2}$. *Ans.*

29. General rules for reducing the functions of any angle to functions of an acute angle. The results of the last seven sections may be stated in compact form as follows, A being an acute angle *:

GENERAL RULES

I. *Whenever the angle is $180° \pm A$ or $360° \pm A$, the functions of the angle are numerically equal to the **same-named** functions of A.*

II. *Whenever the angle is $90° \pm A$ or $270° \pm A$, the functions of the angle are numerically equal to the **co-named** functions of A.*

III. *In any case the sign of the result is the same as the sign of the given function taken in the quadrant where the given angle lies.*

In Rule I, the angle A is called the *related angle*.

The student is advised to use Rule I wherever possible, since the likelihood of making a mistake is less when the name of the function remains unchanged throughout the operation.

In Arts. 25–28 the formulas found were proved geometrically, and the angles A and B are acute angles. Since the tables give the values of the functions of angles from $0°$ to $90°$, these formulas give a method for finding the numerical value of any function of any angle. But the formulas hold when A and B are not acute. The proofs, which are analytical, are given later. A geometrical proof may be worked out in any given case, as illustrated in Problem 45 following this article.

PROBLEMS

Express the following as functions of a positive acute angle:

1. $\sin 138°$. *Ans.* $\sin 42°$. 2. $\tan 200°$.

3. $\cos(-30°)$. *Ans.* $\cos 30°$. 4. $\tan 883°$.

5. $\cot \dfrac{4\pi}{5}$. *Ans.* $-\cot \dfrac{\pi}{5}$. 6. $\sec\left(-\dfrac{2\pi}{3}\right)$.

---

* In case the given angle is greater than $360°$ we assume that it has first been reduced to a positive angle less than $360°$ by the subtraction of some multiple of $360°$. Or, if the given angle is negative, we assume that it has been reduced to a positive angle by the theorem on page 49.

7. $\cos \dfrac{16\,\pi}{5}.$ *Ans.* $-\cos \dfrac{\pi}{5}.$ **8.** $\sec 260°\,40'.$

9. $\csc 835°.$ *Ans.* $\csc 65°.$ **10.** $\cot 356°\,11'.$

11. $\tan \left(-\dfrac{3\,\pi}{4}\right).$ *Ans.* $\tan \dfrac{\pi}{4}.$ **12.** $\sec (-400°).$

13. $\cos (-135°).$ *Ans.* $-\cos 45°.$ **14.** $\tan 275°\,22'.$

15. $\sin \left(-\dfrac{17\,\pi}{6}\right).$ *Ans.* $-\sin \dfrac{\pi}{6}.$ **16.** $\cos 1000°.$

Without using tables, find the values of the functions of the following angles. Answers are given in the order sine, cosine, tangent.

17. $480°.$ *Ans.* $\dfrac{\sqrt{3}}{2}, -\dfrac{1}{2}, -\sqrt{3},$ etc.   **18.** $-60°.$

19. $\dfrac{3\,\pi}{4}.$ *Ans.* $\dfrac{\sqrt{2}}{2}, -\dfrac{\sqrt{2}}{2}, -1,$ etc.   **20.** $-225°.$

21. $-\dfrac{\pi}{6}.$ *Ans.* $-\dfrac{1}{2}, \dfrac{\sqrt{3}}{2}, -\dfrac{\sqrt{3}}{3},$ etc.   **22.** $420°.$

23. $-150°.$ *Ans.* $-\dfrac{1}{2}, -\dfrac{\sqrt{3}}{2}, \dfrac{\sqrt{3}}{3},$ etc.   **24.** $780°.$

25. $-495°.$ *Ans.* $-\dfrac{\sqrt{2}}{2}, -\dfrac{\sqrt{2}}{2}, 1,$ etc.   **26.** $-315°.$

27. $-\dfrac{4\,\pi}{3}.$ *Ans.* $\dfrac{\sqrt{3}}{2}, -\dfrac{1}{2}, -\sqrt{3},$ etc.   **28.** $-270°.$

Using the table on page 10, find the values of the following functions:

29. $\sin 128°.$ *Ans.* $0.7880.$ **30.** $\cos 147°.$

31. $\tan 235°.$ *Ans.* $1.4281.$ **32.** $\sec 100°.$

33. $\cos (-95°).$ *Ans.* $-0.0872.$ **34.** $\tan 687°.$

35. $\sin 275°.$ *Ans.* $-0.9962.$ **36.** $\cot 1055°.$

37. $\cos \dfrac{15\,\pi}{4}.$ *Ans.* $0.7071.$ **38.** $\tan \left(-\dfrac{4\,\pi}{3}\right).$

39. $\csc 302°.$ *Ans.* $-1.1792.$ **40.** $\sin 316°.$

41. $\cot \dfrac{16\,\pi}{5}.$ *Ans.* $1.3764.$ **42.** $\cos 1500°.$

43. $\cos (-211°).$ *Ans.* $-0.8572.$ **44.** $\sec (-7\,\pi).$

45. Derive geometrically the formulas which express the functions of $90° + B$ in terms of the functions of B, if B lies in the second quadrant.

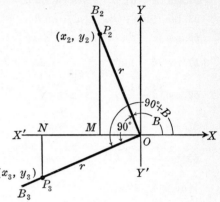

Solution. In the figure, let OB_2 be the terminal side of any angle lying in the second quadrant whose measure is B.

Construct

$$\angle XOB_3 = 90° + B.$$

Take $OP_3 = OP_2 = r$, and draw the ordinates MP_2 and NP_3. Denote the position of P_2 by (x_2, y_2), and the position of P_3 by (x_3, y_3). Then the right triangles OMP_2 and ONP_3 are congruent. Therefore $x_3 = - y_2$ and $y_3 = x_2$.

From the definitions of the functions, we now have

$$\sin (90° + B) = \frac{y_3}{r} = \frac{x_2}{r} = \cos B;$$

$$\cos (90° + B) = \frac{x_3}{r} = - \frac{y_2}{r} = - \sin B;$$

$$\tan (90° + B) = \frac{y_3}{x_3} = - \frac{x_2}{y_2} = - \cot B;$$

$$\cot (90° + B) = \frac{x_3}{y_3} = - \frac{y_2}{x_2} = - \tan B;$$

$$\sec (90° + B) = \frac{r}{x_3} = - \frac{r}{y_2} = - \csc B;$$

$$\csc (90° + B) = \frac{r}{y_3} = \frac{r}{x_2} = \sec B.$$

Thus we see that the formulas on page 42 are also true if B lies in the second quadrant. By this method it is readily shown that these formulas are likewise true if B lies in the third or the fourth quadrant and hence are true for *all* values of B.

46. Derive geometrically the formulas which express the functions of $90° + B$ in terms of the functions of B

(*a*) if B lies in the third quadrant;

(*b*) if B lies in the fourth quadrant.

47. Derive geometrically the formulas for the functions of $180° - A$

(*a*) if A lies in the second quadrant;

(*b*) if A lies in the third quadrant.

By constructing figures in each case for θ (Greek letter "theta") lying in the second, third, and fourth quadrants respectively, derive the formulas for the functions of each of the following angles in terms of the functions of θ.

48. $180° + \theta.$ **49.** $270° - \theta.$ **50.** $270° + \theta.$

Express each of the following functions as a function of θ:

51. $\sin(\pi + \theta)$.   *Ans.* $-\sin\theta$.   **52.** $\cos(270° - \theta)$.

53. $\tan(540° + \theta)$.   *Ans.* $\tan\theta$.   **54.** $\cot(630° - \theta)$.

55. $\sec(\pi - \theta)$.   *Ans.* $-\sec\theta$.   **56.** $\sin(\theta + 450°)$.

57. $\cos(\theta - 180°)$.   *Ans.* $-\cos\theta$.   **58.** $\tan\left(\dfrac{3\pi}{2} - \theta\right)$.

59. $\csc\left(\theta - \dfrac{3\pi}{2}\right)$.   *Ans.* $\sec\theta$.   **60.** $\cot\left(\dfrac{11\pi}{2} + \theta\right)$.

61. $\cos\left(\theta - \dfrac{5\pi}{2}\right)$.   *Ans.* $\sin\theta$.   **62.** $\sin(\theta - 900°)$.

63. $\tan\left(-\dfrac{\pi}{2} - \theta\right)$.   *Ans.* $\cot\theta$.   **64.** $\sec\left(-\theta - \dfrac{3\pi}{2}\right)$.

Prove the following:

65. $\sin 420° \cdot \cos 390° + \cos(-300°) \cdot \sin(-330°) = 1$.

66. $\cos 570° \cdot \sin 510° - \sin 330° \cdot \cos 390° = 0$.

67. $a\cos(90° - x) + b\cos(90° + x) = (a - b)\sin x$.

68. $m\cos\left(\dfrac{\pi}{2} - x\right) \cdot \sin\left(\dfrac{\pi}{2} - x\right) = m\sin x\cos x$.

69. $(a-b)\tan(90°-x) + (a+b)\cot(90°+x) = (a-b)\cot x - (a+b)\tan x$.

70. $\sin\left(\dfrac{\pi}{2} + x\right)\sin(\pi + x) + \cos\left(\dfrac{\pi}{2} + x\right)\cos(\pi - x) = 0$.

71. $\cos(\pi+x)\cos\left(\dfrac{3\pi}{2} - y\right) - \sin(\pi+x)\sin\left(\dfrac{3\pi}{2} - y\right) = \cos x\sin y - \sin x\cos y$.

72. $\tan x + \tan(-y) - \tan(\pi - y) = \tan x$.

73. $\cos(90° + a)\cos(270° - a) - \sin(180° - a)\sin(360° - a) = 2\sin^2 a$.

74. $\dfrac{\sin(180° - y)}{\sin(270° - y)}\tan(90° + y) + \dfrac{1}{\sin^2(270° - y)} = 1 + \sec^2 y$.

75. $3\tan 210° + 2\tan 120° = -\sqrt{3}$.   **78.** $\tan\frac{1}{2}(2\pi + x) = \tan\frac{1}{2}x$.

76. $5\sec^2 135° - 6\cot^2 300° = 8$.   **79.** $\csc\frac{1}{4}(x - 2\pi) = -\sec\frac{1}{4}x$.

77. $\cos\frac{1}{3}(x - 270°) = \sin\frac{1}{3}x$.   **80.** $\cos\frac{1}{3}(y - 810°) = -\sin\frac{1}{3}y$.

Express the following as functions of an acute angle less than 45°:

81. $\sin 263°$.   *Ans.* $-\cos 7°$.   **82.** $\cos 284°$.

83. $\cot 333.3°$.   *Ans.* $-\cot 26.7°$.   **84.** $\tan 462° \, 15'$.

85. $\cos 642° \, 10'$.   *Ans.* $\sin 12° \, 10'$.   **86.** $\csc 614.4°$.

87. $\tan\dfrac{17\pi}{10}$.   *Ans.* $-\cot\dfrac{\pi}{5}$.   **88.** $\cot\dfrac{8\pi}{3}$.

89. $\sec\dfrac{9\pi}{14}$.   *Ans.* $-\csc\dfrac{\pi}{7}$.   **90.** $\sin\dfrac{37\pi}{14}$.

CHAPTER III

LINE DEFINITIONS AND GRAPHS

30. Line definitions of the trigonometric functions. The definitions of the functions in Art. 13 as ratios are fundamental. For some purposes, however, it is convenient to use a graphical method of representing the values of the functions by means of *directed line-segments*.

A directed line-segment is one for which direction is taken into account. If its extremities are the points A and B, then the directed line-segments AB and BA differ in sign.

In the figure below, the line-segments defining the six trigonometric functions are labeled. The circle has its radius equal to the unit of length. It is called a *unit circle*.

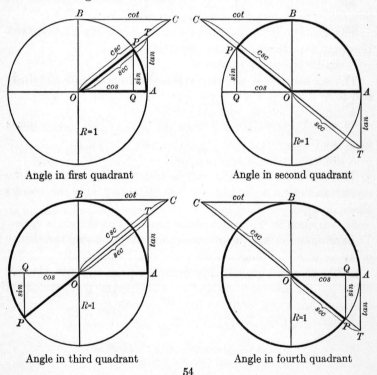

Angle in first quadrant   Angle in second quadrant

Angle in third quadrant   Angle in fourth quadrant

54

In each figure, the coördinates of the point P on the terminal side are $x = OQ$, $y = QP$. The distance $r = OP = 1$.

Applying the ratio definitions of Art. 13, we get

$$\sin AOP = \frac{QP}{OP(=1)} = \boldsymbol{QP};$$

$$\cos AOP = \frac{OQ}{OP(=1)} = \boldsymbol{OQ};$$

$$\tan AOP = \frac{QP}{OQ} = \frac{AT}{OA(=1)}{}^{*} = \boldsymbol{AT};$$

$$\sec AOP = \frac{OP}{OQ} = \frac{OT}{OA(=1)}{}^{*} = \boldsymbol{OT};$$

$$\cot AOP = \frac{OQ}{QP} = \frac{BC}{OB(=1)}{}^{\dagger} = \boldsymbol{BC};$$

$$\csc AOP = \frac{OP}{QP} = \frac{OC}{OB(=1)}{}^{\dagger} = \boldsymbol{OC}.$$

The line-segments QP, OQ, etc. in the above equations are *directed*. The statements covering this point are as follows:

The segment QP is *positive* or *negative* according as the direction from Q to P is *upward* or *downward*.

A similar statement applies to AT.

The segment OQ is *positive* or *negative* according as the direction from O to Q is to the *right* or to the *left*.

A similar statement applies to BC.

The segment OT is *positive* or *negative* according as the directions from O to T and O to P are the *same* or *opposite*.

A similar statement applies to OC.

The line-segments in the line definitions above now give the correct numerical values of the functions and also the correct algebraic signs.

31. Variation in the values of the functions as the angle varies. The line values in Art. 30 are convenient for discussing the change in the value of any function when the angle varies.

a. The sine and cosine. The figure on page 56 shows the line values of the sine and cosine for angles between 0° and 360°. It shows clearly the results of Art. 20, namely,

$$\sin 0° = 0, \ \cos 0° = 1, \ \sin 90° = 1, \ \text{etc.}$$

---

* Since triangles OQP and OAT are similar.
† Since triangles OQP and OBC are similar.

We readily see the truth of the following statements:

When the angle x increases from 0° to 90°,

sin x increases from 0 to 1,

cos x decreases from 1 to 0.

When the angle x increases from 90° to 180°,

sin x decreases from 1 to 0,

cos x decreases from 0 to − 1.

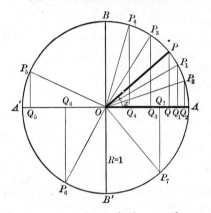

When the angle x increases from 180° to 270°,

sin x decreases from 0 to − 1,

cos x increases from − 1 to 0.

When the angle x increases from 270° to 360°,

sin x increases from − 1 to 0,

cos x increases from 0 to 1.

b. The tangent. Let x denote the variable acute angle AOT.

As x decreases, the tangent decreases through the values AT_1, AT_2, etc. Thus we see, as in Art. 20, that

$$\tan 0° = 0.$$

As x increases from 0° and approaches 90° as a limit, the tangent is positive and increases from zero through the values AT_3, AT_4, etc., without limit, that is, beyond any numerical value. This is written

$$\tan 90° = + \infty.*$$

Now suppose the angle x to be equal to the angle AOP (greater than 90°) and let it decrease and approach 90°; then the corre-

---

* $+ \infty$ is read *plus infinity.* $- \infty$ is read *minus infinity.* ∞ is read simply *infinity.*

sponding tangent AT_6 is negative and increases in numerical value without limit. This is written

$$\tan 90° = - \infty.$$

We see, then, that the tangent will become $+ \infty$ or $- \infty$ according as x is increasing or decreasing as it approaches 90°. As one statement these last two results are written

$$\tan 90° = \infty,$$

when, as in this book, no distinction is made for the manner in which the angle approaches the limit 90°.

Also, from the figure,

$$\tan 180° = 0, \quad \tan 270° = \infty,$$

as in Art. 20.

When the angle x increases from 0° to 90°,

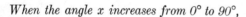

tan x increases from 0 and becomes infinite.

When the angle x increases and has any value except 90° or 270°, tan x increases.

c. The secant. In the above figure, in which x denotes the variable acute angle AOT, sec $x = OT$. Then

$$\sec 0° = OA = 1.$$

By a discussion precisely the same as for tan x, we find

$$\sec 90° = \infty, \quad \sec 270° = \infty.$$

Also $$\sec 180° = - 1.$$

These results agree with Art. 20.

When x increases from 0° to 90°, sec x increases from 1 and becomes infinite.

When x is greater than 90° and increases, the discussion of the variation of sec x is left for the reader.

d. The cotangent. Let x denote the variable angle AOC (p. 58).

As x decreases, the cotangent increases through the values BC_1, BC_2, etc., and as x approaches 0°, the cotangent increases without limit. This is written $$\cot 0° = \infty.$$

In the same manner, we find

$$\cot 180° = \infty.$$

Also, as can be seen from the figure,

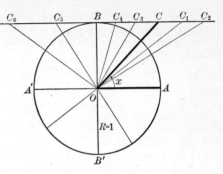

$$\cot 90° = 0,$$
$$\cot 270° = 0.$$

These results agree with Art. 20.

When x increases and has any value except 0° or 180°, cot x decreases.

e. The cosecant. Using the last figure, we see that as x decreases, the cosecant increases through the values OC_1, OC_2, etc., and as x approaches 0°, the cosecant increases without limit. This is written

$$\csc 0° = \infty.$$

In the same manner, we get

$$\csc 180° = \infty.$$

Also, from the figure,

$$\csc 90° = 1, \quad \csc 270° = -1.$$

These results agree with Art. 20.

When x is a small positive angle and increases to 90°, csc x decreases and becomes 1. For other values of x the discussion is left to the reader.

32. Graphs of functions. The relation between the assumed values of a variable and the corresponding values of a function of that variable are very clearly shown by a geometrical representation where the assumed values of the variable are taken as the abscissas, and the corresponding values of the function as the ordinates of points in a plane. A smooth curve drawn through these points in order is called the *graph of the function.* Following are

GENERAL DIRECTIONS FOR PLOTTING THE GRAPH OF A FUNCTION

First step. Place y equal to the function.

Second step. Assume different values for the variable ($= x$) and calculate the corresponding values of the function ($= y$), writing down the results in tabulated form.

Third step. Plot the points having the values of x as abscissas and the corresponding values of y as ordinates.

Fourth step. A smooth curve drawn through these points in order is called the graph of the function.

EXAMPLE 1. Plot the graph of $2x - 6$.

Solution. *First step.* Let $y = 2x - 6$.

Second step. Assume different values for x and compute the corresponding values of y. Thus, if

$$x = 0, \quad y = -6; \qquad x = -1, \quad y = -8;$$
$$x = 1, \quad y = -4; \qquad x = -2, \quad y = -10;$$
$$x = 2, \quad y = -2; \qquad \text{etc.}$$

Arranging these results in tabulated form, the first two columns give the corresponding values of x and y when we assume positive values of x, and the

x	y	x	y
0	− 6	0	− 6
1	− 4	− 1	− 8
2	− 2	− 2	− 10
3	0	− 3	− 12
4	2	− 4	− 14
5	4	− 5	− 16
6	6	− 6	− 18
etc.	etc.	etc.	etc.

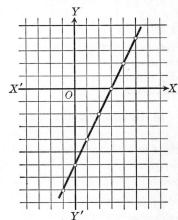

last two columns when we assume negative values of x. For the sake of symmetry $x = 0$ is placed in both pairs of columns.

Third step. Plot the points found.

Fourth step. Drawing a smooth curve through these points gives the graph of the function, which in this case is a straight line.

EXAMPLE 2. Plot the graph of $x^2 - 2x - 3$.

Solution. *First step.* Let

$$y = x^2 - 2x - 3.$$

Second step. Computing y by assuming values of x, we find the following table of values:

x	y	x	y
0	− 3	0	− 3
1	− 4	− 1	0
2	− 3	− 2	5
3	0	− 3	12
4	5	− 4	21
5	12	etc.	etc.
6	21		
etc.	etc.		

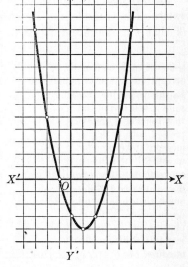

Third step. Plot the points found.

Fourth step. Drawing a smooth curve through these points gives the graph of the function.

PROBLEMS

Plot the graphs of the following functions:

1. $x + 2$.

2. $6 - 3x$.

3. x^2.

4. $\dfrac{1}{x}$.

5. $\dfrac{4}{x - 2}$.

6. 2^x.

7. $2x^2 - 4$.

8. $8 - x^2$.

9. $x^3 - 4x + 3$.

10. $x^3 - 4x$.

33. Graphs of the trigonometric functions. To find the graph of a trigonometric function we assume values for the angle; the circular measures of these angles are taken as the abscissas, and the corresponding values of the function are taken as the ordinates of points on the graph.

EXAMPLE. Plot the graph of $\sin x$.

Solution. *First step.* Let $y = \sin x$.

Second step. Assuming values of x differing by 30°, we calculate the corresponding values of y from the table on page 10 and from Art. 29. In tabulating the results it will be noticed that the angles are expressed both in degree measure and in circular measure. It is most convenient to use the degree measure of an angle when looking up its function, while in plotting it is necessary to use its circular measure.

x		y	x		y
0°	0	0	0°	0	0
30°	$\dfrac{\pi}{6}$	0.50	$-30°$	$-\dfrac{\pi}{6}$	-0.50
60°	$\dfrac{\pi}{3}$	0.87	$-60°$	$-\dfrac{\pi}{3}$	-0.87
90°	$\dfrac{\pi}{2}$	1.00	$-90°$	$-\dfrac{\pi}{2}$	-1.00
120°	$\dfrac{2\pi}{3}$	0.87	$-120°$	$-\dfrac{2\pi}{3}$	-0.87
150°	$\dfrac{5\pi}{6}$	0.50	$-150°$	$-\dfrac{5\pi}{6}$	-0.50
180°	π	0	$-180°$	$-\pi$	0
210°	$\dfrac{7\pi}{6}$	-0.50	$-210°$	$-\dfrac{7\pi}{6}$	0.50
240°	$\dfrac{4\pi}{3}$	-0.87	$-240°$	$-\dfrac{4\pi}{3}$	0.87
270°	$\dfrac{3\pi}{2}$	-1.00	$-270°$	$-\dfrac{3\pi}{2}$	1.00
300°	$\dfrac{5\pi}{3}$	-0.87	$-300°$	$-\dfrac{5\pi}{3}$	0.87
330°	$\dfrac{11\pi}{6}$	-0.50	$-330°$	$-\dfrac{11\pi}{6}$	0.50
360°	2π	0	$-360°$	-2π	0

Third step. In plotting the points we must use the circular measure of the angles for abscissas. The most convenient way of doing this is to lay off distances $\pi = 3.1416$ to the right and left of the origin and then divide each of these into six equal parts. Then when

$$x = 0, \qquad\qquad y = 0;$$

$$x = \frac{\pi}{6} = 0.52, \qquad\qquad y = 0.50 = AB;$$

$$x = \frac{\pi}{3} = 1.05, \qquad\qquad y = 0.87 = CD;$$

$$x = \frac{\pi}{2} = 1.57, \qquad\qquad y = 1.00 = EF; \text{ etc.}$$

Also, when $\quad x = -\frac{\pi}{6} = -0.52, \qquad y = -0.50 = GH; \text{ etc.}$

In the figure, three small divisions (either axis) = 1.

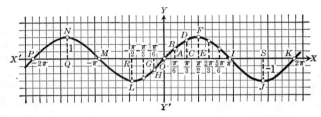

Fourth step. Drawing a smooth curve through these points, we get the graph of sin x for values of x between -2π and 2π. It is called the *sine curve* or *sinusoid*.

Discussion. *a.* Since $\sin(x \pm 2\pi) = \sin x$, it follows that

$$y = \sin x = \sin(x \pm 2\pi),$$

that is, the value of y is *unchanged* if we replace x by $x \pm 2\pi$. This means, however, that every point is moved a distance 2π to the right or left. Hence the arc $PNMLO$ may be moved parallel to XX' until P falls at O. Then N will fall at F, M at I, etc. That is, $PNMLO$ will take the position $OFIJK$, and it will be a part of the curve in its new position. In the case of the sine curve it is, then, only necessary to plot points, say, from $x = -\pi$ to $x = \pi$, giving the arc or double undulation $MLOFI$. The sine curve consists of an indefinite number of such arcs extending to the right and left.

b. From the graph we see that the maximum value of $\sin x (= y)$ is $1 (= EF = QN$, etc.) and the minimum value is $-1 (= SJ = RL$, etc.), while x can take on any value whatever.

c. Since the graph crosses the axis of x an infinite number of times, we see that the equation $\qquad\qquad \sin x = 0$

has an infinite number of real roots, namely, $x = 0, \pm 2\pi, \pm 4\pi$, etc.

34. Periodicity of the trigonometric functions.

From the graph of $\sin x$ in the above example we saw that as the angle increased from 0 to 2π radians, the sine first increased from 0 to 1, then decreased from 1 to -1, and finally increased from -1 to 0. As the angle increased from 2π radians to 4π radians, the sine again went through the same series of changes, and so on. Thus the sine goes through all its changes while the angle changes 2π radians in value. This is expressed by saying that the *period of the sine is 2π.*

Similarly, the cosine, secant, or cosecant passes through all its values while the angle changes 2π radians.

The tangent or cotangent, however, passes through all its values while the angle changes by π radians. Hence, *the **period** of the sine, cosine, secant, or cosecant is **2π radians**; while the **period** of the tangent or cotangent is **π radians**.*

PROBLEMS

1. Give by quadrants a complete statement of the variation of each of the trigonometric functions as the angle increases from $0°$ to $360°$.

2. Give by quadrants a complete statement of the variation of the function $4\cos\theta + 3$ as θ increases from $0°$ to $360°$.

3. From a figure showing the line values for the functions of θ and for $180° - \theta$, write the formulas which express the functions of $180° - \theta$ in terms of the functions of θ.

4. Following the method of Art. 33, plot the graph of (*a*) $\cos x$; (*b*) $\tan x$.

5. Using the graph of $\sin x$ and the relation $\cos x = \sin\left(\dfrac{\pi}{2} + x\right)$, draw the graph of $\cos x$.

6. Using the graph of $\sin x$, draw the graph of $\csc x$ from the reciprocal relation $\csc x = \dfrac{1}{\sin x}$.

7. Using the graphs of $\cos x$ and of $\tan x$, draw the graphs of $\sec x$ and of $\cot x$ from the reciprocal relations $\sec x = \dfrac{1}{\cos x}$, $\cot x = \dfrac{1}{\tan x}$.

8. Verify the relation $\cos\left(x + \dfrac{\pi}{2}\right) = -\sin x$ by comparing the graph of $\cos x$ with the graph of $\sin x$.

Plot the graphs of the following functions and compare them with the graph of $\sin x$:

9. $\frac{1}{2}\sin x$.   **10.** $2\sin x$.   **11.** $\sin 2x$.   **12.** $\sin 3x$.

Plot the graphs of the following functions at intervals of $\frac{1}{2}$ a radian:

13. $\cos\dfrac{\pi x}{2}$.   **15.** $\frac{1}{2}\tan\dfrac{\pi x}{3}$.

14. $4\sin\dfrac{\pi x}{3}$.   **16.** $2\sec\dfrac{\pi x}{2}$.

17. Plot the graphs of sin x and cos x with reference to the same axes. By adding geometrically the ordinates corresponding to the same abscissas draw the graph of sin $x +$ cos x. Is this function periodic?

35. Graphs of trigonometric functions plotted by means of the unit circle. The following example will illustrate how we may plot the graph of a trigonometric function without using any table of numerical values of the function for different angles such as given on page 10.

EXAMPLE 1. Plot the graph of sin x.

Solution. Let $y =$ sin x. Draw a unit circle.

Divide the circumference of the circle into any number of equal parts (12 in this case). At the several points of division drop perpendiculars to the horizontal diameter. Then the sine of the angle AOB, or, what amounts to the same thing,

$$\text{sine of arc } AB = QB,$$
$$\text{sine of arc } AE = NE,$$
$$\text{sine of arc } AJ = OJ, \text{ etc.}$$

 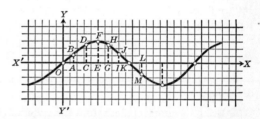

It is evident that if we take the lengths of the arcs as the abscissas and the corresponding lengths of the perpendiculars as the ordinates of points in a plane, these points will lie on the graph of sin x. If we choose the same scale as in the example in Art. 33, p. 60, the two graphs can be made to coincide. When different scales are chosen, the main features of the two graphs of sin x are the same and the discussion is the same for both.

	In Circle	In Graph		In Circle	In Graph
When	$x =$ arc zero $=$ zero,			$y =$ zero $=$ zero;	
	$x =$ arc $AB = OA$,			$y = QB = AB$;	
	$x =$ arc $AC = OC$,			$y = PC = CD$;	
	$x =$ arc $AD = OE$,			$y = OD = EF$;	
	$x =$ arc $AE = OG$,			$y = NE = GH$;	
	$x =$ arc $AF = OI$,			$y = MF = IJ$;	
	$x =$ arc $AG = OK$,			$y =$ zero $=$ zero;	
	$x =$ arc $AH = OL$,			$y = MH = LM$, etc.	

EXAMPLE 2. Plot the graph of cos *x*.

Solution. Let $y = \cos x$. The *cosine curve* is found to be as follows:

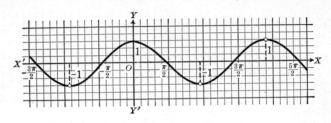

To plot the graph of cos *x* by means of the unit circle we may use the circle on page 63. Taking the abscissas as arcs zero, *AB*, *AC*, *AD*, etc., and the corresponding ordinates as *OA*, *OQ*, *OP*, zero, etc., respectively, we shall get points lying on the cosine curve.

EXAMPLE 3. Plot the graph of tan *x*.

Solution. The *tangent curve* is given below.

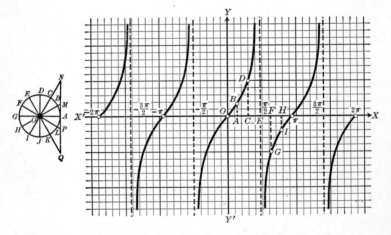

To construct the tangent curve from the unit circle shown, we have

	In Circle	In Graph		In Circle	In Graph
When	$x = \text{arc zero} = \text{zero},$			$y = \text{zero} = \text{zero};$	
	$x = \text{arc } AB = OA,$			$y = AM = AB;$	
	$x = \text{arc } AC = OC,$			$y = AN = CD;$	
	$x = \text{arc } AD = OE,$			$y = \infty = \infty;$	
	$x = \text{arc } AE = OF,$			$y = AQ = FG, \text{ etc.}$	

EXAMPLE 4. Plot the graph of sec x.

Solution. The *secant curve* is given below.

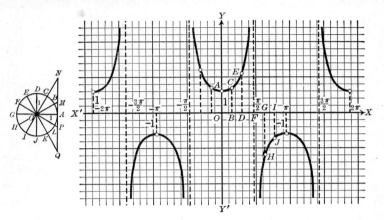

Using the unit circle, we have

		In Circle	In Graph		In Circle	In Graph
When	$x = $ arc zero $=$ zero,			$y = OA$		$= OA$;
	$x = $ arc AB	$= OB,$		$y = OM$		$= BC$;
	$x = $ arc AC	$= OD,$		$y = ON$		$= DE$;
	$x = $ arc AD	$= OF,$		$y = \infty$		$= \infty$;
	$x = $ arc AE	$= OG,$		$y = OQ$		$= GH$, etc.

EXAMPLE 5. Plot the *cotangent curve.*

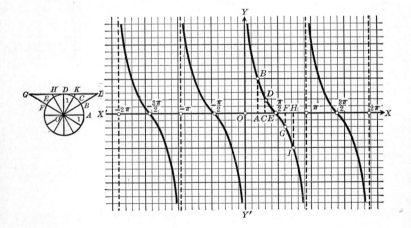

EXAMPLE 6. Plot the *cosecant curve.*

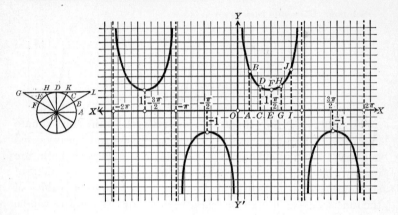

PROBLEM

Using the method of this article, draw the graphs of

a. $\sin x + \cos x.$ *d.* $\tan 2x.$

b. $\cos x - \sin x.$ *e.* $\sin x \cos x.$

c. $\sin 2x.$

CHAPTER IV

APPLICATIONS

36. Object of the chapter; computations with approximate numbers. Many problems in which the given and the required quantities are measurements of lengths or of angles, or both, are readily solved by the use of trigonometric functions. A variety of such problems is presented in this chapter. A table of values of the functions of acute angles was given on page 10, and this will be made use of in Art. 37. A more extensive table will be referred to later (Arts. 38–39).

Significant figures. From the table of Art. 7 we have

$$\sin 2° = 0.0349, \quad \tan 46° = 1.0355, \quad \sec 88° = 28.654.$$

The "significant figures" in the right-hand members are, respectively, 349, 10355, 28654.

The decimal point is ignored in determining significant figures, and for numbers less than unity, zeros immediately to the right of the decimal point are omitted.

The values given above are approximate, but the errors are in each case less than half a unit in the last place of decimals. That is, the *exact* values are as follows:

of sin 2°, between 0.03485 and 0.03495;

of tan 46°, between 1.03545 and 1.03555;

of sec 88°, between 28.6535 and 28.6545.

Calculations made in this chapter employ the four operations of arithmetic — addition, subtraction, multiplication, and division. In making a calculation from data having only four significant figures, it is important to remember that *only four significant figures of the result* are, in general, of any value. To illustrate, let it be required to calculate a from the formula

(1) $$a = c \sin A,$$

given $$c = 267, \quad A = 35°.$$

From the table of Art. 7,

$$\sin 35° = 0.5736,$$

to four significant figures. Hence

(2) $\qquad\qquad a = 267 \times 0.5736.$

Multiplying,
$$
\begin{array}{r}
0.5736 \\
267 \\
\hline
40152 \\
34416 \\
11472 \\
\hline
a = 153.1512
\end{array}
$$

This result has seven figures, but we shall see that four figures only are significant. For, from a five-place table, we have

$$\sin 35° = 0.57358$$

to five significant figures. Using this value in (1), we have

$$
\begin{array}{r}
0.57358 \\
267 \\
\hline
401506 \\
344148 \\
114716 \\
\hline
a = 153.14586
\end{array}
$$

The two results agree to four significant figures only. Hence we have in the first calculation

$$267 \times 0.5736 = 153.1,$$

discarding the figures to the right of tenths' place.

When we apply the principles of trigonometry to the solution of practical problems, — engineering problems, for instance, — it is usually necessary to use data which have been found by actual measurement and therefore are subject to error. In taking these measurements one should carefully see that they are made with about the same degree of accuracy. Thus, it would evidently be folly to measure one side of a triangle with much greater care than another, for, in combining these measurements in a calculation, the result would at best be no more accurate than the worst measurement. Similarly, the angles of a triangle should be measured with the same care as the sides.

The number of significant figures in a measurement is supposed to indicate the care that was intended when the measurement was made, and any two measurements showing the same number of significant figures will, in general, show about the same relative care in measurement. If the sides of a rectangle are about 936 ft. and 8 ft., the short side should be measured to at least two decimal places. A neglected 4 in the tenths' place will alter the area by 374 sq. ft.

The following directions will help us to make consistent measurements and avoid unnecessary work in our calculations:

1. Let all measured lines and calculated lines show the same number of significant figures, as a rule.

2. When the lines show only one significant figure, let the angles read to the nearest 5°.

3. When the lines show two significant figures, let the angles read to the nearest half degree.

4. When the lines show three significant figures, let the angles read to the nearest 5'.

5. When the lines show four significant figures, let the angles read to the nearest minute.

37. Problems depending upon right triangles. The solution of a given problem will depend often upon "solving a triangle." A triangle is composed of six parts, three sides and three angles. To solve a triangle is to find the parts not given. A triangle can be solved if three parts, at least one of which is a side, are given.* A right triangle has one angle, the right angle, always given; hence a right triangle can be solved if two sides, or one side and an acute angle, are given. One of the most important applications of trigonometry† is the solution of triangles, and we shall now take up the *solution of right triangles.*

GENERAL DIRECTIONS FOR SOLVING RIGHT TRIANGLES

First step. Draw a figure as accurately as possible representing the triangle in question.

Second step. When one acute angle is known, subtract it from 90° to get the other acute angle.

Third step. To find an unknown part, select from (1) to (6), Art. 4, a formula involving the unknown part and two known parts, and then solve for the unknown part.

---

* It is assumed that the given conditions are consistent, that is, that it is possible to construct the triangle from the given parts.

† The name *trigonometry* is derived from two Greek words which taken together mean "I measure a triangle."

Fourth step. Check the values found by noting whether they satisfy relations different from those already employed in the third step. A convenient numerical check is the relation

$$a^2 = c^2 - b^2 = (c + b)(c - b).$$

Large errors may be detected by measurement.

The directions above will now be illustrated by examples.

EXAMPLE 1. Given $A = 35°$, $c = 267$; solve the right triangle. Also find its area.

Solution. *First step.* Draw a figure of the triangle indicating the known and unknown parts.

Second step. $B = 90° - A = 90° - 35° = 55°$.

Third step. To find a, use formula (1), p. 2, namely,

$$\sin A = \frac{a}{c}.$$

Substituting the value of $\sin A = \sin 35° = 0.5736$ (found from the table) and $c = 267$, we have

$$0.5736 = \frac{a}{267}.$$

Hence $a = 267 \times 0.5736 = 153.1$.

To find b, use formula (2), p. 2, namely,

$$\cos A = \frac{b}{c}.$$

Substituting as before, we have

$$0.8192 = \frac{b}{267},$$

since from the table $\cos A = \cos 35° = 0.8192$. Hence
$$b = 0.8192 \times 267 = 218.7.$$

Fourth step. By measurements we now check the results to see that there are no large errors. As a numerical check we find that the values of a, b, c satisfy the condition
$$c^2 = a^2 + b^2.$$

To find the area of the triangle we have

$$\text{area} = \frac{ab}{2} = \frac{153.1 \times 218.7}{2} = 16{,}741.$$

EXAMPLE 2. A ladder 30 ft. long leans against the side of a building, its foot being 15 ft. from the building. What angle does the ladder make with the ground?

Solution. Our figure shows a right triangle with hypotenuse and side adjacent to the required angle $(= x)$ given. Hence

$$\cos x = \tfrac{15}{30} = \tfrac{1}{2}.$$

Hence, by Art. 5, $x = 60°$. *Ans.*

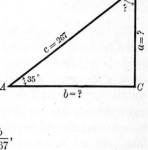

We shall now derive three formulas by means of which the work of solving right triangles may be simplified. From (1), (2), (3), p. 2,

$$\sin A = \frac{a}{c},$$

or, $\qquad a = c \sin A$;

$$\cos A = \frac{b}{c},$$

or, $\qquad b = c \cos A$;

$$\tan A = \frac{a}{b},$$

or, $\qquad a = b \tan A.$

These results may be stated as follows:

(38) **Side opposite an acute angle = hypotenuse × sine of the angle.**

(39) **Side adjacent to an acute angle = hypotenuse × cosine of the angle.**

(40) **Side opposite an acute angle = adjacent side × tangent of the angle.**

Solution of isosceles triangles. An isosceles triangle is divided by the perpendicular from the vertex to the base into two congruent right triangles; hence the solution of an isosceles triangle can be made to depend on the solution of one of these right triangles. The following examples will illustrate the method:

EXAMPLE 3. The equal sides of an isosceles triangle are each 40 in. long, and the equal angles at the base are each 25°. Solve the triangle and find its area.

Solution. $B = 180° - (A + C) = 180° - 50° = 130°.$
Drop the perpendicular BD to AC.

$AD = AB \cos A$

$\quad = 40 \cos 25° \qquad$ by **(39)**

$\quad = 40 \times 0.9063$

$\quad = 36.25.$

Therefore $\qquad AC = 2\,AD = 72.50$ in.

To find the area, we need in addition the altitude BD.

$$BD = AB \sin A = 40 \sin 25° \qquad\qquad \text{by (38)}$$
$$= 40 \times 0.4226 = 16.9.$$

Check. $BD = AD \tan 25° = 36.25 \times 0.4663 = 16.9.$ $\qquad$ By **(40)**

Also, $\qquad\qquad$ area $= \frac{1}{2} AC \times BD = 612.6$ sq. in.

EXAMPLE 4. A barn 60 ft. wide has a gable roof whose rafters are $30\sqrt{2}$ ft. long. What is the pitch of the roof, and how far above the eaves is the ridge-pole?

Solution. Drop a perpendicular from B to AD. Then

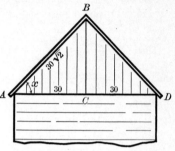

$$\cos x = \frac{AC}{AB} = \frac{30}{30\sqrt{2}} = \frac{1}{\sqrt{2}}.$$

Hence $x = 45° =$ pitch of the roof.

Also, $BC = AB \sin x$ by (**38**)

$$= 30\sqrt{2} \cdot \frac{1}{\sqrt{2}}$$

$$= 30 \text{ ft.}$$

   = height of the ridgepole above the eaves.

Check. $AB = \sqrt{\overline{AC}^2 + \overline{BC}^2} = \sqrt{(30)^2 + (30)^2} = \sqrt{1800} = 30\sqrt{2}.$

Solution of regular polygons. Lines drawn from the center of a regular polygon of n sides to the vertices are the radii of the cir-cumscribed circle and divide the polygon into n equal isosceles tri-angles. The perpendiculars from the center to the sides of the poly-gon are the radii of the inscribed circle and divide these n equal isos-celes triangles into $2n$ equal right triangles. Hence the solution of a regular polygon depends on the solution of one of these right triangles.

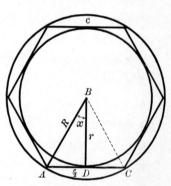

From geometry we know that the central angle $ABC = \dfrac{360°}{n}$; hence in the right triangle ABD the

$$\text{angle } x = \frac{180°}{n}.$$

Also, $AD = \dfrac{c}{2} =$ half the length of one side,

         $AB = R =$ radius of circumscribed circle,

         $BD = r =$ radius of inscribed circle,

         $p = nc =$ perimeter of polygon,

         $\dfrac{pr}{2} =$ area of polygon.

EXAMPLE 5. One side of a regular decagon is 10 in.; find the radii of the inscribed and circumscribed circles and the area of the polygon.

Solution. Since $n = 10$, in this example we have

$$x = \frac{180°}{n} = \frac{180°}{10} = 18°.$$

Then $R = \dfrac{5}{\sin 18°} = \dfrac{5}{0.3090} = 16.18$ in.,

and $r = \dfrac{5}{\tan 18°} = \dfrac{5}{0.3249} = 15.39$ in.

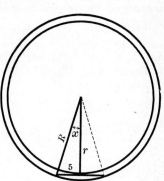

Check. $r = R \cos 18° = 16.18 \times 0.9511$

$= 15.39.$

Also, $p = 10 \times 10 = 100$ in.

$= \text{perimeter of polygon};$

hence $\dfrac{pr}{2} = \dfrac{100 \times 15.39}{2} = 769.5$ sq. in.

$= \text{area}.$

PROBLEMS

Solve the following right triangles ($C = 90°$), given:

1. $A = 20°$, $c = 80$. — *Ans.* $B = 70°$, $a = 27.36$, $b = 75.18$.

2. $B = 51°$, $c = 250$.

3. $A = 36°$, $c = 1$. *Ans.* $B = 54°$, $a = 0.5878$, $b = 0.8090$.

4. $A = 25°$, $a = 30$.

5. $A = 10°$, $b = 30$. *Ans.* $B = 80°$, $a = 5.289$, $c = 30.46$.

6. $B = 55°$, $b = 10$.

7. $A = 75°$, $a = 80$. *Ans.* $B = 15°$, $b = 21.43$, $c = 82.82$.

8. $a = 2$, $c = 2.8284$.

9. $c = 43$, $a = 38.31$. *Ans.* $A = 63°$, $B = 27°$, $b = 19.52$.

10. $a = 36.4$, $b = 100$.

11. $a = 23.32$, $b = 50$. *Ans.* $A = 25°$, $B = 65°$, $c = 55.17$.

12. $b = 9.696$, $c = 20$.

13. $a = 30.21$, $c = 33.33$. *Ans.* $A = 65°$, $B = 25°$, $b = 14.085$.

14. $a = 13.40$, $b = 50$.

15. A tree is broken by the wind so that its two parts form with the ground a right-angled triangle. The upper part makes an angle of 35° with the ground, and the distance on the ground from the trunk to the top of the tree is 50 ft. Find the length of the tree. *Ans.* 96.05 ft.

16. In order to find the breadth of a river, a distance AB was measured along the bank, the point A being directly opposite a tree C on the other side. If the angle ABC was observed to be 55° and AB 100 ft., find the breadth of the river.

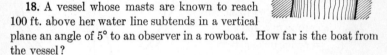

17. Two forts defending a harbor are 2 mi. apart. From one a hostile battleship is observed due south and from the other 15° east of south. How far is the battleship from the nearest fort?

Ans. 7.464 mi.

18. A vessel whose masts are known to reach 100 ft. above her water line subtends in a vertical plane an angle of 5° to an observer in a rowboat. How far is the boat from the vessel?

19. The central pole of a circular tent is 20 ft. high, and its top is fastened by ropes 40 ft. long to stakes set in the ground. How far are the stakes from the foot of the pole? What is the inclination of the ropes to the ground? *Ans.* 34.6 ft.; 30°.

20. The equal angles of an isosceles triangle are each 35°, and the base is 393.18 in. Find the remaining parts of the triangle.

21. The base of an isosceles triangle is 300 ft. and its altitude is 150 ft. Solve the triangle.
Ans. Vertex angle = 90°, equal angles = 45°, equal sides = 212.13 ft.

22. The base of an isosceles triangle is 24 in. long, and the vertex angle is 48°; find the remaining parts and the area.

23. The base of an isosceles triangle is 100 ft., and its altitude is 35.01 ft. Solve the triangle. *Ans.* 61.04 ft.; 35°, 110°.

24. The ground plan of a barn measures 40 ft. by 80 ft. and the pitch of the roof is 45°. Find the length of the rafters and the area of the whole roof, the horizontal projection of the cornice being 1 ft.

25. The side of a regular pentagon is 24 ft.; find R, r, and area.
Ans. 20.42 ft., 16.52 ft., 991.2 sq. ft.

Find the remaining parts and the area of a regular polygon, having given

26. $n = 9$, $c = 12$.

27. $n = 18$, $R = 10$.   *Ans.* $r = 9.848$, $c = 3.472$, area = 307.7.

28. $n = 20$, $R = 20$.

29. $n = 12$, $r = 8$.   *Ans.* $R = 8.28$, $c = 4.29$, area = 206.

30. The side of a regular pentagon is 21.78 ft. Find the length of a diagonal.

31. The side of a regular hexagon is 24 ft. Find the radii of the inscribed and circumscribed circles; also find the difference between the areas of the hexagon and the inscribed circle, and the difference between the areas of the hexagon and the circumscribed circle.

Ans. $R = 24$ ft., $r = 20.8$ ft.; 138.4 sq. ft., 312 sq. ft.

32. If c is the side of a regular polygon of n sides, show that

$$R = \frac{1}{2} c \csc \frac{180°}{n} \text{ and } r = \frac{1}{2} c \cot \frac{180°}{n}.$$

33. If r is the radius of a circle, show that the side of the regular inscribed polygon of n sides is $2 r \sin \frac{180°}{n}$, and that the side of the regular circumscribed polygon is $2 r \tan \frac{180°}{n}$.

38. Table of values of the sine and cosine; interpolation. Table IV, pp. 40 and 41 of the tables,* gives the values of the sine and cosine of angles ranging from 0° to 90° at intervals of 10′. These values are expressed decimally to the nearest ten-thousandth. An inspection of the table will readily reveal the manner in which these values are tabulated. For the sine, the degrees appear in the first column on the left of each page and are read downward. The tens of minutes in excess of a given number of degrees are read in rows from left to right. For the cosine, the degrees appear in the last column on the right of each page and are read upward. The tens of minutes are read from right to left.

The difference between any two successive tabulated values is called the **tabular difference**.

This table and Table V are used in two ways: (1) given an angle, to find the corresponding value of a function of this angle, and (2) given the value of a function, to find the corresponding angle.

The following examples illustrate the use of the table:

EXAMPLE 1. Find sin 28° 40′. On page 40, in the column headed **Ang., deg.,** we find 28°. Proceeding to the right into the column headed **40′**, we find the number 0.4797.

Hence $\quad\quad\quad$ sin 28° 40′ = 0.4797. *Ans.*

---

*The tables referred to in this book are *Four-Place Tables* by Granville, Smith, and Mikesh (Ginn and Company).

EXAMPLE 2. Find cos 77° 10′. On page 40, in the degree column on the right, reading upward, we find 77°. We now proceed to the left into the column in which 10′ appears at the bottom. We find the number 0.2221. Hence
$$\cos 77° \, 10′ = 0.2221. \ Ans.$$

In case the given angle is such that the corresponding value of a function is not tabulated, it becomes necessary to find this value by a separate process. This process is called **interpolation**. The following examples illustrate interpolation :

EXAMPLE 3. Find sin 62° 46′. On page 41 we find
$$\sin 62° \, 50′ = 0.8897$$
and
$$\sin 62° \, 40′ = 0.8884.$$

We see that an increase of 10′ in the angle produces an increase of 0.0013 in the sine. If we assume that the increase in the sine is proportional to the increase in the angle, the increase in the sine corresponding to an increase of 6′ in the angle is $0.6 \times 0.0013 = 0.00078$. This number is now "rounded off" to the accuracy of our table, that is, to four decimal places. Thus, we round off 0.00078 to 0.0008. Hence
$$\sin 62° \, 46′ = 0.8884 + 0.0008 = 0.8892. \ Ans.$$

We must note at this point, however, that the increase in the sine of an angle is not exactly proportional to the increase in the angle. But since the change in the angle is small, our interpolation is sufficiently accurate.

EXAMPLE 4. Find cos 57° 23′. From page 40 we have
$$\cos 57° \, 30′ = 0.5373$$
$$\underline{\cos 57° \, 20′ = 0.5398}$$
$$10′ \quad 0.0025$$

The interpolation is done as in the preceding example. But since the cosine decreases as the angle increases, we must subtract the proportional part. Now $0.3 \times 0.0025 = 0.00075$. In rounding off to four places we may write with equal accuracy either 0.0007 or 0.0008. In long computations we raise to the next higher digit the number preceding a 5 in the fifth place only if it is odd. In this way the errors will tend to balance each other. Hence
$$\cos 57° \, 23′ = 0.5398 - 0.0008 = 0.5390. \ Ans.$$

PROBLEMS

Find the values of the following functions :

1. sin 43° 18′.   *Ans.* 0.6858.   2. cos 23° 16′.

3. cos 79° 54′.   *Ans.* 0.1754.   4. sin 65° 36′.

5. sin 8° 2′.   *Ans.* 0.1398.   6. cos 45° 45′.

The examples which follow illustrate the process of finding an angle corresponding to a given function :

EXAMPLE 5. Given $\sin A = 0.8150$, find A.

On page 41 we find that 0.8150 lies between 0.8141 and 0.8158. And

$$\begin{array}{r} \sin 54° \; 40' = 0.8158 \\ \sin 54° \; 30' = 0.8141 \\ \hline 10' \quad 0.0017 \end{array}$$

An increase of 0.0017 in the sine produces an increase of 10' in the angle. An increase of $0.8150 - 0.8141$, or 0.0009, in the sine will produce an increase of $\frac{9}{17}$ of $10' = 5.3'$. A four-place table, however, gives the corresponding accuracy in the angle to the nearest minute only. Hence

$$A = 54° \; 30' + 5' = 54° \; 35'. \quad Ans.$$

EXAMPLE 6. Given $\cos A = 0.3362$, find A.

On page 40 we find

$$\begin{array}{r} \cos 70° \; 30' = 0.3338 \\ \cos 70° \; 20' = 0.3365 \\ \hline 10' \quad 0.0027 \end{array}$$

A decrease of 0.0027 in the cosine produces an increase of 10' in the angle. Hence the proportional part $\frac{3}{27}$ of 10', or 1', is added to the smaller angle. Hence

$$A = 70° \; 21'. \quad Ans.$$

PROBLEMS

Find the value of A in the first quadrant corresponding to each of the following functions:

1. $\sin A = 0.3365$. *Ans.* 19° 40'.   2. $\sin A = 0.5032$.

3. $\cos A = 0.8613$. *Ans.* 30° 32'.   4. $\cos A = 0.3372$.

5. $\sin A = 0.9956$. *Ans.* 84° 37'.   6. $\cos A = 0.1630$.

39. Table of values of the tangent and the cotangent. Table V, pp. 42 and 43 of the tables, gives the values of the tangent and cotangent of angles ranging from 0° to 90° at intervals of 10'. The arrangement of this table is the same as that of Table IV. Interpolation is performed in the same manner as for the sine and cosine.

EXAMPLE. Find $\cot 34° \; 48'$. From page 43 we have

$$\begin{array}{r} \cot 34° \; 50' = 1.437 \\ \cot 34° \; 40' = 1.446 \\ \hline 10' \quad 0.009 \end{array}$$

The decrease 0.009 in the cotangent is produced by an increase of 10' in the angle. The proportional part 0.8×0.009, or 0.007, is subtracted. That is,

$$\cot 34° \; 48' = 1.446 - 0.007 = 1.439. \quad Ans.$$

Interpolation should not be made for the tangent of an angle between 82° and 90°, nor for the cotangent of an angle between 0° and 7°.

PROBLEMS

Find the value of each of the following functions:

1. tan 15° 24'. *Ans.* 0.2755.   2. cot 35° 18'.

3. tan 80° 12'. *Ans.* 5.789.   4. sin 75° 16'.

5. cot 55° 43'. *Ans.* 0.6817.   6. cos 25° 47'.

7. cot 169° 19'. *Ans.* − 5.301.   8. sin 217° 17'.

9. tan 333° 33'. *Ans.* − 0.4975.   10. cos (− 46° 25').

11. tan 163° 42'. *Ans.* − 0.2925.   12. cot (− 273° 55').

Find the value of A in the first quadrant corresponding to each of the following functions:

13. tan A = 0.7673. *Ans.* 37° 30'.   14. cot A = 0.4452.

15. cot A = 0.5730. *Ans.* 60° 11'.   16. tan A = 2.666.

17. sin A = 0.9678. *Ans.* 75° 26'.   18. cos A = 0.4182.

19. tan A = 0.3589. *Ans.* 19° 45'.   20. cot A = 3.298.

21. cos A = 0.7121. *Ans.* 44° 36'.   22. sin A = 0.7121.

23. tan A = 4.200. *Ans.* 76° 36'.   24. cot A = 1.028.

Find the values of x from 0° to 360° which satisfy each of the following equations:

25. cos x = − $\frac{1}{2}$. *Ans.* 120°, 240°.   26. sin x = 0.3420.

27. cos x = 0.3420. *Ans.* 70°, 290°.   28. tan x = 0.4822.

29. sin x = − 0.9442. *Ans.* 250° 46', 289° 14'.   30. cos x = − 0.4183.

40. Terms occurring in trigonometric problems. *The vertical line* at a point is the line which coincides with the plumb line through that point.

A horizontal line at a point is a line which is perpendicular to the vertical line through that point.

A vertical plane at a point is a plane which contains the vertical line through that point.

The horizontal plane at a point is the plane which is perpendicular to the vertical line through that point.

A vertical angle is one lying in a vertical plane.

A horizontal angle is one lying in a horizontal plane.

The angle of elevation of an object above the horizontal plane of the observer is the vertical angle between the line drawn from the observer's eye to the object and a horizontal line through the eye.

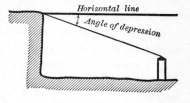

The angle of depression of an object below the horizontal plane of the observer is the vertical angle between the line drawn from the observer's eye to the object and a horizontal line through the eye.

The horizontal distance between two points is the distance from one of the two points to the vertical line drawn through the other.

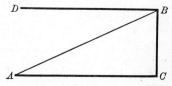

The vertical distance between two points is the distance from one of the two points to the horizontal plane through the other.

Thus, let *BC* be the vertical line at *B*, and let the horizontal plane at *A* cut this vertical line in *C*; then *AC* is called the horizontal distance between *A* and *B* and *BC* the vertical distance.

The Mariner's Compass is divided into 32 equal parts; hence each part $= 360° \div 32 = 11\frac{1}{4}°$. The figure at the right shows how the different divisions are designated. North, south, east, and west are called the *cardinal points*, and on paper these directions are usually taken as upward, downward, to the right, and to the left respectively. The direction of an object

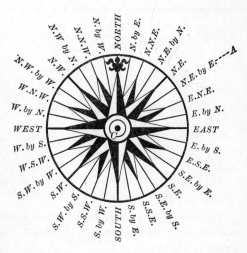

from an observer at *C* may be given in several ways. Thus, *A* in the figure is said to bear N.E. by E. from *C*, or from *C* the bearing of *A* is N.E. by E. In the same way the bearing of *C* from *A* is

S.W. by W. The point A is 3 points north of east and 5 points east of north. Also, E. $33\frac{3}{4}°$ N. means the same as N.E. by E.

In order to illustrate the application of the trigonometric functions (ratios) to the solution of practical examples, we shall now give a variety of problems on finding heights, distances, angles, areas, etc. In solving these problems it is best to follow some definite plan. In general we may proceed as follows:

1. Construct a drawing to some convenient scale which will show the relations between the given and the required lines and angles.

2. If necessary draw any auxiliary lines that will aid in the solution, and decide on the simplest steps that will solve the problem.

3. Write down the formulas needed, make the calculations, and check the results.

PROBLEMS

Solve the right triangles which have the following given parts. Express the angles to the nearest minute. Check your solutions. In each case $C = 90°$.

1. $a = 60$, $c = 100$.   *Ans.* $A = 36° 52'$, $B = 53° 8'$, $b = 80$.

2. $a = 147$, $c = 184$.

3. $A = 38° 40'$, $a = 50.6$.   *Ans.* $B = 51° 20'$, $c = 80.98$, $b = 63.24$.

4. $A = 38° 50'$, $c = 13.5$.

5. $B = 6° 12'$, $c = 37.2$.   *Ans.* $A = 83° 48'$, $a = 36.98$, $b = 4.018$.

6. $B = 43° 48'$, $b = 50.95$.

7. $a = 12.3$, $b = 20.2$.   *Ans.* $A = 31° 20'$, $B = 58° 40'$, $c = 23.7$.

8. $a = 101$, $b = 116$.

9. $B = 68° 50'$, $a = 729.3$.   *Ans.* $A = 21° 10'$, $b = 1884$, $c = 2020$.

10. $B = 10° 51'$, $c = 0.7264$.

11. $A = 64° 1'$, $b = 200$.   *Ans.* $B = 26° 59'$, $a = 410.4$, $c = 456.5$.

12. $b = 1.438$, $c = 3.465$.

13. The length of a kite string is 250 yd., and the angle of elevation of the kite is 40°. Find the height of the kite, supposing the line of the kite string to be straight.   *Ans.* 160.7 yd.

14. At a point 200 ft. in a horizontal line from the foot of a tower the angle of elevation of the top of the tower is observed to be 60°. Find the height of the tower.

15. A stick 10 ft. in length stands vertically on a horizontal plane, and the length of its shadow is 8.391 ft. Find the angle of elevation of the sun.

Ans. 50°.

16. From the top of a rock that rises vertically 80 ft. out of the water the angle of depression of a boat is found to be 30°; find the distance of the boat from the foot of the rock.

17. From the top of a tower 120 ft. high the angle of depression of an object on a level with the base of the tower is 27° 43'. What is the distance of the object from the top and bottom of the tower?

Ans. 258 ft., 228 ft.

18. What is the angle of elevation of an inclined plane if it rises 1 ft. in a horizontal distance of 40 ft.?

19. In order to find the width of a river, a base line AC is measured along one bank to be 350 ft. On the opposite bank a point B is located so that CB is perpendicular to AC. The angle CAB is measured and found to be 52° 12'. Find the width of the river. *Ans.* 451.4 ft.

20. From the top of a tower the angle of depression of the extremity of a horizontal base line 1000 ft. in length, measured from the foot of the tower, is observed to be 21° 16'. Find the height of the tower.

21. What angle does a diagonal of a cube make with the diagonal of a face of the cube drawn from the same vertex? *Ans.* 35° 16'.

22. The length of the side of a regular octagon is 12 in. Find the radii of the inscribed and circumscribed circles.

23. If a chord of 41.36 ft. subtends an arc of 145° 37', what is the radius of the circle? *Ans.* 21.65 ft.

24. If the diameter of a circle is 3268 ft., find the angle at the center subtended by an arc whose chord is 1027 ft.

25. A ship is sailing due N.E. at the rate of 10 mi. an hour. Find the rate at which she is moving due north. *Ans.* 7.07 mi. per hour.

26. A ship is sailing due east at the rate of 7.8 mi. an hour. A lighthouse is observed to be due north at 10:37 A.M. and 33° west of north at 12:43 P.M. Find the distance of the lighthouse from each point of observation.

27. A ship is sailing due east at a uniform rate of speed. At 7 A.M. a lighthouse is observed bearing due north, 10.32 mi. distant, and at 7:30 A.M. it bears 18° 13' west of north. Find the rate of sailing of the ship and the bearing of the lighthouse at 10 A.M. *Ans.* 6.79 mi. per hour, 63° 8' W. of N.

28. A ladder 40 ft. long may be so placed that it will reach a window 33 ft. high on one side of the street, and by turning it over without moving its foot it will reach a window 21 ft. high on the other side. Find the breadth of the street.

29. At a point midway between two towers on a horizontal plane the angles of elevation of their tops are 30° and 60° respectively. Show that one tower is three times as high as the other.

30. A man in a balloon observes that the bases of two towers, which are a mile apart on a horizontal plane, subtend an angle of 70°. If he is exactly above the middle point between the towers, find the height of the balloon.

31. Two buoys are observed in a direction due south from a cliff the top of which is 312 ft. above the level of the water. Find the distance between the buoys if their angles of depression from the top of the cliff are 46° 18′ and 27° 15′ respectively.   *Ans.* 307.8 ft.

32. Two towns, A and B, are on a highway which runs north and south. A town C, 11 mi. from this highway, bears 25° west of south from A and 35° west of south from B. How far is the town A from the town B if the towns and the highway are on the same horizontal plane?

33. From each of two stations east and west of each other and 1 mi. apart, the angle of elevation of a balloon is observed to be 45°. If the balloon bears N.W. and N.E. from the stations, respectively, how high is it?   *Ans.* 3733 ft.

34. In approaching a fort situated on a plain, a reconnoitering party finds at one place that the fort subtends an angle of 10°, and at a place 200 ft. nearer the fort that it subtends an angle of 15°. How high is the fort and what is the distance to it from the second place of observation?

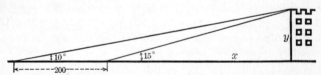

Hint. Denoting the height by y and the distance by x, we have

$$y = x \tan 15°,$$ by **(40)**, p. 71

also, $$y = (x + 200) \tan 10°.$$ By **(40)**, p. 71

Solve these two simultaneous equations for x and y, substituting the values of $\tan 15°$ and $\tan 10°$ from the table on page 10.   *Ans.* $x = 385$ ft., $y = 103$ ft.

35. In order to measure the height, h, of an object, the distance between two points, A and B, along a line through its base in a horizontal plane is measured and found to be l feet long. The angles of elevation of the top of the object from A and B are found to be α and β respectively, A being nearer the base. Show that the height is given by the formula

$$h = \frac{l}{\cot \beta - \cot \alpha}$$ if A and B are on the same side, and by $$h = \frac{l}{\cot \beta + \cot \alpha}$$ if A and B are on opposite sides of the base.

36. A flagstaff 25 ft. high stands on the top of a house. From a point on the plain on which the house stands, the angles of elevation of the top and the bottom of the flagstaff are observed to be 60° and 45° respectively. Find the height of the house.

37. The pilot in an airplane observes the angle of depression of a light directly below his line of flight to be 30°. A minute later its angle of depression is 45°. If he is flying horizontally in a straight course at the rate of 90 mi. per hour, find

    (**a**) the altitude at which he is flying;

    (**b**) his distance from the light at the first point of observation.

        Ans. (**a**) 2.049 mi.; (**b**) 4.098 mi.

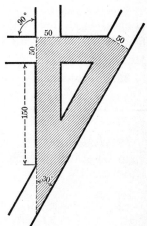

38. A cord is stretched around two wheels with radii of 7 ft. and 1 ft. respectively, and with their centers 12 ft. apart. Prove that the length of the cord is $12\sqrt{3} + 10\,\pi$ ft.

39. Find the number of square feet of pavement required for the shaded portion of the streets shown in the figure, all the streets being 50 ft. wide.

        Ans. $\dfrac{28750}{\sqrt{3}} + 7500 = 24094$.

41. Solution of oblique triangles. In plane geometry the student has already been taught how to solve triangles graphically. That is, it has been shown how to construct a triangle, having given

    CASE I. *Two angles and one side.*

    CASE II. *Two sides and an angle opposite one of the sides.*

    CASE III. *Two sides and the included angle.*

    CASE IV. *Three sides.*

From such a construction of the required triangle the parts not given may be found by actual measurement with a graduated ruler and a protractor. On account of the limitations of the observer and the imperfections of the instruments used, however, the results from such measurements will, in general, be only more or less rough approximations. After having constructed the triangle from the given parts by geometric methods, it will be seen that trigonometry teaches us how to find the unknown parts of the triangle to any degree of accuracy desired, and the two methods may then serve as checks on each other.

The student should always bear in mind, when solving triangles, the two following geometrical properties which are common to all triangles:

(41) **The sum of the three angles equals 180°.**

(42) **The greater side lies opposite the greater angle, and conversely.**

The trigonometric solution of oblique triangles depends upon the application of three laws, — the law of sines, the law of cosines, and the law of tangents, to the derivation of which we now turn our attention.

42. Law of sines.

Theorem. *The sides of a triangle are proportional to the sines of the opposite angles.*

Proof. Fig. 1 represents a triangle all of whose angles are acute, while Fig. 2 represents a triangle one angle of which is obtuse (as A).

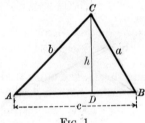

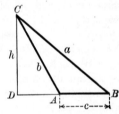

FIG. 1   FIG. 2

By the theorem, we have to prove

(43)
$$\frac{a}{\sin A} = \frac{b}{\sin B} = \frac{c}{\sin C}.$$

Draw the perpendicular CD $(= h)$ on AB or AB produced. From either figure, using the right triangle ACD,

(A)
$$\sin A = \frac{h}{b}.$$

[In Fig. 2, $\sin A = \sin (180° - A) = \sin CAD$ (Art. 25).]

Also, using the right triangle BCD,

(B)
$$\sin B = \frac{h}{a}.$$

Dividing (A) by (B) gives

$$\frac{\sin A}{\sin B} = \frac{a}{b},$$

or, by alternation in proportion,

(C) $$\frac{a}{\sin A} = \frac{b}{\sin B}.$$

Similarly, by drawing perpendiculars from A and B we get

(D) $$\frac{b}{\sin B} = \frac{c}{\sin C}$$

and

(E) $$\frac{c}{\sin C} = \frac{a}{\sin A}$$

respectively. Writing (C), (D), (E) as a single statement, we get (**43**).

Each of these equal ratios has a simple geometrical meaning, as may be shown if the *law of sines* is proved as follows:

Circumscribe a circle about the triangle ABC as shown in the figure, and draw the radii OB, OC. Denote the radius of the circle by R. Draw OM perpendicular to BC.

Since the inscribed angle A is measured by one half of the arc BC and the central angle BOC is measured by the whole arc BC, it follows that the angle $BOC = 2\,A$, or,

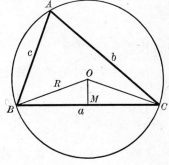

angle $BOM = A$.

Then $BM = R \sin BOM = R \sin A,$
by (**38**), Art. 37

and $a = 2\,BM = 2\,R \sin A,$

or, $2\,R = \dfrac{a}{\sin A}.$

In like manner it may be shown that

$$2\,R = \frac{b}{\sin B} \text{ and } 2\,R = \frac{c}{\sin C}.$$

Hence, by equating the results, we get

$$2\,R = \frac{a}{\sin A} = \frac{b}{\sin B} = \frac{c}{\sin C}.$$

The ratio of any side of a triangle to the sine of the opposite angle is numerically equal to the diameter of the circumscribed circle.

It is evident that a triangle may be solved by the aid of the law of sines *if two of the three known elements are a side and its opposite angle.* The case of two angles and the included side being given may also be brought under this head, since by (41), Art. 41, we may find the third angle, which lies opposite the given side.

EXAMPLE. Given $A = 65°$, $B = 40°$, $a = 50$ ft.; solve the triangle.

Solution. Construct the triangle. Since two angles are given, we get the third angle at once from (41), Art. 41. Thus,

$$C = 180° - (A + B) = 180° - 105° = 75°.$$

Since we know the side a and the opposite angle A, we may use the law of sines, but we must be careful to choose such ratios in (43) that *only one unknown quantity is involved.* Thus, to find the side b use

$$\frac{a}{\sin A} = \frac{b}{\sin B}.$$

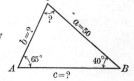

Clearing of fractions and solving for the only unknown quantity b, we get

$$b = \frac{a \sin B}{\sin A}.$$

Substituting the numerical values of $\sin A$ and $\sin B$ from the table on page 10, and $a = 50$ ft., we get

$$b = \frac{50 \times 0.6428}{0.9063} = 35.46 \text{ ft.}$$

Similarly, to find the side c, use

$$\frac{a}{\sin A} = \frac{c}{\sin C}.$$

Clearing of fractions and solving for c, we get

$$c = \frac{a \sin C}{\sin A} = \frac{50 \times 0.9659}{0.9063} = 53.29 \text{ ft.}$$

By measurements on the figure we now check the results to see that there are no large errors.

Since we now know all the sides and angles of the triangle, the triangle is said to be solved.

PROBLEMS

Solve the following triangles:

1. Given $a = 50$, $A = 65°$, $B = 40°$. *Ans.* $C = 75°$, $b = 35.46$, $c = 53.29$.

2. Given $b = 7.07$, $A = 30°$, $C = 105°$.

3. Given $c = 60$, $A = 50°$, $B = 75°$. *Ans.* $C = 55°$, $b = 70.7$, $a = 56.1$.

4. Given $a = 20$, $B = 45°$, $C = 60°$.

5. Given $a = 550$, $A = 10° 12'$, $B = 46° 36'$.

Ans. $C = 123° 12'$, $b = 2257$, $c = 2599$.

6. Given $B = 100° 10'$, $C = 45° 40'$, $c = 3060$.

43. The ambiguous case when two sides and the angle opposite one of them are given. The solution of the triangle in this case will depend on the law of sines. We must first find the unknown angle which lies opposite one of the given sides. But when only the sine of an angle is given, the angle may have either of two values which are supplements of each other, and either value may be taken unless excluded by the conditions of the problem (Art. 25).

Let a and b be the given sides and A (opposite the side a) the given angle.

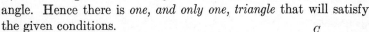

If $a > b$, then, by geometry, $A > B$, and B must be acute whatever be the value of A, for a triangle can have only one obtuse angle. Hence there is *one, and only one, triangle* that will satisfy the given conditions.

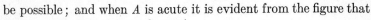

If $a = b$, then, by geometry, $A = B$, both A and B must be acute, and *the required triangle is isosceles.*

If $a < b$, then, by geometry, $A < B$, and A must be acute in order that the triangle shall be possible; and when A is acute it is evident from the figure that *the two triangles ACB and ACB'*

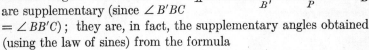

will satisfy the given conditions provided a is greater than the perpendicular CP; that is, provided

$$a > b \sin A.$$

The angles ABC and $AB'C$ are supplementary (since $\angle B'BC = \angle BB'C$); they are, in fact, the supplementary angles obtained (using the law of sines) from the formula

$$\sin B = \frac{b \sin A}{a}.$$

That is, we get the corresponding acute value B from a table of sines, and the supplementary obtuse value from

$$B' = 180° - B.$$

If, however, $a = b \sin A = CP$, then $\sin B = 1$, $B = 90°$, and *the triangle required is a right triangle.*

If $a < b \sin A$ (that is, less than CP), then $\sin B > 1$, and *the triangle is impossible.*

These results may be stated in compact form as follows:

Two solutions: *If A is acute and the value of a lies between b and b sin A.*

No solution: *If A is acute and $a < b \sin A$, or if A is obtuse and $a < b$ or $a = b$.*

One solution: *In all other cases.*

The number of solutions can usually be determined by inspection on constructing the triangle. In case of doubt find the value of $b \sin A$ and test as above.

EXAMPLE 1. Given $a = 21$, $b = 32$, $A = 115°$; find the remaining parts.

Solution. In this case $a < b$ and $A > 90°$; hence the triangle is impossible and there is no solution.

EXAMPLE 2. Given $a = 32$, $b = 86$, $A = 30°$; find the remaining parts.

Solution. Here $b \sin A = 86 \times \frac{1}{2} = 43$; hence $a < b \sin A$ and there is no solution.

EXAMPLE 3. Given $a = 40$, $b = 30$, $A = 75°$; find the remaining parts.

Solution. Since $a > b$ and A is acute there is one solution only.

By the law of sines,

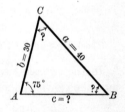

$$\frac{a}{\sin A} = \frac{b}{\sin B},$$

or,
$$\sin B = \frac{b \sin A}{a} = \frac{30 \times 0.9659}{40}.$$

$$\therefore \sin B = 0.7244,$$

or,
$$B = 46° \, 25', \text{ the only admissible value of } B.$$

Then
$$C = 180° - (A + B) = 180° - 121° \, 25' = 58° \, 35'.$$

To find c, we get, by the law of sines,

$$\frac{c}{\sin C} = \frac{a}{\sin A},$$

or,
$$c = \frac{a \sin C}{\sin A} = \frac{40 \times 0.8534}{0.9659} = 35.3.$$

Check the results by measurements on the figure.

EXAMPLE 4. Solve the triangle, having given $b = 15$, $a = 12$, $A = 52°$.

Solution. Here $b \sin A = 15 \times 0.7880 = 11.82$; hence, since A is acute and a lies between b and $b \sin A$, there are two solutions. That is, there are two triangles, ACB_1 and ACB_2, which satisfy the given conditions. By the law of sines,

$$\frac{a}{\sin A} = \frac{b}{\sin B_1},$$

or,
$$\sin B_1 = \frac{b \sin A}{a} = \frac{15 \times 0.7880}{12} = 0.9850.$$

This gives $B_1 = 80° 4'$, and the supplementary angle
$$B_2 = 180° - B_1 = 99° 56'.$$

Let us first solve completely the triangle AB_1C.
$$C_1 = 180° - (A + B_1) = 47° 56'.$$

By the law of sines,

$$\frac{a}{\sin A} = \frac{c_1}{\sin C_1},$$

or,
$$c_1 = \frac{a \sin C_1}{\sin A} = \frac{12 \times 0.7423}{0.7880} = 11.3.$$

Now, solving the triangle AB_2C,
$$C_2 = 180° - (A + B_2) = 28° 4'.$$

By the law of sines,

$$\frac{a}{\sin A} = \frac{c_2}{\sin C_2},$$

or,
$$c_2 = \frac{a \sin C_2}{\sin A} = \frac{12 \times 0.4705}{0.7880} = 7.2.$$

The solutions then are

For triangle AB_1C | For triangle AB_2C
$B_1 = 80° 4'$, | $B_2 = 99° 56'$,
$C_1 = 47° 56'$, | $C_2 = 28° 4'$,
$c_1 = 11.3.$ | $c_2 = 7.2.$

Check the results by measurements on the figure.

In the ambiguous case care should be taken to properly combine the calculated sides and angles.

PROBLEMS

Find the number of solutions in the following triangles, having given

1. **a.** $a = 80$, $b = 100$, $A = 30°$. *Ans.* Two.
   b. $a = 50$, $b = 100$, $A = 30°$. One.
   c. $a = 40$, $b = 100$, $A = 30°$. None.
   d. $a = 13$, $b = 11$, $A = 69°$. One.

2. **a.** $a = 70$, $b = 75$, $A = 60°$.
   b. $a = 134$, $b = 84$, $B = 52°$.
   c. $a = 200$, $b = 100$, $A = 30°$.
   d. $b = 300$, $C = 45°$, $c = 250$.

Solve the following triangles:

3. Given $a = 18$, $b = 20$, $A = 55° 24'$.

Ans. $B_1 = 66° 10'$, $C_1 = 58° 26'$, $c_1 = 18.6$.
$B_2 = 113° 50'$, $C_2 = 10° 46'$, $c_2 = 4.08$.

4. Given $a = 3\sqrt{2}$, $b = 2\sqrt{3}$, $A = 60°$.

test **5.** Given $b = 19$, $c = 18$, $C = 15°\ 49'$.

        Ans. $B_1 = 16°\ 43'$, $A_1 = 147°\ 28'$, $a_1 = 35.5$.

             $B_2 = 163°\ 17'$, $A_2 = 0°\ 54'$, $a_2 = 1.04$.

6. Given $a = 119$, $b = 97$, $A = 50°$.

7. Given $a = 120$, $b = 80$, $A = 60°$.

        Ans. $B = 35°\ 16'$, $C = 84°\ 44'$, $c = 138.0$.

8. It is required to find the horizontal distance from a point A to an inaccessible point B on the opposite bank of a river. We measure off any convenient horizontal distance, as AC, and then measure the angles CAB and ACB.

Let $AC = 283$ ft., angle $CAB = 38°$, and angle $ACB = 66°\ 18'$.

Solve the triangle ABC for the side AB.

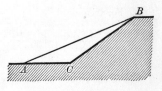

9. A railroad embankment stands on a horizontal plane and it is required to find the distance from a point A in the plane to the top B of the embankment. Select a point C at the foot of the embankment lying in the same vertical plane as A and B, and measure the distances AC and CB, and the angle BAC.

Let $AC = 48.5$ ft., $BC = 84$ ft., and angle $BAC = 21°\ 30'$. Solve the triangle for the side AB.   Ans. 127.2 ft.

10. A tree A is observed from two points B and C, 270 ft. apart, on a straight road. The angle BCA is $55°$ and the angle $CBA = 65°$. Find the distance from the tree to the nearer point B.

11. To determine the distance of a hostile fort A from a place B, a line BC and the angles ABC and BCA were measured and found to be 1006 yd., $44°$, and $70°$ respectively. Find the distance AB.

        Ans. 1034.8 yd.

12. A triangular lot has two sides of lengths 140.5 ft. and 170.6 ft., and the angle opposite the former is $40°$. Find the length of a fence around it.

13. Two buoys are 64.2 yd. apart, and a boat is 74.1 yd. from the nearer buoy. The angle between the lines from the buoys to the boat is $27°\ 18'$. How far is the boat from the farther buoy?   Ans. 120.3 yd.

14. If R is the radius of the circumscribed circle, prove the following for any triangle [$s = \frac{1}{2}(a + b + c)$]:

a. $R (\sin A + \sin B + \sin C) = s$.

b. $\dfrac{1}{s-a} + \dfrac{1}{s-b} + \dfrac{1}{s-c} - \dfrac{1}{s} = \dfrac{4R}{\sqrt{s(s-a)(s-b)(s-c)}}$.

15. Prove the following for any triangle:

    a. $a = b \cos C + c \cos B,$
        $b = a \cos C + c \cos A,$
        $c = a \cos B + b \cos A.$

    b. $\sqrt{bc \sin B \sin C} = \dfrac{b^2 \sin C + c^2 \sin B}{b + c}.$

    c. $\dfrac{\sin A + 2 \sin B}{a + 2b} = \dfrac{\sin C}{c}.$

    d. $\dfrac{\sin^2 A - m \sin^2 B}{a^2 - mb^2} = \dfrac{\sin^2 C}{c^2}.$

44. Law of tangents.

Theorem. *The sum of two sides of a triangle is to their difference as the tangent of half the sum of the opposite angles is to the tangent of half the difference of these angles.*

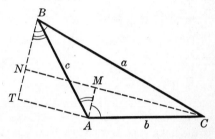

Taking the sides a and b of the triangle ABC in the figure, we have to prove

(44) $$\frac{a + b}{a - b} = \frac{\tan \frac{1}{2}(A + B)}{\tan \frac{1}{2}(A - B)}.$$

Proof. In the figure, NC is the bisector of the angle C. BN and AM are perpendicular to NC, and AT is drawn parallel to NC to meet BN produced. Then

$$\angle NBC = \angle MAC = \tfrac{1}{2}(A + B),$$
$$\angle TBA = \angle MAB = \tfrac{1}{2}(A - B).$$

For $\angle NBC = \angle MAC = 90° - \tfrac{1}{2} C = \dfrac{180° - C}{2}.$

But $$180° - C = A + B.$$

Hence

(1) $$\angle NBC = \angle MAC = \tfrac{1}{2}(A + B).$$

Also,

(2) $\quad \angle TBA = \angle MAB = A - \tfrac{1}{2}(A + B) = \tfrac{1}{2}(A - B).$

Now $\quad \tan \angle TBA = \dfrac{TA}{BT} = \dfrac{NM}{BT} = \dfrac{NC - MC}{BN + NT}.$

Hence, since $NT = AM$,

$$(3) \qquad \tan \angle TBA = \frac{NC - MC}{BN + AM}.$$

In the right triangle BNC,

$$(4) \qquad NC = a \sin \angle NBC = a \sin \tfrac{1}{2}(A + B). \qquad \text{By (1)}$$

$$(5) \qquad BN = a \cos \angle NBC = a \cos \tfrac{1}{2}(A + B). \qquad \text{By (1)}$$

In the right triangle ACM,

$$(6) \qquad MC = b \sin \angle MAC = b \sin \tfrac{1}{2}(A + B). \qquad \text{By (1)}$$

$$(7) \qquad MA = b \cos \angle MAC = b \cos \tfrac{1}{2}(A + B). \qquad \text{By (1)}$$

Substituting from (4)–(7) in the right-hand member of (3), and using (2), we get

$$(8) \qquad \tan \tfrac{1}{2}(A - B) = \frac{(a - b) \sin \tfrac{1}{2}(A + B)}{(a + b) \cos \tfrac{1}{2}(A + B)}.$$

Hence, by (16), Art. 17,

$$\tan \tfrac{1}{2}(A - B) = \frac{a - b}{a + b} \tan \tfrac{1}{2}(A + B).$$

Writing this in the form of a proportion, we get (44).

If $b > a$, then $B > A$, making $a - b$ and $A - B$ negative. The formula still holds true, but to avoid negative quantities it is better to write the formula in the form

$$\frac{b + a}{b - a} = \frac{\tan \tfrac{1}{2}(B + A)}{\tan \tfrac{1}{2}(B - A)}.$$

Similarly,

$$\frac{c + a}{c - a} = \frac{\tan \tfrac{1}{2}(C + A)}{\tan \tfrac{1}{2}(C - A)},$$

$$\frac{b + c}{b - c} = \frac{\tan \tfrac{1}{2}(B + C)}{\tan \tfrac{1}{2}(B - C)}. \; *$$

When two sides and the included angle are given, as a, b, C, the law of tangents may be employed in finding the two unknown angles A and B. Since $a + b$, $a - b$, $A + B \,(= 180° - C)$, and therefore also $\tan \tfrac{1}{2}(A + B)$ are known, we clear (44) of fractions and solve for the unknown quantity $\tan \tfrac{1}{2}(A - B)$. This gives

$$(45) \qquad \tan \tfrac{1}{2}(A - B) = \frac{a - b}{a + b} \tan \tfrac{1}{2}(A + B).$$

We shall illustrate the process by means of examples.

* These may also be found by changing the letters in cyclical order (see footnote, p. 95).

EXAMPLE 1. Having given $a = 872.5$, $b = 632.7$, $C = 80°$, solve the triangle.

Solution. $a + b = 1505.2$, $a - b = 239.8$, $A + B = 180° - C = 100°$, and $\frac{1}{2}(A + B) = 50°$.

From (45), since $\tan \frac{1}{2}(A + B) = \tan 50° = 1.192$,

$$\tan \tfrac{1}{2}(A - B) = \frac{a-b}{a+b} \tan \tfrac{1}{2}(A + B) = \frac{239.8}{1505.2} \times 1.192 = 0.1898.$$

$$\therefore \tfrac{1}{2}(A - B) = 10° 45'.$$

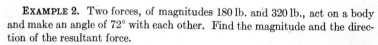

Adding this result to $\frac{1}{2}(A + B) = 50°$ gives

$$A = 60° 45'.$$

Subtracting the result from $\frac{1}{2}(A+B) = 50°$ gives

$$B = 39° 15'.$$

To find the side c, use the law of sines. Thus,

$$c = \frac{a \sin C}{\sin A} = \frac{872.5 \times 0.9848}{0.8725} = 984.8.$$

EXAMPLE 2. Two forces, of magnitudes 180 lb. and 320 lb., act on a body and make an angle of 72° with each other. Find the magnitude and the direction of the resultant force.

Solution. By the principle known as the *Parallelogram Law of Forces*, if AB and AD represent the given forces, the magnitude and the direction of the resultant is represented by the diagonal AC of the parallelogram of which AB and AD are two sides. The action of the single force AC at A is equivalent to the combined action of the two forces AB and AD.

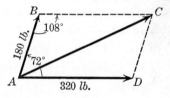

We are required to find AC and the angle BAC or the angle CAD. For this purpose we shall solve the triangle ABC. Let $b = AC$, $c = AB$, $a = BC = AD$, $A =$ angle BAC and $C =$ angle BCA, and apply the law of tangents. Then $a + c = 500$, $a - c = 140$, $B = 180° - 72° = 108°$, $A + C = 72°$, $\frac{1}{2}(A + C) = 36°$.

$$\tan \tfrac{1}{2}(A - C) = \frac{a-c}{a+c} \tan \tfrac{1}{2}(A + C) = \frac{140}{500} \tan 36°,$$

$$= 0.28 \times 0.7265 = 0.2034.$$

$$\therefore \tfrac{1}{2}(A - C) = 11° 30'.$$

But $\frac{1}{2}(A + C) = 36°$.

Hence $A = 47° 30'$, and $C =$ angle $CAD = 24° 30'$.
To find b, we use the law of sines. We have

$$b = \frac{c \sin B}{\sin C} = \frac{180 \times 0.9511}{0.4147} = 412.8.$$

Hence the resultant force is 412.8 lb. and makes an angle of 24° 30' with the greater of the two given forces. *Ans.*

45. Law of cosines.

Theorem. *In any triangle the square of any side is equal to the sum of the squares of the other two sides minus twice the product of these two sides into the cosine of their included angle.*

Proof. Suppose we want to find the side a in terms of the other two sides b and c and their included angle A. By the theorem, we have to prove

$$(46) \qquad a^2 = b^2 + c^2 - 2\,bc \cos A.$$

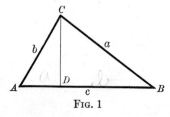 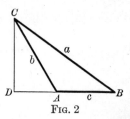

Fig. 1   Fig. 2

In either figure, $\quad a^2 = \overline{CD}^2 + \overline{DB}^2,$
$$b^2 = \overline{CD}^2 + \overline{AD}^2.$$

Subtracting these equations, we find

$$(1) \qquad a^2 - b^2 = \overline{DB}^2 - \overline{AD}^2.$$

In Fig. 1, $DB = c - AD$. Squaring and substituting in the right-hand member of (1), we get (since $\overline{AD}^2$ cancels out)

$$(2) \qquad a^2 - b^2 = c^2 - 2\,c \cdot AD.$$

In Fig. 2, $DB = AD + c$. Squaring and substituting in the right-hand member of (1), the result is

$$(3) \qquad a^2 - b^2 = c^2 + 2\,c \cdot AD.$$

But, from the right triangle CAD in Fig. 1, we have

$$(4) \qquad\qquad AD = b \cos A. \qquad\qquad \text{By (39), Art. 37}$$

Substituting this value for AD in the right-hand member of (2), and solving for a^2, we find

$$(5) \qquad\qquad a^2 = b^2 + c^2 - 2\,bc \cos A.$$

And, from the right triangle CAD in Fig. 2,

$$(6) \qquad\qquad AD = b \cos \angle DAC. \qquad\qquad \text{By (39), Art. 37}$$

But $A = 180° - \angle DAC$, and hence

$$\cos A = - \cos \angle DAC. \qquad\qquad \text{By Art. 25}$$

Then, by (6), $AD = -b \cos A$ (in Fig. 2).

Substituting this value for AD in the right-hand member of (3), and solving for a^2, we get (5), as before. Hence, in either figure,
$$a^2 = b^2 + c^2 - 2\,bc\cos A.$$

Similarly, we may find

(47) $$b^2 = a^2 + c^2 - 2\,ac\cos B,$$

(48) $$c^2 = a^2 + b^2 - 2\,ab\cos C.^*$$

Observe that if $A = 90°$, then $\cos A = 0$, and (46) becomes $a^2 = b^2 + c^2$, which is the known relation between the sides of a right triangle where A is the right angle.

Solving (46) to (48) for the cosines of the angles, we get

(49) $$\cos A = \frac{b^2 + c^2 - a^2}{2\,bc},$$

(50) $$\cos B = \frac{a^2 + c^2 - b^2}{2\,ac},$$

(51) $$\cos C = \frac{a^2 + b^2 - c^2}{2\,ab}.$$

These formulas are useful in finding the angles of a triangle, having given its sides.

Formulas (46) to (48) may be used for finding the third side of a triangle when two sides and the included angle are given. The other angles may then be found either by the law of sines or by formulas (49) to (51).

EXAMPLE 1. Having given $A = 47°$, $b = 8$, $c = 10$, solve the triangle.

Solution. To find the side a use (46).

$$a^2 = b^2 + c^2 - 2\,bc\cos A$$
$$= 64 + 100 - 2 \times 8 \times 10 \times 0.6820$$
$$= 54.88.$$
$$\therefore a = \sqrt{54.88} = 7.408.$$

To find the angles C and B use the law of sines.

$$\sin B = \frac{b\sin A}{a} = \frac{8 \times 0.7314}{7.408} = 0.7898. \quad \therefore B = 52°\,10'.$$

$$\sin C = \frac{c\sin A}{a} = \frac{10 \times 0.7314}{7.408} = 0.9872. \quad \therefore C = 80°\,50'.$$

Check. $\qquad A + B + C = 47° + 52°\,10' + 80°\,50' = 180°.$

---

* Since a and A, b and B, c and C stand for *any side* of a triangle and the *opposite angle*, from any formula expressing a general relation between these parts another formula may be deduced by *changing the letters in cyclical order*. Thus, in (46) by changing a to b, b to c, c to a, and A to B we obtain (47); and in (47) by changing b to c, c to a, a to b, and B to C we get (48). This is a great help in memorizing some sets of formulas.

EXAMPLE 2. Having given $a = 7, b = 3, c = 5$, solve the triangle.

Solution. Using formulas **(49)**, **(50)**, **(51)** to find the angles, we get

$$\cos A = \frac{b^2 + c^2 - a^2}{2\,bc} = \frac{3^2 + 5^2 - 7^2}{2 \cdot 3 \cdot 5} = -\frac{1}{2} = -0.5000. \quad \therefore A = 120°.$$

$$\cos B = \frac{a^2 + c^2 - b^2}{2\,ac} = \frac{7^2 + 5^2 - 3^2}{2 \cdot 7 \cdot 5} = \frac{13}{14} = 0.9286. \qquad \therefore B = 21°\ 47'.$$

$$\cos C = \frac{a^2 + b^2 - c^2}{2\,ab} = \frac{7^2 + 3^2 - 5^2}{2 \cdot 7 \cdot 3} = \frac{11}{14} = 0.7857. \qquad \therefore C = 38°\ 13'.$$

Check. $A + B + C = 120° + 21°\ 47' + 38°\ 13' = 180°.$

PROBLEMS

1. Given $a = 2, b = 3, C = 45°$; find c.   *Ans.* 2.12.

2. Given $b = 8, c = 5, A = 60°$; find a, cos B, and cos C.

3. Given $a = 4, c = 5, B = 120°$; find b.   *Ans.* 7.81.

4. Given $a = 24, b = 16, C = 44°$; find c.

5. Given $b = 10, c = 11, A = 133°$; find a.   *Ans.* 19.3.

6. Given $a = 21, b = 24, c = 27$; solve the triangle.

7. Given $a = 2, b = 3, c = 4$; find the cosine of the largest angle.

                                      Ans. $-\frac{1}{4}$.

8. The sides of a triangle are 4, 7, and 10. Find the largest angle of the triangle.

9. If the two sides of a triangle are 10 and 11 and the included angle is 50°, find the third side.   *Ans.* 8.92.

10. The sides of a triangle are 3, 8, and 9. Find the altitude of the triangle from the vertex of the smallest angle.

11. The two diagonals of a parallelogram are 10 and 12 and they form an angle of 49° 18'; find the sides.   *Ans.* 10 and 4.68.

12. In order to find the distance between two objects, A and B, separated by a pond, a station C was chosen, and the distances $CA = 426$ yd., $CB = 322.4$ yd., together with the angle $ACB = 68°\ 42'$, were measured. Find the distance from A to B.

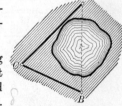

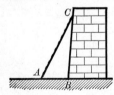

13. A ladder 52 ft. long is set 20 ft. from the foot of an inclined buttress, and reaches 46 ft. up its face. Find the inclination of the face of the buttress.

                          Ans. 95° 52'.

14. Under what visual angle is an object 7 ft. long seen by an observer whose eye is 5 ft. from one end of the object and 8 ft. from the other end?

15. Two stations, A and B, on opposite sides of a mountain, are both visible from a third station C. The distance $AC = 11.5$ mi., $BC = 9.4$ mi., and angle $ACB = 59°\ 30'$. Find the distance between A and B. *Ans.* 10.5 mi.

16. Two vessels leave a port at the same time. One travels in the direction $62°\ 15'$ east of north at the rate of 24 mi. an hour; the other travels in the direction $18°\ 20'$ west of south at the rate of 20 mi. an hour. How far apart will the vessels be at the end of two hours? In what direction will the faster vessel be from the slower at that time?

17. Prove the following for any triangle:

  a. $a(b^2 + c^2)\cos A + b(c^2 + a^2)\cos B + c(a^2 + b^2)\cos C = 3\ abc.$

  b. $\dfrac{b + c}{a} = \dfrac{\cos B + \cos C}{1 - \cos A}.$

  c. $a + b + c = (b + c)\cos A + (c + a)\cos B + (a + b)\cos C.$

  d. $\dfrac{\cos A}{a} + \dfrac{\cos B}{b} + \dfrac{\cos C}{c} = \dfrac{a^2 + b^2 + c^2}{2\ abc}.$

  e. $a^2 + b^2 + c^2 = 2(ab \cos C + bc \cos A + ca \cos B).$

46. Trigonometric functions of the half-angles of a triangle in terms of the sides. Formulas **(49)** to **(51)** are not convenient for computation when a, b, c are large numbers. These may be replaced, as will now be shown, by other formulas, which involve the half-angles of a triangle. We first prove the

Theorem. *If x is an acute angle or an obtuse angle,* then*

  (1) $$\sin^2 \tfrac{1}{2}\,x = \tfrac{1}{2}(1 - \cos x),$$
  (2) $$\cos^2 \tfrac{1}{2}\,x = \tfrac{1}{2}(1 + \cos x).$$

Proof. (For both figures.) In Fig. 1, x is an acute angle. In Fig. 2, x is an obtuse angle. The vertex O is the center of a unit circle $(R = 1)$. MP is perpendicular to the horizontal diameter BA. Then $$\angle ABP = \tfrac{1}{2}\,x.$$

[Being inscribed in the arc AP.]

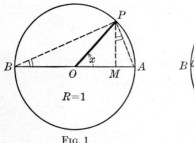
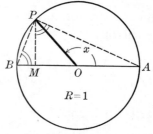

FIG. 1   FIG. 2

* These relations are true for any angle x, as is shown in Chap. VI.

Also, $OM = \cos x.$ By Art. 30

The right triangles ABP and MPA are similar.

Hence $\angle ABP = \angle MPA = \frac{1}{2}x.$

Therefore

(3) $\qquad \sin \frac{1}{2}x = \dfrac{AP}{BA} = \dfrac{AP}{2}$ (in triangle ABP).

(4) $\qquad \sin \frac{1}{2}x = \dfrac{MA}{AP}$ (in triangle MPA).

Hence, by multiplication, from (3) and (4),

(5) $\qquad \sin^2 \frac{1}{2}x = \frac{1}{2}MA.$

But on the line BA, $MA = OA - OM = 1 - \cos x$, since the line-segments are directed (Art. 30). Hence

(6) $\qquad \sin^2 \frac{1}{2}x = \frac{1}{2}(1 - \cos x).$

Then, making use of (**18**), Art. 17,

(7) $\qquad \cos^2 \frac{1}{2}x = 1 - \sin^2 \frac{1}{2}x = \frac{1}{2}(1 + \cos x).$

To derive the required formulas, we now proceed as follows. Denote half the sum of the sides of a triangle (that is, half the perimeter) by s. Then

(8) $\qquad 2s = a + b + c.$

Subtracting $2c$ from both sides,

$\qquad 2s - 2c = a + b + c - 2c,$

or,

(9) $\qquad 2(s - c) = a + b - c.$

Similarly,

(10) $\qquad 2(s - b) = a - b + c,$

(11) $\qquad 2(s - a) = -a + b + c.$

In (1) and (2), replace x by A. This gives

(12) $\qquad 2\sin^2 \frac{1}{2}A = 1 - \cos A,$

(13) $\qquad 2\cos^2 \frac{1}{2}A = 1 + \cos A.$

$\sin^2 \frac{1}{2}x = \frac{1}{2}(1 - \cos x)$

$\cos^2 \frac{1}{2}x = \frac{1}{2}(1 + \cos x)$

$s = \dfrac{a + b + c}{2}$

$\sin \frac{1}{2}A = \sqrt{\dfrac{(s-b)(s-c)}{bc}}$

But from (49), p. 95, $\cos A = \dfrac{b^2 + c^2 - a^2}{2bc}$; hence (12) becomes

$$2 \sin^2 \tfrac{1}{2} A = 1 - \frac{b^2 + c^2 - a^2}{2bc}$$

$$= \frac{2bc - b^2 - c^2 + a^2}{2bc}$$

$$= \frac{a^2 - (b^2 - 2bc + c^2)}{2bc}$$

$$= \frac{a^2 - (b - c)^2}{2bc}$$

$$= \frac{(a + b - c)(a - b + c)}{2bc}$$

[$a^2 - (b - c)^2$ being the product of the sum and difference of a and $b - c$.]

$$= \frac{2(s - c)\,2(s - b)}{2bc}. \qquad \text{By (9), (10)}$$

(52) $\qquad \therefore \sin \tfrac{1}{2} A = \sqrt{\dfrac{(s - b)(s - c)}{bc}}.$

Similarly, (13) becomes

$$2 \cos^2 \tfrac{1}{2} A = 1 + \frac{b^2 + c^2 - a^2}{2bc}$$

$$= \frac{2bc + b^2 + c^2 - a^2}{2bc}$$

$$= \frac{(b + c)^2 - a^2}{2bc}$$

$$= \frac{(b + c + a)(b + c - a)}{2bc}$$

$$= \frac{2s \cdot 2(s - a)}{2bc}.$$

(53) $\qquad \therefore \cos \tfrac{1}{2} A = \sqrt{\dfrac{s(s - a)}{bc}}.$

Since $\tan \tfrac{1}{2} A = \dfrac{\sin \tfrac{1}{2} A}{\cos \tfrac{1}{2} A}$, we get, by substitution from (52) and (53),

(54) $\qquad \tan \tfrac{1}{2} A = \sqrt{\dfrac{(s - b)(s - c)}{s(s - a)}}.$

Since any angle of a triangle must be less than 180°, $\tfrac{1}{2} A$ must be less than 90° and all the functions of $\tfrac{1}{2} A$ must be positive. Hence only the positive signs of the radicals in (52), (53), and (54) have been taken.

Similarly, we may get

$$\sin \tfrac{1}{2} B = \sqrt{\frac{(s-a)(s-c)}{ac}}, \qquad \sin \tfrac{1}{2} C = \sqrt{\frac{(s-a)(s-b)}{ab}},$$

$$\cos \tfrac{1}{2} B = \sqrt{\frac{s(s-b)}{ac}}, \qquad \cos \tfrac{1}{2} C = \sqrt{\frac{s(s-c)}{ab}},$$

$$\tan \tfrac{1}{2} B = \sqrt{\frac{(s-a)(s-c)}{s(s-b)}}, \qquad \tan \tfrac{1}{2} C = \sqrt{\frac{(s-a)(s-b)}{s(s-c)}}.\;^{*}$$

There is, then, a choice of three different formulas for finding the value of each angle. If half the angle is very near 0°, the formula for the cosine will not give a very accurate result, because the cosines of angles near 0° differ little in value; and the same holds true of the formula for the sine when half the angle is very near 90°. Hence in the first case the formula for the sine, in the second that for the cosine, should be used. In general, however, the formula for the tangent is to be preferred.

When two angles, as A and B, have been found, the third angle, C, may be found by the relation $A + B + C = 180°$, but it is best to compute all the angles from the formulas, so that we may use the sum of the angles as a test of the accuracy of the results.

It is customary to use a second form of **(54)**, found as follows:

$$\tan \tfrac{1}{2} A = \sqrt{\frac{(s-b)(s-c)}{s(s-a)}}$$

$$= \sqrt{\frac{(s-a)(s-b)(s-c)}{s(s-a)^2}}$$

$$\left[\begin{array}{l}\text{Multiplying both numerator and denomina-}\\\text{tor of the fraction under the radical by } s-a.\end{array}\right]$$

$$= \frac{1}{s-a}\sqrt{\frac{(s-a)(s-b)(s-c)}{s}}.$$

Denoting the radical part of the expression by r,

(55) $$r = \sqrt{\frac{(s-a)(s-b)(s-c)}{s}},$$

and we get

(56) $$\tan \tfrac{1}{2} A = \frac{r}{s-a}.$$

* Also found by changing the letters in cyclical order.

Similarly,

(57) $$\tan \tfrac{1}{2} B = \frac{r}{s-b},$$

(58) $$\tan \tfrac{1}{2} C = \frac{r}{s-c}.$$

By proving one of the last three formulas geometrically it may be shown that r is the radius of the inscribed circle.

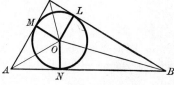

Proof. Since angle $NAO = \tfrac{1}{2} A$,

(14) $$\tan \tfrac{1}{2} A = \frac{NO}{AN}.$$

If s denotes half the perimeter, we have

$$2s = AN + NB + BL + LC + CM + MA.$$

But $NB = BL$, $CM = LC$, $MA = AN$; therefore

$$2s = 2 AN + 2 BL + 2 LC,$$

or, $$s = AN + (BL + LC) = AN + a.$$

This gives $AN = s - a$.

Substituting in (14), $\tan \tfrac{1}{2} A = \dfrac{NO}{s-a}.$

Comparing this result with (56) and (55), we see that

$$NO = r = \sqrt{\frac{(s-a)(s-b)(s-c)}{s}}.$$

EXAMPLE. Solve the triangle whose sides are 13, 14, 15.

Solution. Let $a = 13$, $b = 14$, $c = 15$.

Then $$2s = a + b + c = 42,$$

or, $$s = 21.$$

Also, $$s - a = 8, \quad s - b = 7, \quad s - c = 6.$$

From (55), $$r = \sqrt{\frac{(s-a)(s-b)(s-c)}{s}} = \sqrt{\frac{8 \cdot 7 \cdot 6}{21}} = \sqrt{16} = 4.$$

From (56), $$\tan \tfrac{1}{2} A = \frac{r}{s-a} = \frac{4}{8} = \frac{1}{2} = 0.5000.$$

$$\therefore \tfrac{1}{2} A = 26° \ 34', \text{ or } A = 53° \ 8'.$$

From (57), $$\tan \tfrac{1}{2} B = \frac{r}{s-b} = \frac{4}{7} = 0.5714.$$

$$\therefore \tfrac{1}{2} B = 29° \ 45', \text{ or } B = 59° \ 30'.$$

From (58), $$\tan \tfrac{1}{2} C = \frac{r}{s-c} = \frac{4}{6} = \frac{2}{3} = 0.6667.$$

$$\therefore \tfrac{1}{2} C = 33° \ 41', \text{ or } C = 67° \ 22'.$$

Check. $A + B + C = 53° \ 8' + 59° \ 30' + 67° \ 22' = 180°.*$

* An excess, or defect, of 2′ in the sum of the angles would not necessarily mean an error in the calculation. In interpolation small errors may arise.

PROBLEMS

Using the law of tangents to find the remaining angles, solve the following triangles:

1. $a = 94$, $b = 56$, $C = 29°$. *Ans.* $A = 119° 54'$, $B = 31° 6'$, $c = 52.56$.

2. $b = 200$, $c = 125$, $A = 68° 18'$.

3. $a = 100$, $c = 130$, $B = 51° 49'$.

Ans. $A = 49° 4'$, $C = 79° 7'$, $b = 104.1$.

4. $a = 42$, $b = 92$, $C = 112° 12'$.

5. A lighthouse is 16 mi. in the direction 29° 30′ east of north from a cliff. Another lighthouse is 12 mi. in the direction 72° 45′ west of south from the cliff. In what direction is the first lighthouse from the second? *Ans.* 47° 54′ east of north.

6. Two forces, of magnitudes 400 lb. and 600 lb., act on a body and make an angle of 112° 15′ with each other. Find the magnitude and direction of the resultant force.

Using formulas (55) to (58), pp. 100 and 101, find the angles of each of the following triangles. Check your answers.

7. Given $a = 2$, $b = 3$, $c = 4$.

Ans. $A = 28° 58'$, $B = 46° 34'$, $C = 104° 28'$.

8. Given $a = 4$, $b = 7$, $c = 10$.

9. Given $a = 21$, $b = 24$, $c = 27$.

Ans. $A = 48° 11'$, $B = 58° 25'$, $C = 73° 24'$.

10. If R and r denote the radii of the circumscribed and inscribed circles respectively, prove the following for any triangle:

a. $r = \dfrac{a \sin \frac{1}{2} B \sin \frac{1}{2} C}{\cos \frac{1}{2} A}$.

c. $\dfrac{1}{bc} + \dfrac{1}{ca} + \dfrac{1}{ab} = \dfrac{1}{2 rR}$.

b. $R = \dfrac{abc}{4\sqrt{s(s-a)(s-b)(s-c)}}$.

d. $R = \dfrac{1}{2} \sqrt[3]{\dfrac{abc}{\sin A \sin B \sin C}}$.

e. $abcr = 4 R(s - a)(s - b)(s - c)$.

47. Formulas for finding the area of an oblique triangle.

CASE I. *When two sides and the included angle are known.*

Theorem. *The area of a triangle equals half the product of any two sides multiplied by the sine of the included angle.*

Proof. Let b, c, and A be known. Take c as the base. Denote the altitude by h and the area by S. Then, by geometry,

$$S = \tfrac{1}{2} ch.$$

But, in both figures below, $h = b \sin A$; hence

(59) $$S = \tfrac{1}{2} bc \sin A.$$

Similarly, $S = \tfrac{1}{2} ac \sin B = \tfrac{1}{2} ab \sin C.$

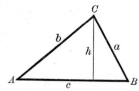 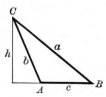

EXAMPLE 1. Find the area of a triangle, having given $b = 20$ in., $c = 15$ in., $A = 60°$.

Solution. Substituting in (59),

$$S = \frac{1}{2} bc \sin A = \frac{1}{2} \times 20 \times 15 \times \frac{\sqrt{3}}{2} = 75\sqrt{3} \text{ sq. in. } Ans.$$

CASE II. *When the three sides are known.*

The triangle ABC, p. 101, is the sum of the three triangles OBC, OCA, OAB, whose areas are, respectively, $\tfrac{1}{2} ar$, $\tfrac{1}{2} br$, $\tfrac{1}{2} cr$. Their sum is $S = \tfrac{1}{2} r(a + b + c) = rs.$

Substituting the value of r from (55), p. 100, we get

(60) $$S = \sqrt{s(s - a)(s - b)(s - c)}.$$

EXAMPLE 2. Having given $a = 13$, $b = 14$, $c = 15$, find the area.

Solution. $s = \tfrac{1}{2}(a + b + c) = 21$, $s - a = 8$, $s - b = 7$, $s - c = 6$. Substituting in (60),

$$S = \sqrt{s(s - a)(s - b)(s - c)} = \sqrt{21 \times 8 \times 7 \times 6} = 84. \ Ans.$$

CASE III. *Problems which do not fall under Cases I or II directly may be solved by Case I, if we first find an additional side or angle by the law of sines.*

EXAMPLE 3. Given $a = 10\sqrt{3}$, $b = 10$, $A = 120°$; find the area of the triangle.

Solution. By the law of sines,

$$\sin B = \frac{b \sin A}{a} = \frac{10 \times \tfrac{1}{2}\sqrt{3}}{10\sqrt{3}} = \frac{1}{2}.$$

Therefore $B = 30°$ and $C = 180° - (A + B) = 30°$.

We now have the two sides a and b and the included angle C. Hence

$$S = \tfrac{1}{2} ab \sin C = \tfrac{1}{2} \times 10\sqrt{3} \times 10 \times \tfrac{1}{2} = 25\sqrt{3}. \ Ans.$$

PROBLEMS

Find the areas of the following triangles:

1. $b = 8$, $c = 5$, $A = 60°$.   *Ans.* 17.32.

2. $a = 10$, $b = 12$, $C = 60°$.

3. $a = 40$, $c = 60$, $B = 30°$.   *Ans.* 600

4. $a = 7$, $c = 5\sqrt{2}$, $B = 135°$.

5. $a = 40$, $b = 13$, $c = 37$.   *Ans.* 240.

6. $a = 5$, $b = 6$, $c = 7$.

7. $a = 409$, $b = 169$, $c = 510$.   *Ans.* 30,600.

8. $b = 149$, $A = 70° 42'$, $B = 39° 18'$.

9. $c = 8$, $B = 100° 6'$, $C = 31° 6'$.   *Ans.* 45.89.

10. $b = 10$, $c = 40$, $A = 75°$.

11. $a = 7$, $c = 3$, $A = 60°$.   *Ans.* 10.39.

12. $a = 140.5$, $b = 170.6$, $A = 40°$.

13. Prove that if a side and two adjacent angles of a triangle are known, the area of the triangle is given by one of the formulas $S = \dfrac{a^2 \sin B \sin C}{2 \sin (B + C)}$, $S = \dfrac{b^2 \sin A \sin C}{2 \sin (A + C)}$, or $S = \dfrac{c^2 \sin A \sin B}{2 \sin (A + B)}$.

14. Show that the area of a parallelogram equals the product of any two adjacent sides multiplied by the sine of the included angle.

15. Find a formula for the area of an isosceles trapezoid in terms of the parallel sides and an acute angle.

16. Show that the area of a quadrilateral equals one half the product of its diagonals by the sine of their included angle.

17. The base of an isosceles triangle is 20, and its area is $100 \div \sqrt{3}$; find its angles.   *Ans.* 30°, 30°, 120°.

18. Prove that the area of any triangle is given by each of the following formulas.

     a. $S = \frac{1}{2} a^2 \sin B \sin C \csc A$.

     b. $S = \dfrac{abc}{4 R}$.

     c. $S = Rr(\sin A + \sin B + \sin C)$.

     d. $S = \dfrac{2 \, abc}{a + b + c} (\cos \frac{1}{2} A \cos \frac{1}{2} B \cos \frac{1}{2} C)$.

48. Concluding remark. In this chapter calculations have been made using Tables IV and V (natural values of the functions) as needed. As shown in Art. 36, four significant figures are obtained in the results. In the next chapter calculations will be made by logarithms, using a four-place table. Results are found automatically to four significant figures, and much useless work is avoided.

CHAPTER V

THEORY AND USE OF LOGARITHMS

49. Need of logarithms * in trigonometry. Many of the problems arising in trigonometry involve computations of considerable length. Since the labor connected with extensive and complicated calculations may be greatly lessened by the use of logarithms, it is advantageous to use them in much of our trigonometric work. Especially is this true of the calculations connected with the solution of triangles. We shall now give the fundamental principles of logarithms and explain the use of logarithmic tables.

Definition of a logarithm. The exponent of the power to which a given number called the base must be raised to equal a second number is called the logarithm of the second number.

Thus, if

(A) $$b^x = N,$$ *(exponential form)*

then $x = $ *the logarithm of N to the base b.* This statement is written in abbreviated form as follows:

(B) $$x = \log_b N.$$ *(logarithmic form)*

(A) and (B) are then simply two different ways of expressing the same relation between b, x, and N.

(A) is called the *exponential form.*
(B) is called the *logarithmic form.*

The fact that a logarithm is an exponent may be emphasized by writing (A) in the form

$$(\text{base})^{\log} = \text{number}.$$

For example, the following relations in exponential form, namely,

$$3^2 = 9, \qquad 2^5 = 32, \qquad (\tfrac{1}{2})^3 = \tfrac{1}{8}, \qquad x^y = z,$$

are written, respectively, in the logarithmic form

$$2 = \log_3 9, \quad 5 = \log_2 32, \quad 3 = \log_{\frac{1}{2}} \tfrac{1}{8}, \quad y = \log_x z ;$$

where   2, 5, 3, y are the logarithms (exponents),
          3, 2, $\tfrac{1}{2}$, x are the bases, and
          9, 32, $\tfrac{1}{8}$, z are the numbers respectively.

---

* Logarithms were invented by John Napier (1550–1617), Baron of Merchiston in Scotland, and described by him in 1614.

Similarly, the relations

$$25^{\frac{1}{2}} = \sqrt{25} = 5, \qquad\qquad 10^{-3} = \frac{1}{10^3} = \frac{1}{1000} = 0.001,$$

$$8^{\frac{2}{3}} = \sqrt[3]{8^2} = \sqrt[3]{64} = 4, \qquad\qquad b^0 = \frac{b^n}{b^n} = 1$$

are written in logarithmic form as follows:

$$\tfrac{1}{2} = \log_{25} 5, \quad -3 = \log_{10} 0.001, \quad \tfrac{2}{3} = \log_8 4, \quad 0 = \log_b 1.$$

EXAMPLE. What is the logarithm of 27 to the base 9?

Solution.

Let $\qquad\qquad\qquad x = \log_9 27.$

Then $\qquad\qquad\qquad 9^x = 27,$

or, $\qquad\qquad\qquad 3^{2x} = 3^3.$

Hence $\qquad\qquad\quad 2\,x = 3$

and $\qquad\qquad\qquad x = \tfrac{3}{2}.$ *Ans.*

PROBLEMS

Express the following equations in logarithmic form:

1. $5^2 = 25$. *Ans.* $\log_5 25 = 2$.

2. $10^3 = 1000$.

3. $3^4 = 81$.

4. $(\tfrac{1}{3})^2 = \tfrac{1}{9}$.

5. $\sqrt{9} = 3$.

6. $2^{-4} = \tfrac{1}{16}$.

7. $\sqrt[3]{125} = 5$.

8. $10^{-2} = 0.01$.

9. $(0.01)^2 = 0.0001$.

10. $a^0 = 1$.

11. $p^s = q$.

12. $y = 4^{2x}$.

Express the following equations in exponential form:

13. $\log_4 64 = 3$. *Ans.* $4^3 = 64$.

14. $\log_7 49 = 2$.

15. $\log_6 216 = 3$.

16. $\log_{10} 0.0001 = -4$.

17. $\log_4 2 = \tfrac{1}{2}$.

18. $\log_a a = 1$.

19. $\log_a 1 = 0$.

20. $\log_b a = c$.

21. When the base is 2, what are the logarithms of the numbers 1, 2, $\tfrac{1}{2}$, 4, $\tfrac{1}{4}$, 8, 64, 128?

22. When the base is 5, what are the logarithms of the numbers 1, 5, 25, 125, $\tfrac{1}{5}$, $\tfrac{1}{25}$, $\tfrac{1}{625}$?

23. When the base is 10, what are the logarithms of the numbers 1, 10, 100, 1000, 10,000, 0.1, 0.01, 0.001, 0.0001?

24. When the base is 4 and the logarithms are 0, 1, 2, 3, -1, -2, $\tfrac{1}{2}$, what are the numbers?

Find the value of x in each of the following equations:

25. $x = \log_3 9$. *Ans.* 2. **26.** $x = \log_3 \frac{1}{9}$.

27. $x = \log_8 16$. *Ans.* $\frac{4}{3}$. **28.** $x = \log_{100} 1000$.

29. $x = \log_{10} \sqrt{10}$. *Ans.* $\frac{1}{2}$. **30.** $x = \log_4 \sqrt[3]{16}$.

31. $\log_2 x = 3$. *Ans.* 8. **32.** $\log_3 x = -3$.

33. $2 \log_{25} x = -3$. *Ans.* $\frac{1}{125}$. **34.** $3 \log_8 x = -4$.

35. $\log_x 16 = 2$. *Ans.* 4. **36.** $\log_x 0.001 = -3$.

37. $\log_x 6\frac{1}{4} = -2$. *Ans.* $\frac{2}{5}$. **38.** $\log_x 10 \sqrt[3]{10} = \frac{4}{3}$.

Verify the following statements:

39. $\log_{10} 1000 + \log_{10} 100 + \log_{10} 10 + \log_{10} 1 = 6$.

40. $\log_{10} 0.001 - \log_{10} 0.01 + \log_{10} 0.1 = -2$.

41. $2 \log_a a + 2 \log_a \frac{1}{a} + \log_a 1 = 0$.

42. $3 \log_{27} 3 - \frac{1}{3} \log_3 27 + \log_9 3 = \frac{1}{2}$.

43. $4 \log_2 \sqrt{0.125} + 6 \log_{10} \frac{\sqrt{10}}{10} = -9$.

44. $a^{\log_a x} = x$.

45. $\log_a a^x = x$.

50. Theorems on logarithms. Since a logarithm is simply a new name for an exponent, it follows that the properties of logarithms must be found from the laws in algebra governing exponents.

Theorem I. The logarithm of the **product** of two factors equals the **sum** of the logarithms of the two factors.

Proof. Let the two factors be M and N, and let x and y be their logarithms to the common base b. Then

(A) $\log_b M = x$, and $\log_b N = y$.

Writing these in the exponential form,

(B) $b^x = M$, and $b^y = N$.

Multiplying together the corresponding members of equations (B),

$$b^{x+y} = MN.$$

Writing this in the logarithmic form gives

$$\log_b MN = x + y = \log_b M + \log_b N. \qquad \text{From } (A)$$

By successive applications this theorem may evidently be extended to the product of any number of factors. Thus

$$\log_b MNPQ = \log_b M \cdot NPQ = \log_b M + \log_b NPQ \qquad \text{Theorem I}$$
$$= \log_b M + \log_b N + \log_b PQ$$
$$= \log_b M + \log_b N + \log_b P + \log_b Q.$$

Theorem II. *The logarithm of the **quotient** of two numbers is equal to the logarithm of the dividend **minus** the logarithm of the divisor.*

Proof. As in Theorem I, let

(A) $\qquad\qquad \log_b M = x, \quad \text{and} \quad \log_b N = y.$

Writing these in the exponential form,

(B) $\qquad\qquad b^x = M, \quad \text{and} \quad b^y = N.$

Dividing the corresponding members of equations (B), we get

$$b^{x-y} = \frac{M}{N}.$$

Writing this in logarithmic form gives

$$\log_b \frac{M}{N} = x - y = \log_b M - \log_b N. \qquad \text{From } (A)$$

Theorem III. *The logarithm of the **pth power** of a number is equal to **p times** the logarithm of the number.*

Proof. Let $\qquad\qquad \log_b N = x.$

Then $\qquad\qquad\qquad b^x = N.$

Raising both sides to the *p*th power,

$$b^{px} = N^p.$$

Writing this in logarithmic form gives

$$\log_b N^p = px = p \log_b N.$$

Theorem IV. *The logarithm of the **rth root** of a number is equal to the logarithm of the number **divided by** r.*

Proof. Let $\qquad\qquad \log_b N = x.$

Then $\qquad\qquad\qquad b^x = N.$

Extracting the *r*th root of both sides,

$$b^{\frac{x}{r}} = N^{\frac{1}{r}}.$$

Writing this in logarithmic form gives

$$\log_b N^{\frac{1}{r}} = \frac{x}{r} = \frac{\log_b N}{r} = \frac{1}{r} \log_b N.$$

From the preceding four theorems it follows that if we use the logarithms of numbers instead of the numbers themselves, then the operations of *multiplication, division, raising to powers,* and *extracting roots* are replaced by those of *addition, subtraction, multiplication,* and *division* respectively.

EXAMPLE 1. Find the value of $\log_{10} \sqrt{0.001}$.

Solution. $\log_{10} \sqrt{0.001} = \frac{1}{2} \log_{10} 0.001$ Theorem IV

$$= \frac{1}{2} \log_{10} \tfrac{1}{1000} = \frac{1}{2}(-3) = -\frac{3}{2}. \ Ans.$$

EXAMPLE 2. Write $\log_b \sqrt[3]{\dfrac{27 \times 0.235 \times 7.63}{63.2 \times 7.86}}$ in expanded form.

Solution.

$$\log_b \sqrt[3]{\frac{27 \times 0.235 \times 7.63}{63.2 \times 7.86}} = \frac{1}{3} \log_b \frac{27 \times 0.235 \times 7.63}{63.2 \times 7.86}$$

$$= \tfrac{1}{3}[\log_b (27 \times 0.235 \times 7.63) - \log_b (63.2 \times 7.86)]$$

$$= \tfrac{1}{3} [\log_b 27 + \log_b 0.235 + \log_b 7.63 - (\log_b 63.2 + \log_b 7.86)].$$

PROBLEMS

Find the value of each of the following expressions:

1. $\log_{10} \sqrt{1000} + \log_{10} \sqrt{0.01}$.   *Ans.* $\frac{1}{2}$.

2. $\log_{10} (0.1)^4 - \log_{10} \sqrt[3]{0.001}$.

3. $\log_{10} \sqrt{\tfrac{1}{10}} + \log_{10} \sqrt{10}$.   *Ans.* 0.

4. $\log_{10} \sqrt[3]{100} - \log_{10} (0.01)^2$.

5. $\log_2 \sqrt{8} + \log_3 (\tfrac{1}{3})^2$.   *Ans.* $-\frac{1}{2}$.

6. $\log_2 (0.5)^3 - \log_4 \sqrt[3]{16}$.

7. $\log_5 \sqrt{125} + \log_{11} \sqrt[3]{121}$.   *Ans.* $\frac{13}{6}$.

8. $\log_8 (2)^5 + \log_7 (\tfrac{1}{49})^{\frac{1}{3}}$.

Write the following logarithmic expressions in expanded form:

9. $\log_{10} \dfrac{4.12 \times 7.34}{6.28}$.

10. $\log_{10} \sqrt{\dfrac{6.72}{93.1 \times 0.065}}$.

11. $\log_m \sqrt{\dfrac{s(s-b)(s-c)}{s-a}}$.

12. $\log_m \dfrac{ab \sin C}{z}$.

13. $\log_{10} P(1+r)^n$.

14. $\log_{10} \dfrac{a^3 b^2 c^{\frac{1}{2}}}{4 \sqrt[3]{d}}$.

Write the following logarithmic expressions in contracted form:

15. $2 \log x + \frac{1}{2} \log y - 3 \log z.$

16. $\frac{5}{3} \log(x - 1) - \frac{2}{3} \log x - \frac{1}{6} \log (x + 2) + \log c.$

17. $\log y - \frac{1}{2} \log (y^2 + 4) + \log c.$

18. $\frac{1}{3}\{2 \log (x - 1) + 3 \log (x + 1) + \frac{1}{2} \log x - \frac{2}{3} \log (x^2 + 1)\}.$

51. Common* logarithms. Any positive number except unity may be taken as the base, and to every particular base chosen there corresponds a set or system of logarithms. In common logarithms the base is 10, and it is the one most convenient to use with our decimal system of numbers. In what follows, when the base is omitted the base 10 is understood. Thus $\log_{10} 100 = 2$ is written $\log 100 = 2$, etc.

The common logarithm of a given number is then the answer to the question

What power of 10 will equal the given number?

The following table indicates what numbers have integers for logarithms in the common system.

	Exponential Form		Logarithmic Form
Since	$10^4 = 10,000$	we have	$\log 10,000 = 4$
	$10^3 = 1000$		$\log 1000 = 3$
	$10^2 = 100$		$\log 100 = 2$
	$10^1 = 10$		$\log 10 = 1$
	$10^0 = 1$		$\log 1 = 0$
	$10^{-1} = 0.1$		$\log 0.1 = -1$
	$10^{-2} = 0.01$		$\log 0.01 = -2$
	$10^{-3} = 0.001$		$\log 0.001 = -3$
	$10^{-4} = 0.0001$		$\log 0.0001 = -4$
	etc.		etc.

Assuming that as a number increases its logarithm also increases, we see that a number between 100 and 1000 has a logarithm lying between 2 and 3. Similarly, the logarithm of a number between 0.1 and 0.01 has a logarithm lying between -1 and -2. In fact the logarithm of any number not an exact power of 10 consists, in general, of a *whole-number* part and a *decimal* part.

---

* Also called the Briggs System, from Henry Briggs (1561–1630), professor at Gresham College, London, and later at Oxford. He modified the new invention of logarithms so as to make it convenient for practical use.

Thus, since 4587 is a number lying between 10^3 and 10^4, we have

$$\log 4587 = 3 + \text{a decimal.}$$

Similarly, since 0.0067 is a number lying between 10^{-3} and 10^{-2},

$$\log 0.0067 = - (2 + \text{a decimal})$$
$$= - 2 - \text{a decimal.}$$

For practical reasons the logarithm of a number is always written in such a form that the decimal part is positive. When the logarithm as a whole is negative, the decimal part may be made positive by adding plus unity to it. Then, so as not to change the value of the logarithm, we add minus unity to the whole part. Thus, in the last example,

$$\log 0.0067 = (- 2) + (- \text{a decimal})$$
$$= (- 1 - 2) + (1 - \text{a decimal})$$
$$= - 3 + \text{a new decimal.}$$

To emphasize the fact that only the whole part of a logarithm is negative, the minus sign is usually written over the whole part. For example,

$$\log 0.004712 = - 2.3268$$
$$= - 2 - 0.3268$$
$$= (- 1 - 2) + (1 - 0.3268)$$
$$= \bar{3}.6732.$$

The whole-number part of a logarithm is called the *characteristic* of the logarithm.

The decimal part of a logarithm is called the *mantissa* of the logarithm.

Thus, if $\log 357 = 2.5527$ and $\log 0.004712 = \bar{3}.6732$, 2 and $- 3$ are the characteristics and 0.5527 and 0.6732 the mantissas.

From the previous explanations and by inspection of the table on the opposite page we get the following:

52. Rules for determining the characteristic of a common logarithm.

The characteristic for a number greater than unity is positive, and one less than the number of digits in the number to the left of the decimal point.

The characteristic for a number less than unity is negative, and is one greater numerically than the number of zeros between the decimal point and the first significant figure of the number.

EXAMPLE 1. Write down the characteristics of the logarithms of the numbers 27,683, 456.2, 9.67, 436,000, 26, 0.04, 0.0000612, 0.7963, 0.8, 0.0012.

Ans. 4, 2, 0, 5, 1, − 2, − 5, − 1, − 1, − 3.

Theorem V. *Numbers with the same significant figures * (and which therefore differ only in the position of the decimal point) have the same mantissa.*

Proof. Consider, for example, the numbers 54.37 and 5437.

Let $10^x = 54.37$.

If we multiply both members of this equation by 100 (= 10^2), we have $10^2 \cdot 10^x = 10^{x+2} = 5437,$

or, $x + 2 = \log 5437.$

Hence the logarithm of one number differs from that of the other merely in its whole part (characteristic).

Thus, if $\log 47{,}120 = 4.6732,$

then $\log 47.12 = 1.6732,$

and $\log 0.004712 = \bar{3}.6732.$

Since the mantissa is always positive, it is desirable in some computations to add to and subtract from the characteristic the same multiples of 10. Thus, $\bar{2}.3416$ may be written in the form $8.3416 - 10$. In this instance 10 was added to and subtracted from the characteristic − 2. The following examples will illustrate the advantage of writing characteristics in this form.

EXAMPLE 2. Add the logarithms $\bar{2}.4069$ and $\bar{1}.9842$.

Adding and subtracting 10, we write

$$8.4069 - 10$$
$$\underline{9.9842 - 10}$$
$$18.3911 - 20$$

or, $\bar{2}.3911.$ *Ans.*

EXAMPLE 3. Subtract $\bar{3}.4492$ from 2.1163.

We write

$$12.1163 - 10$$
$$\underline{7.4492 - 10}$$
$$4.6671.$$ *Ans.*

EXAMPLE 4. Multiply $\bar{2}.7012$ by 3.

$$8.7012 - 10$$
$$\underline{3}$$
$$26.1036 - 30$$

or, $\bar{4}.1036.$ *Ans.*

* See Art. 36.

EXAMPLE 5. Divide $\bar{2}.2411$ by 3.

Here we first add and then subtract 30.

$$3\lfloor 28.2411 - 30$$
$$9.4137 - 10$$

or, $\qquad\qquad \bar{1}.4137.$ *Ans.*

PROBLEMS

Given $\log 62.63 = 1.7968$ and $\log 7194 = 3.8569$; find the logarithms of the following numbers:

1. 6263.	*Ans.* 3.7968.	**2.** 7.194.	
3. 0.006263.	*Ans.* $\bar{3}.7968$.	**4.** 62630.	
5. 0.7194.	*Ans.* $\bar{1}.8569$.	**6.** 626.3×71.94.	
7. $(6.263)^2$.	*Ans.* 1.5936.	**8.** $\sqrt{719.4}$.	
9. $0.06263\sqrt[3]{7.194}$.	*Ans.* $\bar{1}.0824$.	**10.** $\sqrt{\dfrac{71940}{62.63}}$.	

Given $\log 5.664 = 0.7531$ and $\log 0.7182 = \bar{1}.8562$; find the numbers which correspond to the following logarithms:

11. 1.7531.	*Ans.* 56.64.	**12.** 2.8562.	
13. $8.7531 - 10$.	*Ans.* 0.05664.	**14.** $\bar{1}.7531$.	
15. 5.8562.	*Ans.* 718200.	**16.** $7.7531 - 10$.	
17. $9.8562 - 10$.	*Ans.* 0.7182.	**18.** 3.8562.	

Given $\log 2 = 0.3010$ and $\log 3 = 0.4771$; find the values of the following logarithms:

19. $\log 8$.	*Ans.* 0.9030.	**20.** $\log 27$.	
21. $\log 6$.	*Ans.* 0.7781.	**22.** $\log 48$.	
23. $\log 2\sqrt{3}$.	*Ans.* 0.5396.	**24.** $\log \dfrac{3\sqrt{6}}{2}$.	
25. $\log \sqrt{0.125}$.	*Ans.* $9.5485 - 10$.	**26.** $\log \sqrt[3]{1.5}$.	
27. $\log 2000\sqrt{30}$.	*Ans.* 4.0396.	**28.** $\log \dfrac{\sqrt{0.03}}{40}$.	

53. Tables of logarithms. The common system (having the base 10) of logarithms is the one used in practical computations. For the convenience of the calculator the common logarithms of numbers up to a certain number of significant figures have been computed and arranged in tabulated forms called logarithmic tables. The common system has two great advantages.

1. *The characteristic of the logarithm of a number may be written down on mere inspection by following the rules on page 111.*

Hence, as a rule, only the mantissas of the logarithms of numbers are printed in the tables.

2. *The logarithms of numbers having the same significant part have the same mantissa (Theorem V, p. 112).*

Hence a change in the position of the decimal point in a number affects the characteristic alone, and it is sufficient to tabulate the mantissas * of integers only. Thus,

$$\log 3104 = 3.4920, \qquad \log 31.04 = 1.4920,$$
$$\log .03104 = \overline{2}.4920, \qquad \log 310{,}400 = 5.4920\,;$$

in fact, the mantissa of any number whatever having 3104 as its significant part will have .4920 as the mantissa of its logarithm.

54. To find the logarithm of a given number. Table I, pp. 2, 3,† gives immediately the mantissas of the logarithms of all numbers whose first significant figure is 1 and whose significant part consists of four or fewer digits; and on pages 4, 5 are found the mantissas of the logarithms of all numbers whose first significant figure is greater than 1 and whose significant part consists of three or fewer digits.

The following examples will illustrate the finding of logarithms of numbers for which the mantissas are given directly in the tables.

The characteristic in all cases is determined by the position of the decimal point according to the rules of Art. 52, p. 111.

EXAMPLE 1. Find log 1387.

Solution. From the rule on page 111 we see that the characteristic is + 3.

On page 2, Table I, we find 138 in column *No.* The required mantissa will be found in the same horizontal row with 138 and in the vertical column which has 7 at the top. This gives the mantissa .1421.

Therefore $\qquad\qquad \log 1387 = 3.1421. \; Ans.$

EXAMPLE 2. Find log 17.

Solution. The characteristic is 1.

To find the mantissa of 17 we look up the mantissa of 1700. On page 3, Table I, we locate 170 in column *No.* The required mantissa is found in the same horizontal row with 170 and in the vertical column having 0 at the top. This gives the mantissa .2304.

Therefore $\qquad\qquad \log 17 = 1.2304. \; Ans.$

---

* In order to save space the decimal point in front of each mantissa is usually omitted in the tables.

† The tables referred to in this book are *Four-Place Tables* by Granville, Smith, and Mikesh (Ginn and Company).

EXAMPLE 3. Find log 0.00152.

Solution. The characteristic is -3, that is, negative and one greater numerically than the number of zeros (two) immediately after the decimal point.

Locate 152 in column *No.*, Table I, p. 3. In the same horizontal row with 152 and in the vertical column with 0 at the top we find the required mantissa .1818.

Therefore $\log 0.00152 = \overline{3}.1818 = 7.1818 - 10.$ *Ans.*

EXAMPLE 4. Find log 5.63.

Solution. The characteristic is zero.

On page 4, Table I, we locate 56 in column *No.* In the horizontal row with 56 and in the vertical column with 3 at the top we find the required mantissa .7505.

Therefore $\log 5.63 = 0.7505.$ *Ans.*

EXAMPLE 5. Find log 0.08.

Solution. The characteristic is -2.

Using 800, we find that the mantissa is .9031.

Therefore $\log 0.08 = \overline{2}.9031 = 8.9031 - 10.$ *Ans.*

PROBLEMS

Find the logarithms of the following numbers:

1. 1872.   *Ans.* 3.2723.   **2.** 5.

3. 0.7.   *Ans.* $\overline{1}$.8451.   **4.** 20,000.

5. 1.808.   *Ans.* 0.2572.   **6.** 0.000032.

7. 0.01011. *Ans.* $\overline{2}$.0048.   **8.** 9.95.

9. 17.35.   *Ans.* 1.2393.   **10.** 0.1289.

11. 2500.   *Ans.* 3.3979.   **12.** 1.002.

When the first significant figure of a number is 1 and the number of digits in its significant part is greater than 4, its mantissa cannot be found in Table I; nor can the mantissa of a number be found when its first significant figure is greater than 1 and the number of digits in its significant part is greater than 3.

By *interpolation*,* however, we may find the mantissa, in the first case, of a number having a fifth significant figure, and in the second case, of a number having a fourth significant figure. In this book no attempt is made to find the logarithms of numbers with more significant figures, since our four-place tables are in general accurate only to that extent.

* Illustrated by examples in Arts. 38–39 in the case of trigonometric functions.

We shall now illustrate the process of interpolation by means of examples.

EXAMPLE 6. Find log 2445.

Solution. By the rule on page 111 the characteristic is **3**. The required mantissa is not found in our table. We have

$$\log 2450 = 3.3892$$

and
$$\log 2440 = \underline{3.3874}$$
$$\text{Difference in logarithms} = 0.0018$$

Since 2445 lies between 2440 and 2450, it is clear that its logarithm must lie between 3.3874 and 3.3892. Because 2445 is just halfway between 2440 and 2450 we assume that its logarithm is halfway between the two logarithms.* We then take half (or 0.5) of their difference, 0.0018 (called the tabular difference), and add this to log 2440 = 3.3874. This gives

$$\log 2445 = 3.3874 + 0.5 \times 0.0018 = 3.3883. \; Ans.$$

If we had to find log 2442, we should take not half the difference but 0.2 of the difference between the logarithms of 2440 and 2445, since 2442 is not halfway between them but two tenths of the way.

In order to save work in interpolating, when looking up the logarithms of numbers whose mantissas are not found in the table, each tabular difference occurring in the table has been multiplied by 0.1, 0.2, 0.3, ···, 0.9, and the results are printed in the large right-hand column with "Prop. Parts" (proportional parts) at the top. Thus, on page 4, Table I, the first section in the Prop. Parts column shows the products obtained when multiplying the tabular differences 22 and 21 by 0.1, 0.2, 0.3, ···, 0.9. Thus,

Extra Digit	Difference	
	22	21
1	2.2	2.1
2	4.4	4.2
3	6.6	6.3
4	8.8	8.4
5	11.0	10.5
6	13.2	12.6
7	15.4	14.7
8	17.6	16.8
9	19.8	18.9

$$0.1 \times 22 = 2.2 \qquad 0.1 \times 21 = 2.1$$
$$0.2 \times 22 = 4.4 \qquad 0.2 \times 21 = 4.2$$
$$0.3 \times 22 = 6.6 \qquad 0.3 \times 21 = 6.3$$
$$0.4 \times 22 = 8.8 \qquad 0.4 \times 21 = 8.4$$
$$0.5 \times 22 = 11.0 \qquad 0.5 \times 21 = 10.5$$
$$\text{etc.} \qquad\qquad\qquad \text{etc.}$$

* In this process of interpolation we have assumed and used the principle that the increase of the logarithm is proportional to the increase of the number. This principle is not strictly true, though for numbers whose first significant figure is greater than 1 the error is so small as not to appear in the fourth decimal place of the mantissa. For numbers whose first significant figure is 1 this error would often appear, and for this reason Table I, pp. 2, 3, gives the mantissas of all such numbers exact to four decimal places.

EXAMPLE 7. Find log 28.64.

Solution. Since the mantissa of 2864 is not found in our table, we must interpolate.

$$\log 28.60 = 1.4564$$
$$\log 28.70 = 1.4579$$
$$\text{Tabular difference} = \quad 15$$

About halfway down the Prop. Parts column on page 4 we find the block giving the proportional parts corresponding to the tabular difference 15. Under 15 and opposite the extra digit 4 of our number we find 6.0. Then

$$\log 28.60 = 1.4564$$
$$\underline{\quad\quad 6} \quad \text{Prop. Part}$$
$$\log 28.64 = 1.4570. \quad Ans.$$

EXAMPLE 8. Find log 0.12548.

Solution. Since the mantissa of 12,548 is not found in our table, we interpolate.

$$\log 0.12540 = \bar{1}.0983$$
$$\log 0.12550 = \bar{1}.0986$$
$$\text{Tabular difference} = \quad 3$$

In the Prop. Parts column on page 2 we find the block giving the proportional parts corresponding to the tabular difference 3. Under 3 and opposite the extra digit 8 we find 2.4 (= 2). Then

$$\log 0.12540 = \bar{1}.0983$$
$$\underline{\quad\quad 2} \quad \text{Prop. Part}$$
$$\log 0.12548 = \bar{1}.0985. \quad Ans.$$

PROBLEMS

Find the logarithms of the following numbers:

1. 4583.   *Ans.* 3.6612.
2. 16.426.
3. 0.09688.   *Ans.* $\bar{2}$.9862.
4. 0.10108.
5. 1000.7.   *Ans.* 3.0003.
6. 724,200.
7. 9.496.   *Ans.* 0.9775.
8. 0.0004586.

55. To find the number corresponding to a given logarithm. The following examples illustrate the process of finding the number when its logarithm is given.

EXAMPLE 1. Find the number whose logarithm is 2.1892.

Solution. The problem may also be stated thus: find x, having given

$$\log x = 2.1892.$$

On page 3, Table I, we find this mantissa, .1892 exactly, in the same horizontal row with 154 in the *No.* column and in the vertical column with 6 at the top. Hence the first four significant figures of the required number are 1546. Since

the characteristic is 2, we place the decimal point so that there will be three digits to the left of the decimal point, that is, we place it between 4 and 6. Hence
$$x = 154.6. \quad Ans.$$

EXAMPLE 2. Find the number whose logarithm is 4.8409.

Solution. That is, given $\log x = 4.8409$, to find x. Since the mantissa .8409 is not found exactly in our table, we interpolate.

The given mantissa, .8409, is found to lie between .8407 and .8414 on page 4, Table I.

The first three significant figures of the number corresponding to the lesser one, that is, to .8407, are 693.

The tabular difference between .8407 and .8414 is 7, and the difference between .8407 and the given mantissa .8409 is 2.

In the Prop. Parts column under the block corresponding to the tabular difference 7, we find that the proportional part 2.1 is nearest to 2 in value. Immediately to the left of 2.1 we find 3, the (extra) figure to be annexed to the number 693 found in the second step. Hence the first four significant figures of the required number are 6933.

Since the characteristic of the given logarithm is 4, we annex one zero and place the decimal point after it in order to have five digits of the number to the left of the decimal point. Hence
$$x = 69,330. \quad Ans.$$

PROBLEMS

Find the numbers corresponding to the following logarithms:

1. 1.8055.	*Ans.* 63.90.	**2.** $\bar{1}$.4487.	
3. 0.2164.	*Ans.* 1.646.	**4.** 2.9487.	
5. $\bar{2}$.0529.	*Ans.* 0.011295.	**6.** 5.2668.	
7. 3.9774.	*Ans.* 9493.	**8.** $\bar{4}$.0010.	
9. 8.4430 − 10.	*Ans.* 0.02773.	**10.** 9.4975 − 10.	

56. The use of logarithms in computations. The following examples will illustrate how logarithms are used in actual calculations.

EXAMPLE 1. Calculate 243×13.49, using logarithms.

Solution. Let $\qquad x = 243 \times 13.49.$

Taking the logarithms of both sides,
$$\log x = \log 243 + \log 13.49. \qquad \text{Th. I, Art. 50}$$
We have
$$\log 243 = 2.3856$$
$$\log 13.49 = \underline{1.1300}$$
Adding, $\qquad \log x = 3.5156$
$$x = 3278. \quad Ans.$$

EXAMPLE 2. Calculate $\dfrac{1375 \times 0.06423}{76,420}$.

Solution. Let $\qquad\qquad x = \dfrac{1375 \times 0.06423}{76,420}$.

Then $\qquad\qquad \log x = \log 1375 + \log 0.06423 - \log 76,420$
$\qquad\qquad\qquad\qquad\qquad\qquad\qquad\qquad\qquad$ Th. I and Th. II, Art. 50

$$\log 1375 = \;\; 3.1383$$
$$\log 0.06423 = \;\; 8.8077 - 10$$
Adding, $\qquad\qquad\qquad \overline{11.9460 - 10}$
$$\log 76,420 = \;\; 4.8832$$
Subtracting, $\qquad\quad \log x = \;\; \overline{7.0628 - 10}$
$$x = 0.0011555. \; \textit{Ans.}$$

EXAMPLE 3. Calculate $(5.664)^3$.

Solution. Let $\qquad\qquad x = (5.664)^3$.

Then $\qquad\qquad\quad \log x = 3 \log 5.664.$ $\qquad$ Th. III, Art. 50
$$\log 5.664 = 0.7531$$
$$\underline{\qquad\qquad\qquad 3}$$
$$\log x = \overline{2.2593}$$
$$x = 181.67. \; \textit{Ans.}$$

EXAMPLE 4. Calculate $\sqrt[3]{0.7182}$.

Solution. Let $\qquad\qquad x = \sqrt[3]{0.7182} = (0.7182)^{\frac{1}{3}}$.

Then $\qquad\qquad\quad \log x = \tfrac{1}{3} \log 0.7182.$ $\qquad$ Th. IV, Art. 50
$$\log 0.7182 = \bar{1}.8562$$
$$= 29.8562 - 30. \qquad \text{Example 5, p. 113}$$
$$3 \,\underline{|\, 29.8562 - 30}$$
$$\log x = \;\; 9.9521 - 10$$
$$x = 0.8956. \; \textit{Ans.}$$

EXAMPLE 5. Calculate $\sqrt[3]{\dfrac{\sqrt{7194 \times 87}}{98,080,000}}$.

Solution. Let $\qquad x = \sqrt[3]{\dfrac{\sqrt{7194 \times 87}}{98,080,000}} = \left[\dfrac{(7194)^{\frac{1}{2}} \times 87}{98,080,000}\right]^{\frac{1}{3}}$.

Then $\qquad\qquad\quad \log x = \tfrac{1}{3}\left[\tfrac{1}{2}\log 7194 + \log 87 - \log 98,080,000\right].$

$$\log 7194 = 3.8569$$
$$2\,\underline{|\, 3.8569}$$
$$\tfrac{1}{2}\log 7194 = 1.9285$$
$$\log 87 = \underline{1.9395}$$
$$3.8680$$
or, $\qquad\qquad\qquad\qquad\qquad\qquad 13.8680 - 10$
$$\log 98,080,000 = \underline{7.9916}$$
Subtracting, $\qquad\qquad\qquad\quad 5.8764 - 10$
or, $\qquad\qquad\qquad\qquad\qquad 25.8764 - 30 \qquad \text{Example 5, p. 113}$
$$3\,\underline{|\, 25.8764 - 30}$$
$$\log x = 8.6255 - 10$$
$$\therefore x = 0.04222. \; \textit{Ans.}$$

EXAMPLE 6. Calculate $\dfrac{8 \times 62.73 \times 0.052}{56 \times 8.793}$.

Solution. Let $\qquad x = \dfrac{8 \times 62.73 \times 0.052}{56 \times 8.793}$.

Then $\log x = [\log 8 + \log 62.73 + \log 0.052] - [\log 56 + \log 8.793]$.

$$
\begin{aligned}
\log 8 &= 0.9031 \\
\log 62.73 &= 1.7975 \\
\log 0.052 &= 8.7160 - 10 \\
\log \text{numerator} &= 11.4166 - 10 \\
\log \text{denominator} &= 2.6924 \\
\log x &= 8.7242 - 10
\end{aligned}
$$

$$
\begin{aligned}
\log 56 &= 1.7482 \\
\log 8.793 &= 0.9442 \\
\log \text{denominator} &= 2.6924
\end{aligned}
$$

$$\therefore x = 0.05299. \quad Ans.^*$$

57. Cologarithms. The logarithm of the reciprocal of a number is called its *cologarithm* (abbreviated *colog*). Hence if N is any positive number,

$$\operatorname{colog} N = \log \frac{1}{N} = \log 1 - \log N \qquad \text{Th. II, p. 108}$$

$$= 0 - \log N = - \log N.$$

That is, the cologarithm of a number equals *minus* the logarithm of the number, the minus sign affecting the entire logarithm, both characteristic and mantissa. In order to avoid a negative mantissa in the cologarithm, it is customary to subtract the logarithm of the number from $10.0000 - 10$. Thus, taking 25 as the number,

$$\operatorname{colog} 25 = \log \tfrac{1}{25} = \log 1 - \log 25.$$

But $\qquad\qquad\qquad \log 1 = 0,$

that is, $\qquad\qquad\quad \log 1 = 10.0000 - 10.$

Also, $\qquad\qquad\quad\; \log 25 = \underline{1.3979}$

hence $\qquad\qquad\quad\; \operatorname{colog} 25 = 8.6021 - 10$

---

* Instead of looking up the logarithms at once when we write down log 8, log 62.73, etc., it is better to write down an outline or skeleton of the computation before using the tables at all. Thus, for the above example,

$$
\begin{aligned}
\log 8 &= 0. \\
\log 62.73 &= 1. \\
\log 0.052 &= 8. \qquad - 10 \\
\log \text{numerator} &= \\
\log \text{denominator} &= \underline{} \\
\log x &= \\
\therefore x &=
\end{aligned}
$$

$$
\begin{aligned}
\log 56 &= 1. \\
\log 8.793 &= 0.\underline{} \\
\log \text{denominator} &=
\end{aligned}
$$

It saves time to look up all the logarithms at once, and, besides, the student is not so apt to forget to put down the characteristics.

Since dividing by a number is the same as multiplying by the reciprocal of the number, it is evident that when we are calculating by means of logarithms we may either subtract the logarithm of a divisor or add its cologarithm. When a computation is to be made in which several factors occur in the denominator of a fraction, it is more convenient to add the cologarithms of the factors than to subtract their logarithms. Hence the

Rule. *Instead of subtracting the logarithm of a divisor, we may add its cologarithm. The cologarithm of any number is found by subtracting its logarithm from 10.0000 − 10.*

EXAMPLE 1. Find colog 52.63.

Solution.
$$
\begin{array}{r}
10.0000 - 10 \\
\log 52.63 = \underline{1.7212} \\
\text{colog } 52.63 = 8.2788 - 10. \ \textit{Ans.}
\end{array}
$$

EXAMPLE 2. Find colog 0.016548.

Solution.
$$
\begin{array}{r}
10.0000 - 10 \\
\log 0.016548 = \underline{8.2187 - 10} \\
\text{colog } 0.016548 = 1.7813. \ \textit{Ans.}
\end{array}
$$

Thus we see that the mantissa of the cologarithm may be obtained from the logarithm by subtracting the last significant figure of the mantissa from 10 and each of the others from 9.

In order to show how the use of cologarithms exhibits the written work in more compact form, let us calculate the expression in Example 6, on the preceding page, namely,

$$
x = \frac{8 \times 62.73 \times 0.052}{56 \times 8.793}.
$$

Solution. Using cologarithms,

$$
\log x = \log 8 + \log 62.73 + \log 0.052 + \text{colog } 56 + \text{colog } 8.793.
$$

$$
\begin{array}{rl}
\log 8 = & 0.9031 \\
\log 62.73 = & 1.7975 \\
\log 0.052 = & 8.7160 - 10 \\
\text{colog } 56 = & 8.2518 - 10 \quad \text{since} \quad \log 56 = 1.7482 \\
\text{colog } 8.793 = & \underline{9.0558 - 10} \quad \text{since} \quad \log 8.793 = 0.9442 \\
\log x = & 28.7242 - 30 \\
= & \bar{2}.7242.
\end{array}
$$

$$
\therefore x = 0.05299. \ \textit{Ans.}
$$

PROBLEMS

Using logarithms, find the value of each of the following expressions:

1. 9.238×0.9152. *Ans.* 8.454. **2.** 4.832×4938.

3. $336.8 \div 7984$. *Ans.* 0.04218. **4.** $353.6 \div 423.2$.

5. $0.002934 \times 48.4 \times 47.37$. *Ans.* 6.727. **6.** 410.2×0.12594.

7. $\dfrac{1500.8 \times 0.0843}{0.06376 \times 4.248}$. *Ans.* 467.1. **8.** $\dfrac{12.34 \times 186.42}{2.520 \times 23.26}$.

9. $(0.07396)^5$. *Ans.* 0.000002213. **10.** $(1.2134)^4$.

11. $\sqrt{2}$. *Ans.* 1.414. **12.** $\sqrt[3]{69.26}$.

13. $\sqrt[4]{5}$. *Ans.* 1.495. **14.** $\sqrt[6]{0.24}$.

15. $\sqrt[3]{0.02305}$. *Ans.* 0.2846. **16.** $\sqrt[4]{0.007777}$.

17. $\sqrt[3]{\dfrac{0.03296}{7.962}}$. *Ans.* 0.1606. **18.** $\sqrt[3]{\dfrac{529}{134 \times 25.9}}$.

19. $\left(\dfrac{0.08726}{0.1321}\right)^{\frac{5}{3}}$. *Ans.* 0.5010. **20.** $\left(\dfrac{35}{113}\right)^{\frac{3}{8}}$.

21. $\dfrac{1}{3}\sqrt{\dfrac{43.32}{968.5}}$. *Ans.* 0.0705. **22.** $\dfrac{1}{5}\sqrt[3]{\dfrac{1}{32.6}}$.

23. $\dfrac{12 \times 86.1 \times \sqrt{345}}{0.087 \times 411}$. *Ans.* 536.7. **24.** $\left(\dfrac{2\sqrt{31.2}}{17.3}\right)^3$.

25. $\sqrt[8]{2} \times \sqrt[5]{3} \times \sqrt[7]{0.01}$. *Ans.* 0.7035. **26.** $\dfrac{14\sqrt[3]{163}}{(21.2)^2}$.

27. $\dfrac{-401.8\,^*}{52.37}$. *Ans.* -7.672. **28.** $\dfrac{(-41.2)^3}{6.1 \times 0.072}$.

29. $\dfrac{(-2563)(0.03442)}{(714.8)(-0.511)}$. *Ans.* 0.2415. **30.** $\dfrac{1}{2\sqrt[3]{-0.012}}$.

31. The volume of a sphere is given by the formula $V = \frac{4}{3}\pi R^3$. What is the radius of a sphere whose volume is 473.8 cu. ft.? $(\pi = 3.142)$

Ans. 4.837 ft.

32. Given the formula $s = \frac{1}{2}gt^2$, in which $g = 32.16$. Find t when $s = 1200$.

33. If interest is compounded annually, the compound amount, A, of P dollars at $r\%$ for n years is given by the formula $A = P(1 + r)^n$. Find the compound amount of $2345 for 6 yr. at 4%. *Ans.* $2966.

---

* From the definition of a logarithm, Art. 49, it is evident that a *negative number* can have no logarithm. If negative numbers do occur in a computation, they should be treated as if they were positive, and the sign of the result determined by the rules for signs in algebra, irrespective of the logarithmic work.

34. Given the formula $T = \pi\sqrt{\dfrac{l}{g}}$ in which $g = 32.16$. Find T when $l = 4.12$.

35. Given the formula $R = \dfrac{abc}{4\sqrt{s(s-a)(s-b)(s-c)}}$ in which $s = \frac{1}{2}(a+b+c)$. Find R when $a = 231$, $b = 315$, $c = 396$.

Ans. 198.05.

58. Change of base in logarithms. We have seen how the logarithm of a number to the base 10 may be found in our tables. It is sometimes necessary to find the logarithm of a number to a base different from 10. For the sake of generality let us assume that the logarithms of numbers to the base a (greater than zero) have been computed. We wish to find the logarithm of a number, as N, to a new base b (greater than zero); that is, we seek to express $\log_b N$ in terms of logarithms to the base a.

Suppose
$$\log_b N = x,$$
that is,
$$b^x = N.$$

Taking the logarithms of both sides of this equation to the base a, we get
$$\log_a b^x = \log_a N,$$
or,
$$x \log_a b = \log_a N. \qquad \text{Th. III, p. 108}$$

Solving,
$$x = \frac{\log_a N}{\log_a b}.$$

But
$$\log_b N = x.$$

$$\therefore \log_b N = \frac{\log_a N}{\log_a b}.$$

Theorem VI. *The logarithm of a number to the new base b equals the logarithm of the same number to the original base a, divided by the logarithm of b to the base a.*

This formula is also written in the form
$$\log_b N = M \cdot \log_a N,$$
where $M = \dfrac{1}{\log_a b}$ is called the **modulus** *of the new system with respect to the original one.*

If, then, we have given the logarithms of numbers to a certain base a, and we wish to find the logarithms of the same numbers to a new base b, we multiply the given logarithms by the constant multiplier (modulus) $M = \dfrac{1}{\log_a b}$. Thus, having given the common logarithms (base 10) of numbers, we can reduce them to the logarithms of the same numbers to the base $e (= 2.718)$ by multiplying them by $M = \dfrac{1}{\log_{10} e} = 2.3026$.

The number M does not depend on the particular number N, but only on the two bases a and b.

In actual computations $a = 10$, since the tables we use are computed to the base 10.

EXAMPLE. Find $\log_3 21$.

Solution.

Let $$x = \log_3 21.$$

Then $$3^x = 21,$$

and $$x \log 3 = \log 21.$$

$$\therefore x = \frac{\log 21}{\log 3} = \frac{1.3222}{0.4771} = 2.771. \quad Ans.$$

PROBLEMS

Find the following logarithms:

1. $\log_2 7$. $Ans.$ 2.807.   2. $\log_3 4$.

3. $\log_4 9$. $Ans.$ 1.585.   4. $\log_5 7$.

5. $\log_9 8$. $Ans.$ 0.9464.   6. $\log_8 5$.

7. $\log_7 14$. $Ans.$ 1.356.   8. $\log_5 102$.

9. $\log_3 10$. $Ans.$ 2.096.   10. $\log_5 100$.

11. $\log_3 0.1$. $Ans.$ -2.096.   12. $\log_5 0.01$.

13. Find the logarithm of $\frac{7}{11}$ to the base 0.5. $Ans.$ 0.6521.

14. Find the base of the system in which the logarithm of 8 is $\frac{2}{3}$.

15. Prove that $\log_b a \cdot \log_a b = 1$.

16. Prove that $\log_N 10 = \dfrac{1}{\log_{10} N}$.

59. Exponential equations. These are equations in which the unknown quantities occur in the exponents. Such equations may often be solved by the use of logarithms, as illustrated in the following examples:

EXAMPLE 1. Given $81^x = 10$; find the value of x.

Solution. Taking the logarithms of both members,

$$\log 81^x = \log 10,$$

or, $$x \log 81 = \log 10.$$

Solving, $$x = \frac{\log 10}{\log 81} = \frac{1.0000}{1.9085} = 0.524. \quad Ans.$$

EXAMPLE 2. Express the solution of

$$a^{2x+3}b^x = c$$

in terms of logarithms.

Solution. Taking the logarithms of both members,

$$\log a^{2x+3} + \log b^x = \log c. \qquad \text{Th. I, p. 107}$$

$$(2x+3)\log a + x \log b = \log c. \qquad \text{Th. III, p. 108}$$

$$2x \log a + 3 \log a + x \log b = \log c.$$

$$x(2 \log a + \log b) = \log c - 3 \log a.$$

$$x = \frac{\log c - 3 \log a}{2 \log a + \log b}. \quad \textit{Ans.}$$

EXAMPLE 3. Solve the simultaneous equations

(A) $$2^x \cdot 3^y = 100.$$

(B) $$x + y = 4.$$

Solution. Taking the logarithms of both members of (A), and multiplying (B) through by log 2, we get

$$x \log 2 + y \log 3 = 2$$

$$\underline{x \log 2 + y \log 2 = 4 \log 2}$$

Subtracting, $$\qquad y(\log 3 - \log 2) = 2 - 4 \log 2$$

Solving, $$\qquad y = \frac{2 - 4 \log 2}{\log 3 - \log 2} = \frac{2 - 1.2040}{0.4771 - 0.3010}$$

$$y = \frac{0.7960}{0.1761} = 4.52.$$

Substituting in (B), $$\qquad x = -0.52.$$

PROBLEMS

Solve the following equations:

1. $5^x = 12.$ *Ans.* 1.54.   2. $7^x = 25.$

3. $(0.4)^{-x} = 7.$ *Ans.* 2.12.   4. $10^{x-1} = 4.$

5. $4^{x-1} = 5^{x+1}.$ *Ans.* $-13.43.$ 6. $4^x = 40.$

7. $(1.3)^x = 7.2.$ *Ans.* 7.53.   8. $(0.9)^{\frac{1}{x^2}} = (4.7)^{-\frac{1}{3}}.$

9. $7^{x+3} = 5.$ *Ans.* $-2.1729.$ 10. $2^{2x+3} - 6^{x-1} = 0.$

Solve the following simultaneous equations:

11. $4^x \cdot 3^y = 8,$ *Ans.* $x = 0.9005,$ 12. $3^x \cdot 4^y = 15{,}552,$
     $2^x \cdot 8^y = 9.$ $y = 0.7565.$ $4^x \cdot 5^y = 128{,}000.$

13. $2^x \cdot 2^y = 2^{22},$ *Ans.* $x = 13,$ 14. $2^x \cdot 3^y = 18,$
     $x - y = 4.$ $y = 9.$ $5^x \cdot 7^y = 245.$

15. $a^{2x-3} \cdot a^{3y-2} = a^8,$ *Ans.* $x = 5,$
      $3x + 2y = 17.$ $y = 1.$

Express the solution of each of the following equations in terms of logarithms:

16. $A = P(1 + r)^x$.

17. $a^{x^2+2x} = b$. $Ans.\ -1 \pm \sqrt{\dfrac{\log ab}{\log a}}$.

18. $a^x \cdot b^y = m$,
$c^x \cdot d^y = n$.

60. Tables of logarithms of trigonometric functions. When we are using logarithms in calculations involving trigonometric functions it saves much labor to have the logarithms of these functions in tabulated form.* Two complete sets of such logarithms of the trigonometric functions are given. Table II, pp. 8–16, should be used when the given or required angle is expressed in degrees, minutes, and the decimal part of a minute, and Table III, pp. 20–37, when the given or required angle is expressed in degrees and the decimal part of a degree. In both tables the following directions hold true :

Angles between 0° and 45° are in the extreme *left-hand* column on each page,† and the logarithm of the function of any angle will be found in the same horizontal row with the angle and in the vertical column with the name of the function at the top.

Angles between 45° and 90° are in the extreme *right-hand* column on each page,‡ and the logarithm of the function of any angle between 45° and 90° will be found in the same horizontal row with the angle and in the vertical column with the name of the function at the bottom.

In order to avoid the printing of negative characteristics, the number 10 has been added to every logarithm in the first, second, and fourth columns (those with log sin, log tan, and log cos at the top). Hence any logarithm taken from these three columns should have − 10 written after it. Logarithms taken from the third column (with "log cot" at the top) should be used as printed. Thus,

$$\log \sin 38° 30' = 9.7941 - 10 = \bar{1}.7941. \qquad \text{p. 16}$$
$$\log \cot 0° 10' = 2.5363 \qquad = 2.5363. \qquad \text{p. 8}$$
$$\log \tan 75.6° = 0.5905 \qquad = 0.5905. \qquad \text{p. 31}$$
$$\log \cos 2.94° = 9.9994 - 10 = \bar{1}.9994. \qquad \text{p. 25}$$

---

*To distinguish between the two kinds of tables, that on pages 40–43 is called a Table of Natural Functions, while the logarithms of these functions arranged in tabulated form is called a Table of Logarithmic Functions. The tables referred to are *Four-Place Tables* by Granville, Smith, and Mikesh (Ginn and Company).

† The angles increase as we read downwards.

‡ The angles increase as we read upwards.

61. Use of Table II, the given or required angle being expressed in degrees and minutes.* This table gives the logarithms of the sines, cosines, tangents, and cotangents of all angles from 0° to 5° and from 85° to 90° for each minute on pages 8–12, and of all angles from 5° to 85° at intervals of 10 minutes on pages 13–16.

The small columns headed "diff. 1′" immediately to the right of the columns headed "log sin" and "log cos" contain the differences, called tabular differences, in the logarithms of the sines and cosines corresponding to a difference of 1′ in the angle. Similarly, the small column headed "com. diff. 1′" contains the tabular differences for both tangent and cotangent corresponding to a difference of 1′ in the angle. It will be observed that any tabular difference is not in the same horizontal row with a logarithm, but midway between the two particular logarithms whose difference it is. Of course that tabular difference should always be taken which corresponds to the interval in which the angle in question lies. Thus, in finding log sin 78° 16′, the tabular difference corresponding to the interval between 78° 10′ and 78° 20′ is .2.

62. To find the logarithm of a function of an angle when the angle is expressed in degrees and minutes. The following examples illustrate the process of finding the logarithm of a trigonometric function when the angle is expressed in degrees and minutes. In interpolating we assume that the differences in the logarithms are proportional to the differences in the corresponding angles. Unless the angle is very near 0° or 90°, this is in general sufficiently accurate.

EXAMPLE 1. Find log tan 32° 30′.

Solution. On page 15, Table II, we find the angle 32° 30′ exactly; hence we read immediately from the table

$$\log \tan 32° 30' = 9.8042 - 10. \text{ Ans.}$$

EXAMPLE 2. Find log cot 88° 17′.

Solution. Reading upward on page 9 in Table II, we find the angle 88° 17′ exactly; hence

$$\log \cot 88° 17' = 8.4767 - 10. \text{ Ans.}$$

---

* In case the given angle involves seconds, first reduce the seconds to the decimal part of a minute by dividing by 60. Thus,

$$88° 18' 42'' = 88° 18.7', \quad \text{since} \quad 42'' = \tfrac{42}{60} = 0.7';$$
$$2° 0' 16'' = 2° 0.27', \quad \text{since} \quad 16'' = \tfrac{16}{60} = 0.266' \cdots.$$

If the angle is given in degrees and the decimal parts of a degree, and it is desired to use Table II, the angle may be quickly found in degrees and minutes by making use of the Conversion Table on page 17.

EXAMPLE 3. Find log sin 23° 26'.

Solution. The exact angle 23° 26' is not found in Table II; hence we interpolate as follows, using page 14.

$$\begin{array}{l} \log \sin 23°\ 30' = 9.6007 - 10 \\ \log \sin 23°\ 20' = 9.5978 - 10 \\ \hline 10' 29 \end{array}$$

Since an increase of 10' produces an increase of 29 (ten-thousandths) in the mantissa, an increase of 6' will produce an increase of $0.6 \times 29 = 17.4$, that is, 17.

Hence

$$\log \sin 23°\ 26' = 9.5978 - 10 + 0.0017$$
$$= 9.5995 - 10.\ \textit{Ans.}$$

Using the tabulated difference, the process appears as follows:

$$\begin{array}{l} \log \sin 23°\ 20' = 9.5978 - 10 \\ \text{corr. for } 6' = 17 \\ \hline \log \sin 23°\ 26' = 9.5995 - 10.\ \textit{Ans.} \end{array}$$
Tab. diff. = 2.9
Excess = 6
Corr. = 17.4

EXAMPLE 4. Find log cos 54° 42' 18".

Solution. Since 18" is less than half a minute, we drop it, and from page 16, Table II,

$$\begin{array}{l} \log \cos 54°\ 40' = 9.7622 - 10 \\ \text{corr. for } 2' = 4 \\ \hline \log \cos 54°\ 42' = 9.7618 - 10.^*\ \textit{Ans.} \end{array}$$
Tab. diff. = 1.8
Excess = 2
Corr. = 3.6*
that is = 4

EXAMPLE 5. Find log cot 1° 34.42'.

Solution. From page 9, Table II,

$$\begin{array}{l} \log \cot 1°\ 34' = 1.5630 \\ \text{corr. for } .4' = 18 \\ \hline \log \cot 1°\ 34.4' = 1.5612.\ \textit{Ans.} \end{array}$$
Tab. diff. = 46
Excess = .4
Corr. = 18.4

When the angles are given in the table at intervals of 10', it is only necessary to take our angle to the nearest minute, while if the angles are given for every minute, we take our angle to the nearest tenth of a minute. Thus, in Example 4, we find cos 54° 42', dropping the seconds; and in Example 5 we find log cot 1° 34.4', dropping the final 2.

PROBLEMS

Find the following logarithms:

1. log tan 35° 50'. *Ans.* 9.8586 − 10.   2. log sin 67° 20'.

3. log sin 61° 58'. *Ans.* 9.9458 − 10.   4. log tan 72° 13'.

5. log tan 82° 3'. *Ans.* 0.8550.   6. log sin 17° 36'.

7. log cos 44° 33'. *Ans.* 9.8528 − 10.   8. log cot 54° 18'.

* The sine and tangent increase as the angle increases, hence we add the correction; the cosine and cotangent, however, decrease as the angle increases, hence we subtract the correction. Of course this is true only for acute angles.

9. log tan 12° 53′.   *Ans.* 9.3593 − 10.   **10.** log sin 3° 3.3′.

11. log tan 87° 15.6′.   *Ans.* 1.3201.   **12.** log sin 86° 42′ 24″.

13. log cos 27° 28′.   *Ans.* 9.9480 − 10.   **14.** log cot 36° 54′.

15. log cot 51° 49′.   *Ans.* 9.8957 − 10.   **16.** log cos 72° 38′.

17. log sin 85° 56′ 18″.   *Ans.* 9.9989 − 10.   **18.** log tan 4° 4′ 4″.

19. log cot 24° 17′ 24″.   *Ans.* 0.3456.   **20.** log cos 73° 3′ 48″.

21. log sin 123° 54′.   *Ans.* 9.9191 − 10.   **22.** log tan 211° 21′.

23. log tan 243° 42′ 15″.   *Ans.* 0.3061.   **24.** log cos 333° 33′ 11″.

63. To find the angle in degrees and minutes which corresponds to a given logarithmic function. In searching in the table for the given logarithm, attention must be paid to the fact that the functions are found in different columns according as the angle is less or greater than 45°. If, for example, the logarithmic sine is found in the column with "log sin" at the top, the degrees and minutes must be taken from the *left-hand* column, but if it is found in the column with "log sin" at the bottom, the degrees and minutes must be taken from the *right-hand* column; similarly, for the other functions. Thus, if the logarithmic cosine is given, we look for it in two columns on each page, the one having "log cos" at the top and also the one having "log cos" at the bottom.

EXAMPLE 1. Find the angle whose log tan = 9.6946 − 10.

Solution. This problem may also be stated as follows : Having given log tan x = 9.6946 − 10, to find the angle x. Looking up and down the columns having "log tan" at top or bottom, we find 9.6946 exactly on page 15, Table II, in the column with "log tan" at top. The corresponding angle is then found in the same horizontal row to the left and is $x = 26° 20′$. *Ans.*

EXAMPLE 2. Find the angle whose log sin = 9.6652 − 10.

Solution. That is, having given log sin x = 9.6652 − 10, to find the angle x. Looking up and down the columns having "log sin" at top or bottom, we do not find 9.6652 exactly; but the next less logarithm in such a column is found on page 15, Table II, to be 9.6644, which corresponds to the angle 27° 30′, and the corresponding tabular difference for 1′ is 2.4. Hence

$$\begin{array}{ll} \text{log sin } x = 9.6652 - 10 & \text{Tab. diff. 1′} \mid \text{Excess} \mid \text{Corr.} \\ \text{log sin } 27° 30′ = \underline{9.6644 - 10} & \underline{\quad 2.4 \quad} \mid \underline{\quad 8.0 \quad} \mid \underline{\quad 3 \quad} \\ \text{excess} = \qquad 8 & \qquad\qquad \frac{72}{8} \end{array}$$

Since the function involved is the sine, we add this correction, giving

$$x = 27° 30′ + 3′ = 27° 33′. \quad Ans.$$

EXAMPLE 3. Find the angle whose log cos = 9.3705 − 10.

Solution. That is, having given log cos x = 9.3705 − 10, to find the angle x. Looking up and down the columns having "log cos" at top or bottom, we do not find 9.3705 exactly; but the next less logarithm in such a column is found on page 13, Table II, to be 9.3682, which corresponds to the angle 76° 30′, and the corresponding tabular difference for 1′ is 5.2. Hence

$$\begin{array}{ll}
\log \cos x = 9.3705 - 10 \\
\log \cos 76° 30′ = 9.3682 - 10 \\
\text{excess} = \qquad 23
\end{array}$$

Tab. diff. 1′	Excess	Corr.
5.2	23.0	4
	208	
	22	

Since the function involved is the cosine, we subtract this correction, giving

$$x = 76° 30′ - 4′ = 76° 26′. \textit{ Ans.}$$

EXAMPLE 4. Given log tan x = 8.7570 − 10; find x.

Solution. The next less logarithmic tangent is found on page 11, Table II.

$$\begin{array}{ll}
\log \tan x = 8.7570 - 10 \\
\log \tan 3° 16′ = 8.7565 - 10 \\
\text{excess} = \qquad 5
\end{array}$$

Tab. diff. 1′	Excess	Corr.
22	5.0	.2
	44	
	6	

Hence $\qquad x = 3° 16′ + .2′ = 3° 16.2′. \textit{ Ans.}$

EXAMPLE 5. Given cot x = $(1.01)^5$; find x.

Solution. Taking the logarithms of both sides,

$$\log \cot x = 5 \log 1.01.$$

But $\qquad\qquad \log 1.01 = 0.0043$

and, multiplying by 5, $\qquad\qquad \dfrac{5}{}$

$$\log \cot x = 0.0215; \text{ to find } x.$$

The next less logarithmic cotangent is found on p. 16, Table II.

$$\begin{array}{ll}
\log \cot x = 0.0215 \\
\log \cot 43° 40′ = 0.0202 \\
\text{excess} = \qquad 13
\end{array}$$

Tab. diff. 1′	Excess	Corr.
2.6	13.0	5
	13.0	

Hence $\qquad x = 43° 40′ - 5′ = 43° 35′. \textit{ Ans.}$

EXAMPLE 6. Given 184 $\sin^3 x = (12.03)^2 \cos 57° 20′$; find x.

Solution. First we solve for sin x, giving

$$\sin x = \sqrt[3]{\frac{(12.03)^2 \cos 57° 20′}{184}}.$$

Taking the logarithms of both sides,

$$\log \sin x = \tfrac{1}{3}[2 \log 12.03 + \log \cos 57° 20′ + \text{colog } 184].$$

$$\begin{array}{ll}
2 \log 12.03 = \quad 2.1606 & \text{since log 12.03} = 1.0803 \\
\log \cos 57° 20′ = \quad 9.7322 - 10 \\
\text{colog } 184 = \quad \underline{7.7352 - 10} & \text{since log 184} = 2.2648 \\
\qquad\qquad\quad 19.6280 - 20 \\
3\,\overline{)\,29.6280 - 30} \\
\log \sin x = \quad 9.8760 - 10
\end{array}$$

$$\therefore x = 48° 44′. \textit{ Ans.}$$

PROBLEMS

Find the acute angle x from each of the following equations:

1. $\log \sin x = 9.5443 - 10.$ *Ans.* 20° 30′.   2. $\log \cos x = 9.8884 - 10.$

3. $\log \cos x = 9.7531 - 10.$ *Ans.* 55° 30′.   4. $\log \sin x = 9.9702 - 10.$

5. $\log \tan x = 9.9570 - 10.$ *Ans.* 42° 10′.   6. $\log \cot x = 8.8960 - 10.$

7. $\log \cot x = 1.0034.$ *Ans.* 5° 40′.   8. $\log \tan x = 1.4289.$

9. $\log \tan x = 9.5261 - 10.$ *Ans.* 18° 34′.   10. $\log \sin x = 9.5430 - 10.$

11. $\log \cos x = 8.7918 - 10.$ *Ans.* 86° 27′.   12. $\log \cot x = 0.2200.$

13. $\log \sin x = 9.8500 - 10.$ *Ans.* 45° 4′.   14. $\log \tan x = 0.3801.$

15. $\log \cot x = 0.6380.$ *Ans.* 12° 58′.   16. $\log \cos x = 9.9910 - 10.$

17. $\log \tan x = 0.0035.$ *Ans.* 45° 14′.   18. $\log \sin x = 8.9081 - 10.$

19. $\log \sin x = 9.8230 - 10.$ *Ans.* 41° 42′.   20. $\log \tan x = 9.8372 - 10.$

21. $\log \cos x = 9.9000 - 10.$ *Ans.* 37° 25′.   22. $\log \cot x = 9.5670 - 10.$

23. $\log \cot x = \overline{3}.9732.$ *Ans.* 89° 27.7′.   24. $\log \cos x = 8.8741 - 10.$

Using logarithms, find the value of x in each of the following equations:

25. $x = 13.4 \times \sin 47° 32′.$ *Ans.* 9.883.

26. $x = 0.734 \div \cos 13° 45′.$

27. $x = \sin 127° \div 0.0272.$ *Ans.* 29.36.

28. $x = \sqrt{42.63 \tan 73° 12′}.$

29. $x = \sqrt[3]{96.5 \cos 123°}.$ *Ans.* $-3.745.$

30. $\dfrac{65.92}{\sin 31° 15′} = \dfrac{x}{\sin 72° 44′}.$

31. $\dfrac{32.4}{x} = \dfrac{\tan 17° 44′}{\tan 72° 15′}.$ *Ans.* 316.4.

32. $x = \dfrac{4.236 \cos 52° 19′}{13.087 \sin 48° 5′}.$

33. $x = \sqrt{\cos 10° 5′ \tan 73° 11′}.$ *Ans.* 1.805.

34. $1.5 \cot 82° = x^2 \sin 12° 15′.$

35. $x = \dfrac{\sin 24° 13′ \cot 58° 2′}{\cos 33° 17′ \tan 199° 58′}.$ *Ans.* 0.8426.

36. $x = \dfrac{(\sin 213° 18′)^3 \sqrt{\cot 71° 20′}}{10.658 \tan 63° 54′}.$

37. $x = \sqrt{1.632 - \sin 67° 38′}.$ *Ans.* 0.8410.

38. $x = \frac{1}{3} \sqrt[3]{0.2426 + \cos 212° 40′}.$

39. $2 x^2 = 4.33 \sin \dfrac{2 \pi}{5}.$ *Ans.* 1.4350.

40. $x = \sqrt[3]{\dfrac{(0.8123)^2 \tan \dfrac{5\pi}{6}}{62.62}}$.

41. If $A = 38° 18'$ and $x = 0.0421$, find the value of $\sqrt[3]{\dfrac{\sin A \cos 3 A}{2 x \tan^2 2 A}}$.

Ans. -0.5603.

42. If $A = 36° 45'$ and $x = 3.23$, find the value of $\dfrac{1}{3}\sqrt{\dfrac{x^3 \cos 2 A}{\tan A \sin 3 A}}$.

Find the acute angle x which satisfies each of the following equations:

43. $\cos x = (0.009854)^{\frac{1}{3}}$. *Ans.* $77° 37'$.

44. $\sin x = (0.9361)^{10}$.

45. $\dfrac{13.42}{\sin 27° 48'} = \dfrac{26.95}{\sin x}$. *Ans.* $69° 28'$.

46. $\tan x = \dfrac{64.3 \tan 47° 18'}{197.4}$.

Find the values of x from $0°$ to $360°$ which satisfy each of the following equations:

47. $3 \cot x = \sqrt[5]{0.7}$. *Ans.* $72° 45'$, $252° 45'$.

48. $50 \tan x = \sqrt[4]{0.2584}$.

49. $2 \sin^3 x = \sin 111° 20'$. *Ans.* $50° 49'$, $129° 11'$.

50. $\cos x = \dfrac{31.3 \sqrt{\cos \dfrac{\pi}{5}}}{54.6}$.

64. Use of Table III, the given or required angle being expressed in degrees and the decimal part of a degree. This table gives on pages 20–29 the logarithms of the sines, cosines, tangents, and cotangents of all angles from $0°$ to $5°$ and from $85°$ to $90°$ for every hundredth part of a degree, and on pages 30–37 those of all angles from $5°$ to $85°$ for every tenth of a degree.

The tabular differences between the logarithms given in the table are given in the same manner as were the tabular differences in Table II, and the general arrangement is the same.

The following examples illustrate the use of this table:

EXAMPLE 1. Find log sin 27.4°.

Solution. On page 34, Table III, we find the angle 27.4° exactly; hence
$$\log \sin 27.4° = 9.6629 - 10. \ Ans.$$

EXAMPLE 2. Find log cot 3.17°.

Solution. On page 26, Table III, we find the angle 3.17° exactly; hence we get immediately from the table
$$\log \cot 3.17° = 1.2566. \ Ans.$$

EXAMPLE 3. Find log tan 61.87°.

Solution. The exact angle 61.87° is not found in our tables. The next less angle is 61.8°, the extra digit of the given angle being 7, and we have, from page 34, Table III,

$$\log \tan 61.8° = 10.2707 - 10.$$

The tabular difference between log tan 61.8° and log tan 61.9° is 18. In the Prop. Parts column under 18 and opposite the extra digit 7 we find the proportional part 12.6 (= 13). Then

$$\log \tan 61.80° = 0.2707$$
$$\underline{\qquad 13 \quad \text{Prop. Part}}$$
$$\log \tan 61.87° = 0.2720. \; Ans.$$

EXAMPLE 4. Find log cot 2.158°.

Solution. The exact angle 2.158° is not found in our tables. The next less angle is 2.15°, the extra digit of the given angle being 8, and we have, from page 24, Table III,

$$\log \cot 2.15° = 1.4255.$$

The tabular difference between log cot 2.15° and log cot 2.16° is 20. In the Prop. Parts column under 20 and opposite the extra digit 8 we find the proportional part 16. Then

$$\log \cot 2.150° = 1.4255$$
$$\underline{\qquad 16 \quad \text{Prop. Part}}$$
$$\log \cot 2.158° = 1.4239. \; Ans.$$

PROBLEMS

Find the following logarithms:

1. log tan 37.6°. *Ans.* 9.8865 − 10.

2. log sin 3.13°.

3. log sin 63.87°. *Ans.* 9.9532 − 10.

4. log tan 27.73°.

5. log cos 45.68°. *Ans.* 9.8443 − 10.

6. log cot 74.13°.

7. log tan 3.867°. *Ans.* 8.8299 − 10.

8. log sin 2.352°.

9. log cot 34.84°. *Ans.* 0.1574.

10. log cos 64.62°.

11. log sin 155.42°. *Ans.* 9.6191 − 10.

12. log tan 211.35°.

13. log tan 196.85°. *Ans.* 9.4813 − 10.

14. log sin 121.67°.

EXAMPLE 5. Having given log tan x = 9.5364 − 10, to find the angle x.

Solution. Looking up and down the columns having "log tan" at top or bottom, we do not find 9.5364 exactly. We locate it between 9.5345 and 9.5370, on page 32, Table III. Except for the last digit the required angle will be the lesser of the two corresponding angles, that is, 18.9°. Then

$$\log \tan 18.9° = 9.5345 - 10$$
$$\log \tan x = \underline{9.5364 - 10}$$
$$19 = \text{difference}$$

The corresponding tabular difference being 25, we find in the Prop. Parts column that 20 is the proportional part under 25 which is nearest 19. To the left of 20 is the last (extra) digit 8 of the required angle. Hence x = 18.98°. *Ans.*

EXAMPLE 6. Having given log cos $x = 8.6820 - 10$, find x.

Solution. On page 25, Table III, we locate 8.6820 between 8.6810 and 8.6826. Except for the last digit, the required angle must be the lesser of the two corresponding angles, that is, 87.24°. Then

$$\log \cos 87.24° = 8.6826 - 10$$
$$\log \cos x = \underline{8.6820 - 10}$$
$$6 = \text{difference}$$

The corresponding tabular difference being 16, we find in the Prop. Parts column that 6.4 is the proportional part under 16 which is nearest 6. To the left of 6.4 is the last (extra) digit 4 of the required angle. Hence $x = 87.244°$. *Ans.*

EXAMPLE 7. Given $\tan x = (1.018)^{12}$; find x.

Solution. Taking the logarithms of both sides,

$$\log \tan x = 12 \log 1.018.$$
$$\log 1.018 = 0.0077$$
$$\underline{12}$$
$$\log \tan x = 0.0924$$

On page 36 we locate 0.0924 between 0.0916 and 0.0932. **Then**

$$\log \tan 51.0° = 0.0916$$
$$\log \tan x = \underline{0.0924}$$
$$8 = \text{difference}$$

The tabular difference is 16. In the Prop. Parts column under 16 we find 8.0 exactly. To the left of 8.0 we find the last digit 5 of the required angle. Hence $x = 51.05°$. *Ans.*

EXAMPLE 8. Given $56.4 \tan^5 x = (18.65)^5 \cos 69.8°$; find x.

Solution. First we solve for $\tan x$, giving

$$\tan x = \sqrt[5]{\frac{(18.65)^5 \cos 69.8°}{56.4}}.$$

Taking the logarithms of both sides,

$$\log \tan x = \tfrac{1}{5}[5 \log 18.65 + \log \cos 69.8° + \text{colog } 56.4].$$

$5 \log 18.65 =$	6.3535	since $\log 18.65 = 1.2707$
$\log \cos 69.8° =$	$9.5382 - 10$	
colog $56.4 =$	$\underline{8.2487 - 10}$	since $\log 56.4 = 1.7513$
	$24.1404 - 20$	
	$5\overline{)54.1404 - 50}$	
$\log \tan x =$	$10.8281 - 10.$	
	$\therefore x = 81.55°.$ *Ans.*	

PROBLEMS

Using Table III, find the acute angle x in each case:

1. log sin $x = 9.6371 - 10$. *Ans.* 25.7°.　　**2.** log cos $x = 9.9873 - 10$.

3. log tan $x = 8.9186 - 10$. *Ans.* 4.74°.　　**4.** log cot $x = 1.1597$.

5. log cos $x = 9.9629 - 10$. *Ans.* 23.35°.　　**6.** log sin $x = 9.5052 - 10$.

7. log tan $x = 9.8380 - 10$. *Ans.* 34.55°.　　**8.** log sin $x = 9.9671 - 10$.

9. log cot $x = 9.3361 - 10$. *Ans.* 77.77°.　　**10.** log cos $x = 9.8490 - 10$.

11. $\log \sin x = 8.6852 - 10$.   *Ans.* 2.776°.   **12.** $\log \tan x = 1.6261$.

13. $\log \cos x = 9.8000 - 10$.   *Ans.* 50.88°.   **14.** $\log \cot x = 9.3680 - 10$.

15. $\log \tan x = 0.0035$.   *Ans.* 45.23°.   **16.** $\log \sin x = 9.8498 - 10$.

17. $\log \cot x = 2.0000$.   *Ans.* 0.573°.   **18.** $\log \cos x = 8.8941 - 10$.

Using logarithms, find the value of x in each of the following equations:

19. $x = 39.3 \sin^2 42.32°$.   *Ans.* 17.815.

20. $x = \dfrac{0.2136}{0.173 \cos 72.38°}$.

21. $x = \dfrac{26.52 \tan 33.86°}{100.85 \cot 88.963°}$.   *Ans.* 9.745.

22. $\dfrac{x}{\sin 22.45°} = \dfrac{123.45}{\sin 72.44°}$.

23. $\sqrt{3} \sin 48.06° = x^3 \cos 2.143°$.   *Ans.* 1.0885.

24. $x^2 \sin 63.75° = \sqrt{211} \cot 39.63°$.

25. $x = \sqrt[3]{21.72 \cos 122.16°}$.   *Ans.* -2.261.

26. $x = \sqrt{361 \tan 267.5° \sin 9.53°}$.

Find the acute angle x which satisfies each of the following equations:

27. $\cos x = \sqrt{0.9681}$.   *Ans.* 10.25°.

28. $5 \cot x = \sqrt[3]{0.4083}$.

29. $\sin x = \dfrac{\sqrt{83} \cos 52.82°}{(13.382)^2}$.   *Ans.* 1.762°.

30. $\tan x = \sqrt{\dfrac{4.2 \tan 47.22°}{\cos 17.55°}}$.

When we consider the complex nature of the expressions submitted for our computation in the last two groups of problems, and in the problems on pages 122–123, we recognize the great advantage of the use of logarithms in numerical work. Multiplication and division are replaced by the simpler tasks of addition and subtraction. Raising to powers and the extraction of roots are replaced by the use of either a multiplier or a divisor consisting rarely of more than a single digit.

We shall now apply logarithms to the solution of triangles.

65. Use of logarithms in the solution of right triangles. The principles involved in the analysis of problems dealing with the right triangle, and the solution of such problems by means of natural functions, have already been considered (see Art. 37).

The following examples will illustrate the best plan to follow in solving right triangles by the aid of logarithms:

EXAMPLE 1. Solve the right triangle if $A = 48° 17'$, $c = 324$. Also find the area.

Solution. Draw a figure of the triangle indicating the known and unknown parts.
$$B = 90° - A = 41° 43'.$$

To find a, use $\qquad a = c \sin A$.

Taking the logarithms of both sides,
$$\log a = \log c + \log \sin A.$$

Hence, from Tables I and II,*

$$
\begin{aligned}
\log c &= 2.5105 \\
\log \sin A &= \underline{9.8730 - 10} \\
\log a &= 12.3835 - 10 \\
&= 2.3835. \\
\therefore a &= 241.8.
\end{aligned}
$$

To find b, use $\qquad b = c \cos A$.

Taking the logarithms of both sides,
$$\log b = \log c + \log \cos A.$$

Hence, from Tables I and II,

$$
\begin{aligned}
\log c &= 2.5105 \\
\log \cos A &= \underline{9.8231 - 10} \\
\log b &= 12.3336 - 10 \\
&= 2.3336. \\
\therefore b &= 215.6.
\end{aligned}
$$

Check. To check these results numerically, let us see if a, b, c satisfy the equation
$$a^2 = c^2 - b^2 = (c + b)(c - b),$$
or, using logarithms,
$$2 \log a = \log (c + b) + \log (c - b),$$
that is,
$$\log a = \tfrac{1}{2}[\log (c + b) + \log (c - b)].$$
Here $c + b = 539.6$ and $c - b = 108.4$.

$$
\begin{aligned}
\log (c + b) &= 2.7321 \\
\log (c - b) &= \underline{2.0350} \\
2 \log a &= 4.7671 \\
\log a &= 2.3835.
\end{aligned}
$$

Since this value of $\log a$ is the same as that obtained above, the answers are probably correct.

To find the area, use formula
$$\text{area} = \frac{ab}{2}.$$

$$
\begin{aligned}
\log \text{area} &= \log a + \log b - \log 2. \\
\log a &= 2.3835 \\
\log b &= \underline{2.3336} \\
& 4.7171 \\
\log 2 &= \underline{0.3010} \\
\log \text{area} &= 4.4161 \\
\therefore \text{area} &= 26{,}070.
\end{aligned}
$$

* If we wish to use Table III instead of Table II, we reduce 17' to the decimal part of a degree. Thus, $A = 48° 17' = 48.28°$.

EXAMPLE 2. Solve the right triangle, having given $b = 15.12$, $c = 30.81$.

Solution. Here we first find an acute angle; to find A, use

$$\cos A = \frac{b}{c}.$$

$$\log \cos A = \log b - \log c.$$

$$\log b = 11.1796 - 10$$
$$\log c = \underline{\quad 1.4887 \quad}$$
$$\log \cos A = \quad 9.6909 - 10$$
$$\therefore A = 60° \ 36'.$$

Hence $B = 90° - A = 29° \ 24'.$

To find a, we may use

$$a = b \tan A.$$

$$\log a = \log b + \log \tan A.$$

$$\log b = 1.1796$$
$$\log \tan A = \underline{0.2491}$$
$$\log a = 1.4287$$
$$\therefore a = 26.84.$$

Check. $a^2 = (c + b)(c - b).$

$$\log a = \tfrac{1}{2} [\log (c + b) + \log (c - b)].$$

$$c + b = 45.93 \quad \text{and} \quad c - b = 15.69.$$

$$\log (c + b) = 1.6621$$
$$\log (c - b) = \underline{1.1956}$$
$$2 \log a = 2.8577$$

$$\log a = 1.4288.$$

This, we see, agrees substantially with the above result.

EXAMPLE 3. Solve the right triangle, having given $B = 2.325°$, $a = 1875.3$.

Solution. $A = 90° - B = 87.675°.$

$$\sin A = \frac{a}{c}.$$

Solving for the unknown side c,

$$c = \frac{a}{\sin A}.$$

$$\log c = \log a - \log \sin A.$$

Hence, from Tables I and III,*

$$\log a = 13.2731 - 10$$
$$\log \sin A = \underline{\ 9.9996 - 10}$$
$$\log c = \quad 3.2735$$
$$\therefore c = 1877.$$

$$\tan A = \frac{a}{b}.$$

* If we wish to use Table II instead of Table III, we reduce $2.325°$ to degrees and minutes. Thus, $B = 2.325° = 2° \ 19.5'$.

Solving for the unknown side b,

$$b = \frac{a}{\tan A}.$$

$$\log b = \log a - \log \tan A.$$

$$\log a = 13.2731 - 10$$
$$\log \tan A = \underline{11.3915 - 10}$$
$$\log b = 1.8816$$

$$\therefore b = 76.13.$$

To check the work, we may use formulas

$$a^2 = (c + b)(c - b)$$

or, $b = c \sin B,$

since neither one was used in the above calculations.

PROBLEMS

Solve the following right triangles using Tables I and II.* In each case $C = 90°$. Check the solutions.

1. $A = 43° 30'$, $c = 11.2$.   *Ans.* $B = 46° 30'$, $a = 7.709$, $b = 8.124$.

2. $A = 67° 10'$, $c = 402$.

3. $B = 62° 56'$, $b = 47.7$.   *Ans.* $A = 27° 4'$, $a = 24.37$, $c = 53.56$.

4. $B = 17° 44'$, $b = 0.727$.

5. $a = 0.624$, $c = 0.910$.   *Ans.* $A = 43° 18'$, $B = 46° 42'$, $b = 0.6623$.

6. $a = 142.7$, $c = 743.2$.

7. $A = 72° 7'$, $a = 83.4$.   *Ans.* $B = 17° 53'$, $b = 26.91$, $c = 87.64$.

8. $A = 21° 44'$, $a = 0.7683$.

9. $A = 52° 41'$, $b = 4247$.   *Ans.* $B = 37° 19'$, $a = 5571$, $c = 7007$.

10. $A = 44° 44'$, $b = 0.7272$.

11. $b = 2.887$, $c = 5.110$.   *Ans.* $B = 34° 24'$, $A = 55° 36'$, $a = 4.216$.

12. $b = 59.31$, $c = 73.12$.

13. $a = 101$, $b = 116$.   *Ans.* $A = 41° 2'$, $B = 48° 58'$, $c = 153.8$.

* For the sake of clearness and simplicity, one set of triangle examples is given which are adapted to practice in using Table II, the given and required angles being expressed in degrees and minutes; and another set is given for practice in the use of Table III, the given and required angles being expressed in degrees and the decimal part of a degree. There is no reason why the student should not work out the examples in the first set using Table III, and those in the second set using Table II, if he so desires, except that it may involve a trifle more labor. This extra work of reducing minutes to the decimal part of a degree, or the reverse, may be reduced to a minimum by making use of the Conversion Tables on page 17. It is possible, however, that an answer thus obtained may differ from the one given here by one unit in the last decimal place. This practice of giving one set of triangle examples for each of the Tables II and III will be followed throughout this book when solving triangles.

14. $a = 0.4623$, $b = 0.3015$.

15. $B = 10° 51'$, $c = 0.7264$. *Ans.* $A = 79° 9'$, $a = 0.7133$, $b = 0.1367$.

16. $B = 67° 45'$, $c = 525.4$.

17. $B = 21° 34'$, $a = 0.8211$. *Ans.* $A = 68° 26'$, $b = 0.3245$, $c = 0.8829$.

18. $B = 69° 12'$, $a = 742.3$.

19. $a = 10.107$, $b = 17.303$.   *Ans.* $A = 30° 18'$, $B = 59° 42'$, $c = 20.04$.

20. $a = 7627$, $b = 2823$.

21. Find the areas of the triangles in Problems 1, 2, and 3.

Ans. (1) 31.32; (2) 686,900; (3) 581.3.

22. Find the areas of the triangles in Problems 4 and 5.

Solve the following right triangles using Tables I and III. Check the solutions.

23. $a = 273$, $b = 418$.   *Ans.* $A = 33.15°$, $B = 56.85°$, $c = 499.3$.

24. $a = 0.505$, $b = 0.303$.

25. $A = 58.65°$, $c = 35.73$.   *Ans.* $B = 31.35°$, $a = 30.51$, $b = 18.59$.

26. $B = 26.33°$, $c = 7.623$.

27. $B = 23.15°$, $b = 75.48$.   *Ans.* $A = 66.85°$, $a = 176.5$, $c = 191.9$.

28. $B = 46.32°$, $b = 0.6241$.

29. $A = 31.75°$, $a = 48.04$.   *Ans.* $B = 58.25°$, $b = 77.64$, $c = 91.28$.

30. $A = 51.23°$, $c = 900.6$.

31. $b = 512$, $c = 900$.   *Ans.* $A = 55.32°$, $B = 34.68°$, $a = 740.2$.

32. $b = 0.6723$, $c = 0.9251$.

33. $a = 52$, $c = 60$.   *Ans.* $A = 60.06°$, $B = 29.94°$, $b = 29.94$.

34. $a = 0.4261$, $c = 1.0432$.

35. $A = 88.426°$, $b = 9$.   *Ans.* $B = 1.574°$, $a = 327.5$, $c = 327.6$.

36. $A = 2.327°$, $b = 1000$.

37. $B = 85.475°$, $c = 80$.   *Ans.* $A = 4.525°$, $a = 6.313$, $b = 79.74$.

38. $B = 4.444°$, $a = 72.63$.

In the following problems use Tables I and II:

39. Solve the following isosceles triangles, in which A, B, C are the angles and a, b, c the sides opposite respectively, a and b being the equal sides.

  a. $A = 68° 57'$, $b = 35.09$.   *Ans.* $C = 42° 6'$, $c = 25.21$.

  b. $B = 27° 8'$, $c = 3.088$.

  c. $C = 80° 47'$, $b = 2103$.   *Ans.* $A = 49° 37'$, $c = 2725$.

  d. $a = 79.24$, $c = 106.62$.

  e. $C = 151° 28'$, $c = 95.47$.   *Ans.* $A = 14° 16'$, $a = 49.25$.

40. Find the areas of the triangles in (*a*), (*c*), and (*d*) of Problem 39.

41. One side of a regular octagon is 24 ft. Find its area and the radii of the inscribed and circumscribed circles.

Ans. Area = 2782 sq. ft., r = 28.97 ft., R = 31.36 ft.

42. The perimeter of a regular polygon of 11 sides is 23.47 ft. Find the radius of the circumscribed circle.

43. The radius of a circle is 12,732 ft., and the length of a chord is 18,321 ft. Find the angle the chord subtends at the center. *Ans.* 92° 2′.

44. If the radius of a circle is 10 in., what is the length of a chord which subtends an angle of 77° 18′ at the center?

45. A rock on the bank of a river is 132 ft. above the level of the water. From a point just opposite the rock on the other bank of the river the angle of elevation of the top of the rock is 14° 36′. Find the width of the river. *Ans.* 506.8 ft.

46. The shadow of a vertical cliff 113 ft. high just reaches a boat 93 ft. from its base. Find the altitude of the sun.

47. An observer on the top of the Empire State Building, which is 1248 ft. high, finds the angle of depression of the top of a building 752 ft. high to be 22° 16′. If the two buildings are on the same horizontal level, find the distance between them. *Ans.* 1211.5 ft.

48. Two buoys are directly south from a lighthouse 178 ft. high. Their angles of depression from the top of the lighthouse are 18° 22′ and 11° 36′. How far apart are the buoys?

49. A car travels at a rate of 30 mi. an hour up a grade which makes an angle of 10° with the horizontal. How long does it take the car to rise 200 ft.? *Ans.* 26.17 sec.

50. The lifting arm of a derrick is 45 ft. long. How high does it lift a steel girder when it turns from 22° 12′ to 38° 46′ with the horizontal?

51. From the top of a lighthouse 205 ft. above the level of the sea at low tide, the angle of depression of a buoy is observed to be 29° 14′ at low tide and 28° 12′ at high tide. How high is the tide? *Ans.* 8.57 ft.

52. In the figure, AC is perpendicular to DC. The values of α and β and the length of h are obtained by measurement. Show that the lengths of $AC = x$, and of $BC = y$, in terms of α, β, and h are given by the formulas

$$x = \frac{h}{\tan \beta - \tan \alpha}, \quad y = \frac{h \tan \alpha}{\tan \beta - \tan \alpha}.$$

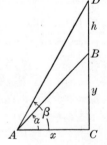

53. A monument 162 ft. high stands on top of a cliff. From a point on the horizontal level of the base of the cliff the angles of elevation of the top and of the bottom of the monument are observed to be 38° 14′ and 31° 52′ respectively. Find the height of the cliff. Use one of the formulas derived in Problem 52. *Ans.* 605.6 ft.

54. An observer on a bridge finds that at a certain point the angle of depression of a rock directly below the bridge is 48° 36′. After walking 40 ft. the rock is still ahead of him and the angle of depression is 53° 14′. How high is the bridge above the rock?

55. A flyer whose speed in still air is 90 mi. an hour flies along a straight course from New York to Washington, a distance of 190 mi. Throughout the trip he contends with a wind having a velocity of 40 mi. an hour at a right angle to his course. Find (*a*) at what angle with his line of flight he directs his plane; (*b*) the time required for the trip.

Ans. (*a*) 26° 23′;
(*b*) 2 hr. 21½ min.

66. Use of logarithms in the solution of oblique triangles. As has already been pointed out, formulas involving principally products, quotients, powers, and roots are well adapted to logarithmic computation; while in the case of formulas involving in the main sums and differences, the labor-saving advantages of logarithmic computation are not so marked. Thus, in solving oblique triangles, the law of sines,

$$\frac{a}{\sin A} = \frac{b}{\sin B} = \frac{c}{\sin C},$$

and the law of tangents,

$$\tan \tfrac{1}{2}(A - B) = \frac{a - b}{a + b} \tan \tfrac{1}{2}(A + B),$$

are well adapted to the use of logarithms, while this is not the case with the law of cosines, namely,

$$a^2 = b^2 + c^2 - 2\,bc\,\cos A.$$

In solving oblique triangles by logarithmic computation, it is convenient to classify the problems as follows:

CASE I. *When two angles and a side are given.*

CASE II. *When two sides and the angle opposite one of them are given (ambiguous case).*

CASE III. *When two sides and the included angle are given.*

CASE IV. *When all three sides are given.*

CASE I. *When two angles and a side are given.*

First step. *To find the third angle, subtract the sum of the two given angles from 180°.*

Second step. *To find an unknown side, choose a pair of ratios from the law of sines,*

$$\frac{a}{\sin A} = \frac{b}{\sin B} = \frac{c}{\sin C},$$

which involve only one unknown part, and solve for that part.

Check. *See if the sides found satisfy the law of tangents.*

EXAMPLE. Given $b = 20$, $A = 104°$, $B = 19°$; solve the triangle.

Solution. Drawing a figure of the triangle on which we indicate the known and unknown parts, we see that the problem comes under Case I.

First step. $C = 180° - (A + B) = 180° - 123° = 57°.$

Second step. Solving $\dfrac{a}{\sin A} = \dfrac{b}{\sin B}$ for a, we get

$$a = \frac{b \sin A}{\sin B},$$

or, $\log a = \log b + \log \sin A - \log \sin B.$

$$\begin{array}{rl}
\log b = & 1.3010 \\
\log \sin A = & 9.9869 - 10* \\
\hline
& 11.2879 - 10 \\
\log \sin B = & 9.5126 - 10 \\
\hline
\log a = & 1.7753
\end{array}$$

$$\therefore a = 59.61.$$

Solving $\dfrac{b}{\sin B} = \dfrac{c}{\sin C}$ for c, we get

$$c = \frac{b \sin C}{\sin B},$$

or, $\log c = \log b + \log \sin C - \log \sin B.$

$$\begin{array}{rl}
\log b = & 1.3010 \\
\log \sin C = & 9.9236 - 10 \\
\hline
& 11.2246 - 10 \\
\log \sin B = & 9.5126 - 10 \\
\hline
\log c = & 1.7120
\end{array}$$

$$\therefore c = 51.52.$$

Check.

$$a + c = 111.13, \qquad a - c = 8.09;$$
$$A + C = 161°, \qquad A - C = 47°;$$
$$\tfrac{1}{2}(A + C) = 80° \; 30', \quad \tfrac{1}{2}(A - C) = 23° \; 30'.$$

* Sin $A = \sin 104° = \sin (180° - 104°) = \sin 76°$. Hence $\log \sin 104° = \log \sin 76° = 9.9869 - 10$.

Here $\qquad \tan \frac{1}{2}(A - C) = \dfrac{a - c}{a + c} \tan \frac{1}{2}(A + C),$

or, $\qquad \log \tan \frac{1}{2}(A - C) = \log (a - c) + \log \tan \frac{1}{2}(A + C) - \log (a + c).$

$$\begin{aligned}
\log (a - c) &= 0.9079 \\
\log \tan \tfrac{1}{2}(A + C) &= \underline{10.7764 - 10} \\
&\ 11.6843 - 10 \\
\log (a + c) &= \underline{2.0458} \\
\log \tan \tfrac{1}{2}(A - C) &= 9.6385 - 10 \\
\therefore\ \tfrac{1}{2}(A - C) &= 23°\ 31',
\end{aligned}$$

which agrees substantially with the above results.

PROBLEMS

Using Tables I and II, solve the oblique triangles which have the following given parts. Check the solutions.

1. $a = 795,\ A = 79°\ 59',\ B = 44°\ 41'.$
   > *Ans.* $C = 55°\ 20',\ b = 567.6,\ c = 664.0.$

2. $a = 400,\ A = 54°\ 28',\ C = 60°.$

3. $b = 0.8037,\ B = 52°\ 20',\ C = 101°\ 40'.$
   > *Ans.* $A = 26°,\ a = 0.4450,\ c = 0.9942.$

4. $c = 161,\ A = 35°\ 15',\ C = 123°\ 39'.$

5. $b = 29.01,\ A = 87°\ 40',\ C = 33°\ 15'.$
   > *Ans.* $B = 59°\ 5',\ a = 33.78,\ c = 18.54.$

6. $a = 5.421,\ B = 42°\ 17',\ C = 82°\ 28'.$

7. $c = 2071,\ A = 31°\ 9',\ B = 115°\ 24'.$
   > *Ans.* $C = 33°\ 27',\ a = 1943,\ b = 3394.$

8. $b = 47.21,\ A = 22°\ 16',\ B = 81°\ 42'.$

9. $c = 370.2,\ B = 23°\ 48',\ C = 47°\ 19'.$
   > *Ans.* $A = 108°\ 53',\ a = 476.4,\ b = 203.3.$

10. $b = 0.2828,\ B = 108°\ 25',\ C = 58°\ 27'.$

Using Tables I and III, solve the oblique triangles (Problems 11 to 20) which have the following given parts. Check the solutions.

11. $a = 500,\ A = 10.2°,\ B = 46.6°.$
    > *Ans.* $C = 123.2°,\ b = 2051,\ c = 2363.$

12. $a = 45,\ A = 36.8°,\ C = 62°.$

13. $b = 5685,\ B = 48.63°,\ C = 83.26°.$
    > *Ans.* $A = 48.11°,\ a = 5640,\ c = 7523.$

14. $b = 0.6244,\ B = 34.22°,\ C = 80.61°.$

15. $a = 76.08,\ B = 126°,\ C = 12.44°.$
    > *Ans.* $A = 41.56°,\ b = 92.80,\ c = 24.70.$

16. $b = 129.38,\ A = 19.42°,\ C = 64°.$

17. $b = 8000$, $A = 24.5°$, $B = 86.495°$.

$\qquad\qquad\qquad$ *Ans.* $C = 69.005°$, $a = 3324$, $c = 7483$.

18. $c = 9500$, $A = 2.086°$, $B = 112°$.

19. $b = 2.876$, $B = 107.52°$, $C = 62.3°$.

$\qquad\qquad\qquad$ *Ans.* $A = 10.18°$, $a = 0.5331$, $c = 2.671$.

20. $c = 10.345$, $A = 20.85°$, $B = 111.11°$.

21. A ship at the point S can be seen from each of two points, A and B, on the shore. By measurement $AB = 800$ ft., angle $SAB = 67° \ 43'$, and angle $SBA = 74° \ 21'$. Find the distance of the ship from the point A.

$\qquad\qquad\qquad\qquad\qquad$ *Ans.* 1253 ft.

22. Two observers 5 mi. apart on a plain, and facing each other, find that the angles of elevation of a balloon in the same vertical plane with them are 55° and 58° respectively. Find the distance of the balloon from each of the observers.

23. A lighthouse observed from a ship was found to be in the direction 34° east of north. After the ship sailed due south a distance of 3 mi., the direction of the lighthouse was 23° east of north. Find the distance of the ship from the lighthouse at each point of observation.

$\qquad\qquad\qquad\qquad$ *Ans.* 6.143 mi., 8.792 mi.

24. To determine the distance of an inaccessible point A from a point B, a line BC and the angles ABC and BCA were measured and found to be 322.6 yd., 60° 34′, and 56° 10′ respectively. Find the distance AB.

CASE II. *When two sides and the angle opposite one of them are given, as a, b, A (ambiguous case*).*

First step. *Using the law of sines as in Case I, calculate log sin B.*

If log sin B = 0, sin B = 1, B = 90°; it is a right triangle.

If log sin B > 0, sin B > 1 (impossible); there is no solution.

If log sin B < 0 and b < a, only the acute value of B found from the table can be used; there is one solution.†

If log sin B < 0 and b > a, the acute value of B found from the table, and also its supplement, should be used; there are two solutions.‡

Second step. *Find C (one or two values according as we have one or two values of B) from*

$$C = 180° - (A + B).$$

Third step. *Find c (one or two values), using the law of sines.*

Check. *Use the law of tangents.*

---

* In this connection the student should read over Art. 43.

† For if $b < a$, B must be less than A, and hence B must be acute.

‡ Since $b > a$, A must be acute, and hence B may be either acute or obtuse.

EXAMPLE 1. Given $a = 36$, $b = 80$, $A = 28°$; solve the triangle.

Solution. In attempting to draw a figure of the triangle, the construction appears impossible. To verify this, let us find log sin B in order to apply our tests.

Solving $\dfrac{a}{\sin A} = \dfrac{b}{\sin B}$ for sin B,

$$\sin B = \frac{b \sin A}{a},$$

or, $\log \sin B = \log b + \log \sin A - \log a.$

$$
\begin{array}{rl}
\log b = & 1.9031 \\
\log \sin A = & 9.6716 - 10 \\
\hline
 & 11.5747 - 10 \\
\log a = & 1.5563 \\
\hline
\log \sin B = & 10.0184 - 10 \\
 = & 0.0184.
\end{array}
$$

Since log sin $B > 0$, sin $B > 1$ (which is impossible), and there is no solution.

EXAMPLE 2. Given $a = 7.42$, $b = 3.39$, $A = 105°$; solve the triangle.

Solution. Draw the figure.
First step. From the law of sines,

$$\sin B = \frac{b \sin A}{a},$$

or, $\log \sin B = \log b + \log \sin A - \log a.$

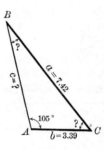

$$
\begin{array}{rl}
\log b = & 0.5302 \\
\log \sin A = & 9.9849 - 10* \\
\hline
 & 10.5151 - 10 \\
\log a = & 0.8704 \\
\hline
\log \sin B = & 9.6447 - 10
\end{array}
$$

$$\therefore B = 26° 11'.$$

Using Table II

Since log sin $B < 0$ and $b < a$, there is only one solution.

Second step. $C = 180° - (A + B) = 180° - 131° 11' = 48° 49'.$

Third step. By the law of sines,

$$c = \frac{a \sin C}{\sin A},$$

or, $\log c = \log a + \log \sin C - \log \sin A.$

$$
\begin{array}{rl}
\log a = & 0.8704 \\
\log \sin C = & 9.8766 - 10 \\
\hline
 & 10.7470 - 10 \\
\log \sin A = & 9.9849 - 10 \\
\hline
\log c = & 0.7621
\end{array}
$$

$$\therefore c = 5.783.$$

* Sin $A = \sin 105° = \sin (180° - 105°) = \sin 75°$. Hence log sin $A = \log \sin 75°$ $= 9.9849 - 10$.

Check. Use the law of tangents.

$$\tan \tfrac{1}{2}(C - B) = \frac{c - b}{c + b} \tan \tfrac{1}{2}(C + B),$$

or, $\log \tan \tfrac{1}{2}(C - B) = \log (c - b) + \log \tan \tfrac{1}{2} (C + B) - \log (c + b).$

Substituting, we find that this equation is satisfied.

EXAMPLE 3. Given $a = 732$, $b = 1015$, $A = 40°$; solve the triangle.

Solution. It appears from the construction of the triangle that there are two solutions.

By the law of sines,

$$\sin B = \frac{b \sin A}{a},$$

or, $\log \sin B = \log b + \log \sin A - \log a.$

$$
\begin{aligned}
\log b &= \ 3.0065 \\
\log \sin A &= \ \underline{9.8081 - 10} \\
&= \ 12.8146 - 10 \\
\log a &= \ \underline{2.8645} \\
\log \sin B &= \ 9.9501 - 10
\end{aligned}
$$

Since $\log \sin B < 0$ and $b > a$, we have two solutions, which test verifies our construction. From Table II we find the first value of B to be

$$B_1 = 63° \ 3'.$$

Hence the second value of B is

$$B_2 = 180° - B_1 = 116° \ 57'.$$
$$C_1 = 180° - (A + B_1) = 180° - 103° \ 3' = 76° \ 57'.$$
$$C_2 = 180° - (A + B_2) = 180° - 156° \ 57' = 23° \ 3'.$$

From the law of sines,

$$c_1 = \frac{a \sin C_1}{\sin A},$$

or, $\log c_1 = \log a + \log \sin C_1 - \log \sin A.$

$$
\begin{aligned}
\log a &= \ 2.8645 \\
\log \sin C_1 &= \ \underline{9.9886 - 10} \\
&= \ 12.8531 - 10 \\
\log \sin A &= \ \underline{9.8081 - 10} \\
\log c_1 &= \ 3.0450
\end{aligned}
$$

$$\therefore c_1 = 1109.3.$$

In the same manner, from $c_2 = \dfrac{a \sin C_2}{\sin A}$

we get $c_2 = 445.9.$

Check. Use $\tan \tfrac{1}{2}(C - B) = \dfrac{c - b}{c + b} \tan \tfrac{1}{2}(C + B)$ for both solutions.

PROBLEMS

In the following problems use Tables I and II. Determine the number of possible solutions for each set of data and solve completely all possible triangles.

1. $a = 50$, $c = 66$, $A = 123°\ 11'$.   *Ans.* Impossible.

2. $b = 3069$, $c = 1223$, $C = 55°\ 52'$.

3. $a = 32.16$, $c = 27.08$, $C = 52°\ 24'$.
$$\text{\textit{Ans.}}\ A_1 = 70°\ 12',\ B_1 = 57°\ 24',\ b_1 = 28.79.$$
$$A_2 = 109°\ 48',\ B_2 = 17°\ 48',\ b_2 = 10.45.$$

4. $a = 62.24$, $b = 74.83$, $A = 27°\ 18'$.

5. $b = 0.2337$, $c = 0.1982$, $B = 109°$.
$$\text{\textit{Ans.}}\ A = 17°\ 41',\ C = 53°\ 19',\ a = 0.07508.$$

6. $a = 975.2$, $b = 603.6$, $A = 108°\ 54'$.

7. $b = 5.161$, $c = 6.840$, $B = 44°\ 3'$.
$$\text{\textit{Ans.}}\ A_1 = 68°\ 47',\ C_1 = 67°\ 10',\ a_1 = 6.920.$$
$$A_2 = 23°\ 7',\ C_2 = 112°\ 50',\ a_2 = 2.913.$$

8. $a = 6.061$, $b = 7.083$, $A = 47°\ 25'$.

9. $a = 8.656$, $c = 10$, $A = 59°\ 57'$.   *Ans.* $B = 30°\ 3'$, $C = 90°$, $b = 5.009$.

10. $a = 107$, $c = 171$, $C = 31°\ 53'$.

In the following problems (11 to 20) use Tables I and III. Determine the number of possible solutions for each set of data and solve completely all possible triangles.

11. $a = 55.55$, $c = 66.66$, $C = 77.7°$.
$$\text{\textit{Ans.}}\ A = 54.5°,\ B = 47.8°,\ b = 50.54.$$

12. $a = 973.5$, $b = 612.8$, $A = 108.43°$.

13. $a = 72.63$, $b = 117.48$, $A = 80°$.   *Ans.* Impossible.

14. $b = 0.0482$, $c = 0.0621$, $B = 57.62°$.

15. $a = 177$, $b = 216$, $A = 35.6°$.
$$\text{\textit{Ans.}}\ B_1 = 45.27°,\ C_1 = 99.13°,\ c_1 = 300.3.$$
$$B_2 = 134.73°,\ C_2 = 9.67°,\ c_2 = 51.09.$$

16. $b = 70.71$, $c = 78.14$, $B = 60.32°$.

17. $b = 91.06$, $c = 77.04$, $B = 51.12°$.
$$\text{\textit{Ans.}}\ A = 87.69°,\ C = 41.19°,\ a = 116.88.$$

18. $a = 0.1234$, $b = 0.1412$, $B = 38.13°$.

19. $a = 17{,}060$, $b = 14{,}050$, $B = 40°$.
$$\text{\textit{Ans.}}\ A_1 = 51.32°,\ C_1 = 88.68°,\ c_1 = 21{,}850.$$
$$A_2 = 128.68°,\ C_2 = 11.32°,\ c_2 = 4290.$$

20. $b = 35.36$, $c = 39.18$, $B = 59.42°$.

21. One side of a parallelogram is 35 ft. long and a diagonal is 63 ft. long. Find the length of the other diagonal if the angle between the diagonals is 21° 37′. *Ans.* 124.62 ft.

22. Two buoys are 2789 ft. apart, and a boat is 4325 ft. from one of them. The angle between the lines from the buoys to the boat is 16° 13′. How far is the boat from the other buoy? How many solutions does this problem have? If we knew that the nearer buoy was 4325 ft. from the boat, how many solutions of the problem would there be?

23. The point P is 60.5 in. from the center O of a circle whose radius is 24.2 in. A secant is drawn making an angle of 18° 42′ with the line OP. How far is the nearer point of intersection of the secant with the circle from P? *Ans.* 42.85 in.

24. The distance from B to C is 145 ft. and from A to C it is 178 ft. The angle ABC is 41° 10′. Find the distance from A to B.

CASE III. *When two sides and the included angle are given, as a, b, C.* *

First step. *Calculate* $a + b$, $a - b$; *also* $\frac{1}{2}(A + B)$ *from* $A + B = 180° - C$.

Second step. *From the law of tangents,*

$$\tan \tfrac{1}{2}(A - B) = \frac{a - b}{a + b} \tan \tfrac{1}{2}(A + B),$$

we find $\frac{1}{2}(A - B)$. *Adding this result to* $\frac{1}{2}(A + B)$ *gives A, and subtracting it gives B.*

Third step. *To find side c use the law of sines; for instance,*

$$c = \frac{a \sin C}{\sin A}.$$

Check. *Use the law of sines,*† *that is, see if*

$$\log a - \log \sin A = \log B - \log \sin B = \log c - \log \sin C.$$

---

* In case any other two sides and included angle are given, simply change the cyclic order of the letters throughout. Thus, if b, c, A are given, use

$$\tan \tfrac{1}{2}(B - C) = \frac{b - c}{b + c} \tan \tfrac{1}{2}(B + C), \text{ etc.}$$

† From the law of sines, $\dfrac{a}{\sin A} = \dfrac{b}{\sin B} = \dfrac{c}{\sin C}$.

EXAMPLE 1. Given $a = 540$, $b = 420$, $C = 52°\ 6'$; solve the triangle, using Tables I and II.

Solution. Drawing a figure of the triangle on which we indicate the known and unknown parts, we see that the problem comes under Case III, since two sides and the included angle are given.

First step.

$a = 540$	540	$180°$
$b = \underline{420}$	$\underline{420}$	$C = \underline{52°\ 6'}$
$a + b = 960$	$a - b = 120$	$A + B = 127°\ 54'$
		$\therefore \frac{1}{2}(A + B) = 63°\ 57'.$

Second step. $\tan \frac{1}{2}(A - B) = \dfrac{a - b}{a + b} \tan \frac{1}{2}(A + B),$

or, $\log \tan \frac{1}{2}(A - B) = \log (a - b) + \log \tan \frac{1}{2}(A + B) - \log (a + b).$

$$\log (a - b) = 2.0792$$
$$\log \tan \tfrac{1}{2}(A + B) = \underline{10.3108 - 10}$$
$$12.3900 - 10$$
$$\log (a + b) = \underline{2.9823}$$
$$\log \tan \tfrac{1}{2}(A - B) = 9.4077 - 10$$

$$\therefore \tfrac{1}{2}(A - B) = 14°\ 21'.$$

$\frac{1}{2}(A + B) = 63°\ 57'$		$63°\ 57'$
$\frac{1}{2}(A - B) = \underline{14°\ 21'}$		$\underline{14°\ 21'}$
Adding, $\quad A = 78°\ 18'$	Subtracting,	$B = 49°\ 36'$

Third step. $\qquad c = \dfrac{a \sin C}{\sin A}.$ $\qquad$ From $\dfrac{c}{\sin C} = \dfrac{a}{\sin A}$

$$\log c = \log a + \log \sin C - \log \sin A.$$

$$\log a = 2.7324$$
$$\log \sin C = \underline{9.8971 - 10}$$
$$12.6295 - 10$$
$$\log \sin A = \underline{9.9909 - 10}$$
$$\log c = 2.6386$$

$$\therefore c = 435.1.$$

Check. By the law of sines,

$\log a = 12.7324 - 10$	$\log b = 12.6232 - 10$	$\log c = 12.6386 - 10$
$\log \sin A = \underline{9.9909 - 10}$	$\log \sin B = \underline{9.8817 - 10}$	$\log \sin C = \underline{9.8971 - 10}$
2.7415	2.7415	2.7415

EXAMPLE 2. Given $a = 167$, $c = 82$, $B = 98°$; solve the triangle, using Tables I and III.

Solution. *First step.*

$a = 167$	167	$180°$
$c = \underline{82}$	$\underline{82}$	$B = \underline{98°}$
$a + c = 249$	$a - c = 85$	$A + C = 82°$
		$\therefore \frac{1}{2}(A + C) = 41°.$

Second step. $\tan \frac{1}{2}(A - C) = \dfrac{a - c}{a + c} \tan \frac{1}{2}(A + C),$

or, $\log \tan \frac{1}{2}(A - C) = \log (a - c) + \log \tan \frac{1}{2}(A + C) - \log (a + c).$

$$\begin{aligned}
\log (a - c) = \ & 1.9294 \\
\log \tan \tfrac{1}{2}(A + C) = \ & \underline{9.9392 - 10} \\
& 11.8686 - 10 \\
\log (a + c) = \ & \underline{2.3962} \\
\log \tan \tfrac{1}{2}(A - C) = \ & 9.4724 - 10
\end{aligned}$$

$$\therefore \tfrac{1}{2}(A - C) = 16.53°.$$

$$\begin{array}{ll}
\tfrac{1}{2}(A + C) = 41.00° & \qquad\qquad 41.00° \\
\tfrac{1}{2}(A - C) = \underline{16.53°} & \qquad\qquad \underline{16.53°}
\end{array}$$

Adding, $\qquad A = 57.53°$ $\qquad$ Subtracting, $C = 24.47°$

Third step. $\qquad b = \dfrac{a \sin B}{\sin A}.$ $\qquad$ From $\dfrac{b}{\sin B} = \dfrac{a}{\sin A}$

$$\log b = \log a + \log \sin B - \log \sin A.$$

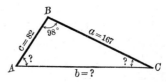

$$\begin{aligned}
\log a = \ & 2.2227 \\
\log \sin B = \ & \underline{9.9958 - 10*} \\
& 12.2185 - 10 \\
\log \sin A = \ & \underline{9.9262 - 10} \\
\log b = \ & 2.2923 \\
\therefore b = \ & 196.
\end{aligned}$$

Check. By the law of sines,

$$\begin{array}{lll}
\log a = 12.2227 - 10 & \log b = 12.2923 - 10 & \log c = 11.9138 - 10 \\
\log \sin A = \underline{9.9262 - 10} & \log \sin B = \underline{9.9958 - 10} & \log \sin C = \underline{9.6172 - 10} \\
\qquad 2.2965 & \qquad 2.2965 & \qquad 2.2966
\end{array}$$

which substantially agree.

PROBLEMS

Using Tables I and II, solve the following triangles. Check the solutions.

1. $a = 27$, $c = 15$, $B = 46°$. $\quad$ *Ans.* $A = 100° 57'$, $C = 33° 3'$, $b = 19.8$.

2. $a = 486$, $b = 347$, $C = 51° 36'$.

3. $b = 2.302$, $c = 3.567$, $A = 62°$.

$\qquad\qquad\qquad$ *Ans.* $B = 39° 16'$, $C = 78° 44'$, $a = 3.211$.

4. $a = 597.3$, $c = 702.4$, $B = 39° 42'$.

5. $a = 77.99$, $b = 83.39$, $C = 72° 16'$.

$\qquad\qquad$ *Ans.* $A = 51° 14.5'$, $B = 56° 29.5'$, $c = 95.24$.

6. $b = 0.8782$, $c = 0.4973$, $A = 32° 24'$.

7. $b = 1192.1$, $c = 356.3$, $A = 26° 16'$.

$\qquad\qquad$ *Ans.* $B = 143° 29'$, $C = 10° 15'$, $a = 886.6$.

8. $a = 88.79$, $b = 15.13$, $C = 110° 22'$.

*Sin $B = \sin 98° = \sin (180° - 98°) = \sin 82°$. $\therefore \log \sin 98° = \log \sin 82° = 9.9958 - 10$.

9. $a = 51.38$, $c = 67.94$, $B = 79°\ 13'$.

Ans. $A = 40°\ 52'$, $C = 59°\ 55'$, $b = 77.14$.

10. $b = 4625$, $c = 5484$, $A = 4°\ 16.2'$.

11. $b = 0.02668$, $c = 0.05092$, $A = 115°\ 47'$.

Ans. $B = 21°\ 1'$, $C = 43°\ 12'$, $a = 0.06699$.

12. $a = 87.91$, $b = 9.464$, $C = 4°\ 56'$.

Using Tables I and III, solve the triangles in Problems 13 to 22. Check the solutions.

13. $a = 17$, $b = 12$, $C = 59.3°$.   *Ans.* $A = 77.2°$, $B = 43.5°$, $c = 15.0$.

14. $b = 101$, $c = 158$, $A = 37.38°$.

15. $a = 0.0850$, $c = 0.0042$, $B = 56.5°$.

Ans. $A = 121.07°$, $C = 2.43°$, $b = 0.0828$.

16. $b = 3.272$, $c = 2.854$, $A = 79.32°$.

17. $b = 0.9486$, $c = 0.8852$, $A = 84.6°$.

Ans. $B = 49.88°$, $C = 45.52°$, $a = 1.235$.

18. $a = 21.82$, $b = 48.27$, $C = 12.23°$.

19. $a = 42,930$, $c = 73,480$, $B = 24.8°$.

Ans. $A = 27.56°$, $C = 127.64°$, $b = 38,920$.

20. $a = 500.2$, $c = 700.7$, $B = 111.11°$.

21. $a = 5.767$, $b = 8.323$, $C = 124.33°$.

Ans. $A = 22.37°$, $B = 33.30°$, $c = 12.510$.

22. $b = 70.25$, $c = 5.632$, $A = 66.66°$.

23. In order to find the distance between two objects, A and B, separated by a swamp, a station C was chosen and the distances CA and CB were measured and found to be 3825 yd. and 3476 yd. respectively. The angle ACB was observed to be $62°\ 31'$. Find the distance from A to B.

Ans. 3800 yd.

24. At a point 3 mi. from one end of an island and 7 mi. from the other end, the island subtends an angle of $33°\ 56'$. Find the length of the island.

25. In a parallelogram the two diagonals are 5 ft. and 6 ft. long and form an angle of $49°\ 18'$. Find the sides of the parallelogram.

Ans. 5.004 ft., 2.339 ft.

26. The sides of a parallelogram are 172.43 ft. and 101.31 ft. long, and the angle included by them is $61°\ 16'$. Find the lengths of the diagonals.

27. Two yachts start at the same time from the same point. One sails due north at the rate of 10.44 mi. an hour, and the other due northeast at the rate of 7.71 mi. an hour. How far apart are they at the end of 40 min.?

Ans. 4.93 mi.

28. Find the direction of the slower yacht from the faster yacht in Problem 27.

CASE IV. *When all the sides, a, b, c, are given.*

First step. *Calculate* $s = \frac{1}{2}(a+b+c)$, $s-a$, $s-b$, $s-c$.

Second step. *Find log r from*

$$r = \sqrt{\frac{(s-a)(s-b)(s-c)}{s}}. \quad \text{(55) to (58), Art. 46}$$

Third step. *Find angles A, B, C from*

$$\tan \tfrac{1}{2} A = \frac{r}{s-a}, \quad \tan \tfrac{1}{2} B = \frac{r}{s-b}, \quad \tan \tfrac{1}{2} C = \frac{r}{s-c}.$$

Check. See if $A + B + C = 180°$.

EXAMPLE. Given $a = 51$, $b = 65$, $c = 20$; solve the triangle.

Solution. **First step.**

	Hence		
$a = 51$			
$b = 65$	$s = 68$	$s = 68$	$s = 68$
$c = 20$	$a = 51$	$b = 65$	$c = 20$
$2s = 136$	$s - a = 17$	$s - b = 3$	$s - c = 48$
$s = 68.$			

Second step. $\quad r = \sqrt{\dfrac{(s-a)(s-b)(s-c)}{s}},$

or, $\quad \log r = \tfrac{1}{2}[\log(s-a) + \log(s-b) + \log(s-c) - \log s].$

From the table of logarithms,

$\log(s-a) = 1.2304$
$\log(s-b) = 0.4771$
$\log(s-c) = \underline{1.6812}$
$ 3.3887$
$\log s = 1.8325$
$2\boxed{1.5562}$
$\log r = 0.7781$

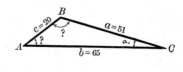

Third step. From the formula $\tan \tfrac{1}{2} A = \dfrac{r}{s-a}$,

$$\log \tan \tfrac{1}{2} A = \log r - \log(s-a).$$

$\log r = 10.7781 - 10$
$\log(s-a) = \underline{1.2304}$
$\log \tan \tfrac{1}{2} A = 9.5477 - 10$

$\tfrac{1}{2} A = 19° \; 27',$ using Table II*

or, $A = 38° \; 54'.$

* If we use Table III instead, we get

     $\tfrac{1}{2} A = 19.44°,$ $\tfrac{1}{2} B = 63.43°,$ $\tfrac{1}{2} C = 7.12°,$

and $A = 38.88°,$ $B = 126.86°,$ $C = 14.24°.$

Check. $A + B + C = 179.98°.$

From the formula $\tan \frac{1}{2} B = \dfrac{r}{s-b}$,

$$\log \tan \tfrac{1}{2} B = \log r - \log (s - b).$$

$$\log r = 10.7781 - 10$$
$$\log (s - b) = \underline{0.4771}$$
$$\log \tan \tfrac{1}{2} B = 10.3010 - 10$$

$$\tfrac{1}{2} B = 63°\ 26', \qquad\qquad \text{using Table II}$$

$$B = 126°\ 52'.$$

From the formula $\tan \frac{1}{2} C = \dfrac{r}{s-c}$,

$$\log \tan \tfrac{1}{2} C = \log r - \log (s - c).$$

$$\log r = 10.7781 - 10$$
$$\log (s - c) = \underline{1.6812}$$
$$\log \tan \tfrac{1}{2} C = 9.0969 - 10$$

$$\tfrac{1}{2} C = 7°\ 8', \qquad\qquad \text{using Table II}$$

$$C = 14°\ 16'.$$

Check.
$$
\begin{aligned}
A &= 38°\ 54' \\
B &= 126°\ 52' \\
C &= \underline{14°\ 16'} \\
A + B + C &= 180°\ 2'
\end{aligned}
$$

PROBLEMS

Using Tables I and II, solve the following triangles and check the solutions:

1. $a = 2$, $b = 3$, $c = 4$. *Ans.* $A = 28°\ 58'$, $B = 46°\ 34'$, $C = 104°\ 28'$.

2. $a = 2.50$, $b = 2.79$, $c = 2.33$.

3. $a = 5.6$, $b = 4.3$, $c = 4.9$.
Ans. $A = 74°\ 40'$, $B = 47°\ 46'$, $C = 57°\ 34'$.

4. $a = 111$, $b = 145$, $c = 40$.

5. $a = 0.321$, $b = 0.361$, $c = 0.402$.
Ans. $A = 49°\ 24'$, $B = 58°\ 38'$, $C = 71°\ 58'$.

6. $a = 168.3$, $b = 205.2$, $c = 291.8$.

7. $a = 3019$, $b = 6731$, $c = 4228$.
Ans. $A = 18°\ 12'$, $B = 135°\ 51'$, $C = 25°\ 57'$.

8. $a = 68.23$, $b = 39.72$, $c = 41.26$.

9. $a = 513.4$, $b = 726.8$, $c = 931.3$.
Ans. $A = 33°\ 16'$, $B = 50°\ 56'$, $C = 95°\ 48'$.

10. $a = 7.440$, $b = 9.063$, $c = 6.181$.

Using Tables I and III, solve the triangles in Problems 11 to 18 and check the solutions:

11. $a = 4, b = 7, c = 6.$ *Ans.* $A = 34.78°, B = 86.42°, C = 58.82°.$

12. $a = 0.43, b = 0.50, c = 0.57.$

13. $a = 61.3, b = 84.7, c = 47.6.$
Ans. $A = 45.20°, B = 101.38°, C = 33.44°.$

14. $a = 328.6, b = 422.4, c = 643.2.$

15. $a = 30.19, b = 67.31, c = 42.28.$
Ans. $A = 18.20°, B = 135.86°, C = 25.94°.$

16. $a = 8001, b = 7002, c = 9003.$

17. $a = 0.0291, b = 0.0184, c = 0.0358.$
Ans. $A = 54.06°, B = 30.80°, C = 95.16°.$

18. $a = 6.727, b = 3.871, c = 4.032.$

19. The sides of a triangular field are 7 rd., 11 rd., and 9.6 rd. long. Find the angle opposite the longest side.   *Ans.* 81° 22′.

20. Find the smallest angle of the triangle whose sides are 1.68 ft., 2.04 ft., and 2.91 ft. long.

21. Under what visual angle is an object 7 ft. long seen when the eye of the observer is 5 ft. from one end of the object and 8 ft. from the other end?   *Ans.* 60°.

22. The point P is 135.81 ft. from one end of a wall 123.42 ft. long, and 100.25 ft. from the other end. What angle does the wall subtend at the point P?

23. Two sides of a parallelogram are 52.1 ft. and 68.5 ft. long. The length of the shorter diagonal is 31.6 ft. Find the length of the longer diagonal.   *Ans.* 117.54 ft.

24. The diagonals of a parallelogram are 842 ft. and 1426 ft. long. The shorter side is 824 ft. long. Find the length of the longer side.

67. Use of logarithms in finding the area of an oblique triangle. From Art. 47 we have the following three cases.

CASE I. *When two sides and the included angle are given, use one of the formulas*

$$S = \frac{ab \sin C}{2}, \quad S = \frac{bc \sin A}{2}, \quad S = \frac{ac \sin B}{2},$$

where $S = $ *area of the triangle.*

EXAMPLE 1. Given $a = 25.6$, $b = 38.2$, $C = 41°\ 56'$; find the area of the triangle.

Solution.
$$S = \frac{ab \sin C}{2}.$$

$$\log S = \log a + \log b + \log \sin C - \log 2.$$

$$
\begin{array}{ll}
\log a = & 1.4082 \\
\log b = & 1.5821 \\
\log \sin C = & \underline{9.8249 - 10} \\
& 12.8152 - 10 \\
\log 2 = & \underline{0.3010} \\
\log S = & 12.5142 - 10 \\
& = 2.5142.
\end{array}
$$

$$\therefore S = 326.8. \quad Ans.$$

CASE II. *When the three sides are given, use formula*

$$S = \sqrt{s(s - a)(s - b)(s - c)},$$

where $S = area\ of\ the\ triangle,$

and $s = \frac{1}{2}(a + b + c).$

EXAMPLE 2. Find the area of a triangle, having given $a = 12.53$, $b = 24.9$, $c = 18.91$.

Solution.

$$
\begin{array}{llll}
a = 12.53 & \text{Hence} & & \\
b = 24.9 & s = 28.17 & s = 28.17 & s = 28.17 \\
c = \underline{18.91} & a = \underline{12.53} & b = \underline{24.9} & c = \underline{18.91} \\
2\,s = 56.34 & s - a = 15.64 & s - b = 3.27 & s - c = 9.26 \\
s = 28.17. & & &
\end{array}
$$

$$S = \sqrt{s(s - a)(s - b)(s - c)}.$$

$$\log S = \tfrac{1}{2}[\log s + \log (s - a) + \log (s - b) + \log (s - c)].$$

$$
\begin{array}{l}
\log s = 1.4498 \\
\log (s - a) = 1.1942 \\
\log (s - b) = 0.5145 \\
\log (s - c) = \underline{0.9666} \\
 2\boxed{4.1251} \\
\log S = 2.0626
\end{array}
$$

$$\therefore S = 115.5. \quad Ans.$$

CASE III. *Area problems which do not fall directly under Cases I or II may be solved by Case I, if we first find an additional side or angle by the law of sines.*

EXAMPLE 3. Given $A = 34°\ 22'$, $B = 66°\ 11'$, $c = 78.35$; find the area of the triangle.

Solution. This does not now come directly under either Case I or Case II. But
$$C = 180° - (A + B) = 180° - 100°\ 33' = 79°\ 27'.$$

And, by the law of sines,

$$a = \frac{c \sin A}{\sin C}.$$

$$\log a = \log c + \log \sin A - \log \sin C.$$

$$
\begin{aligned}
\log c &= \ 1.8941 \\
\log \sin A &= \ \underline{9.7517 - 10} \\
&\ \ \ 11.6458 - 10 \\
\log \sin C &= \ \underline{9.9926 - 10} \\
\log a &= \ 1.6532
\end{aligned}
$$

Now it comes under Case I.

$$S = \frac{ac \sin B}{2}.$$

$$\log S = \log a + \log c + \log \sin B - \log 2.$$

$$
\begin{aligned}
\log a &= \ 1.6532 \\
\log c &= \ 1.8941 \\
\log \sin B &= \ \underline{9.9614 - 10} \\
&\ \ \ 13.5087 - 10 \\
\log 2 &= \ \underline{0.3010} \\
\log S &= \ 13.2077 - 10 \\
&= \ 3.2077 \\
\therefore S &= \ 1613.3. \ \ \textit{Ans.}
\end{aligned}
$$

PROBLEMS

Find the areas of the following triangles. Use Tables I and II for Problems 1 to 10, and Tables I and III for Problems 11 to 18.

1. $a = 38.0$, $c = 61.2$, $B = 67° 56'$.   *Ans.* 1078.

2. $b = 116.1$, $c = 100.0$, $A = 118° 16'$.

3. $b = 2.07$, $A = 70°$, $B = 36° 23'$.   *Ans.* 3.257.

4. $a = 3.123$, $A = 53° 11'$, $B = 13° 57'$.

5. $a = 0.3228$, $c = 0.9082$, $B = 60° 16'$.   *Ans.* 0.1273.

6. $a = 86.84$, $b = 73.41$, $C = 56° 31'$.

7. $a = 95.0$, $b = 142.8$, $c = 89.6$.   *Ans.* 4174.

8. $a = 6.295$, $b = 3.093$, $c = 4.123$.

9. $a = 18.063$, $A = 96° 30'$, $B = 35°$.   *Ans.* 70.55.

10. $b = 62.83$, $c = 40.95$, $B = 28° 19'$.

11. $a = 100$, $B = 60.25°$, $C = 54.5°$.   *Ans.* 3891.

12. $c = 2.35$, $A = 30.21°$, $B = 46.42°$.

13. $a = 145$, $b = 178$, $B = 41.17°$.   *Ans.* 12,383.

14. $b = 28.51$, $c = 40.23$, $C = 77.76°$.

15. $a = 23.1$, $b = 19.7$, $c = 25.2$.   *Ans.* 215.9.

16. $a = 7.464$, $b = 9.326$, $c = 10.937$.

17. $a = 960$, $b = 720$, $C = 25.67°$.   *Ans.* 149,730.

18. $b = 0.6275$, $c = 0.4921$, $A = 121.32°$.

19. Find the area of the largest circular flower bed which can be made in a triangular grass plot whose sides are 124.62 ft., 40.86 ft., and 97.92 ft. long.   *Ans.* 518.24 sq. ft.

20. The area of a triangle is one acre, and two of its sides are 127 yd. and 150 yd. Find the angle included between the given sides.

21. The side AB of a field $ABCD$ is 37 rd., BC is 63 rd., and DA is 20 rd. long. The diagonals AC and BD are 75 rd. and 42 rd. long respectively. Find the area of the field.   *Ans.* 1570 sq. rd.

22. In a field $ABCD$ the sides AB, BC, CD, and DA are 155 rd., 236 rd., 252 rd., and 105 rd. respectively. The diagonal AC is 311 rd. long. Find the area of the field.

68. Measurement of land areas. The following example illustrates the nature of the measurements made by surveyors in determining land areas, and the usual method employed for calculating the area from the data found. The Gunter's chain is 4 rd., or 66 ft., in length. An acre equals 10 sq. chains, or 160 sq. rd.

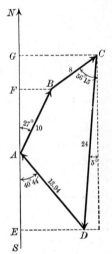

EXAMPLE. A surveyor starting from a point A runs N. 27° E. 10 chains to B, thence N.E. by E. (see page 79) 8 chains to C, thence S. 5° W. 24 chains to D, thence N. 40° 44′ W. 13.94 chains to A. Calculate the area of the field $ABCD$.

Solution. Draw an accurate figure of the field. Through the extreme westerly point of the field draw a north-and-south line. From the figure, area $ABCD =$ area trapezoid * $GCDE -$ (area trapezoid $GCBF +$ area triangle $FBA +$ area triangle ADE) $= 13.9$ acres. *Ans.*

PROBLEMS

1. A surveyor measures S. 50° 25′ E. 6.04 chains, thence S. 58° 10′ W. 4.15 chains, thence N. 28° 12′ W. 5.1 chains, thence to the starting point. Determine the direction and distance of the starting point from the last station, and find area of the field inclosed.

                    Ans. N. 39° 42′ E. 2 chains; 1.66 acres.

---

* From geometry the area of a trapezoid equals one half the sum of the parallel sides times the altitude. Thus, area $GCDE = \frac{1}{2}(GC + ED)GE$.

2. One side of a field runs N. 83° 30′ W. 10.5 chains, the second side S. 22° 15′ W. 11.67 chains, the third side N. 71° 45′ E. 12.9 chains, and the fourth side completes the circuit of the field. Find the direction and length of the fourth side, and calculate the area of the field.

3. From station No. 1 to station No. 2 is S. 7° 20′ W. 4.57 chains, thence to station No. 3 S. 61° 55′ W. 7.06 chains, thence to station No. 4 N. 3° 10′ E. 5.06 chains, thence to station No. 5 N. 33° 50′ E. 325 chains, and thence to station No. 1. Find the direction and distance of station No. 1 from No. 5, and calculate the area of the field inclosed.

Ans. E. 1° 15′ N. 4.7 chains; 3.55 acres.

69. Parallel sailing. When a vessel sails due east or due west, that is, always travels on the same parallel of latitude, it is called *parallel sailing.* The distance sailed is the *departure,** and it is

 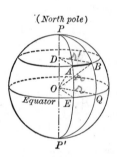

expressed in geographical† miles. Thus, in the figure, arc AB is the departure between A and B. The latitudes of A and B are the same, that is, arc EA = angle EOA = arc QB = angle QOB. The difference in longitude of A and B = arc EQ. The relation between *latitude, departure,* and *difference in longitude* may be found as follows: By geometry,

$$\frac{\text{arc } AB}{\text{arc } EQ} = \frac{DA}{OE} = \frac{DA}{OA} = \cos OAD = \cos AOE = \cos \text{latitude}.$$

$$\therefore \text{arc } AB = \text{arc } EQ \cos \text{latitude},$$

or,

(61) Diff. long. $= \dfrac{\text{departure}}{\cos \text{latitude}}.$

* The *departure* between two meridians is the arc of a parallel of latitude comprehended between those meridians. It diminishes as the distance from the equator increases.

† A *geographical mile* or *knot* is the length of an arc of one minute on a great circle of the earth.

EXAMPLE. A ship whose position is lat. 25° 20′ N., long. 36° 10′ W., sails due west 140 knots. Find the longitude of the place reached.

Solution. Here   departure = 140,

and   latitude = 25° 20′ N.

Substituting in above formula (**61**),

$$\text{diff. long.} = \frac{140}{\cos 25° 20′}.$$

$$
\begin{aligned}
\log 140 &= 12.1461 - 10 \\
\log \cos 25° 20′ &= \underline{9.9561 - 10} \\
\log \text{diff. long.} &= 2.1900
\end{aligned}
$$

diff. long. = 154.9′ = 2° 34.9′.

Hence longitude of place reached = 36° 10′ + 2° 34.9′ = 38° 44.9′ W. *Ans.*

PROBLEMS

1. A ship in lat. 42° 16′ N., long. 72° 16′ W., sails due east a distance of 149 geographical miles. What is the position of the point reached?

Ans. Long. 68° 55′ W.

2. A vessel in lat. 44° 49′ S., long. 119° 42′ E., sails due west until it reaches long. 117° 16′ E. Find the departure.

3. A ship in lat. 36° 48′ N., long. 56° 15′ W., sails due east 226 mi. Find the longitude of the place reached.   *Ans.* Long. 51° 33′ W.

4. A vessel in lat. 48° 54′ N., long. 10° 55′ W., sails due west until it is in long. 15° 12′ W. Find the number of knots sailed.

70. Plane sailing. When a ship sails in such a manner as to cross successive meridians at the same angle, it is said to sail on a *rhumb line.* This angle is called the course, and the *distance* between two places is measured on a rhumb line. Thus, in the figure, if a ship travels from *A* to *B* on a rhumb line,

arc *AB* = distance,

angle *CAB* = course,

arc *CB* = departure,

arc *AC* = difference in latitude between *A* and *B.*

(*North Pole*)

An approximate relation between the quantities involved is obtained by regarding the surface of the earth as a *plane* surface, that is, regarding *ACB* as a plane right triangle, the angle *ACB* being the right angle. This right triangle is called the *triangle of plane sailing.*

From this plane right triangle we get

$$CB = AB \sin A,$$

and $$AC = AB \cos A;$$

or,

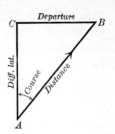

(62)　　**Departure = distance × sin course,**

and

(63)　　**Diff. lat. = distance × cos course.**

If AB is long, the error caused by neglecting the curvature of the earth will be too great to make these results of any value. In that case AB may be divided into parts, such as AE, EG, GI, IB (figure on page 159), which are so small that the curvature of the earth may be neglected.

EXAMPLE. A ship sails from lat. 8° 45′ S., on a course N. 36° E., 345 geographical miles. Find the latitude reached and the departure made.

Solution. Here distance = 345 and course = 36°.

∴ departure = 345 sin 36°.　　　　diff. lat. = 345 cos 36°.

log 345 = 2.5378	log 345 = 2.5378
log sin 36° = 9.7692 − 10	log cos 36° = 9.9080 − 10
log departure = 2.3070	log diff. lat. = 2.4458

∴ departure = 202.8 mi.　　　　diff. lat. = 279.1′ = 4° 39.1′.

As the ship is sailing in a northerly direction, she will have reached latitude 8° 45′ − 4° 39.1′ = 4° 5.9′ S.

PROBLEMS

1. A ship sails from lat. 32° 18′ N., on a course between N. and W., a distance of 344 mi., and a departure of 103 mi. Find the course and the latitude reached.　　　　*Ans.*　Course N. 17° 25′ W., lat. 37° 46′ N.

2. A ship sails from lat. 43° 45′ S., on a course N. by E., 2345 mi. Find the latitude reached and the departure made.

3. A ship sails on a course between S. and E. 244 mi., leaving lat. 2° 52′ S. and reaching lat. 5° 8′ S. Find the course and the departure.
　　　　　　Ans.　Course S. 56° 8′ E., departure = 202.6 mi.

71. Middle latitude sailing. Here we take the departure between two places to be measured on that parallel of latitude which lies halfway between the parallels of the two places. Thus, in the figure on page 159 the departure between A and B is LM, measured on a parallel of latitude midway between the parallels of A and B.

This will be sufficiently accurate for ordinary purposes if the run is not of great length nor too far away from the equator. The *middle latitude* is then the mean of the latitudes of A and B. The formula (61) on page 158 will then become

(64) $$\text{Diff. long.} = \frac{\text{departure}}{\cos \text{mid. lat.}}.$$

EXAMPLE. A ship in lat. 42° 30′ N., long. 58° 51′ W., sails S. 33° 45′ E. 300 knots. Find the latitude and longitude of the position reached.

Solution. We know the latitude of the starting point A. To get the latitude of the final position B, we first find diff. in lat. from (63). This gives

diff. lat. = 300 cos 33° 45′.

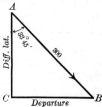

log 300 = 2.4771
log cos 33° 45′ = 9.9198 − 10
log diff. lat. = 2.3969
diff. lat. = 249.4′ = 4° 9.4′.

Since the ship sails in a southerly direction, she will have reached latitude = 42° 30′ − 4° 9.4′ = 38° 20.6′ N.

To get the longitude of B, we must first calculate the departure and middle latitude for substitution in (64). From (62),

departure = 300 sin 33° 45′.

log 300 = 2.4771
log sin 33° 45′ = 9.7448 − 10
log departure = 2.2219
departure = 166.7′.

middle latitude = $\frac{1}{2}$(42° 30′ + 38° 20.6′) = 40° 25.3′.

Substituting in (64),   diff. long. = $\dfrac{166.7}{\cos 40° 25.3′}$.

log 166.7 = 12.2219 − 10
log cos 40° 25.3′ = 9.8815 − 10
log diff. long. = 2.3404
diff. long. = 219′ = 3° 39′.

Since the ship sails in an easterly direction, she will have reached longitude = 58° 51′ − 3° 39′ = 55° 12′ W.

PROBLEMS

1. A vessel in lat. 26° 15′ N., long. 61° 43′ W., sails N.W. 253 knots. Find the latitude and longitude of the position reached.

Ans. Lat. 29° 13.9′ N.; long. 65° 5.1′ W.

2. A ship leaves lat. 31° 14′ N., long. 42° 19′ W., and sails E.N.E. 325 mi. Find the position reached.

3. Leaving lat. 42° 30′ N., long. 58° 51′ W., a battleship sails S.E. by S. 300 mi. Find the place reached. *Ans.* Lat. 38° 21′ N.; long. 55° 12′ W.

4. A ship sails from a position lat. 49° 56′ N., long. 15° 16′ W., to another lat. 47° 18′ N., long. 20° 10′ W. Find the course and distance.

Hint. The difference in latitude and the difference in longitude are known, also the middle latitude.

5. A torpedo boat in lat. 37° N., long. 32° 16′ W., steams N. 36° 56′ W., and reaches lat. 41° N. Find the distance steamed and the longitude of the position reached.   *Ans.* Distance = 300.3 mi.; long. 36° 8′ W.

6. A ship in lat. 42° 30′ N., long. 58° 51′ W., sails S.E. until her departure is 163 mi. and her latitude 38° 22′ N. Find her course and distance and the longitude of the position reached.

7. A cruiser in lat. 47° 44′ N., long. 32° 44′ W., steams 171 mi. N.E. until her latitude is 50° 2′ N. Find her course and the longitude of the position reached.   *Ans.* Course, N. 36° 11′ E.; long. 30° 10′ W.

8. A vessel in lat. 47° 15′ N., long. 20° 48′ W., sails S.W. 208 mi., the departure being 162 mi. Find the course and the latitude and longitude of the position reached.

$$\sin x + y = \frac{CQ}{OQ} = \frac{CF + FQ}{OQ} = \frac{EP + FQ}{OQ}$$

$$\sin x = \frac{EP}{OQ} \qquad ED = OD \sin x$$

CHAPTER VI

TRIGONOMETRIC ANALYSIS

72. Functions of the sum and of the difference of two angles.
We now proceed to express the trigonometric functions of the sum
and difference of two angles in terms of the trigonometric functions
of the angles themselves.* The fundamental formulas to be derived are the following:

(65) $\qquad \sin (x + y) = \sin x \cos y + \cos x \sin y.$

(66) $\qquad \sin (x - y) = \sin x \cos y - \cos x \sin y.$

(67) $\qquad \cos (x + y) = \cos x \cos y - \sin x \sin y.$

(68) $\qquad \cos (x - y) = \cos x \cos y + \sin x \sin y.$

**73. Sine and cosine of the sum of two angles. Proofs of for-
mulas (65) and (67).** Let the angles x and y be each a positive angle less than 90°. In the unit circle whose center is O, lay off the
angle $AOP = x$ and the angle $POQ = y$. Then the angle $AOQ = x + y$.

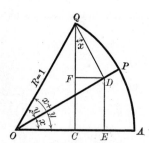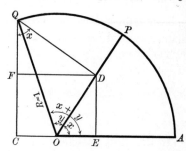

In the first figure the angle $x + y$ is less than 90°, in the second
greater than 90°.

In both figures, QD is perpendicular to OP, QC and DE are perpendicular to OA (or OA produced), and FD is parallel to OA. The
right triangles DFQ and OED are similar. Hence

$$\text{angle } FQD = x.$$

---

* Since x and y are angles, their sum $x + y$ and their difference $x - y$ are also
angles. Thus, if $x = 61°$ and $y = 23°$, then $x + y = 84°$ and $x - y = 38°$. The student should observe that $\sin (x + y)$ is not the same as $\sin x + \sin y$, or $\cos (x - y)$
the same as $\cos x - \cos y$, etc.

163

In the right triangle ODQ,

(1) $$OD = OQ \cos y = \cos y.$$

(2) $$DQ = OQ \sin y = \sin y.$$

Now $$\sin (x + y) = CQ. \hspace{2cm} \text{By Art. 30}$$

But $$CQ = CF + FQ = ED + FQ.$$

Therefore
(3) $$\sin (x + y) = ED + FQ.$$

In the right triangle OED,

(4) $$ED = OD \sin x = \sin x \cos y. \hspace{2cm} \text{By (1)}$$

In the right triangle DFQ,

(5) $$FQ = DQ \cos x = \cos x \sin y. \hspace{2cm} \text{By (2)}$$

Substituting from (4) and (5) in (3), we have

(65) $$\sin (x + y) = \sin x \cos y + \cos x \sin y.$$

Again, $$\cos (x + y) = OC. \hspace{2cm} \text{By Art. 30}$$

But $$OC = OE - CE = OE - FD,$$

in both figures, since the line-segments OC, OE, CE on the horizontal diameter are directed line-segments (Art. 30).

Therefore
(6) $$\cos (x + y) = OE - FD.$$

In the right triangle OED,

(7) $$OE = OD \cos x = \cos x \cos y. \hspace{2cm} \text{By (1)}$$

In the right triangle DFQ,

(8) $$FD = DQ \sin x = \sin x \sin y. \hspace{2cm} \text{By (2)}$$

Substituting from (7) and (8) in (6), we have

(67) $$\cos (x + y) = \cos x \cos y - \sin x \sin y.$$

In deriving formulas (65) and (67) we assumed that each of the angles x and y was positive and less than 90°. It is a fact, however, that these formulas hold true for values of x and y of any magnitude whatever, positive or negative. The work which follows will illustrate how this may be shown for particular cases.

EXERCISE 1. Show that (**67**) is true when x is a positive angle in the second quadrant and y a positive angle in the fourth quadrant.

Proof. Let $x = 90° + x'$ and $y = 270° + y'^*$; then $x + y = 360° + (x' + y')$ and

(9) $x' = x - 90°$, $y' = y - 270°$, $x' + y' = x + y - 360°$.

$$\cos (x + y) = \cos [360° + (x' + y')] = \cos (x' + y') \qquad \text{by Art. 29}$$
$$= \cos x' \cos y' - \sin x' \sin y' \qquad \text{by (67)}$$
$$= \cos (x - 90°) \cos (y - 270°) - \sin (x - 90°) \sin (y - 270°)$$
$$\text{from (9)}$$
$$= \sin x(- \sin y) - (- \cos x \cos y) \qquad \text{by Art. 29}$$
$$= \cos x \cos y - \sin x \sin y. \qquad \text{Q.E.D.}$$

EXERCISE 2. Show that (**65**) is true when x is a positive angle in the first quadrant and y a negative angle in the second quadrant.

Proof. Let $x = 90° - x'$ and $y = - 180° - y'$; then $x + y = - 90° - (x' + y')$ and

(10) $x' = 90° - x$, $y' = - 180° - y$, $x' + y' = - 90° - (x + y)$.

$$\sin (x + y) = \sin [- 90° - (x' + y')] = - \cos (x' + y') \qquad \text{by Art. 29}$$
$$= - [\cos x' \cos y' - \sin x' \sin y'] \qquad \text{by (67)}$$
$$= - [\cos (90° - x) \cos (- 180° - y) - \sin (90° - x) \sin (- 180° - y)]$$
$$\text{from (10)}$$
$$= - [\sin x(- \cos y) - \cos x \sin y] \qquad \text{by Art. 29}$$
$$= \sin x \cos y + \cos x \sin y. \qquad \text{Q.E.D.}$$

EXAMPLE 1. Find $\sin 75°$, using (**65**) and the functions of 45° and 30°.

Solution. Since $75° = 45° + 30°$, we get from (**65**)

$$\sin 75° = \sin (45° + 30°) = \sin 45° \cos 30° + \cos 45° \sin 30°$$

$$= \frac{1}{\sqrt{2}} \cdot \frac{\sqrt{3}}{2} + \frac{1}{\sqrt{2}} \cdot \frac{1}{2} \qquad \text{from Art. 5}$$

$$= \frac{\sqrt{3} + 1}{2\sqrt{2}} = \tfrac{1}{4}(\sqrt{6} + \sqrt{2}). \quad Ans.$$

EXAMPLE 2. Find $\cos (x + y)$, having given $\sin x = \tfrac{3}{5}$ and $\sin y = \tfrac{5}{13}$, x and y being positive acute angles.

Solution. By Art. 17 we find

$$\sin x = \tfrac{3}{5}, \qquad \cos x = \tfrac{4}{5}, \qquad \sin y = \tfrac{5}{13}, \qquad \cos y = \tfrac{12}{13}.$$

Substituting these values in (**67**), we get

$$\cos (x + y) = \tfrac{4}{5} \cdot \tfrac{12}{13} - \tfrac{3}{5} \cdot \tfrac{5}{13} = \tfrac{33}{65}. \quad Ans.$$

* The student should note that x' and y' are acute angles.

PROBLEMS

1. Find the value of cos 75°, using the functions of 45° and 30°.
$$\text{Ans. } \tfrac{1}{4}(\sqrt{6} - \sqrt{2}).$$

2. Find the value of sin 105°, using the functions of 60° and 45°.

3. Verify formula (65) for $A = 210°$ and $B = 120°$.

4. Verify formula (67) for $A = 180°$ and $B = -135°$.

5. If $\tan x = \tfrac{3}{4}$ and $\tan y = \tfrac{7}{24}$, find $\sin (x + y)$ and $\cos (x + y)$ when x and y are acute angles.   Ans. $\sin (x + y) = \tfrac{4}{5}$, $\cos (x + y) = \tfrac{3}{5}$.

6. Given that α and β terminate in the second and in the fourth quadrant respectively, and that $\sin \alpha = \cos \beta = \tfrac{3}{5}$, find $\cos (\alpha + \beta)$.

7. Using the table of natural functions, find (**a**) sin 31° from the functions of 20° and 11°; (**b**) the difference between $\sin (20° + 11°)$ and $\sin 20° + \sin 11°$.   Ans. (**b**) 0.0178.

8. Find $\cos (210° + A)$ if $\sec A = -\sqrt{3}$ and A terminates in the second quadrant.

9. Prove that $\sin 90° = 1$ and $\cos 90° = 0$, using the functions of 60° and 30°.

10. Prove that $\sin 180° = 0$ and $\cos 180° = -1$, using the functions of 120° and 60°.

Show that

11. $\sin (45° + x) = \dfrac{\cos x + \sin x}{\sqrt{2}}$.

12. $\cos (60° + \alpha) = \dfrac{\cos \alpha - \sqrt{3} \sin \alpha}{2}$.

13. $\sin (y + 135°) = \dfrac{\cos y - \sin y}{\sqrt{2}}$.

14. $\cos (210° + x) = \tfrac{1}{2}(\sin x - \sqrt{3} \cos x)$.

15. $\sin (A + B + C) = \sin A \cos B \cos C + \cos A \sin B \cos C$
$$+ \cos A \cos B \sin C - \sin A \sin B \sin C.$$
Hint. $A + B + C = (A + B) + C$.

16. $\cos (A + B + C) = \cos A \cos B \cos C - \sin A \cos B \sin C$
$$- \cos A \sin B \sin C - \sin A \sin B \cos C.$$

17. $\sin (x + y) \cos y - \cos (x + y) \sin y = \sin x.$

18. $\sin (x + 60°) - \cos (x + 30°) = \sin x.$

74. Sine and cosine of the difference of two angles. Proofs of formulas (66) and (68). It was stated in the last section that **(65)** and **(67)** hold true for values of x and y of any magnitude whatever, positive or negative. Hence **(66)** and **(68)** are merely special cases of **(65)** and **(67)** respectively. Thus, from **(65)**,

$$\sin (x + y) = \sin x \cos y + \cos x \sin y.$$

Now replace y by $- y$. This gives

(1) $\qquad \sin (x - y) = \sin x \cos (- y) + \cos x \sin (- y).$

But $\cos (- y) = \cos y$, and $\sin (- y) = - \sin y$.　　From Art. 28

Substituting in (1), we get

(66) $\qquad \sin (x - y) = \sin x \cos y - \cos x \sin y.$

Similarly, from **(67)**,

$$\cos (x + y) = \cos x \cos y - \sin x \sin y.$$

Now replace y by $- y$. This gives

(2) $\qquad \cos (x - y) = \cos x \cos (- y) - \sin x \sin (- y).$

But $\cos (- y) = \cos y$, and $\sin (- y) = - \sin y$.　　From Art. 28

Substituting in (2), we get

(68) $\qquad \cos (x - y) = \cos x \cos y + \sin x \sin y.$

EXAMPLE 1. Find $\cos 15°$, using **(68)** and the functions of $45°$ and $30°$.

Solution. Since $15° = 45° - 30°$, we get from **(68)**

$$\cos 15° = \cos (45° - 30°) = \cos 45° \cos 30° + \sin 45° \sin 30°$$

$$= \frac{1}{\sqrt{2}} \cdot \frac{\sqrt{3}}{2} + \frac{1}{\sqrt{2}} \cdot \frac{1}{2}$$

$$= \frac{\sqrt{3} + 1}{2\sqrt{2}} = \frac{\sqrt{6} + \sqrt{2}}{4}. \quad Ans.$$

The student should work out the above example taking $15° = 60° - 45°$.

EXAMPLE 2. Prove $\sin (60° + x) - \sin (60° - x) = \sin x$.

Solution. $\qquad \sin (60° + x) = \sin 60° \cos x + \cos 60° \sin x.$　　By **(65)**

$\qquad\qquad\qquad \sin (60° - x) = \sin 60° \cos x - \cos 60° \sin x.$　　By **(66)**

$\therefore \sin (60° + x) - \sin (60° - x) = 2 \cos 60° \sin x$　　by subtraction

$$= 2 \cdot \tfrac{1}{2} \cdot \sin x = \sin x. \; Ans.$$

PROBLEMS

1. Find the value of sin 15°, using the functions of 45° and 30°.

$$Ans. \quad \frac{\sqrt{6} - \sqrt{2}}{4}.$$

2. Find $\sin (x - y)$ and $\cos (x - y)$, having given $\sin x = \frac{1}{4}$ and $\sin y = \frac{1}{3}$, x and y being acute angles.

3. Find $\sin (x - y)$ and $\cos (x - y)$, having given $\tan x = \frac{4}{3}$ and $\tan y = \frac{3}{4}$, x terminating in the third quadrant and y in the first quadrant.

$$Ans. \quad \sin (x - y) = -\tfrac{7}{25}, \cos (x - y) = -\tfrac{24}{25}.$$

4. Verify formula (**68**) for $A = 135°$ and $B = 45°$.

Show that

5. $\sin (45° - x) = \dfrac{\cos x - \sin x}{\sqrt{2}}.$

6. $\cos (60° - A) = \dfrac{\cos A + \sqrt{3} \sin A}{2}.$

7. $\cos (x - 315°) = \dfrac{\cos x - \sin x}{\sqrt{2}}.$

8. $\sin (\beta - 120°) = - \dfrac{\sin \beta + \sqrt{3} \cos \beta}{2}.$

9. $\sin (60° + x) - \sin x = \sin (60° - x).$

10. $\cos (30° + y) - \cos (30° - y) = - \sin y.$

11. $\cos (x + 45°) + \cos (x - 45°) = \sqrt{2} \cos x.$

12. $\cos (Q + 45°) + \sin (Q - 45°) = 0.$

13. $\sin (x + y) \sin (x - y) = \sin^2 x - \sin^2 y.$

14. $\cos (x - y + z) = \cos x \cos y \cos z + \cos x \sin y \sin z$
$$- \sin x \cos y \sin z + \sin x \sin y \cos z.$$

75. Tangent and cotangent of the sum and of the difference of two angles. From (**16**), Art. 17, and (**65**) and (**67**), Art. 72, we get

$$\tan (x + y) = \frac{\sin (x + y)}{\cos (x + y)} = \frac{\sin x \cos y + \cos x \sin y}{\cos x \cos y - \sin x \sin y}.$$

Now divide both numerator and denominator by $\cos x \cos y$. This gives

$$\tan (x + y) = \frac{\dfrac{\sin x \cos y}{\cos x \cos y} + \dfrac{\cos x \sin y}{\cos x \cos y}}{\dfrac{\cos x \cos y}{\cos x \cos y} - \dfrac{\sin x \sin y}{\cos x \cos y}}$$

$$= \frac{\dfrac{\sin x}{\cos x} + \dfrac{\sin y}{\cos y}}{1 - \dfrac{\sin x}{\cos x} \cdot \dfrac{\sin y}{\cos y}}.$$

Since $\dfrac{\sin x}{\cos x} = \tan x$ and $\dfrac{\sin y}{\cos y} = \tan y$, we find

$$(69) \qquad \tan (x + y) = \frac{\tan x + \tan y}{1 - \tan x \tan y}.$$

In the same way, from (66) and (68) we find

$$(70) \qquad \tan (x - y) = \frac{\tan x - \tan y}{1 + \tan x \tan y}.$$

From (17), Art. 17, and (65) and (67), Art. 72, we find

$$\cot (x + y) = \frac{\cos (x + y)}{\sin (x + y)} = \frac{\cos x \cos y - \sin x \sin y}{\sin x \cos y + \cos x \sin y}.$$

Now divide both numerator and denominator by $\sin x \sin y$. This gives

$$\cot (x + y) = \frac{\dfrac{\cos x \cos y}{\sin x \sin y} - \dfrac{\sin x \sin y}{\sin x \sin y}}{\dfrac{\sin x \cos y}{\sin x \sin y} + \dfrac{\cos x \sin y}{\sin x \sin y}}$$

$$= \frac{\dfrac{\cos x}{\sin x} \cdot \dfrac{\cos y}{\sin y} - 1}{\dfrac{\cos y}{\sin y} + \dfrac{\cos x}{\sin x}}.$$

Since $\dfrac{\cos x}{\sin x} = \cot x$, and $\dfrac{\cos y}{\sin y} = \cot y$, we get

$$(71) \qquad \cot (x + y) = \frac{\cot x \cot y - 1}{\cot y + \cot x}.$$

In the same way, from (66) and (68) we may show

$$(72) \qquad \cot (x - y) = \frac{\cot x \cot y + 1}{\cot y - \cot x}.$$

Formulas (65) to (72) may be written in a more compact form as follows:

$$\sin (x \pm y) = \sin x \cos y \pm \cos x \sin y,$$

$$\cos (x \pm y) = \cos x \cos y \mp \sin x \sin y,$$

$$\tan (x \pm y) = \frac{\tan x \pm \tan y}{1 \mp \tan x \tan y},$$

$$\cot (x \pm y) = \frac{\cot x \cot y \mp 1}{\cot y \pm \cot x}.$$

The formulas derived in this chapter demonstrate the Addition Theorem for trigonometric functions, namely, that *any trigonometric function of the algebraic sum of two angles is expressible in terms of trigonometric functions of those angles.*

EXAMPLE 1. Find tan 15°, using (70) and the functions of 60° and 45°.

Solution. Since $15° = 60° - 45°$, we get from (70)

$$\tan 15° = \tan(60° - 45°) = \frac{\tan 60° - \tan 45°}{1 + \tan 60° \tan 45°} = \frac{\sqrt{3} - 1}{1 + \sqrt{3}} = 2 - \sqrt{3}. \; Ans.$$

The student should work out the above example taking $15° = 45° - 30°$.

PROBLEMS

1. Find tan 75° from the functions of 45° and 30°.   *Ans.* $2 + \sqrt{3}$.

2. Find cot 105° from the functions of 60° and 45°.

3. Find $\tan(x + y)$ and $\tan(x - y)$, having given $\tan x = \frac{1}{2}$ and $\tan y = \frac{1}{4}$.   *Ans.* $\frac{6}{7}, \frac{2}{9}$.

4. If $\tan(x + y) = \sqrt{3}$ and $\tan x = 1$, find tan y.

Show that

5. $\tan(45° + x) = \dfrac{1 + \tan x}{1 - \tan x}$.

6. $\cot(y - 45°) = \dfrac{1 + \cot y}{1 - \cot y}$.

7. $\tan(A - 60°) = \dfrac{\tan A - \sqrt{3}}{1 + \sqrt{3} \tan A}$.

8. $\cot(B + 210°) = \dfrac{\sqrt{3} \cot B - 1}{\cot B + \sqrt{3}}$.

9. $\dfrac{\sin(x + y)}{\sin(x - y)} = \dfrac{\tan x + \tan y}{\tan x - \tan y}$.

10. $\tan x + \tan y = \dfrac{\sin(x + y)}{\cos x \cos y}$.

11. $\tan(x + 45°) + \cot(x - 45°) = 0$.

12. $\cot A - \cot B = \dfrac{\sin(B - A)}{\sin A \sin B}$.

13. $1 - \tan x \tan y = \dfrac{\cos(x + y)}{\cos x \cos y}$.

14. $\cot P \cot Q - 1 = \dfrac{\cos(P + Q)}{\sin P \sin Q}$.

The reduction formulas of Arts. 25–28 were derived under the assumption that A was an acute angle. The formulas of Art. 72 enable us to show that these formulas are general formulas, that is, true for *any angle* A. The following example illustrates this statement:

EXAMPLE 2. Prove that

(*a*) $$\sin (180° + A) = - \sin A,$$ (see Art. 26)

and

(*b*) $$\tan (270° + B) = - \cot B,$$ (see Art. 27)

when A and B are any angles.

Solution. To prove (*a*), use (65), taking

$$x = 180°, \ y = A.$$

Then $\quad \sin (180° + A) = \sin 180° \cos A + \cos 180° \sin A.$

By Art. 20, $\sin 180° = 0$, $\cos 180° = - 1$. Substituting these values, we get (*a*).

To prove (*b*), we cannot use (69), since, by Art. 20, $\tan 270° = \infty$. But by (16), Art. 17,

(1) $$\tan (270° + B) = \frac{\sin (270° + B)}{\cos (270° + B)}.$$

Now use (65) and (67), taking $x = 270°$, $y = B$. Then

$$\sin (270° + B) = \sin 270° \cos B + \cos 270° \sin B,$$
$$\cos (270° + B) = \cos 270° \cos B - \sin 270° \sin B.$$

By Art. 20, $\sin 270° = - 1$, $\cos 270° = 0$. Hence

$$\sin (270° + B) = - \cos B,$$
$$\cos (270° + B) = \sin B.$$

When these values are substituted in the right-hand member of (1), we get the equation (*b*).

PROBLEMS

Using the formulas of Art. 72, obtain the formulas for the sine, cosine, tangent, and cotangent of the following angles:

1. $90° + A.$ 3. $270° - A.$

2. $180° - A.$ 4. $A - 90°.$

76. Functions of twice an angle in terms of the functions of the angle. Formulas (65) to (72) hold true for all possible values of x and y; hence they must hold true when x equals y.

To find $\sin 2 x$ we take (65),

$$\sin (x + y) = \sin x \cos y + \cos x \sin y.$$

Replace y by x. This gives

$$\sin (x + x) = \sin x \cos x + \cos x \sin x,$$

or,

(73) $$\sin 2 x = 2 \sin x \cos x.$$

To find $\cos 2 x$ we take (67),

$$\cos (x + y) = \cos x \cos y - \sin x \sin y.$$

Replace y by x. This gives

$$\cos (x + x) = \cos x \cos x - \sin x \sin x,$$

or,

(74) $$\cos 2 x = \cos^2 x - \sin^2 x.$$

Since $\cos^2 x = 1 - \sin^2 x$, (74) may be written

(74a) $$\cos 2 x = 1 - 2 \sin^2 x.$$

Or, since $\sin^2 x = 1 - \cos^2 x$, (74) may also be written

(74b) $$\cos 2 x = 2 \cos^2 x - 1.$$

To find $\tan 2 x$ we take (69),

$$\tan (x + y) = \frac{\tan x + \tan y}{1 - \tan x \tan y}.$$

Replace y by x. This gives

$$\tan (x + x) = \frac{\tan x + \tan x}{1 - \tan x \tan x},$$

or,

(75) $$\tan 2 x = \frac{2 \tan x}{1 - \tan^2 x}.$$

77. Functions of multiple angles. The method of the last article may readily be extended to finding the functions of nx in terms of the functions of x if n is an integer.

To find $\sin 3 x$ in terms of $\sin x$ we take (65),

$$\sin (x + y) = \sin x \cos y + \cos x \sin y.$$

Replace y by $2 x$. This gives

$$\sin (x + 2 x) = \sin x \cos 2 x + \cos x \sin 2 x,$$

or, $\sin 3 x = \sin x (\cos^2 x - \sin^2 x) + \cos x (2 \sin x \cos x)$

by (74), (73)

$$= 3 \sin x \cos^2 x - \sin^3 x$$
$$= 3 \sin x (1 - \sin^2 x) - \sin^3 x$$
$$= 3 \sin x - 4 \sin^3 x. \quad Ans.$$

To find $\tan 4 x$ in terms of $\tan x$, we take (69), (75),

$$\tan 4 x = \tan (2 x + 2 x) = \frac{2 \tan 2 x}{1 - \tan^2 2 x} = \frac{4 \tan x (1 - \tan^2 x)}{1 - 6 \tan^2 x + \tan^4 x}. \quad Ans.$$

EXAMPLE. Given $\sin x = \dfrac{2}{\sqrt{5}}$, x lying in the second quadrant; find $\sin 2x$, $\cos 2x$, $\tan 2x$.

Solution. Since $\sin x = \dfrac{2}{\sqrt{5}}$ and x lies in the second quadrant, we get, using the method of Art. 15,

$$\sin x = \frac{2}{\sqrt{5}}, \qquad \cos x = -\frac{1}{\sqrt{5}}, \qquad \tan x = -2.$$

Substituting in (73), we find

$$\sin 2x = 2 \sin x \cos x = 2 \cdot \frac{2}{\sqrt{5}}\left(-\frac{1}{\sqrt{5}}\right) = -\frac{4}{5}.$$

Similarly, we get $\cos 2x = -\frac{3}{5}$ by substituting in (74), and $\tan 2x = \frac{4}{3}$ by substituting in (75).

PROBLEMS

1. Given $\tan x = 2$, x lying in the third quadrant; find $\sin 2x$, $\cos 2x$, $\tan 2x$. *Ans.* $\sin 2x = \frac{4}{5}$, $\cos 2x = -\frac{3}{5}$, $\tan 2x = -\frac{4}{3}$.

2. If $\cot x = k$, express the six trigonometric functions of $2x$ in terms of k.

3. If A lies in the third quadrant, and $\sin A = -\frac{3}{5}$, find

    a. $\cos(90° + A)$.   *Ans.* $\frac{3}{5}$.

    b. $\tan 2A$.   *Ans.* $\frac{24}{7}$.

    c. $\cot(180° - 2A)$.   *Ans.* $-\frac{7}{24}$.

    d. $\sec(270° - 2A)$.   *Ans.* $-\frac{25}{24}$.

4. If θ is an angle in the second quadrant, and $\tan \theta = -\frac{5}{12}$, find

    a. $\cot 2\theta$.

    b. $\sin(180° - \theta)$.

    c. $\cos(270° - 2\theta)$.

    d. $\csc(180° + 2\theta)$.

Considering each of the following as a function of a double angle, express each in terms of functions of the single angle.

5. (*a*) $\sin 6\theta$; (*b*) $\sin 10°$.   *Ans.* (*a*) $2 \sin 3\theta \cos 3\theta$; (*b*) $2 \sin 5° \cos 5°$.

6. (*a*) $\tan 4\theta$; (*b*) $\cos 45°$.

7. (*a*) $\cos \theta$; (*b*) $\tan 400°$.

    Ans. (*a*) $2 \cos^2 \dfrac{\theta}{2} - 1$, also other forms; (*b*) $\dfrac{2 \tan 200°}{1 - \tan^2 200°}$.

8. (*a*) $\cot 3\theta$; (*b*) $\sec \dfrac{\theta}{2}$.

9. Show that $\cos 3x = 4 \cos^3 x - 3 \cos x$.

10. Show that $\tan 3A = \dfrac{3 \tan A - \tan^3 A}{1 - 3 \tan^2 A}$.

11. Express $\cos 4B$ in terms of $\sin B$.   *Ans.* $1 - 8 \sin^2 B + 8 \sin^4 B$.

12. Express $\sin 5\theta$ in terms of $\sin \theta$.

Prove that in a right triangle, C being the right angle, the following relations are true:

13. $\sin 2 A = \sin 2 B.$

14. $\tan 2 A = \dfrac{2 ab}{b^2 - a^2}.$

15. $\cos 2 A = \dfrac{b^2 - a^2}{c^2}.$

16. $\cos 2 A + \cos 2 B = 0.$

17. $\tan B = \cot A + \cos C.$

18. $\sin 3 A = \dfrac{3 ab^2 - a^3}{c^3}.$

19. a. Show that the value of $\sin 2\,\theta$ is less than the value of $2 \sin \theta$ for all values of θ from $0°$ to $90°$.

b. Show that the value of the fraction $\dfrac{\sin 2\,\theta}{2 \sin \theta}$ decreases from 1 to 0 as θ increases from $0°$ to $90°$.

78. Functions of an angle in terms of functions of half the angle. From (**73**),
$$\sin 2 x = 2 \sin x \cos x.$$

Replace $2 x$ by x, or, what amounts to the same thing, replace x by $\dfrac{x}{2}$. This gives

(**76**)
$$\sin x = 2 \sin \frac{x}{2} \cos \frac{x}{2}.$$

From (**74**), $\qquad \cos 2 x = \cos^2 x - \sin^2 x.$

Replace $2 x$ by x, or, what amounts to the same thing, replace x by $\dfrac{x}{2}$. This gives

(**77**)
$$\cos x = \cos^2 \frac{x}{2} - \sin^2 \frac{x}{2}.$$

From (**75**), $\qquad \tan 2 x = \dfrac{2 \tan x}{1 - \tan^2 x}.$

Replace $2 x$ by x, or, what amounts to the same thing, replace x by $\dfrac{x}{2}$. This gives

(**78**)
$$\tan x = \frac{2 \tan \dfrac{x}{2}}{1 - \tan^2 \dfrac{x}{2}}.$$

79. Functions of half an angle in terms of the cosine of the angle. From **(74 a)** and **(74 b)** we get

$$2 \sin^2 x = 1 - \cos 2x,$$

and

$$2 \cos^2 x = 1 + \cos 2x.$$

Solving for $\sin x$ and $\cos x$,

$$\sin x = \pm \sqrt{\frac{1 - \cos 2x}{2}},$$

and

$$\cos x = \pm \sqrt{\frac{1 + \cos 2x}{2}}.$$

Replace $2x$ by x, or, what amounts to the same thing, replace x by $\frac{x}{2}$. This gives

$$(79) \qquad \sin \frac{x}{2} = \pm \sqrt{\frac{1 - \cos x}{2}},$$

and

$$(80) \qquad \cos \frac{x}{2} = \pm \sqrt{\frac{1 + \cos x}{2}}.$$

To get $\tan \frac{x}{2}$ we divide **(79)** by **(80)**. This gives

$$\tan \frac{x}{2} = \frac{\sin \dfrac{x}{2}}{\cos \dfrac{x}{2}} = \frac{\pm \sqrt{\dfrac{1 - \cos x}{2}}}{\pm \sqrt{\dfrac{1 + \cos x}{2}}},$$

or,

$$(81) \qquad \tan \frac{x}{2} = \pm \sqrt{\frac{1 - \cos x}{1 + \cos x}}.$$

Multiplying both numerator and denominator of the right-hand member by $\sqrt{1 + \cos x}$, we get *

$$(82) \qquad \tan \frac{x}{2} = \frac{\sin x}{1 + \cos x};$$

or, multiplying both numerator and denominator by $\sqrt{1 - \cos x}$, we get

$$(83) \qquad \tan \frac{x}{2} = \frac{1 - \cos x}{\sin x}.$$

$* \sqrt{\dfrac{1 - \cos x}{1 + \cos x}} \cdot \dfrac{\sqrt{1 + \cos x}}{\sqrt{1 + \cos x}} = \dfrac{\sqrt{1 - \cos^2 x}}{1 + \cos x} = \dfrac{\sin x}{1 + \cos x}.$

The positive sign only of the radical is taken since $1 + \cos x$ can never be negative and $\tan \frac{x}{2}$ and $\sin x$ always have like signs.

Since tangent and cotangent are reciprocal functions, we have at once, from (81) to (83),

$$\text{(84)} \qquad \cot \frac{x}{2} = \pm \sqrt{\frac{1 + \cos x}{1 - \cos x}}.$$

$$\text{(85)} \qquad \cot \frac{x}{2} = \frac{1 + \cos x}{\sin x}.$$

$$\text{(86)} \qquad \cot \frac{x}{2} = \frac{\sin x}{1 - \cos x}.$$

80. Sums and differences of functions. From Art. 72,

(65) $\sin (x + y) = \sin x \cos y + \cos x \sin y.$

(66) $\sin (x - y) = \sin x \cos y - \cos x \sin y.$

(67) $\cos (x + y) = \cos x \cos y - \sin x \sin y.$

(68) $\cos (x - y) = \cos x \cos y + \sin x \sin y.$

From these equations we find

(a) $\sin (x + y) + \sin (x - y) = 2 \sin x \cos y.$
$$\text{Adding (65) and (66)}$$

(b) $\sin (x + y) - \sin (x - y) = 2 \cos x \sin y.$
$$\text{Subtracting (66) from (65)}$$

(c) $\cos (x + y) + \cos (x - y) = 2 \cos x \cos y.$
$$\text{Adding (67) and (68)}$$

(d) $\cos (x + y) - \cos (x - y) = - 2 \sin x \sin y.$
$$\text{Subtracting (68) from (67)}$$

Let $\quad x + y = A \qquad\qquad\qquad\qquad x + y = A$

and $\quad\; x - y = B \qquad\qquad\qquad\qquad x - y = B$

Adding, $2 x = A + B \qquad\qquad$ Subtracting, $2 y = A - B$

$$x = \tfrac{1}{2}(A + B). \qquad\qquad\qquad\qquad y = \tfrac{1}{2}(A - B).$$

Now replacing the values of $x + y$, $x - y$, x, y in terms of A and B in (a) to (d) inclusive, we get

(87) $\sin A + \sin B = 2 \sin \tfrac{1}{2}(A + B) \cos \tfrac{1}{2}(A - B).$

(88) $\sin A - \sin B = 2 \cos \tfrac{1}{2}(A + B) \sin \tfrac{1}{2}(A - B).$

(89) $\cos A + \cos B = 2 \cos \tfrac{1}{2}(A + B) \cos \tfrac{1}{2}(A - B).$

(90) $\cos A - \cos B = - 2 \sin \tfrac{1}{2}(A + B) \sin \tfrac{1}{2}(A - B).$

An alternative proof of the law of tangents (Art. 44) may be derived by means of (87) and (88). The proof is as follows:

By the law of sines,

$$\frac{a}{\sin A} = \frac{b}{\sin B}, \qquad = \frac{a}{b} + 1 = \frac{\sin A}{\sin B} + 1$$

and by composition and division in proportion,

(e) $$\frac{a+b}{a-b} = \frac{\sin A + \sin B}{\sin A - \sin B}.$$

The desired expression for the right-hand member is obtained from (87) and (88).

Dividing (87) by (88), member for member, we obtain the following:

$$\frac{\sin A + \sin B}{\sin A - \sin B} = \frac{2 \sin \tfrac{1}{2}(A+B) \cos \tfrac{1}{2}(A-B)}{2 \cos \tfrac{1}{2}(A+B) \sin \tfrac{1}{2}(A-B)}$$

$$= \frac{\sin \tfrac{1}{2}(A+B)}{\cos \tfrac{1}{2}(A+B)} \cdot \frac{\cos \tfrac{1}{2}(A-B)}{\sin \tfrac{1}{2}(A-B)}$$

$$= \tan \tfrac{1}{2}(A+B) \cot \tfrac{1}{2}(A-B).$$

But $$\cot \tfrac{1}{2}(A-B) = \frac{1}{\tan \tfrac{1}{2}(A-B)}.$$

Hence

(f) $$\frac{\sin A + \sin B}{\sin A - \sin B} = \frac{\tan \tfrac{1}{2}(A+B)}{\tan \tfrac{1}{2}(A-B)}.$$

Formula (44), Art. 44, follows from (e) and (f).

EXAMPLE 1. Find $\sin 22\tfrac{1}{2}°$, having given $\cos 45° = \dfrac{1}{\sqrt{2}}$.

Solution. From (79), $\qquad \sin \dfrac{x}{2} = \pm \sqrt{\dfrac{1 - \cos x}{2}}.$

Let $x = 45°$, then $\dfrac{x}{2} = 22\tfrac{1}{2}°$, and we get

$$\sin 22\tfrac{1}{2}° = \sqrt{\frac{1 - \dfrac{1}{\sqrt{2}}}{2}} = \tfrac{1}{2}\sqrt{2 - \sqrt{2}}. \quad Ans.$$

EXAMPLE 2. Reduce the sum $\sin 7x + \sin 3x$ to the form of a product.

Solution. From (87),

$$\sin A + \sin B = 2 \sin \tfrac{1}{2}(A+B) \cos \tfrac{1}{2}(A-B).$$

Let $A = 7x$, $B = 3x$. Then $A + B = 10x$, and $A - B = 4x$. Substituting, we get

$$\sin 7x + \sin 3x = 2 \sin 5x \cos 2x. \quad Ans.$$

PROBLEMS

1. Find the cosine and tangent of $22\frac{1}{2}°$. *Ans.* $\frac{1}{2}\sqrt{2+\sqrt{2}}$, $\sqrt{2}-1$.

2. Find the sine, cosine, and tangent of $15°$, using the cosine of $30°$.

3. If A terminates in the third quadrant, and $\cot A = \frac{4}{3}$, find the value of

a. $\sin \dfrac{A}{2}$.   *Ans.* $\dfrac{3\sqrt{10}}{10}$.

b. $\cos \dfrac{A}{2}$.   *Ans.* $-\dfrac{\sqrt{10}}{10}$.

c. $\cot \left(180° - \dfrac{A}{2}\right)$.   *Ans.* $\frac{1}{3}$.

d. $\tan \left(270° - \dfrac{A}{2}\right)$.   *Ans.* $-\frac{1}{3}$.

e. $\cos 2A - \tan \dfrac{A}{2}$.   *Ans.* $\frac{32}{25}$.

4. If θ terminates in the fourth quadrant, and $\sin \theta = -\frac{5}{13}$, find the value of

a. $\tan \dfrac{\theta}{2}$. Use formula (82) or (83).

b. $\csc \dfrac{\theta}{2}$.

c. $\sin \left(90° + \dfrac{\theta}{2}\right)$.

d. $\cot \left(180° + \dfrac{\theta}{2}\right)$.

e. $\sin 2\theta + \cot \dfrac{\theta}{2}$.

Considering the following as functions of half the angle, express each as a function of the angle:

5. (*a*) $\sin 7\frac{1}{2}°$; (*b*) $\tan \dfrac{x}{4}$.   *Ans.* (*a*) $\sqrt{\dfrac{1-\cos 15°}{2}}$; (*b*) $\dfrac{\sin \dfrac{x}{2}}{1+\cos \dfrac{x}{2}}$.

6. (*a*) $\cos 67\frac{1}{2}°$; (*b*) $\cot \theta$.

7. (*a*) $\sin \theta$; (*b*) $\cot \dfrac{3\,\theta}{2}$.   *Ans.* (*a*) $\pm\sqrt{\dfrac{1-\cos 2\theta}{2}}$; (*b*) $\dfrac{1+\cos 3\theta}{\sin 3\theta}$.

8. (*a*) $\tan \theta$; (*b*) $\cos 3\theta$.

9. Express $\sec \dfrac{\alpha}{2}$ in terms of $\sec \alpha$.   *Ans.* $\pm\sqrt{\dfrac{2\sec \alpha}{1+\sec \alpha}}$.

10. Express $\sin x$ in terms of $\tan \dfrac{x}{2}$.

Verify the following equations:

11. $\sin 32° + \sin 28° = \cos 2°$.

12. $\sin 50° - \sin 10° = \sqrt{3} \sin 20°$.

13. $\cos 80° - \cos 20° = - \sin 50°$.

14. $\cos 60° + \cos 30° = \sqrt{2} \cos 15°$.

15. $\sin 40° - \cos 70° = \sqrt{3} \sin 10°$.

16. $\sin (60° + \alpha) + \sin (60° - \alpha) = \sqrt{3} \cos \alpha$.

17. $\cos 5x + \cos 9x = 2 \cos 7x \cos 2x$.

18. $\dfrac{\sin 7x - \sin 5x}{\cos 7x + \cos 5x} = \tan x$.

19. $\dfrac{\sin 33° + \sin 3°}{\cos 33° + \cos 3°} = \tan 18°$.

20. $\dfrac{\sin A - \sin B}{\sin A + \sin B} = \tan \frac{1}{2}(A - B) \cot \frac{1}{2}(A + B)$.

21. $\dfrac{\sin A + \sin B}{\cos A + \cos B} = \tan \frac{1}{2}(A + B)$.

22. $\cos 20° - \sin 10° - \sin 50° = 0$.

Prove that in a right triangle, C being the right angle, the following relations are true:

23. $\sin^2 \dfrac{B}{2} = \dfrac{c - a}{2c}$.

25. $\dfrac{a - b}{a + b} = \tan \frac{1}{2}(A - B)$.

24. $\left(\sin \dfrac{A}{2} + \cos \dfrac{A}{2} \right)^2 = \dfrac{a + c}{c}$.

26. $\tan \dfrac{A}{2} = \dfrac{a}{b + c}$.

81. Trigonometric identities. A trigonometric identity is an equation involving trigonometric functions which is true for all values of the angles for which these functions are defined. Thus the formulas of Art. 17 are trigonometric identities, since they are true for all values of A for which the functions are defined; also formulas (**87**) to (**90**) of Art. 80 are identities, since they are true for all values of A and B.

Let us consider two methods of procedure in proving given identities.

1. We may reduce one member to the form of the other member, by using known identities. In general, the more complicated member is reduced to the form of the simpler member.

2. We may reduce both members, by using known identities, to the same expression. Since, by this method, the two members are equal identically to the same expression, they are identically equal to each other.

No general method can be given which is best to follow in all cases. A thorough knowledge of the fundamental relations (Art. 17) is essential because these relations frequently suggest the reductions to be made. In identities involving functions of multiple angles, fractional angles, or the sums and differences of angles, it is, as a rule, advisable to express these functions as functions of the single angles. If, after this is done, no feasible procedure is apparent, it is usually advantageous to change all functions to sines and cosines.

The two methods considered above are now illustrated.

EXAMPLE 1. Show that
$$1 + \tan 2x \tan x = \sec 2x$$
is an identity.

Solution. *First Method.*

$$1 + \tan 2x \tan x = 1 + \frac{2 \tan^2 x}{1 - \tan^2 x} \qquad \text{by (75), Art. 76}$$

$$= \frac{1 + \tan^2 x}{1 - \tan^2 x}$$

$$= \frac{1 + \dfrac{\sin^2 x}{\cos^2 x}}{1 - \dfrac{\sin^2 x}{\cos^2 x}} \qquad \text{by (16), Art. 17}$$

$$= \frac{\cos^2 x + \sin^2 x}{\cos^2 x - \sin^2 x}$$

$$= \frac{1}{\cos^2 x - \sin^2 x} \qquad \text{by (18), Art. 17}$$

$$= \frac{1}{\cos 2x} \qquad \text{by (74), Art. 76}$$

$$= \sec 2x. \qquad \text{By (23), Art. 17}$$

Second Method.

$$1 + \tan 2x \tan x$$
$$= 1 + \frac{2 \tan^2 x}{1 - \tan^2 x}$$
$$= \frac{1 + \tan^2 x}{1 - \tan^2 x}$$
$$= \frac{1 + \dfrac{\sin^2 x}{\cos^2 x}}{1 - \dfrac{\sin^2 x}{\cos^2 x}}$$
$$= \frac{\cos^2 x + \sin^2 x}{\cos^2 x - \sin^2 x}$$
$$= \frac{1}{\cos^2 x - \sin^2 x}.$$

$$\sec 2x$$
$$= \frac{1}{\cos 2x}$$
$$= \frac{1}{\cos^2 x - \sin^2 x}.$$

$$\therefore 1 + \tan 2x \tan x = \sec 2x \text{ is an identity.}$$

EXAMPLE 2. Show that $\dfrac{\sin(x+y)}{\sin(x-y)} = \dfrac{\tan x + \tan y}{\tan x - \tan y}$ is an identity.

Solution. *Second Method.*

$$\frac{\sin(x+y)}{\sin(x-y)}$$

$$= \frac{\sin x \cos y + \cos x \sin y}{\sin x \cos y - \cos x \sin y}.$$

$$\frac{\tan x + \tan y}{\tan x - \tan y}$$

$$= \frac{\dfrac{\sin x}{\cos x} + \dfrac{\sin y}{\cos y}}{\dfrac{\sin x}{\cos x} - \dfrac{\sin y}{\cos y}}$$

$$= \frac{\sin x \cos y + \cos x \sin y}{\sin x \cos y - \cos x \sin y}.$$

$$\therefore \frac{\sin(x+y)}{\sin(x-y)} = \frac{\tan x + \tan y}{\tan x - \tan y} \text{ is an identity.}$$

PROBLEMS

Show that the following are identities:

1. $\tan x \sin x + \cos x = \sec x.$

2. $\cot x - \sec x \csc x(1 - 2\sin^2 x) = \tan x.$

3. $(\tan x + \cot x)\sin x \cos x = 1.$

4. $\dfrac{\sin y}{1 + \cos y} = \dfrac{1 - \cos y}{\sin y}.$

5. $\sqrt{\dfrac{1 - \sin A}{1 + \sin A}} = \sec A - \tan A.$

6. $\tan x \sin x \cos x + \sin x \cos x \cot x = 1.$

7. $\cot^2 x = \cos^2 x + (\cot x \cos x)^2.$

8. $(\sec y + \csc y)(1 - \cot y) = (\sec y - \csc y)(1 + \cot y).$

9. $\sin^2 z \tan z + \cos^2 z \cot z + 2\sin z \cos z = \tan z + \cot z.$

10. $\sin^3 x + \cos^3 x = (\sin x + \cos x)(1 - \sin x \cos x).$

11. $\sin^6 x + \cos^6 x = \sin^4 x + \cos^4 x - \sin^2 x \cos^2 x.$

12. $\sin B \tan^2 B + \csc B \sec^2 B = 2 \tan B \sec B + \csc B - \sin B.$

13. $\cos(x+y)\cos(x-y) = \cos^2 x - \sin^2 y.$

14. $\sin(A+B)\sin(A-B) = \cos^2 B - \cos^2 A.$

15. $\dfrac{\cos(x-y)}{\cos(x+y)} = \dfrac{1 + \tan x \tan y}{1 - \tan x \tan y}.$

16. $\tan A - \tan B = \dfrac{\sin(A-B)}{\cos A \cos B}.$

17. $\cot x + \cot y = \dfrac{\sin(x+y)}{\sin x \sin y}.$

18. $\sin x \cos(y+z) - \sin y \cos(x+z) = \sin(x-y)\cos z.$

19. $\dfrac{\tan(\theta - \phi) + \tan\phi}{1 - \tan(\theta - \phi)\tan\phi} = \tan\theta.$

20. $\sin(x + y - z) + \sin(x + z - y) + \sin(y + z - x)$
$$= \sin(x + y + z) + 4\sin x \sin y \sin z.$$

21. $\cos x \sin(y - z) + \cos y \sin(z - x) + \cos z \sin(x - y) = 0.$

22. $\cos 5\alpha \cos 4\alpha + \sin 5\alpha \sin 4\alpha = \cos\alpha.$

23. $\sin(x + 75°)\cos(x - 75°) - \cos(x + 75°)\sin(x - 75°) = \frac{1}{2}.$

24. $\cos(2x + y)\cos(x + 2y) + \sin(2x + y)\sin(x + 2y)$
$$= \cos x \cos y + \sin x \sin y.$$

25. $\dfrac{\cot(45° - y)}{\cot(45° + y)} = \dfrac{1 + 2\sin y \cos y}{1 - 2\sin y \cos y}.$

26. $\tan(45° + x) - \tan(45° - x) = 2\tan 2x.$

27. $\tan(45° + C) + \tan(45° - C) = 2\sec 2C.$

28. $\sin 2x = \dfrac{2\tan x}{1 + \tan^2 x}.$

29. $\cos 2x = \dfrac{1 - \tan^2 x}{1 + \tan^2 x}.$

30. $\tan P + \cot P = 2\csc 2P.$

31. $\cos 2x = \cos^4 x - \sin^4 x.$

32. $(\sin x + \cos x)^2 = 1 + \sin 2x.$

33. $\sec 2x = \dfrac{\csc^2 x}{\csc^2 x - 2}.$

34. $2\csc 2s = \sec s \csc s.$

35. $\cot y - \tan y = 2\cot 2y.$

36. $\cos 2x = \dfrac{2 - \sec^2 x}{\sec^2 x}.$

37. $\dfrac{1 + \sin 2x}{1 - \sin 2x} = \left(\dfrac{\tan x + 1}{\tan x - 1}\right)^2.$

38. $\tan x = \dfrac{\sin 2x}{1 + \cos 2x}.$

39. $\cot x = \dfrac{\sin 2x}{1 - \cos 2x}.$

40. $\dfrac{\cot A - 1}{\cot A + 1} = \sqrt{\dfrac{1 - \sin 2A}{1 + \sin 2A}}.$

41. $\cot(A + 45°) = \dfrac{1 - \sin 2A}{\cos 2A}.$

42. $\dfrac{\cos^3 x + \sin^3 x}{\cos x + \sin x} = \dfrac{2 - \sin 2x}{2}.$

43. $\dfrac{\sin 3x - \sin x}{\cos 3x + \cos x} = \tan x.$

44. $\dfrac{\sin 3x - \sin x}{\cos x - \cos 3x} = \cot 2x.$

45. $\sin 3x = 4\sin x \sin(60° + x)\sin(60° - x).$

46. $\dfrac{\sin 4x}{\sin 2x} = 2\cos 2x.$

47. $\dfrac{\sin A + \sin 2A}{1 + \cos A + \cos 2A} = \tan A.$

48. $\sec 2A - \tan 2A = \dfrac{\cos A - \sin A}{\cos A + \sin A}.$

49. $\left(\sin\dfrac{x}{2} - \cos\dfrac{x}{2}\right)^2 = 1 - \sin x.$

50. $\cot \dfrac{x}{4} = \dfrac{\sin \dfrac{x}{2}}{1 - \cos \dfrac{x}{2}}.$

51. $\sin (30^\circ + x) \sin (30^\circ - x) = \tfrac{1}{4}(\cos 2\,x - 2 \sin^2 x).$

52. $\dfrac{\cot (90^\circ + A)}{\cos 2\,A - 1} = \csc 2\,A.$

53. $\cot^2 x\,(1 - \cos 2\,x) + 2 \sin^2 x = 2.$

54. $1 - 4 \sin^4 x - 2 \sin^2 x \cos 2\,x = \cos 2\,x.$

55. $\cos 3\,\alpha - \cos 7\,\alpha = 2 \sin 5\,\alpha \sin 2\,\alpha.$

56. $\dfrac{\sin 5\,x - \sin 2\,x}{\cos 2\,x - \cos 5\,x} = \cot \dfrac{7\,x}{2}.$

57. $\left(\sin \dfrac{x}{2} + \cos \dfrac{x}{2}\right)^2 = 1 + \sin x.$

58. $\dfrac{1 + \sec y}{\sec y} = 2 \cos^2 \dfrac{y}{2}.$

59. $\dfrac{\sin A + \sin B}{\cos A - \cos B} = -\cot \tfrac{1}{2}\,(A - B).$

60. $\dfrac{\cos \theta}{1 - \sin \theta} = \dfrac{1 + \tan \dfrac{\theta}{2}}{1 - \tan \dfrac{\theta}{2}}.$

61. $\cot \dfrac{x}{2} + \tan \dfrac{x}{2} = 2 \csc x.$

62. $\dfrac{1 - \tan^2 \dfrac{x}{2}}{1 + \tan^2 \dfrac{x}{2}} = \cos x.$

63. $1 + \tan x \tan \dfrac{x}{2} = \sec x.$

64. $\tan \dfrac{x}{2} + 2 \sin^2 \dfrac{x}{2} \cot x = \sin x.$

65. $1 + \cot^2 \dfrac{x}{2} = \dfrac{2}{\sin x \tan \dfrac{x}{2}}.$

66. $\dfrac{\tan^2 \dfrac{x}{2} + \cot^2 \dfrac{x}{2}}{\tan^2 \dfrac{x}{2} - \cot^2 \dfrac{x}{2}} = -\dfrac{1 + \cos^2 x}{2 \cos x}.$

67. $\sin \theta + \sin 2\,\theta + \sin 3\,\theta = \sin 2\,\theta(1 + 2 \cos \theta).$

68. $\cos \theta + \cos 2\,\theta + \cos 3\,\theta = \cos 2\,\theta(1 + 2 \cos \theta).$

69. Express $\sin x + \cos y$ as a product.

$Ans.$ $2 \sin\left(45^\circ + \dfrac{x - y}{2}\right) \cos\left(45^\circ - \dfrac{x + y}{2}\right).$

70. Express $\sin x - \cos y$ as a product.

71. Show that the value of $\tan^2 \theta(1 + \cos 2\,\theta) + 2 \cos^2 \theta$ is the same for all values of θ.

72. Give the behavior of $\tan \dfrac{\theta}{2} + 2 \sin^2 \dfrac{\theta}{2} \cot \theta$ as θ increases from 0° to 90°.

Hint. See Problem 64.

73. Give the behavior of $\cos^2 \dfrac{\theta}{2} \left(\tan \dfrac{\theta}{2} - 1 \right)^2$ as θ increases from $0°$ to $90°$.

74. Give the behavior of $\cot \dfrac{\theta}{2} + \tan \dfrac{\theta}{2}$ as θ increases from $0°$ to $90°$.

Show that if A, B, and C are the angles of a triangle, the following relations are true. Note that $C = 180° - (A + B)$.

75. $\sin A + \sin B + \sin C = 4 \cos \dfrac{A}{2} \cos \dfrac{B}{2} \cos \dfrac{C}{2}.$

76. $\tan A + \tan B + \tan C = \tan A \tan B \tan C.$

77. $\sin 2 A + \sin 2 B + \sin 2 C = 4 \sin A \sin B \sin C.$

78. $\cos A + \cos B + \cos C = 4 \sin \dfrac{A}{2} \sin \dfrac{B}{2} \sin \dfrac{C}{2} + 1.$

79. Transform $\sin^4 A$ into $\frac{1}{8} \cos 4 A - \frac{1}{2} \cos 2 A + \frac{3}{8}$.

80. Transform $\cos^4 A$ into $\frac{1}{8} \cos 4 A + \frac{1}{2} \cos 2 A + \frac{3}{8}$.

82. Trigonometric equations. The equation

$$3 \cos^2 x + \sqrt{3} \sin x + 1 = 0$$

is an example of a trigonometric equation. It is not an identity, that is to say, it does not hold for *all* values of x. For example, it is not true when $x = 0°$. In fact, since $\sin 0° = 0$, $\cos 0° = 1$, we see that the left-hand member equals 4 when $x = 0°$ and does *not* equal zero. Thus a trigonometric equation differs from an identity in that it does not hold for all values of the unknown angle involved in it.

To solve a trigonometric equation involving one unknown angle is to find the values of the unknown angle which satisfy the given equation.

No general method can be given for solving trigonometric equations that is best to follow in all cases, but the suggestions in the following article will be found useful.

83. Suggestions for solving a trigonometric equation.

First step. Express all the trigonometric functions in the equation in terms of functions of the same angle, by using known identities. Thus, if $2 x$ and x appear in the equation, express the functions of $2 x$ in terms of functions of x.

Second step. Express all the functions in terms of the same function.

Third step. Solve algebraically (by factoring or otherwise) for the one function now occurring in the equation.

Extraneous roots are frequently introduced by squaring both sides of the equation, or by clearing of fractions. The values of the angle, obtained in such cases, which do not satisfy the given equation must be rejected. Also care must be taken that no roots are lost when extracting the square root of both sides of the equation, or when dividing both sides by a factor.

EXAMPLE 1. Solve the equation

$$\cos 2x \sec x + \sec x + 1 = 0.$$

Solution. Since $\cos 2x = \cos^2 x - \sin^2 x$, we get

First step. $(\cos^2 x - \sin^2 x) \sec x + \sec x + 1 = 0.$

Second step. Since $\sec x = \dfrac{1}{\cos x}$, this becomes

$$\frac{\cos^2 x - \sin^2 x}{\cos x} + \frac{1}{\cos x} + 1 = 0;$$

hence $\cos^2 x - \sin^2 x + 1 + \cos x = 0.$

Since $\sin^2 x = 1 - \cos^2 x$, we have

$$\cos^2 x - 1 + \cos^2 x + 1 + \cos x = 0,$$

or, $2 \cos^2 x + \cos x = 0.$

Third step. $\cos x \,(2 \cos x + 1) = 0.$

Placing each factor equal to zero, we get

(1) $\cos x = 0,$

and

(2) $\cos x + \tfrac{1}{2} = 0 \quad \text{or} \quad \cos x = -\tfrac{1}{2}.$

The values of x between $0°$ and $360°$ which satisfy the equation are, therefore,

from (1), $90°$ and $270°$;   Art. 20

from (2), $120°$ and $240°$.

Changing these values to radians, and arranging them in the order of increasing magnitude, we find the solutions

(3) $\dfrac{\pi}{2}, \dfrac{2\pi}{3}, \dfrac{4\pi}{3}, \dfrac{3\pi}{2}$ radians.

To each of these values in (3) may be added, or subtracted, any multiple of 2π, and in this way *all* solutions are obtained.

EXAMPLE 2. Solve the equation

$$2 \sin^2 x + \sqrt{3} \cos x + 1 = 0.$$

Solution. Since $\sin^2 x = 1 - \cos^2 x$, we get

$$2 - 2 \cos^2 x + \sqrt{3} \cos x + 1 = 0,$$

or, $2 \cos^2 x - \sqrt{3} \cos x - 3 = 0.$

This is a quadratic equation in $\cos x$. Solving, we get

$$\cos x = \sqrt{3} \quad \text{or} \quad -\frac{\sqrt{3}}{2}.$$

No value of x will satisfy $\cos x = \sqrt{3}$, since the value of the cosine cannot exceed 1.

From $\cos x = -\frac{\sqrt{3}}{2}$, we find $x = 150° = \frac{5\,\pi}{6}$, and $x = -150° = -\frac{5\,\pi}{6}$.

Hence all values of x in radians which satisfy the equation are given by the formula $x = 2\,n\pi \pm \frac{5\,\pi}{6}$, where n is any integer, positive or negative.

EXAMPLE 3. Solve the equation $5 \cos x = 4 \sin x + 4$ for all values of x from 0° to 360°.

Solution. To avoid radicals in expressing all functions in terms of the same function, we square both sides, and obtain

$$25 \cos^2 x = 16 \sin^2 x + 32 \sin x + 16.$$

Using the identity $\cos^2 x = 1 - \sin^2 x$, we get

$$25(1 - \sin^2 x) = 16 \sin^2 x + 32 \sin x + 16,$$

or,

(1) $$41 \sin^2 x + 32 \sin x - 9 = 0.$$

Solving this quadratic equation for $\sin x$, we obtain

$$\sin x = \tfrac{9}{41} = 0.2195 \text{ and } - 1.$$

The corresponding values of x between 0° and 360° are

$$x = 12° \, 41', \; 167° \, 19', \text{ and } 270°.$$

These values of x are the solution of equation (1); but since we squared both sides of the given equation, extraneous values might have been introduced. Now $\cos 167° \, 19'$ is negative and $\sin 167° \, 19'$ is positive; thus for this angle the left-hand member of the given equation is negative and the right-hand member is positive. Hence the given equation is not satisfied and $167° \, 19'$ must be rejected. The two remaining angles are found by substitution to satisfy the given equation. Hence the solution is

$$x = 12° \, 41' \text{ and } 270°. \; \textit{Ans.}$$

PROBLEMS

Solve the following equations for values of x from 0° to 360°:

1. $\sin^2 x = \frac{1}{4}$.   *Ans.* 30°, 150°, 210°, 330°.

2. $\csc^2 x = 2$.

3. $\tan^2 x - 3 = 0$.   *Ans.* 60°, 120°, 240°, 300°.

4. $\sec^2 x - 4 = 0$.

5. $\tan 2 x = 1$.   *Ans.* $22\frac{1}{2}°$, $112\frac{1}{2}°$, $202\frac{1}{2}°$, $292\frac{1}{2}°$.

6. $2 \cos 2x + \sqrt{3} = 0$.

7. $\sin^2 2x = 1$.   *Ans.* 45°, 135°, 225°, 315°.

8. $4 \cos^2 2x - 1 = 0$.

9. $\cot^2 \dfrac{x}{2} = 3$.   *Ans.* 60°, 300°.

10. $\sec^2 \dfrac{x}{2} = 2$.

Find, in radians, all angles between 0 and 2π which satisfy the following equations:

11. $(\tan x + 1)(\sqrt{3} \cot x - 1) = 0$.   *Ans.* $\dfrac{\pi}{3}, \dfrac{3\pi}{4}, \dfrac{4\pi}{3}, \dfrac{7\pi}{4}$.

12. $(2 \cos x + 1)(\sin x - 1) = 0$.

13. $(4 \cos^2 \theta - 3)(\csc \theta + 2) = 0$.   *Ans.* $\dfrac{\pi}{6}, \dfrac{5\pi}{6}, \dfrac{7\pi}{6}, \dfrac{11\pi}{6}$.

14. $2 \cot \theta \sin \theta + \cot \theta = 0$.

15. $\tan^2 x - (1 + \sqrt{3}) \tan x + \sqrt{3} = 0$.   *Ans.* $\dfrac{\pi}{4}, \dfrac{\pi}{3}, \dfrac{5\pi}{4}, \dfrac{4\pi}{3}$.

16. $2 \sin^2 x + (2 - \sqrt{3}) \sin x - \sqrt{3} = 0$.

Solve the following equations for values of the angle from 0° to 360°:

17. $2 \sin^2 x + 3 \cos x = 0$.   *Ans.* 120°, 240°.

18. $\cos^2 \alpha - \sin^2 \alpha = \frac{1}{2}$.

19. $2\sqrt{3} \cos^2 \alpha = \sin \alpha$.   *Ans.* 60°, 120°.

20. $\sin^2 y - 2 \cos y + \frac{1}{4} = 0$.

21. $4 \sec^2 y - 7 \tan^2 y = 3$.   *Ans.* 30°, 150°, 210°, 330°.

22. $\tan B + \cot B = 2$.

23. $\sin x + \cos x = 0$.   *Ans.* 135°, 315°.

24. $\sin x + \cos x = 1$.

25. $2 \tan^2 x + 3 \sec x = 0$.   *Ans.* 120°, 240°.

26. $\cos^2 x + 2 \sin x + 2 = 0$.

27. $\cot^2 \theta - 3 \csc \theta + 3 = 0$.   *Ans.* 30°, 90°, 150°.

28. $\tan^2 x + \cot^2 x - 2 = 0$.

29. $\csc x \cot x = 2\sqrt{3}$.   *Ans.* 30°, 330°.

30. $\sin x \cos x + \frac{1}{4} = 0$.

31. $\cos 2x + \cos x = -1$.   *Ans.* 90°, 120°, 240°, 270°.

32. $2 \sin y = \sin 2y$.

33. $\cos 2x = \cos x$.   *Ans.* 0°, 120°, 240°, 360°.

34. $\cos 2x = \cos^2 x$.

35. $\tan (x + 45°) = 1 + \sin 2x$.   *Ans.* 0°, 135°, 180°, 315°.

36. $\sin(60° - x) - \sin(60° + x) = \dfrac{\sqrt{3}}{2}$.

37. $\sin(30° + x) - \cos(60° + x) = -\dfrac{\sqrt{3}}{2}$. *Ans.* 210°, 330°.

38. $\tan(45° - x) + \cot(45° - x) = 4$.

39. $\sin x \sin\dfrac{x}{2} = 1 - \cos x$. *Ans.* 0°, 360°.

40. $\sin\dfrac{x}{2} + \cos x = 1$.

41. $\csc y + \cot y = \sqrt{3}$. *Ans.* 60°.

42. $3(\sec^2 \alpha + \cot^2 \alpha) = 13$.

43. $\sin x = 3 \cos x$. *Ans.* 71° 34', 251° 34'.

44. $2 \cos x = \cos 2x$.

45. $\tan x = \tan 2x$. *Ans.* 0°, 180°, 360°.

46. $3 \cos^2 x + 5 \sin x - 1 = 0$.

47. $3 \sin x \tan x - 5 \sec x + 7 = 0$. *Ans.* 70° 32', 289° 28'.

48. $\csc^2 x(1 + \sin x \cot x) = 2$.

49. $\tan x + \sec^2 x - 3 = 0$. *Ans.* 45°, 116° 34', 225°, 296° 34'.

50. $\sin x + \cos 2x = 4 \sin^2 x - 1$.

51. $\sin(2x - 180°) = \cos x$. *Ans.* 90°, 210°, 270°, 330°.

52. $\sec(x + 120°) + \sec(x - 120°) = 2 \cos x$.

53. $\cos^2 x + 2 \sin x = 0$. *Ans.* 204° 28', 335° 32'.

54. $\sec^2 x - 4 \tan x = 0$.

55. $\sin^2 2x - \sin 2x - 2 = 0$. *Ans.* 135°, 315°.

56. $\tan^2\dfrac{x}{2} - \tan\dfrac{x}{2} - 2 = 0$.

57. $4 \sin x + 3 \cos x = 3$. *Ans.* 0°, 106° 16'.

58. $5 \sin x = 4 \cos x + 4$.

59. $\sin x + \sin 2x + \sin 3x = 0$. *Ans.* 0°, 90°, 120°, 180°, 240°, 270°, 360°.

60. $\tan x + \tan 2x + \tan 3x = 0$.

61. $\sin 4x - \cos 3x = \sin 2x$. *Ans.* 30°, 90°, 150°, 210°, 270°, 330°.

62. $\sin 3x - \sin x = \sin 5x$.

63. What are the acute angles of a right triangle if the difference of the squares of the legs is twice the product of the legs? *Ans.* $22\frac{1}{2}°$, $67\frac{1}{2}°$.

64. What angles between 90° and 270° satisfy the equation
$$\cos(x + 60°) \cos(x - 60°) = -\tfrac{1}{2}?$$

84. General formula for an angle when one function is given.
It is sometimes desirable to write an expression which will include
all angles for which one function has a given value. Such expressions will now be derived. It is convenient to use circular measure
for the angles.

First, we note the following fact from Art. 10.

Since all angles having the same initial and terminal sides have
the same functions, it follows that we can add 2π to the angle or
subtract 2π from the angle as many times as we please without
changing the value of any function. Hence each function of the
angle A is equal to the same function of the angle

$$2 m\pi + A,$$

where m is zero or any positive or negative integer.

We begin by deriving an expression for all angles having the
same sine. These angles will also have the same cosecant, since sine
and cosecant are reciprocal functions. When the given value of the
sine is positive, the angles will lie in the first or in the second
quadrant. When the value of the sine is negative, the angles will
lie in the third or in the fourth quadrant.

Now, if x is any angle, we have

$$\sin (\pi - x) = \sin x. \qquad \text{Arts. 25 and 75}$$

Hence the angles x and $\pi - x$ have equal sines. If the angle x
lies in the first quadrant, then the angle $\pi - x$ will lie in the second
quadrant. If the angle x lies in the third quadrant, the angle $\pi - x$
will lie in the fourth quadrant. Adding $2 m\pi$ to each of these
angles, we get

(1) $$2 m\pi + x$$

and

(2) $$(2 m + 1)\pi - x.$$

Formula (1) gives all angles with the same terminal side as x.
Formula (2) gives all angles with the same terminal side as $\pi - x$.
These formulas may be combined in the single formula

(3) $$n\pi + (- 1)^n x,$$

where n is an integer, positive or negative. In fact, if $n = 2 m$ (an
even number), (3) is the same as (1). If $n = 2 m + 1$, an odd number, (3) is the same as (2).

From the relations

$$\tan (\pi + x) = \tan x, \qquad \text{Arts. 26 and 75}$$
$$\cos (2 \pi - x) = \cos x, \qquad \text{Arts. 27 and 75}$$

we derive, by similar reasoning, expressions for all angles having the same tangent (or cotangent), and for all angles having the same cosine (or secant). The general formulas required are then as follows:

For all angles having the same sine (or cosecant),

(4) $n\pi + (-1)^n x.$

For all angles having the same tangent (or cotangent),

(5) $n\pi + x.$

For all angles having the same cosine (or secant),

(6) $2 n\pi \pm x.$

In (4) to (6), n is any integer, positive or negative.

When formulas to include all solutions of a trigonometric equation are desired, (4) to (6) may be used. (Compare Example 2, Art. 83.)

EXAMPLE 1. Find the four least positive angles whose cosecant equals 2.

Solution. The least positive angle whose cosecant $= 2$ is $30°$, or $\dfrac{\pi}{6}$. Let $x = \dfrac{\pi}{6}$ in (4). This gives

$$n\pi + (-1)^n \frac{\pi}{6}.$$

When $n = 0$, we get $\dfrac{\pi}{6} = 30°.$

When $n = 1$, we get $\pi - \dfrac{\pi}{6} = 150°.$

When $n = 2$, we get $2\pi + \dfrac{\pi}{6} = 390°.$

When $n = 3$, we get $3\pi - \dfrac{\pi}{6} = 510°.$ *Ans.*

EXAMPLE 2. Given $\cos A = -\dfrac{1}{\sqrt{2}}$; find the general formula for A. Also find the five least positive values of A.

Solution. The least positive angle whose cosine $= -\dfrac{1}{\sqrt{2}}$ is $135°$, or $\dfrac{3\pi}{4}$. If we let $x = \dfrac{3\pi}{4}$ in (6), we get

$$A = 2 n\pi \pm \frac{3\pi}{4}.$$

When $n = 0$, $A = \dfrac{3\pi}{4} = 135°.$

When $n = 1$, $A = 2\pi \pm \dfrac{3\pi}{4} = 225°$ and $495°.$

When $n = 2$, $A = 4\pi \pm \dfrac{3\pi}{4} = 585°$ and $855°.$ *Ans.*

PROBLEMS

1. Given $\sin A = \frac{1}{2}$; find the general formula for A. Also find the four least positive values of A.   *Ans.* $n\pi + (-1)^n \dfrac{\pi}{6}$; 30°, 150°, 390°, 510°.

2. Given $\cos A = \dfrac{\sqrt{3}}{2}$; find the general formula for A. Also find all values of A numerically less than 2π.

3. Given $\tan A = 1$; find the general formula for A. Also find the values of A numerically less than 4π.

   Ans. $n\pi + \dfrac{\pi}{4}$; $\dfrac{\pi}{4}$, $-\dfrac{3\pi}{4}$, $\dfrac{5\pi}{4}$, $-\dfrac{7\pi}{4}$, $\dfrac{9\pi}{4}$, $-\dfrac{11\pi}{4}$, $\dfrac{13\pi}{4}$, $-\dfrac{15\pi}{4}$.

4. Given $\sin 2x = \dfrac{1}{2}$; show that $x = \dfrac{n\pi}{2} + (-1)^n \dfrac{\pi}{12}$.

5. Given $\cos 3x = -\dfrac{1}{2}$; show that $x = \dfrac{2n\pi}{3} \pm \dfrac{2\pi}{9}$.

Give the general formulas for the angles which satisfy the following equations:

6. $\sin A = \pm 1$.

7. $\cot x = \pm \sqrt{3}$.   *Ans.* $x = n\pi \pm \dfrac{\pi}{6}$.

8. $\cos y = \pm \frac{1}{2}$.

9. $\tan B = \pm 1$.   *Ans.* $B = n\pi \pm \dfrac{\pi}{4}$.

10. $\csc C = \pm \sqrt{2}$.

11. $\sec A = \pm \dfrac{2}{\sqrt{3}}$.   *Ans.* $A = n\pi \pm \dfrac{\pi}{6}$.

12. $\csc x = 2$.

13. Given $\sin x = -\dfrac{1}{2}$ and $\tan x = \dfrac{1}{\sqrt{3}}$; find the general formula for x.

Solution. Since $\sin x$ is $-$ and $\tan x$ is $+$, x must lie in the third quadrant. The smallest positive angle in the third quadrant which satisfies the condition $\sin x = -\dfrac{1}{2}$ is 210°, or $\dfrac{7\pi}{6}$, and this angle also satisfies $\tan x = \dfrac{1}{\sqrt{3}}$.

Hence $x = 2n\pi + \dfrac{7\pi}{6}$. *Ans.*

14. Given $\cos x = \dfrac{\sqrt{2}}{2}$ and $\cot x = -1$; find the general formula for x.

85. Inverse trigonometric functions. The value of a trigonometric function of an angle depends on the value of the angle; and, conversely, the value of an angle depends on the value of the function. If the angle is given, the sine of the angle can be found;

if the sine is given, the angle can be expressed (Art. 84). It is often convenient to represent an angle by the value of one of its functions. Thus, instead of saying that *an angle is 30°*, we may say (what amounts to the same thing) that *it is the least positive angle whose sine is* $\frac{1}{2}$. That is, we may speak of "the angle whose sine is y," "the angle whose tangent is y," etc. These expressions are replaced by

$$\text{arc sin } y, \quad \text{arc tan } y, \quad \text{etc.,}$$

and they are called *inverse trigonometric functions.*

The equations

$$(1) \qquad y = \sin x, \quad y = \tan x, \quad y = \cos x, \quad \text{etc.,}$$

may also be written

$$(2) \quad x = \text{arc sin } y, \quad x = \text{arc tan } y, \quad x = \text{arc cos } y, \quad \text{etc.}$$

The right-hand members in (2) are read "arc sine y," "arc tangent y," "arc cosine y," etc. In (2), x is an inverse trigonometric function of y. In (1), to a given value of x will correspond one and only one value of y. But in (2), to a given value of y will correspond different values of x unlimited in number, as was shown in Art. 84. Hence

The trigonometric functions are single valued, and the inverse trigonometric functions are many valued.

Definition. *The principal value of an inverse trigonometric function is its smallest numerical value, preference being given to the positive value for the arc cosine and arc secant.*

Examples are

arc sin $\frac{1}{2}$,   principal value 30° ;

arc tan (-1),   principal value $-45°$;

arc cos $(-\frac{1}{2})$,   principal value 120°.

All possible values of an inverse trigonometric function may be expressed by using the principal value and (4) to (6), Art. 84. Thus for

arc sin x, all values are given by $x = n\pi + (-1)^n x_0$,

arc tan x, all values are given by $x = n\pi + x_0$,

arc sec x, all values are given by $x = 2\,n\pi \pm x_0$,

the principal value in each case being x_0.

Since the sine and cosine of an angle cannot be less than -1 nor greater than $+1$, it follows that the expressions

$$\text{arc sin } a \quad \text{and} \quad \text{arc cos } a$$

have no meaning unless a lies between -1 and $+1$ inclusive. Similarly, it is evident that the expressions

$$\text{arc sec } a \quad \text{and} \quad \text{arc csc } a$$

have no meaning for values of a lying between -1 and $+1$.

Equations (2) are sometimes written

(3) $\qquad x = \sin^{-1} y, \quad x = \tan^{-1} y, \quad x = \cos^{-1} y,$

and the right-hand members are read "inverse sine y," "inverse tangent y," "inverse cosine y." The -1 is not an exponent but a part of the symbol. In Example 3, p. 194, and some of the problems that follow, this notation is used.

We shall now show how to prove identities involving inverse trigonometric functions for the principal values of the angles.

EXAMPLE 1. Prove the identity

(a) $\qquad\qquad \text{arc tan } m + \text{arc tan } n = \text{arc tan } \dfrac{m+n}{1-mn}.$

Proof. Let

(b) $\qquad\qquad A = \text{arc tan } m \quad \text{and} \qquad B = \text{arc tan } n.$

(c) Then $\quad \tan A = m \qquad \text{and} \quad \tan B = n.$

Substituting from (b) in the first member of (a), we get

$$A + B = \text{arc tan } \frac{m+n}{1-mn},$$

or, what amounts to the same thing,

(d) $\qquad\qquad \tan (A+B) = \dfrac{m+n}{1-mn}.$

But, from Art. 75,

(e) $\qquad\qquad \tan (A+B) = \dfrac{\tan A + \tan B}{1 - \tan A \tan B}.$

Substituting from (c) in the second member of (e), we get

(f) $\qquad\qquad \tan (A+B) = \dfrac{m+n}{1-mn}.$

Since (d) and (f) are identical, we have proved (a) to be true.

EXAMPLE 2. Prove that

(a) $\qquad\qquad \text{arc sin } \frac{3}{5} + \text{arc cos } \frac{15}{17} = \text{arc sin } \frac{77}{85}.$

Proof. Let

(b) $\qquad A = \text{arc sin } \frac{3}{5} \quad \text{and} \qquad B = \text{arc cos } \frac{15}{17}.$

(c) Then $\sin A = \frac{3}{5} \qquad \text{and} \quad \cos B = \frac{15}{17}.$

(d) Also $\cos A = \frac{4}{5} \qquad \text{and} \quad \sin B = \frac{8}{17}.$ $\qquad$ Art. 15

Substituting from (*b*) in the first member of (*a*), we get

$$A + B = \text{arc sin } \tfrac{77}{85},$$

or, what amounts to the same thing,

(*e*) $$\sin (A + B) = \tfrac{77}{85}.$$

But, from Art. 73,

(*f*) $$\sin (A + B) = \sin A \cos B + \cos A \sin B.$$

Substituting from (*c*) and (*d*) in the second member of (*f*), we get

(*g*) $$\sin (A + B) = \tfrac{3}{5} \cdot \tfrac{15}{17} + \tfrac{4}{5} \cdot \tfrac{8}{17} = \tfrac{77}{85}.$$

Since (*e*) and (*g*) are identical, we have proved (*a*) to be true.

The following example illustrates how some equations involving inverse trigonometric functions may be solved.

EXAMPLE 3. Solve the following equation for x:

$$\tan^{-1} 2\, x + \tan^{-1} 3\, x = \frac{\pi}{4}.$$

Solution. Take the tangent of both sides of the equation. Thus,

$$\tan (\tan^{-1} 2\, x + \tan^{-1} 3\, x) = \tan \frac{\pi}{4},$$

or, $$\frac{\tan (\tan^{-1} 2\, x) + \tan (\tan^{-1} 3\, x)}{1 - \tan (\tan^{-1} 2\, x) \tan (\tan^{-1} 3\, x)} = 1, \qquad \text{from Art. 75}$$

or, $$\frac{2\, x + 3\, x}{1 - 2\, x \cdot 3\, x} = 1.$$

Clearing of fractions and solving for x, we get

$$x = \tfrac{1}{6} \quad \text{or} \quad -1.$$

$x = \tfrac{1}{6}$ satisfies the equation for the principal values of $\tan^{-1} 2\, x$ and $\tan^{-1} 3\, x$. $x = -1$ satisfies the equation for the values

$$\tan^{-1} (-2) = 116.57°,$$
$$\tan^{-1} (-3) = -71.57°.$$

PROBLEMS

Write (in radians) general formulas for the values of the following functions:

1. $\text{arc sin } \dfrac{1}{\sqrt{2}}.$ *Ans.* $n\pi + (-1)^n \dfrac{\pi}{4}.$ 2. $\text{arc sin } \left(-\dfrac{\sqrt{3}}{2}\right).$

3. $\text{arc cos } \dfrac{\sqrt{3}}{2}.$ *Ans.* $2\, n\pi \pm \dfrac{\pi}{6}.$ 4. $\cos^{-1} \left(-\dfrac{1}{2}\right).$

5. $\text{arc tan } \dfrac{1}{\sqrt{3}}.$ *Ans.* $n\pi + \dfrac{\pi}{6}.$ 6. $\text{arc tan } (\pm \sqrt{3}).$

7. $\cot^{-1} (\pm 1).$ *Ans.* $n\pi \pm \dfrac{\pi}{4}.$ 8. $\text{arc cot } \left(\dfrac{1}{\sqrt{3}}\right).$

Prove the following:

9. $\arctan a - \arctan b = \arctan \dfrac{a-b}{1+ab}$.

10. $2\tan^{-1} a = \sin^{-1} \dfrac{2a}{1+a^2}$.

11. $2\arcsin a = \arccos(1 - 2a^2)$.

12. $\arctan a = \arcsin \dfrac{a}{\sqrt{1+a^2}}$.

13. $\tan^{-1} \dfrac{m}{n} - \tan^{-1} \dfrac{m-n}{m+n} = \dfrac{\pi}{4}$.

14. $\arccos \frac{4}{5} + \arctan \frac{3}{5} = \arctan \frac{27}{11}$.

15. $2\tan^{-1} \frac{2}{3} = \tan^{-1} \frac{12}{5}$.

16. $2\arctan a = \arctan \dfrac{2a}{1-a^2}$.

17. $\arcsin a = \arccos \sqrt{1-a^2}$.

18. $\sin^{-1} a = \tan^{-1} \dfrac{a}{\sqrt{1-a^2}}$.

19. $\arctan a = \arccos \dfrac{1}{\sqrt{1+a^2}}$.

20. $\sin^{-1} \frac{3}{5} + \sin^{-1} \frac{8}{17} = \sin^{-1} \frac{77}{85}$.

21. $\arccos \frac{4}{5} + \arccos \frac{12}{13} = \arccos \frac{33}{65}$.

22. $\arctan \frac{1}{7} + \arctan \frac{1}{13} = \arctan \frac{2}{9}$.

Solve the following equations:

23. $\tan^{-1} x + \tan^{-1}(1-x) = \tan^{-1}(\frac{4}{3})$.   *Ans.* $x = \frac{1}{2}$.

24. $\arctan x + 2\operatorname{arc cot} x = \dfrac{2\pi}{3}$.

25. $\tan^{-1} \dfrac{x-1}{x+2} + \tan^{-1} \dfrac{x+1}{x+2} = \dfrac{\pi}{4}$.   *Ans.* $x = \pm \dfrac{\sqrt{10}}{2}$.

26. $\cos^{-1} \dfrac{x^2-1}{x^2+1} + \tan^{-1} \dfrac{2x}{x^2-1} = \dfrac{2\pi}{3}$.

27. $\arctan \dfrac{x+1}{x-1} + \arctan \dfrac{x-1}{x} = \arctan(-7)$.   *Ans.* $x = 2$.

28. $\tan^{-1}(x+1) + \tan^{-1}(x-1) = \tan^{-1} \frac{8}{31}$.

29. $\sin^{-1} x + \sin^{-1} 2x = \dfrac{\pi}{3}$.   *Ans.* $x = \pm \dfrac{\sqrt{21}}{14}$.

30. $\arcsin \dfrac{5}{x} + \arcsin \dfrac{12}{x} = \dfrac{\pi}{2}$.

Find the values of the following:

31. $\sin(\tan^{-1} \frac{5}{12})$.   *Ans.* $\pm \frac{5}{13}$.   32. $\cot(2\arcsin \frac{3}{5})$.

33. $\sin\left(\tan^{-1} \dfrac{1}{2} + \tan^{-1} \dfrac{1}{3}\right)$.   *Ans.* $\pm \dfrac{1}{\sqrt{2}}$.   34. $\cos(2\arccos a)$.

35. $\tan(2\tan^{-1} a)$.   *Ans.* $\dfrac{2a}{1-a^2}$.   36. $\cos(2\arctan a)$.

CHAPTER VII

ACUTE ANGLES NEAR 0° OR 90°

86. The following statement will now be proved:

Theorem. *When the angle x approaches zero as a limit, each of the ratios* $\dfrac{\sin x}{x}$, $\dfrac{\tan x}{x}$, *approaches unity as a limit, x being the circular measure of the angle.*

Proof. Let O be the center of a circle whose radius is unity. Let arc $AP = x$, and let arc $AP' = x$ in numerical value. Draw PP', and let PT and $P'T$ be the tangents drawn to the circle at P and P'. From geometry,

(A) $\qquad\qquad PQP' < PAP' < PTP'.$

But $\quad PQP' = PQ + QP' = 2 \sin x$ in numerical value,

$\qquad PAP' = PA + AP' = 2\,x$ in numerical value,

and $\qquad PTP' = PT + TP' = 2 \tan x$ in numerical value.

Substituting in (A),

$\qquad 2 \sin x < 2\,x < 2 \tan x.$

Dividing through by 2, we have

(B) $\quad \sin x < x < \tan x,$

which proves that

If x be the circular measure of an acute angle, it will always lie between sin x and tan x, being greater than sin x and less than tan x.

Dividing (B) through by $\sin x$, we get

$$1 < \frac{x}{\sin x} < \frac{1}{\cos x}.$$

Or also, using the reciprocal values,

$$1 > \frac{\sin x}{x} > \cos x.$$

196

If we now let x approach zero as a limit, it is seen that the value of

$$\frac{\sin x}{x}$$

lies between the constant 1 and the limiting value of $\cos x$, which is also 1, since $\cos 0 = 1$.

Hence the ratio of $\sin x$ to x approaches unity as a limit when x approaches zero as a limit.

Similarly, if we divide (B) through by $\tan x$, we get

$$\cos x < \frac{x}{\tan x} < 1.$$

As before, if x approaches zero as a limit, the ratio of $\tan x$ to x will approach unity as a limit.

The limits in the theorem just proved are of great importance in both pure and applied mathematics. These results may be stated as follows:

When x is the circular measure of a very small angle, we may replace $\sin x$ and $\tan x$ in approximate calculations by x.

87. Functions of positive acute angles near 0° and 90°. Up to this point we have assumed that the differences in the trigonometric functions are proportional to the differences in the corresponding angles. While this assumption is not strictly true, it is in general sufficiently exact for most practical purposes unless the angles are very near 0° or 90°. In using logarithms we have also assumed that the differences in the logarithms of the trigonometric functions are proportional to the differences in the corresponding angles. This will give results sufficiently accurate for most purposes if we use Tables II or III of the authors' *Four-Place Tables** and confine ourselves to angles between 18′ and 89° 42′ inclusive. If, however, we have an angle between 0° and 18′ or an angle between 89° 42′ and 90°, and are looking for exact results, it is evident that the ordinary method will not do. For example, the tabular difference (Table II) between the logarithmic sine, tangent, or cotangent of 8′ and the logarithm of the corresponding functions of 9′ is 512, while between 9′ and 10′ it is 457. If we interpolate here in the usual way it is evident that our results will be inaccurate.

* Published by Ginn and Company.

To obtain more accurate results, we may use the principle established in the last section, namely:

We may replace sin x and tan x in our calculations by x when x is a very small angle and is expressed in circular measure.

For example, from Table IV giving the natural functions of angles, we have

$$\sin 2° \; 12' = 0.0384,$$

$$\tan 2° \; 12' = 0.0384.$$

Also, $$2° \; 12'(= 2.2°) = 0.0384 \text{ radian.}$$

Thus in any calculation we may replace the sine or tangent of any angle between $0°$ and $2° \; 12'$ by the circular measure of the angle without changing the first four significant figures of the result. Also, since

$$\cos 87° \; 48' = \sin (90° - 87° \; 48') = \sin 2° \; 12' = 0.0384,$$

and

$$\cot 87° \; 48' = \tan (90° - 87° \; 48') = \tan 2° \; 12' = 0.0384,$$

we may replace the cosine or cotangent of any angle between $87° \; 48'$ and $90°$ by the circular measure of the complement of that angle. We may then state the rules of Arts. 88 and 89.

88. Rule for finding the functions of acute angles near 0°.

$$\sin x = circular \; measure \; of \; x,*$$

$$\tan x = circular \; measure \; of \; x,$$

$$\cot x = \frac{1}{circular \; measure \; of \; x},$$

cos x is found from the tables in the usual way.†

* The following equivalents may be used for reducing an angle to circular measure (radians), and in other computations.

$$1° = \frac{\pi}{180} \text{ radian.}$$

$$1° = 0.0174533 \text{ radian.}$$
$$1' = 0.0002909 \text{ radian.}$$
$$1'' = 0.00000485 \text{ radian.}$$

$$\frac{180°}{\pi} = 57.29578° = 1 \text{ radian.}$$

$$\pi = 3.14159$$
$$= \tfrac{22}{7} \text{ approximately.}$$

$$\log 0.0174533 = 8.2419 - 10.$$
$$\log 0.0002909 = 6.4637 - 10.$$
$$\log 0.00000485 = 4.6857 - 10.$$

$$\log 57.29578 = 1.7581.$$

$$\log \pi = 0.4971.$$

† csc x and sec x are simply the reciprocals of sin x and cos x respectively.

89. Rule for finding the functions of acute angles near 90°.

cos x = circular measure of the complement of x,*

cot x = circular measure of the complement of x,

$$tan\ x = \frac{1}{circular\ measure\ of\ the\ complement\ of\ x},$$

sin x is found from the tables in the usual way.†

Since any function of an angle of any magnitude whatever, positive or negative, equals numerically some function of a positive acute angle, it is evident that the above rules, together with those of Art. 29, will suffice for finding the functions of angles near $\pm 90°$, $\pm 180°$, $\pm 270°$, $\pm 360°$.

EXAMPLE 1. Find sine, tangent, and cotangent of 42'.

Solution. Reducing the angle to radians,

$$42' = 42 \times 0.0002909\ radian = 0.01222\ radian.$$

Therefore $\sin 42' = 0.01222,$

$\tan 42' = 0.01222,$

$$\cot 42' = \frac{1}{0.01222} = 81.83.\ \textit{Ans.}$$

EXAMPLE 2. Find cosine, cotangent, and tangent of 89° 34.6'.

Solution. The complement of our angle is $90° - 89° 34.6' = 25.4'$. Reducing this remainder to radians,

$$25.4' = 25.4 \times 0.0002909\ radian = 0.00739\ radian.$$

Therefore $\cos 89° 34.6' = 0.00739,$

$\cot 89° 34.6' = 0.00739,$

$$\tan 89° 34.6' = \frac{1}{0.00739} = 135.3.\ \textit{Ans.}$$

When the function of a positive acute angle near 0° or 90° is given, to find the angle itself we reverse the process illustrated above. For instance:

EXAMPLE 3. Find the angle subtended by a man 6 ft. tall at a distance of 1225 ft.

Solution. From the figure,

$$\tan x = \tfrac{6}{1225}.$$

---

* If the angle is given in degrees, subtract it from 90° and reduce the remainder to circular measure (radians). If the angle is given in circular measure (radians), simply subtract it from $\frac{\pi}{2}$ (= 1.57079).

† csc x and sec x are simply the reciprocals of sin x and cos x respectively.

But, since the angle is very small, we may replace tan x by x, giving

$$x = \tfrac{6}{1225} \text{ radian} = 0.0049 \text{ radian.}$$

Or, reducing the angle to minutes of arc, we get

$$x = \frac{0.0049}{0.0002909} \text{ minutes of arc} = 16.8'. \quad Ans.$$

90. Rules for finding the logarithms of the functions of angles near 0° and 90°.* For use in logarithmic computations the rules which were given in the last two sections may be put in the form shown below.

First, we note that

If the angle is given in degrees, minutes, and seconds, it should first be reduced to degrees and the decimal part of a degree (see Conversion Table on page 17 of tables).

Rule I. To find the logarithms of the functions of an angle near 0°.

$$log \ sin \ x° = \bar{2}.2419 + log \ x.†$$
$$log \ tan \ x° = \bar{2}.2419 + log \ x.$$
$$log \ cot \ x° = 1.7581 - log \ x.‡$$

log cos $x°$ is found from the tables in the usual way.

Rule II. To find the logarithms of the functions of an angle near 90°.

$$log \ cos \ x° = \bar{2}.2419 + log \ (90 - x).$$
$$log \ cot \ x° = \bar{2}.2419 + log \ (90 - x).$$
$$log \ tan \ x° = 1.7581 - log \ (90 - x).$$

log sin $x°$ is found from the tables in the usual way.

---

* These rules will give results accurate to four decimal places for all angles between 0° and 1.1° and between 88.9° and 90°.

† Since 1 degree = 0.017453 radian, the circular measure of

$$x \text{ degrees} = 0.017453 \cdot x \text{ radians.}$$

Hence, from page 198, $\quad sin \ x° = 0.017453 \cdot x,$

and $\quad\quad log \ sin \ x° = log \ 0.017453 + log \ x$
$$= \bar{2}.2419 + log \ x.$$

From page 198, $\quad\quad cot \ x° = \dfrac{1}{0.017453 \cdot x},$

and $\quad\quad log \ cot \ x° = - \ log \ 0.017453 - log \ x$
$$= 1.7581 - log \ x.$$

EXAMPLE 1. Find log tan 0.045°.

Solution. As is indicated in our logarithmic tables, ordinary interpolation will not give accurate results in this case. But from the above rule,

$$\log \tan 0.045° = \overline{2}.2419 + \log 0.045$$
$$= \overline{2}.2419 + \overline{2}.6532.$$
$$\therefore \log \tan 0.045° = \overline{4}.8951. \ Ans.$$

On consulting a much larger table of logarithms, this result is found to be exact to four decimal places. Interpolating in the ordinary way, we get

$$\log \tan 0.045° = \overline{4}.8924,$$

which is correct to only two decimal places.

EXAMPLE 2. Find log tan 89.935°.

Solution. From the above rule,

$$\log \tan 89.935° = 1.7581 - \log (90 - 89.935)$$
$$= 1.7581 - \log 0.065$$
$$= 1.7581 - \overline{2}.8129.$$
$$\therefore \log \tan 89.935° = 2.9452. \ Ans.$$

If the tangent itself is desired, we look up the number in Table I corresponding to this logarithm. This gives

$$\tan 89.935° = 881.4.$$

PROBLEMS

1. The inclination of a railway to the horizontal is 40′. How many feet does it rise in a mile?   *Ans.* 61.43.

2. Given that the moon's distance from the earth is 238,885 mi. and subtends an angle of 31′ 8″ at the earth. Find the diameter of the moon in miles.

3. Given that the sun's distance from the earth is 92,000,000 mi. and subtends an angle of 32′ 4″ at the earth. Find the sun's diameter.
Ans. 858,200 mi.

4. Given that the earth's radius is 3963 mi. and subtends an angle of 57′ 2″ at the moon. Find the distance of the moon from the earth.

5. Given that the radius of the earth is 3963 mi. and subtends an angle of 9″ at the sun. Find the distance of the sun from the earth.
Ans. 90,840,000 mi.

6. Assuming that the sun subtends an angle of 32′ 4″ at the earth, how far from the eye must a dime be held so as to just hide the sun, the diameter of a dime being $\frac{5}{7}$ of an inch?

7. Find the angle subtended by a circular target 5 ft. in diameter at the distance of half a mile.   *Ans.* 6′ 30.6″.

8. Piccard in his balloon reached an altitude of 54,776 ft. Taking the radius of the earth as 3963 mi., find the distance from the balloon to the horizon if the ocean were observed from this altitude.

MISCELLANEOUS PROBLEMS

1. An airplane starts from a station and rises at an angle of 8° 40′ with the horizontal. By how many feet will it clear a vertical wall 110 ft. high and 1000 ft. from the station?   *Ans.* 42.4 ft.

2. An airplane flying at an average speed of 80 mi. an hour rises at an angle of 10° 22′. How high does it rise in 1 min.?

3. From the top of a lighthouse 122.6 ft. high, the angles of depression of two boats in line with the base of the lighthouse are 19° 40′ and 8° 30′ respectively. Find the distance between the boats.   *Ans.* 477.3 ft.

4. From the top of a cliff the angles of depression of the top and of the bottom of a lighthouse 97.25 ft. high are observed to be 23° 17′ and 24° 19′ respectively. How much higher is the cliff than the lighthouse?   *Ans.* 1947 ft.

5. One side of a triangle is 42.32 ft. long and the angles adjacent to this side are 67° 14′ and 38° 24′ respectively. Find the altitude of the triangle upon the given side.   *Ans.* 25.16 ft.

6. In order to find the width of a river, a base line AB is measured along one bank and found to be 326.5 ft. long. An object is located at P on the opposite bank and the angles PAB and PBA are observed to be 121° 14′ and 43° 28′ respectively. Find the width of the river.

7. A balloon is observed simultaneously from two points on the same horizontal level. From one point the balloon is due east and its angle of elevation is 78° 13′; from the other point the balloon is due west and its angle of elevation is 66° 5′. If the two points are 1052 ft. apart, how high is the balloon?   *Ans.* 1613.3 ft.

8. A railroad bridge is 475 ft. long. From one end of the bridge the angle of depression of a rock directly below the bridge is 36° 48′ and from the other end the angle of depression of the rock is 21° 42′. How high above the rock is the bridge?

9. If, in Problem 8, the angles of depression are denoted by α and β respectively, the length of the bridge by l, and the required height by h, show that the height is given by the formula $h = \dfrac{l \sin \alpha \sin \beta}{\sin (\alpha + \beta)}$.

10. If a balloon is due west from two points of observation, and the distance between the two points is denoted by d, the angles of elevation by α and β respectively (α being the greater angle), and the required height by h, show that the height of the balloon is given by the formula

$$h = \frac{d \sin \alpha \sin \beta}{\sin (\alpha - \beta)}.$$

11. A tower stands on a horizontal plane. An observer walking directly toward it finds at one point the angle of elevation of its top to be 10° 22′. After walking 415 ft., the angle of elevation of its top is 15° 16′. How far was he from the base of the tower at each point of observation?

Ans. 1262.4 ft., 847.4 ft.

12. Find the height of the tower in Problem 11.

13. In a parallelogram two sides are 24.6 ft. and 73.8 ft. long respectively, and form an angle of 67° 14′. Find the length of the longer diagonal.

Ans. 86.36 ft.

14. The diagonals of a parallelogram are 420 ft. and 580 ft. long respectively, and form an angle of 47° 24′. Find the length of the longer side of the parallelogram.

15. The sides of a triangle are to each other as $5 : 6 : 9$. Find the largest angle of the triangle.

Hint. Use a property of similar triangles and apply the law of cosines.

Ans. 109° 28′.

16. The angles of a triangle are to each other as $3 : 4 : 6$, and the longest side is 42 ft. long. Find the length of the shortest side.

17. Two vessels start from the same point at the same time. One sails in the direction 20° 14′ west of north at the rate of 21 mi. an hour; the other sails in the direction 38° 42′ east of north at the rate of 14.5 mi. an hour. Find how far apart the vessels are at the end of 2 hr. What is the direction of the slower vessel from the faster?

Ans. 36.71 mi., 62° 49′ east of south.

18. Two forces act on a body, one of 625 lb. and the other of 845 lb., and make an angle of 38° 42′ with each other. Find the magnitude of the resultant and the angle which it makes with the smaller force. (See Example 2, p. 93.)

19. A straight path leading to a monument is inclined 13° to the horizontal. At a point on the path 310 ft. from the base of the monument the monument subtends an angle of 15°. How high is the monument?

Ans. 90.88 ft.

20. A tower 130 ft. high stands on top of an embankment which is inclined 18° to the horizontal. An observer on top of the tower finds the angle of depression of an object directly down the embankment from the base of the tower to be 47°. Find the distance from the object to the base of the tower.

21. Two motor boats start from the same dock at the same time. One travels in the direction 78° east of south at 30 mi. an hour. In what direction must the other travel at 40 mi. an hour in order to be due north from the first?   *Ans.* 47° 11′ east of north.

22. The dock B is 1 mi. due east from the dock A. One motor boat starts from B in the direction 40° east of north and travels at the rate of 30 mi. an hour. One minute later, a second motor boat starts from A and overtakes the first in 5 min. At what rate and in what direction does the second motor boat travel?

23. Find the radius of a circle inscribed in a triangle the lengths of whose sides are 14.5 ft., 18.6 ft., and 25.6 ft.   *Ans.* 4.517 ft.

24. The area of a triangle ABC is 420.5 sq. ft. $BC = 60.5$ ft., and angle $ABC = 40° 36′$. Find the length of AB.

25. Show that for any triangle

$$\sin A = 2 \sin \frac{A}{2} \cos \frac{A}{2} = \frac{2}{bc} \sqrt{s(s-a)(s-b)(s-c)}.$$

26. Show that the radius, R, of a circle circumscribed about a triangle is given by the formula

$$R = \frac{abc}{4\sqrt{s(s-a)(s-b)(s-c)}}.$$ (See Art. 42, p. 85.)

27. The sides of a triangle are 21.2 ft., 32.3 ft., and 40.8 ft. long. Find the radius of the circumscribed circle.   *Ans.* 20.56 ft.

28. If R and r denote the radii of the circumscribed and inscribed circles respectively, prove that for any triangle $abcr = 4\,R(s-a)(s-b)(s-c)$.

29. Find the ratio of the radius of the inscribed circle to the radius of the circumscribed circle for the triangle whose sides are 24.7 ft., 31.9 ft., and 43.8 ft. long.   *Ans.* $r \div R = 0.3462$.

30. A and B are the centers of two circles whose radii are 7 in. and 5 in. respectively. The line of centers AB is 20 in. long. A circle whose center is at C touches the other two circles, and its radius is 8 in. Find the distance CD from C to AB and the distance AD. (This problem presents itself in computations concerning gears.)

31. A torpedo boat is 10 mi. S.W. from a harbor. A vessel sails from the harbor at the rate of 12 mi. an hour in the direction S. 80° E. In what direction and at what rate must the torpedo boat proceed in order to overtake the vessel in $1\frac{1}{2}$ hr.? *Ans.* E. 9° 2′ N.; 16.74 mi. per hour.

32. The angle of elevation of a rock is observed to be 47° 12′. After walking 1000 ft. toward the rock up a slope of 32°, the observer finds the angle of elevation of the rock to be 77° 32′. Find the height of the rock above the level of the first point of observation.

33. A person goes 120 yd. up a slope of 16° from the edge of a river, and observes the angle of depression of an object on the opposite bank to be 6° 30′. Find the width of the river. *Ans.* 174.95 yd.

34. The angle of elevation of a tower at a point due south of it is α, and at another point due west from the first point and at a distance d from the first point, the angle of elevation is β. Prove that the height, h, of the tower is given by the formula

$$h = \frac{d}{\sqrt{\cot^2 \beta - \cot^2 \alpha}} \quad \text{or by} \quad h = \frac{d \sin \alpha \sin \beta}{\sqrt{\sin (\alpha - \beta) \sin (\alpha + \beta)}}.$$

35. The angle of elevation of the top of an inaccessible tower situated on a horizontal plane is 63° 26′. At a point 500 ft. farther from the base of the tower the elevation of its top is 32° 14′. Find the height of the tower. *Ans.* 460.5 ft.

36. At a point 2.5 mi. from one end of a lake and 3.8 mi. from the other end the length of the lake subtends an angle of 110°. Find the length of the lake.

37. The sides of a triangle are $AB = 17.32$ ft., $BC = 12.96$ ft., and $AC = 21.43$ ft. How far from A on AC is the center of a circle which passes through B and C? *Ans.* 10.43 ft.

38. The angle of elevation of the top of a tower which stands on a horizontal plane is twice as large when observed at a point 100 ft. from its base as when observed at a point 300 ft. from its base. How high is the tower?

39. Two beach lights are due east from a dock at distances of 100 yd. and 600 yd. An observer on a boat due south from the dock finds at one point that the difference in the directions of the lights is 45°. After proceeding directly toward the dock for a certain distance, he again finds the difference in the directions of the lights to be 45°. Find the distance between the two points of observation. *Ans.* 100 yd.

40. The angle of elevation of an inaccessible tower situated on a horizontal plane is 63° 26′; at a point 500 ft. farther from the base of the tower the elevation of its top is 32° 14′. Find the height of the tower.

41. Two inaccessible points, A and B, are visible from D, but no other point can be found from which both are visible. Take some point C, from which A and D can be seen, and measure CD, 200 ft.; ADC, 89°; ACD, 50° 30′. Then take some point E, from which D and B are visible, and measure DE, 200 ft.; BDE, 54° 30′; BED, 88° 30′. At D measure ADB, 72° 30′. Compute the distance AB.   *Ans.* 345.4 ft.

42. To compute the horizontal distance between two inaccessible points, A and B, when no point can be found from which both can be seen. Take two points, C and D, distant 200 yd., so that A can be seen from C, and B from D. From C measure CF, 200 yd. to F, from which A can be seen; and from D measure DE, 200 yd. to E, from which B can be seen. Measure AFC, 83°; ACD, 53° 30′; ACF, 54° 31′; BDE, 54° 30′; BDC, 156° 25′; DEB, 88° 30′.

43. A tower is situated on the bank of a river. From the opposite bank the angle of elevation of the tower is 60° 13′, and from a point 40 ft. more distant the elevation is 50° 19′. Find the breadth of the river. *Ans.* 88.9 ft.

44. At a distance of 40 ft. from the foot of a tower on an inclined plane the tower subtends an angle of 41° 19′; at a point 60 ft. farther away the angle subtended by the tower is 23° 45′. Find the height of the tower.

45. A tower makes an angle of 113° 12′ with the inclined plane on which it stands; and at a distance of 89 ft. from its base, measured down the plane, the angle subtended by the tower is 23° 27′. Find the height of the tower.   *Ans.* 51.6 ft.

46. From the top of a hill the angles of depression of two objects situated in the horizontal plane of the base of the hill are 45° and 30°; and the horizontal angle between the two objects is 30°. Show that the height of the hill is equal to the distance between the objects.

47. I observe the angular elevation of the summits of two spires which appear in a straight line to be α, and the angular depressions of their reflections in still water to be β and γ. If the height of my eye above the level of the water is c, then the horizontal distance between the spires is

$$\frac{2\,c\cos^2\alpha\sin(\beta-\gamma)}{\sin(\beta-\alpha)\sin(\gamma-\alpha)}.$$

48. The angular elevation of a tower due south at a place A is 30°, and at a place B, due west of A and at a distance a from it, the elevation is 18°. Show that the height of the tower is $\dfrac{a}{\sqrt{2\sqrt{5}+2}}$.

49. A boy standing c feet behind and opposite the middle of a football goal sees that the angle of elevation of the nearer crossbar is A and the angle of elevation of the farther one is B. Show that the length of the field is $c(\tan A \cot B - 1)$ feet.

50. Prove that in any triangle

$$\frac{a+b}{c} = \frac{\cos \frac{1}{2}(A-B)}{\sin \frac{1}{2}C}.$$

51. Prove that in any triangle

$$\frac{a-b}{c} = \frac{\sin \frac{1}{2}(A-B)}{\cos \frac{1}{2}C}.$$

52. Derive the law of tangents using the formulas of Problem 50 and Problem 51.

53. From a point on a hillside of constant elevation the angle of inclination of the top of an obelisk on its summit is observed to be α, and a feet nearer to the top of the hill to be β. Show that if h is the height of the obelisk, the inclination of the hill to the horizon is

$$\text{arc cos} \left\{ \frac{a \sin \alpha \sin \beta}{h \sin (\beta - \alpha)} \right\}.$$

CHAPTER VIII

RECAPITULATION OF FORMULAS

PLANE TRIGONOMETRY

Right triangles, Arts. 4 and 37.

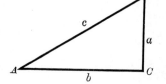

(1) $\sin A = \dfrac{a}{c}$.

(4) $\csc A = \dfrac{c}{a}$.

(2) $\cos A = \dfrac{b}{c}$.

(5) $\sec A = \dfrac{c}{b}$.

(3) $\tan A = \dfrac{a}{b}$.

(6) $\cot A = \dfrac{b}{a}$.

(38) Side opposite an acute angle
$$= \text{hypotenuse} \times \text{sine of the angle.}$$

(39) Side adjacent to an acute angle
$$= \text{hypotenuse} \times \text{cosine of the angle.}$$

(40) Side opposite an acute angle
$$= \text{adjacent side} \times \text{tangent of the angle.}$$

Fundamental relations between the functions, Art. 17.

(13) $\sin A = \dfrac{1}{\csc A}$, $\qquad \csc A = \dfrac{1}{\sin A}$.

(14) $\cos A = \dfrac{1}{\sec A}$, $\qquad \sec A = \dfrac{1}{\cos A}$.

(15) $\tan A = \dfrac{1}{\cot A}$, $\qquad \cot A = \dfrac{1}{\tan A}$.

(16) $\tan A = \dfrac{\sin A}{\cos A}$. $\qquad$ (17) $\cot A = \dfrac{\cos A}{\sin A}$.

(18) $\sin^2 A + \cos^2 A = 1$.

(19) $\sec^2 A = 1 + \tan^2 A$. $\qquad$ (20) $\csc^2 A = 1 + \cot^2 A$.

Law of sines, Art. 42.

(43) $$\dfrac{a}{\sin A} = \dfrac{b}{\sin B} = \dfrac{c}{\sin C}.$$

208

Law of tangents, Art. 44.

(44) $$\frac{a+b}{a-b} = \frac{\tan\frac{1}{2}(A+B)}{\tan\frac{1}{2}(A-B)}.$$

Law of cosines, Art. 45.

(46) $$a^2 = b^2 + c^2 - 2\,bc\cos A.$$

Functions of the half-angles of a triangle in terms of the sides, Art. 46.
$$s = \tfrac{1}{2}(a+b+c).$$

(52) $$\sin\tfrac{1}{2}A = \sqrt{\frac{(s-b)(s-c)}{bc}}.$$

(53) $$\cos\tfrac{1}{2}A = \sqrt{\frac{s(s-a)}{bc}}.$$

(54) $$\tan\tfrac{1}{2}A = \sqrt{\frac{(s-b)(s-c)}{s(s-a)}}.$$

(55) $$r = \sqrt{\frac{(s-a)(s-b)(s-c)}{s}}.$$

(56) $$\tan\tfrac{1}{2}A = \frac{r}{s-a}.$$

(57) $$\tan\tfrac{1}{2}B = \frac{r}{s-b}.$$

(58) $$\tan\tfrac{1}{2}C = \frac{r}{s-c}.$$

Area of a triangle, Art. 47.

(59) $$S = \tfrac{1}{2}\,bc\sin A.$$
(60) $$S = \sqrt{s(s-a)(s-b)(s-c)}.$$

Functions of the sum and of the difference of two angles, Arts. 72–75.

(65) $$\sin(x+y) = \sin x\cos y + \cos x\sin y.$$
(66) $$\sin(x-y) = \sin x\cos y - \cos x\sin y.$$
(67) $$\cos(x+y) = \cos x\cos y - \sin x\sin y.$$
(68) $$\cos(x-y) = \cos x\cos y + \sin x\sin y.$$

(69) $$\tan(x+y) = \frac{\tan x + \tan y}{1 - \tan x\tan y}.$$

(70) $$\tan(x-y) = \frac{\tan x - \tan y}{1 + \tan x\tan y}.$$

$$(71) \qquad \cot (x + y) = \frac{\cot x \cot y - 1}{\cot y + \cot x}.$$

$$(72) \qquad \cot (x - y) = \frac{\cot x \cot y + 1}{\cot y - \cot x}.$$

Functions of twice an angle, Art. 76.

$$(73) \qquad \sin 2x = 2 \sin x \cos x.$$

$$(74) \qquad \cos 2x = \cos^2 x - \sin^2 x.$$

$$(75) \qquad \tan 2x = \frac{2 \tan x}{1 - \tan^2 x}.$$

Functions of an angle in terms of functions of half the angle, Art. 78.

$$(76) \qquad \sin x = 2 \sin \frac{x}{2} \cos \frac{x}{2}.$$

$$(77) \qquad \cos x = \cos^2 \frac{x}{2} - \sin^2 \frac{x}{2}.$$

$$(78) \qquad \tan x = \frac{2 \tan \frac{x}{2}}{1 - \tan^2 \frac{x}{2}}.$$

Functions of half an angle, Art. 79.

$$(79) \quad \sin \frac{x}{2} = \pm \sqrt{\frac{1 - \cos x}{2}}. \qquad (83) \quad \tan \frac{x}{2} = \frac{1 - \cos x}{\sin x}.$$

$$(80) \quad \cos \frac{x}{2} = \pm \sqrt{\frac{1 + \cos x}{2}}. \qquad (84) \quad \cot \frac{x}{2} = \pm \sqrt{\frac{1 + \cos x}{1 - \cos x}}.$$

$$(81) \quad \tan \frac{x}{2} = \pm \sqrt{\frac{1 - \cos x}{1 + \cos x}}. \qquad (85) \quad \cot \frac{x}{2} = \frac{1 + \cos x}{\sin x}.$$

$$(82) \quad \tan \frac{x}{2} = \frac{\sin x}{1 + \cos x}. \qquad (86) \quad \cot \frac{x}{2} = \frac{\sin x}{1 - \cos x}.$$

Sums and differences of functions, Art. 80.

$$(87) \quad \sin A + \sin B = 2 \sin \tfrac{1}{2}(A + B) \cos \tfrac{1}{2}(A - B).$$

$$(88) \quad \sin A - \sin B = 2 \cos \tfrac{1}{2}(A + B) \sin \tfrac{1}{2}(A - B).$$

$$(89) \quad \cos A + \cos B = 2 \cos \tfrac{1}{2}(A + B) \cos \tfrac{1}{2}(A - B).$$

$$(90) \quad \cos A - \cos B = -2 \sin \tfrac{1}{2}(A + B) \sin \tfrac{1}{2}(A - B).$$

SPHERICAL TRIGONOMETRY

CHAPTER I

RIGHT SPHERICAL TRIANGLES

1. Correspondence between the face angles and the diedral angles of a triedral angle and the sides and angles of a spherical triangle. Take any triedral angle $O-A'B'C'$ and let a sphere of any radius, as OA, be described about the vertex O as a center. The

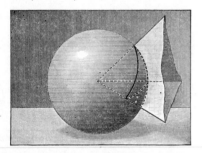 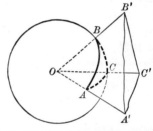

intersections of this sphere with the faces of the triedral angle will be three arcs of great circles of the sphere, forming a spherical triangle, as ABC. The sides (arcs) AB, BC, CA of this triangle measure the face angles $A'OB'$, $B'OC'$, $C'OA'$ of the triedral angle. The angles ABC, BCA, CAB are measured by the plane angles which also measure the diedral angles of the triedral angle; for, by geometry, each is measured by the angle between two straight lines drawn, one in each face, perpendicular to the edge at the same point.

Spherical trigonometry treats of the trigonometric relations between the six elements (three sides and three angles) of a spherical triangle; or, what amounts to the same thing, between the face and diedral angles of the triedral angle which intercepts it, as shown in the figure. Hence we have the

Theorem. *From any property of triedral angles an analogous property of spherical triangles can be inferred, and vice versa.*

211

It is evident that the face and diedral angles of the triedral angle are not altered in magnitude by varying the radius of the sphere; hence the relations between the sides and angles of a spherical triangle are independent of the length of the radius.

The sides of a spherical triangle, being arcs, are usually expressed in degrees.* The length of a side (arc) may be found in terms of any linear unit from the proportion

circumference of great circle : length of arc = 360° : degrees in arc.

A side or an angle of a spherical triangle may have any value from 0° to 360°, but any spherical triangle can always be made to depend on a spherical triangle having each element less than 180°.

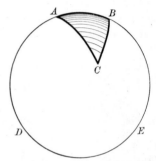

Thus, a triangle such as $ADEBC$ (unshaded portion of hemisphere in figure), which has a side $ADEB$ greater than 180°, need not be considered, for its parts can be immediately found from the parts of the triangle ABC, each of whose sides is less than 180°. For arc $ADEB = 360° -$ arc AB, angle CAD $= 180° -$ angle CAB, etc. Only triangles each of whose elements is less than 180° are considered in this book.

2. Properties of spherical triangles. The proofs of the following properties of spherical triangles may be found in any treatise on spherical geometry :

a. Either side of a spherical triangle is less than the sum of the other two sides.

b. If two sides of a spherical triangle are unequal, the angles opposite them are unequal, and the greater angle lies opposite the greater side, and conversely.

c. The sum of the sides of a spherical triangle is less than 360°.†

d. The sum of the angles of a spherical triangle is greater than 180° and less than 540°.‡

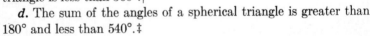

* One of the chief differences between plane trigonometry and spherical trigonometry is that in the former the *sides* of triangles are expressed in linear units, while in the latter *all* the parts are usually expressed in units of arc, that is, degrees, etc.

† In a plane triangle the sum of the sides may have any magnitude.

‡ In a plane triangle the sum of the angles is always equal to 180°.

e. If $A'B'C'$ is the polar triangle * of ABC, then, conversely, ABC is the polar triangle of $A'B'C'$.

f. In two polar triangles each angle of one is the supplement of the side lying opposite to it in the other. Applying this to the last figure, we get

$$A = 180° - a', \quad B = 180° - b', \quad C = 180° - c',$$
$$A' = 180° - a, \quad B' = 180° - b, \quad C' = 180° - c.$$

A spherical triangle which has one or more right angles is called a *right spherical triangle*.

PROBLEMS

Find the sides of the polar triangles of the spherical triangles having the following given angles. Draw a figure in each case.

1. $A = 40°$, $B = 80°$, $C = 110°$.   *Ans.* $a' = 140°$, $b' = 100°$, $c' = 70°$.

2. $A = 52°$, $B = 113°$, $C = 92°$.

3. $A = 70° \ 10'$, $B = 56° \ 20'$, $C = 92° \ 15'$.
$$Ans. \ a' = 109° \ 50', \ b' = 123° \ 40', \ c' = 87° \ 45'.$$

4. $A = 115.6°$, $B = 89.9°$, $C = 72.4°$.

Find the angles of the polar triangles of the spherical triangles having the following given sides:

5. $a = 90°$, $b = 50°$, $c = 100°$.   *Ans.* $A = 90°$, $B = 130°$, $C = 80°$.

6. $a = 74° \ 42'$, $b = 95° \ 6'$, $c = 66° \ 25'$.

7. If each angle of a spherical triangle is a right angle, show that the sides of the triangle are quadrants.

8. Show that if two angles of a spherical triangle are right angles, the sides opposite these angles are quadrants, and the third angle is measured by the opposite side.

9. Find the lengths of the sides of a spherical triangle, if the sides measured in degrees are 60°, 90°, and 150°, when the radius of the sphere is 10 ft.   *Ans.* 10.47 ft., 15.71 ft., 26.18 ft.

10. If the radius of the sphere is 4 ft., find the lengths of the sides of the triangle in Problem 6.

3. Formulas relating to right spherical triangles. From the above Problems 7 and 8, it is evident that the only kind of right spherical triangle that requires further investigation is that which contains *only one* right angle.

---

* The *polar triangle* of any spherical triangle is constructed by describing arcs of great circles about the vertices of the original triangle as poles.

In the figure below let ABC be a right spherical triangle having only one right angle, the center of the sphere being at O. Let C be the right angle, and suppose first that each of the other elements is less than 90°, the radius of the sphere being unity. Pass an auxiliary

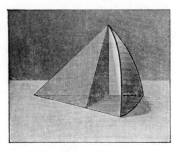
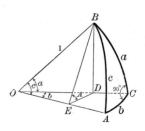

plane through B perpendicular to OA, cutting OA at E and OC at D. Draw BE, BD, and DE. BE and DE are each perpendicular to OA;

[If a straight line is ⊥ to a plane, it is ⊥ to every line in the plane.]

therefore angle BED = angle A. The plane BDE is perpendicular to the plane AOC;

⎡If a straight line is ⊥ to a plane, every plane⎤
⎣passed through the line is ⊥ to the first plane.⎦

hence BD, which is the intersection of the planes BDE and BOC, is perpendicular to the plane AOC,

⎡If two intersecting planes are each ⊥ to a third plane,⎤
⎣their line of intersection is also ⊥ to that plane.⎦

and therefore perpendicular to OC and DE.

In triangle EOD, remembering that angle $EOD = b$, we have

$$\frac{OE}{OD} = \cos b,$$

or, clearing of fractions,

(A) $\qquad\qquad OE = OD \cdot \cos b.$

But $\qquad\qquad OE = \cos c \ (= \cos EOB),$

and $\qquad\qquad OD = \cos a \ (= \cos DOB).$

Substituting in (A), we get

(1) $\qquad\qquad \cos c = \cos a \cos b.$

In triangle BED, remembering that angle BED = angle A, we have

$$\frac{BD}{BE} = \sin A,$$

or, clearing of fractions,

(B) $\qquad\qquad BD = BE \cdot \sin A.$

But $\qquad\qquad BD = \sin a \; (= \sin DOB)$,

and $\qquad\qquad BE = \sin c \; (= \sin EOB)$.

Substituting in (B), we get

(2) $\qquad\qquad \sin a = \sin c \sin A.$

Similarly, if we had passed the auxiliary plane through A perpendicular to OB,

(3) $\qquad\qquad \sin b = \sin c \sin B.$

Again, in the triangle BED,

(C) $\qquad\qquad \cos A = \dfrac{DE}{BE}.$

But $\qquad\qquad DE = OD \sin b$, $\qquad\qquad$ from $\sin b = \dfrac{DE}{OD}$

$\qquad\qquad\qquad OD = \cos a \; (= \cos DOB)$,

and $\qquad\qquad BE = \sin c \; (= \sin EOB)$.

Substituting in (C),

(D) $\qquad\qquad \cos A = \dfrac{OD \sin b}{\sin c} = \cos a \cdot \dfrac{\sin b}{\sin c}.$

But from (3), $\dfrac{\sin b}{\sin c} = \sin B.$ Therefore

(4) $\qquad\qquad \cos A = \cos a \sin B.$

Similarly, if we had passed the auxiliary plane through A perpendicular to OB,

(5) $\qquad\qquad \cos B = \cos b \sin A.$

The above five formulas are fundamental; that is, from them we may derive all other relations expressing any one part of a right spherical triangle in terms of two others. For example, to find a relation between A, b, c, proceed thus:

From (4), $\qquad \cos A = \cos a \sin B$

$$= \frac{\cos c}{\cos b} \cdot \frac{\sin b}{\sin c}$$

$$\left[\text{Since } \cos a = \tfrac{\cos c}{\cos b} \text{ from (1), and } \sin B = \tfrac{\sin b}{\sin c} \text{ from (3).} \right]$$

$$= \frac{\sin b}{\cos b} \cdot \frac{\cos c}{\sin c}.$$

(6) $\qquad\qquad \therefore \cos A = \tan b \cot c.$

Similarly, we may get

(7) $\cos B = \tan a \cot c.$

(8) $\sin b = \tan a \cot A.$

(9) $\sin a = \tan b \cot B.$

(10) $\cos c = \cot A \cot B.$

These ten formulas are sufficient for the solution of right spherical triangles. In deriving these formulas we assumed all the elements except the right angle to be less than 90°. But the formulas hold when this assumption is not made. For instance, let

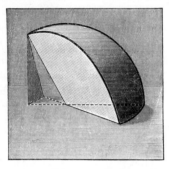 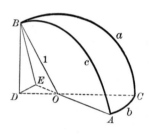

us suppose that a is greater than 90°. In this case the auxiliary plane BDE will cut CO and AO produced beyond the center O, and we have, in the triangle EOD,

$$(E) \quad \cos DOE \ (= \cos b) = \frac{OE}{OD}.$$

But $OE = \cos EOB = -\cos AOB = -\cos c,$

and $OD = \cos DOB = -\cos COB = -\cos a.$

Substituting in (E), we get

$$\cos b = \frac{\cos c}{\cos a}, \text{ or } \cos c = \cos a \cos b,$$

which is the same as (1).

Likewise, the other formulas will hold true in this case. Similarly, they may be shown to hold true in all cases.

If the two sides including the right angle are either both less or both greater than 90° (that is, $\cos a$ and $\cos b$ are either both positive or both negative), then the product

(F) $\cos a \cos b$

will always be positive, and therefore $\cos c$, from (1), will always be positive, that is, c will always be less than 90°. If, however, one of the sides including the right angle is less and the other is greater than 90°, the product (F), and therefore also cos c, will be negative, and c will be greater than 90°.

Hence we have

Theorem I. *If the two sides including the right angle of a right spherical triangle are both less or both greater than 90°, the hypotenuse is less than 90°; if one side is less and the other is greater than 90°, the hypotenuse is greater than 90°.*

From (**4**) and (**5**),

$$\sin B = \frac{\cos A}{\cos a}, \quad \text{and} \quad \sin A = \frac{\cos B}{\cos b}.$$

Since A and B are less than 180°, sin A and sin B must always be positive. But then cos A and cos a must have the same sign, that is, A and a are either both less than 90° or both greater than 90°. Similarly, for B and b. Hence we have

Theorem II. *In a right spherical triangle an oblique angle and the side opposite are either both less or both greater than 90°.*

4. Napier's rules of circular parts. The ten formulas derived in the last article express the relations between the three sides and the two oblique angles of a right spherical triangle. All these relations may be shown to follow from two very useful rules discovered by Baron Napier, the inventor of logarithms.

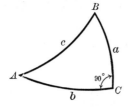 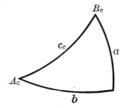

For this purpose the right angle (not entering the formulas) is not taken into account, and we replace the hypotenuse and the two oblique angles by their respective *complements*; so that the five parts, called the *circular parts*, used in Napier's rules are a, b, A_c, c_c, B_c. The subscript c indicates that the complement is to be used. The first figure illustrates the ordinary method of representing a right spherical triangle. To emphasize the circular parts employed in Napier's rules, the same triangle might be represented as shown in the second figure on page 217. It is not necessary, however, to draw the triangle at all when using Napier's rules; in fact, it is found to be more convenient simply to write down the five parts in their proper order as on the circumference of a circle, as shown at the right (hence the name *circular parts*).

$$c_c$$

$$A_c \qquad\qquad B_c$$

$$a \qquad\qquad b$$

Any one of these parts may be called a *middle* part; then the two parts immediately adjacent to it are called *adjacent* parts, and the other two *opposite* parts. Thus, if a is taken as a middle part, A_c and b are the adjacent parts, while c_c and B_c are the opposite parts.

NAPIER'S RULES OF CIRCULAR PARTS

Rule I. *The sine of any middle part is equal to the product of the tangents of the adjacent parts.*

Rule II. *The sine of any middle part is equal to the product of the cosines of the opposite parts.*

These rules are easily remembered if we associate the first one with the expression "*tan-adj.*" and the second one with "*cos-opp.*" *

Napier's rules may easily be verified by applying them in turn to each one of the five circular parts taken as a middle part and comparing the results with (1) to (10).

For example, let c_c be taken as a middle part; then A_c and B_c are the adjacent parts, while a and b are the opposite parts.

Then, by Rule I,

$$\sin c_c = \tan A_c \tan B_c,$$

or, $$\cos c = \cot A \cot B,$$

$$c_c$$

which agrees with (10), p. 216.

By Rule II,

$$A_c \qquad\qquad B_c$$

$$\sin c_c = \cos a \cos b,$$

or, $$\cos c = \cos a \cos b,$$

which agrees with (1), p. 214.

The student should verify Napier's rules in this manner by taking each one of the other four circular parts as the middle part.

---

* Or by noting that a is the first vowel in the words "tangent" and "adjacent," while o is the first vowel in the words "cosine" and "opposite."

Writers on trigonometry differ as to the practical value of Napier's rules. However, it is generally conceded that they are a great aid to the memory in applying formulas (1) to (10) to the solution of right spherical triangles, and we shall so employ them in our work.

5. Solution of right spherical triangles. In order to solve a right spherical triangle, two elements (parts) must be given in addition to the right angle. For the sake of uniformity we shall continue to denote the right angle in a right spherical triangle ABC by the letter C.

General directions for solving right spherical triangles.

c_c		c_c		c_c		$\underline{c_c}$	
A_c	B_c	$\underline{A_c}$	B_c	$\underline{A_c}$	B_c	A_c	$\underline{B_c}$
b	a	$\underline{b}$	$\underline{a}$	$\underline{b}$	$\underline{a}$	$\underline{b}$	a

First step. *Write down the five circular parts as in the first figure above.*

Second step. *Underline the two given parts and the required unknown part. Thus, if A_c and a are given, to find b, we underline all three as is shown in the second figure.*

Third step. *Pick out the middle part (in this case b) and cross the line under it as indicated in the third figure.*

Fourth step. *Use Rule I if the other two parts are adjacent to the middle part (as in the case illustrated), or Rule II if they are opposite, and solve for the unknown part.*

Check. *Check with that rule which involves the three required parts.**

Careful attention must be paid to the algebraic signs of the functions when solving spherical triangles, the cosines, tangents, and cotangents of angles or arcs greater than 90° being negative. When computing with logarithms we shall write (n) after the logarithms when the functions are negative. If the number of negative factors is even, the result will be positive; if it is odd, the result will be negative and (n) should be written after the resulting logarithm. In order to show our computations in compact form, we

---

* Thus, in the above case, A_c and a are given; therefore we underline the three required parts and cross b as the middle part. Applying Rule II, c_c and B_c being opposite parts, we get $\sin b = \cos c_c \cos B_c$, or, $\sin b = \sin c \sin B$.

shall write down all the logarithms of the trigonometric functions just as they are given in our table; that is, when a logarithm has a negative characteristic we shall not write down -10 after it.*

NOTE. The tables referred to in this book are *Four-Place Tables* by Granville, Smith, and Mikesh (Ginn and Company).

EXAMPLE 1. Solve the right spherical triangle, having given $B = 33° 50'$, $a = 108°$.

Solution. Follow the above general directions.

To find A	To find b	To find c

c_c c_c $\underline{c_c}$

$\underset{/}{A_c}$ $\underline{B_c}$ A_c $\underline{B_c}$ A_c $\underset{/}{\underline{B_c}}$

b a $\underline{b}$ $\underset{/}{a}$ b a

Using Rule II,   Using Rule I,   Using Rule I,

Using Rule II,	Using Rule I,	Using Rule I,
$\sin A_c = \cos B_c \cos a$	$\sin a = \tan B_c \tan b$	$\sin B_c = \tan c_c \tan a$
$\cos A = \sin B \cos a$	$\tan b = \sin a \tan B$	$\cot c = \cos B \cot a$
$\log \sin B = 9.7457$	$\log \sin a = 9.9782$	$\log \cos B = 9.9194$
$\log \cos a = \underline{9.4900}\,(n)$	$\log \tan B = \underline{9.8263}$	$\log \cot a = \underline{9.5118}\,(n)$
$\log \cos A = 9.2357\,(n)$	$\log \tan b = 9.8045$	$\log \cot c = 9.4312\,(n)$
$\therefore 180° - A\dagger = 80° 6'$	$\therefore b = 32° 31'.$	$\therefore 180° - c = 74° 54'$
and $A = 99° 54'.$		and $c = 105° 6'.$

Check. Using Rule I,

$$\sin A_c = \tan b \tan c_c$$
$$\cos A = \tan b \cot c$$

$$\log \tan b = 9.8045$$
$$\log \cot c = \underline{9.4312}\,(n)$$
$$\log \cos A = 9.2357\,(n)$$

$\underline{c_c}$

$\underset{/}{A_c}$ B_c

$\underline{b}$ a

The value of $\log \cos A$ found in the check is the same value as that found in our first computation. The student should observe that in checking our work in this example it was not necessary to look up any new logarithms. Hence the check in this case is only on the correctness of the logarithmic work involved.‡

---

* For example, as in the table, we shall write $\log \sin 24° = 9.6093$. To be exact, this should be written $\log \sin 24° = 9.6093 - 10$, or, $\log \sin 24° = \overline{1}.6093$.

† Since $\cos A$ is negative, we get the supplement of A from the table.

‡ In order to be sure that the angles and sides have been correctly taken from the tables, in such an example as this, we should use them together with some of the given data in relations not already employed.

In logarithmic computations the student should always write down an outline or skeleton of the computation before using his logarithmic table at all. In the last example this outline would be as follows:

$\log \sin B =$	$\log \sin a =$	$\log \cos B =$
$\log \cos a =$ (n)	$\log \tan B =$ ____	$\log \cot a =$ (n)
$\log \cos A =$ (n)	$\log \tan b =$	$\log \cot c =$ (n)
$\therefore 180° - A =$	$\therefore b =$	$\therefore 180° - c =$
and $A =$		and $c =$

It saves time to look up all the logarithms at once, and besides it reduces the liability of error to thus separate the theoretical part of the work from that which is purely mechanical. Students should be drilled in writing down forms like that given above before attempting to solve examples.

EXAMPLE 2. Solve the right spherical triangle, having given $c = 70° 30'$, $A = 100°$.

Solution. Follow the general directions.

To find a	To find b	To find B
Using Rule II,	Using Rule I,	Using Rule I,
$\sin a = \cos c_c \cos A_c$	$\sin A_c = \tan b \tan c_c$	$\sin c_c = \tan A_c \tan B_c$
$\sin a = \sin c \sin A$	$\tan b = \cos A \tan c$	$\cot B = \cos c \tan A$
$\log \sin c = 9.9743$	$\log \cos A = 9.2397$ (n)	$\log \cos c = 9.5235$
$\log \sin A = 9.9934$	$\log \tan c = 0.4509$	$\log \tan A = 0.7537$ (n)
$\log \sin a = 9.9677$	$\log \tan b = 9.6906$ (n)	$\log \cot B = 0.2772$ (n)
$\therefore 180° - a* = 68° 10'$	$\therefore 180° - b = 26° 8'$	$\therefore 180° - B = 27° 51'$
and $a = 111° 50'$.	and $b = 153° 52'$.	and $B = 152° 9'$.

The work of verifying the results is left to the student.

6. The ambiguous case. Two solutions. When the given parts of a right spherical triangle are an oblique angle and its opposite side, there are two triangles which satisfy the given conditions.

---

* Since a is determined from its sine, it is evident that it may have the value 68° 10' found from the table or the supplementary value 111° 50'. Since $A > 90°$, however, we know from Theorem II, p. 217, that $a > 90°$; hence $a = 111° 50'$ is the only solution.

For, in the triangle ABC, let $C = 90°$, and let A and $CB (= a)$ be the given parts. If we extend the arcs AB and AC to A', it is evident that the triangle $A'BC$ also satisfies the given conditions, since $BCA' = 90°$, $A' = A$, and $BC = a$. The remaining parts in $A'BC$ are supplementary to the respective remaining parts in ABC. Thus

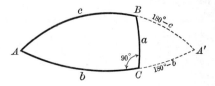

$$A'B = 180° - c, \qquad A'C = 180° - b, \qquad A'BC = 180° - ABC.$$

This ambiguity also appears in the solution of the triangle, as is illustrated in the following example:

EXAMPLE. Solve the right spherical triangle, having given $A = 105° 59'$, $a = 128° 33'$.

Solution. We proceed as in the previous examples.

To find b	*To find B*	*To find c*
c_c	c_c	$\underline{c_c}$
$\underline{A_c} \qquad B_c$	$A_{\!\!\!/c} \qquad B_c$	$\underline{A_c} \qquad B_c$
$\underset{\diagup}{b} \qquad a$	$b \qquad a$	$b \qquad \underset{\diagup}{a}$
$\sin b = \tan a \tan A_c$	$\sin A_c = \cos a \cos B_c$	$\sin a = \cos A_c \cos c_c$
$\sin b = \tan a \cot A$	$\sin B = \dfrac{\cos A}{\cos a}$	$\sin c = \dfrac{\sin a}{\sin A}$
$\log \tan a = 0.0986\ (n)$	$\log \cos A = 9.4399\ (n)$	$\log \sin a = 9.8932$
$\log \cot A = \underline{9.4570}\ (n)$	$\log \cos a = \underline{9.7946}\ (n)$	$\log \sin A = \underline{9.9828}$
$\log \sin b = 9.5556$	$\log \sin B = 9.6453$	$\log \sin c = 9.9104$
$\therefore b = 21° 4'$, or,	$\therefore B = 26° 14'$, or,	$\therefore c' = 54° 27'$, or,
$180° - b = 158°56' = b'.*$	$180° - B = 153°46' = B'.$†	$180° - c' = 125° 33' = \dot c.$ ‡

Hence the two solutions are (see Theorem II, p. 217)

1. $b = 21° 4'$, $\qquad c = 125° 33'$, $\qquad B = 26° 14'$ (triangle ABC).
2. $b' = 158° 56'$, $\qquad c' = 54° 27'$, $\qquad B' = 153° 46'$ (triangle $A'BC$).

It is not necessary to check both solutions. We leave this to the student.

* Since $\sin b$ is positive and b is not known, we cannot remove the ambiguity. Hence the acute angle taken from the table and its supplement must both be retained.

† The two values of B must be retained, since b has two values which are supplementary.

‡ Since $a > 90°$ and b has two values, one greater than $90°$ and the other less than $90°$, it follows from Theorem I, p. 217, that c will have two values, the first one less than $90°$ and the second greater than $90°$.

PROBLEMS

Solve the following right spherical triangles:

No.	GIVEN PARTS		REQUIRED PARTS		
1	$a = 25° 18'$	$b = 32° 41'$	$A = 41° 12'$	$B = 56° 20'$	$c = 40° 27'$
2	$a = 159°$	$c = 137° 20'$			
3	$A = 50° 20'$	$B = 122° 40'$	$a = 40° 42'$	$b = 134° 31'$	$c = 122° 7'$
4	$a = 115° 7'$	$b = 123° 7'$			
5	$A = 107° 30'$	$a = 132° 25'$	$B = 153° 31'$ $c = 50° 43'$ $b = 159° 49'$; or		
			$B' = 26° 29'$ $c' = 129° 17'$ $b' = 20° 11'$		
6	$B = 80°$	$b = 67° 40'$			
7	$B = 112°$	$c = 81° 50'$	$A = 109° 23'$	$a = 110° 58'$	$b = 113° 22'$
8	$a = 61° 40'$	$b = 144° 10'$			
9	$B = 144° 54'$	$b = 146° 32'$	$A = 78° 47'$ $a = 70° 10'$ $c = 106° 28'$; or		
			$A' = 101° 13'$ $a' = 109° 50'$ $c' = 73° 32'$		
10	$A = 99° 50'$	$a = 112°$			
11	$b = 15°$	$c = 152° 20'$	$A = 120° 44'$	$a = 156° 30'$	$B = 33° 53'$
12	$A = 62° 59'$	$B = 37° 4'$			
13	$A = 73° 7'$	$c = 114° 32'$	$a = 60° 31'$	$B = 143° 50'$	$b = 147° 32'$
14	$B = 72° 24'$	$c = 48° 18'$			
15	$A = 161° 52'$	$b = 131° 8'$	$a = 166° 9'$	$B = 101° 49'$	$c = 50° 18'$
16	$b = 168° 14'$	$c = 150° 9'$			
17	$a = 102° 35'$	$B = 112° 14'$	$b = 112° 43'$	$c = 85° 10'$	$A = 101° 38'$
18	$a = 69° 12'$	$c = 82° 35'$			
19	$A = 122° 59'$	$B = 104° 18'$	$a = 124° 11'$	$b = 107° 7'$	$c = 80° 29'$

7. Solution of isosceles and quadrantal triangles. Plane isosceles triangles were solved by dividing each one into two equal right triangles and then solving one of the right triangles. Similarly, we may solve an *isosceles spherical triangle* by dividing it into two symmetrical (equal) right spherical triangles by an arc drawn from the vertex perpendicular to the base, and then solving one of the right spherical triangles.

A *quadrantal triangle* is a spherical triangle one side of which is a quadrant (= 90°). By *f*, p. 213, the polar triangle of a quadrantal triangle is a right triangle. Therefore, to solve a quadrantal triangle we have only to solve its polar triangle and take the *supplements* of the parts obtained by the calculation.

EXAMPLE. Solve the triangle, having given $c = 90°$, $a = 67° 38'$, $b = 48° 50'$.

Solution. This is a quadrantal triangle since one side $c = 90°$. We then find the corresponding elements of its polar triangle by *f*, p. 213. They are $C' = 90°$, $A' = 112° 22'$, $B' = 131° 10'$. We solve this right triangle in the usual way.

Construct the polar (right) triangle.

Given $A' = 112° 22'$, $B' = 131° 10'$:

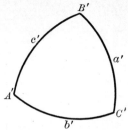

To find a'
c'_c

$\overset{A'_c}{\underset{7}{\not{}}}$ $\qquad$ $\overset{B'_c}{\underline{}}$

b' $\qquad$ $\underline{a'}$

$\sin A'_c = \cos a' \cos B'_c$

$\cos a' = \dfrac{\cos A'}{\sin B'}.$

$\log \cos A' = 9.5804 \; (n)$
$\log \sin B' = \underline{9.8767}$
$\log \cos a' = 9.7037 \; (n)$

$180° - a' = 59° 38'.$
$\qquad a' = 120° 22'.$

Similarly, we get

$\qquad b' = 135° 23', \quad c' = 68° 55'.$

Hence in the given quadrantal triangle we have

$A = 180° - a' = 59° 38',$
$B = 180° - b' = 44° 37',$
$C = 180° - c' = 111° 5'.$

PROBLEMS

Solve the following quadrantal triangles:

No.	Given Parts			Required Parts		
1	$A = 69° 45'$	$B = 94° 40'$	$c = 90°$	$a = 69° 49'$	$b = 94° 23'$	$C = 88° 23'$
2	$A = 139° 10'$	$b = 142° 50'$	$c = 90°$			
3	$a = 30° 20'$	$C = 42° 40'$	$c = 90°$	$A = 20° 1'$	$B = 141° 30'$	$b = 113° 17'$
4	$B = 71° 22'$	$C = 110° 10'$	$c = 90°$			
5	$A = 105° 53'$	$a = 104° 54'$	$c = 90°$	$B = 69° 16'$	$b = 70°$	$C = 84° 30'$; or
				$B = 110° 44'$	$b = 110°$	$C = 95° 30'$
6	$a = 159°$	$b = 95° 18'$	$c = 90°$			

Solve the following isosceles spherical triangles:

No.	Given Parts			Required Parts		
7	$a = 33° 28'$	$C = 110°$	$A = B$	$b = 33° 28'$	$A = B = 40° 1'$	$c = 53° 42'$
8	$a = b = 54° 20'$	$c = 72° 54'$				
9	$A = B = 50° 17'$	$a = b = 66° 29'$		$C = 128° 42'$		$c = 111° 30'$
10	$c = 156° 40'$	$C = 187° 46'$	$A = B$			

Prove the following relations between the parts of a right spherical triangle ($C = 90°$):

11. $\cos^2 A \sin^2 c = \sin (c + a) \sin (c - a).$ $\qquad$ **12.** $\tan a \cos c = \sin b \cot B.$

13. $\sin^2 A = \cos^2 B + \sin^2 a \sin^2 B.$

14. $\sin (b + c) = 2 \cos^2 \tfrac{1}{2} A \cos b \sin c.$

15. $\sin (c - b) = 2 \sin^2 \tfrac{1}{2} A \cos b \sin c.$

CHAPTER II

OBLIQUE SPHERICAL TRIANGLES

8. Fundamental formulas. In this chapter some relations between the sides and angles of any spherical triangle (whether right angled or oblique) will be derived.

9. Law of sines. *In a spherical triangle the sines of the sides are proportional to the sines of the opposite angles.*

Proof. Let ABC be any spherical triangle, and draw the arc CD perpendicular to AB. There will be two cases according as CD falls

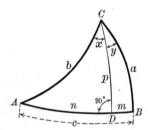 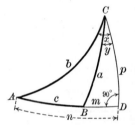

upon AB (first figure) or upon AB produced (second figure). For the sake of brevity let $CD = p$, $AD = n$, $BD = m$, angle $ACD = x$, angle $BCD = y$.

In the right triangle ADC (either figure)

(A) $$\sin p = \sin b \sin A.$$ Rule II, p. 218

In the right triangle BCD (first figure)

(B) $$\sin p = \sin a \sin B.$$ Rule II, p. 218

This also holds true in the second figure, for

$$\sin DBC = \sin (180° - B) = \sin B.$$

Equating the values of $\sin p$ from (A) and (B),

$$\sin a \sin B = \sin b \sin A,$$

or, dividing through by $\sin A \sin B$,

(C) $$\frac{\sin a}{\sin A} = \frac{\sin b}{\sin B}.$$

225

In like manner, by drawing perpendiculars from A and B, we get

(D) $$\frac{\sin b}{\sin B} = \frac{\sin c}{\sin C},$$

and

(E) $$\frac{\sin c}{\sin C} = \frac{\sin a}{\sin A},$$

respectively.

Writing (C), (D), (E) as a single statement, we get the **law of sines**,

(11) $$\frac{\sin a}{\sin A} = \frac{\sin b}{\sin B} = \frac{\sin c}{\sin C}. *$$

10. Law of cosines. *In a spherical triangle the cosine of any side is equal to the product of the cosines of the other two sides plus the product of the sines of these two sides and the cosine of their included angle.*

Proof. Using the same figures as in the last article, we have, in the right triangle BDC,

$$\cos a = \cos p \cos m \qquad\qquad \text{Rule II, p. 218}$$
$$= \cos p \cos (c - n)$$
$$= \cos p \{\cos c \cos n + \sin c \sin n\}$$
(A) $$= \cos p \cos c \cos n + \cos p \sin c \sin n.$$

In the right triangle ADC,

(B) $$\cos p \cos n = \cos b.$$

Whence $$\cos p = \frac{\cos b}{\cos n},$$

and, multiplying both sides by $\sin n$,

(C) $$\cos p \sin n = \frac{\cos b}{\cos n} \cdot \sin n = \cos b \tan n.$$

But $$\cos A = \tan n \cot b, \qquad\qquad \text{Rule I, p. 218}$$

or,

(D) $$\tan n = \tan b \cos A.$$

Substituting the value of $\tan n$ from (D) in (C), we have

(E) $$\cos p \sin n = \cos b \tan b \cos A = \sin b \cos A.$$

Substituting the value of $\cos p \cos n$ from (B) and the value of $\cos p \sin n$ from (E) in (A), we get the law of cosines,

(F) $$\cos a = \cos b \cos c + \sin b \sin c \cos A.$$

Similarly, for the sides b and c we may obtain

(G) $$\cos b = \cos c \cos a + \sin c \sin a \cos B,$$

(H) $$\cos c = \cos a \cos b + \sin a \sin b \cos C.$$

* Compare with the law of sines in the authors' *Plane Trigonometry*, Art. 42.

11. Principle of Duality. Given any relation involving one or more of the sides a, b, c and the angles A, B, C of any general spherical triangle. Now the polar triangle (whose sides are denoted by a', b', c' and angles by A', B', C') is also in this case a general spherical triangle, and the given relation must hold true for it also; that is, the given relation applies to the polar triangle if accents are placed upon the letters representing the sides and angles. Thus (F), (G), (H) of the last article give us the following law of cosines for the polar triangle:

(A) $\qquad \cos a' = \cos b' \cos c' + \sin b' \sin c' \cos A'.$

(B) $\qquad \cos b' = \cos c' \cos a' + \sin c' \sin a' \cos B'.$

(C) $\qquad \cos c' = \cos a' \cos b' + \sin a' \sin b' \cos C'.$

But by f, p. 213,

$$a' = 180° - A, \qquad b' = 180° - B, \qquad c' = 180° - C,$$
$$A' = 180° - a, \qquad B' = 180° - b, \qquad C' = 180° - c.$$

Making these substitutions in (A), (B), (C), which refer to the polar triangle, we get

(D) $\cos (180° - A) = \cos (180° - B) \cos (180° - C)$
$\qquad \qquad \qquad + \sin (180° - B) \sin (180° - C) \cos (180° - a),$

(E) $\cos (180° - B) = \cos (180° - C) \cos (180° - A)$
$\qquad \qquad \qquad + \sin (180° - C) \sin (180° - A) \cos (180° - b),$

(F) $\cos (180° - C) = \cos (180° - A) \cos (180° - B)$
$\qquad \qquad \qquad + \sin (180° - A) \sin (180° - B) \cos (180° - c),$

which involve the sides and angles of the original triangle.

The result of the preceding discussion may then be stated in the following form:

Theorem. *In any relation between the parts of a general spherical triangle, each part may be replaced by the supplement of the opposite part, and the relation thus obtained will hold true.*

The Principle of Duality now follows readily.

Let the supplements of the angles of the triangle be denoted by the Greek letters α ("alpha"), β ("beta"), γ ("gamma")*; that is,

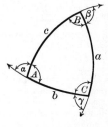

$$\alpha = 180° - A, \ \beta = 180° - B, \ \gamma = 180° - C,$$

or,

$$A = 180° - \alpha, \ B = 180° - \beta, \ C = 180° - \gamma.$$

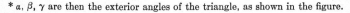

* α, β, γ are then the exterior angles of the triangle, as shown in the figure.

When we apply the above theorem to a relation between the sides and supplements of the angles of a triangle, we, in fact,

replace a by α $(= 180° - A)$,

replace b by β $(= 180° - B)$,

replace c by γ $(= 180° - C)$,

replace α $(= 180° - A)$ by $180° - (180° - a) = a$,

replace β $(= 180° - B)$ by $180° - (180° - b) = b$,

replace γ $(= 180° - C)$ by $180° - (180° - c) = c$,

or, what amounts to the same thing, *interchange the Greek and Roman letters.* For instance, substitute

$$A = 180° - \alpha, \qquad B = 180° - \beta, \qquad C = 180° - \gamma$$

in (F), (G), (H) of the last article. This gives the law of cosines for the sides in the new form

(12) $\cos a = \cos b \cos c - \sin b \sin c \cos \alpha,$

(13) $\cos b = \cos c \cos a - \sin c \sin a \cos \beta,$

(14) $\cos c = \cos a \cos b - \sin a \sin b \cos \gamma.$

[Since $\cos A = \cos (180° - \alpha) = - \cos \alpha$, etc.]

If we now apply the above theorem to these formulas, we get the law of cosines for the angles, namely,

(15) $\cos \alpha = \cos \beta \cos \gamma - \sin \beta \sin \gamma \cos a,$

(16) $\cos \beta = \cos \gamma \cos \alpha - \sin \gamma \sin \alpha \cos b,$

(17) $\cos \gamma = \cos \alpha \cos \beta - \sin \alpha \sin \beta \cos c,$

that is, we have derived three new relations between the sides and supplements of the angles of the triangle.* We may now state the

---

* If we had employed the interior angles of the triangle in our formulas (as has been the almost universal practice of writers on spherical trigonometry), the two sets of cosine formulas would not have been of the same form. That the method used here has many advantages will become more and more apparent as the reading of the text is continued. Not only are the resulting formulas much easier to memorize, but much labor is saved in that, when we have derived one set of formulas for the angles (or sides), the corresponding set of formulas for the sides (or angles) may be written down at once by mere inspection by applying this Principle of Duality. The great advantage of using this Principle of Duality was first pointed out by Möbius (1790–1868).

Principle of Duality. *If the sides of a general spherical triangle are denoted by the Roman letters a, b, c, and the supplements of the corresponding opposite angles by the Greek letters α, β, γ, then, from any given formula involving any of these six parts, we may write down a* **dual** *formula by simply interchanging the corresponding Greek and Roman letters.*

The immediate consequence of this principle is that formulas in spherical trigonometry occur in *pairs*, either one of a pair being the *dual* of the other.

Thus (**12**) and (**15**) are dual formulas; also (**13**) and (**16**), or (**14**) and (**17**).

If we substitute

$$A = 180° - \alpha, \qquad B = 180° - \beta, \qquad C = 180° - \gamma$$

in the law of sines (p. 226), we get

$$\frac{\sin a}{\sin \alpha} = \frac{\sin b}{\sin \beta} = \frac{\sin c}{\sin \gamma}.$$

[Since $\sin A = \sin (180° - \alpha) = \sin \alpha$, etc.]

Applying the Principle of Duality to this relation, we get

$$\frac{\sin \alpha}{\sin a} = \frac{\sin \beta}{\sin b} = \frac{\sin \gamma}{\sin c},$$

which is essentially the same as the previous form. That is, the law of sines is self-dual.

The forms of the law of cosines that we have derived involve algebraic sums. As these are not convenient for logarithmic calculations, we will reduce them to the form of products.

12. Trigonometric functions of half the supplements of the angles of a spherical triangle in terms of its sides. Denote half the sum of the sides of a triangle (that is, half the perimeter) by s. Then

(A) $$2 s = a + b + c,$$

or, $$s = \tfrac{1}{2}(a + b + c).$$

Subtracting $2 c$ from both sides of (A),

$$2 s - 2 c = a + b + c - 2 c,$$

or,

(B) $$s - c = \tfrac{1}{2}(a + b - c).$$

Similarly,

(*C*) $s - b = \frac{1}{2}(a - b + c),$

and

(*D*) $s - a = \frac{1}{2}(-a + b + c) = \frac{1}{2}(b + c - a).$

From plane trigonometry,

(*E*) $2 \sin^2 \frac{1}{2} \alpha = 1 - \cos \alpha,$

(*F*) $2 \cos^2 \frac{1}{2} \alpha = 1 + \cos \alpha.$

But from (12), p. 228, solving for $\cos \alpha$,

$$\cos \alpha = \frac{\cos b \cos c - \cos a}{\sin b \sin c};$$

hence (*E*) becomes

$$2 \sin^2 \tfrac{1}{2} \alpha = 1 - \frac{\cos b \cos c - \cos a}{\sin b \sin c}$$

$$= \frac{\sin b \sin c - \cos b \cos c + \cos a}{\sin b \sin c}$$

$$= \frac{\cos a - (\cos b \cos c - \sin b \sin c)}{\sin b \sin c}$$

$$= \frac{\cos a - \cos (b + c)}{\sin b \sin c}$$

$$= \frac{-2 \sin \tfrac{1}{2}(a + b + c) \sin \tfrac{1}{2}(a - b - c)}{\sin b \sin c},*$$

or,

(*G*) $2 \sin^2 \tfrac{1}{2} \alpha = \dfrac{2 \sin \tfrac{1}{2}(a + b + c) \sin \tfrac{1}{2}(b + c - a)}{\sin b \sin c}.$

[Since $\sin \tfrac{1}{2}(a - b - c) = -\sin \tfrac{1}{2}(-a + b + c) = -\sin \tfrac{1}{2}(b + c - a)$.]

Substituting from (*A*) and (*D*) in (*G*), we get

$$\sin^2 \tfrac{1}{2} \alpha = \frac{\sin s \sin (s - a)}{\sin b \sin c},$$

or,

(18) $\sin \frac{1}{2} a = \sqrt{\dfrac{\sin s \sin (s - a)}{\sin b \sin c}}.$

---

* Let

$A = a$	$A = a$
$B = b + c$	$B = b + c$
$A + B = a + b + c$	$A - B = a - b - c$
$\frac{1}{2}(A + B) = \frac{1}{2}(a + b + c).$	$\frac{1}{2}(A - B) = \frac{1}{2}(a - b - c).$

Hence, substituting in (90), Art. 80, of the authors' *Plane Trigonometry*, namely,

$$\cos A - \cos B = -2 \sin \tfrac{1}{2}(A + B) \sin \tfrac{1}{2}(A - B),$$

we get $\cos a - \cos (b + c) = -2 \sin \tfrac{1}{2}(a + b + c) \sin \tfrac{1}{2}(a - b - c).$

Similarly, (F) becomes

$$2 \cos^2 \tfrac{1}{2} \alpha = 1 + \frac{\cos b \cos c - \cos a}{\sin b \sin c}$$

$$= \frac{\sin b \sin c + \cos b \cos c - \cos a}{\sin b \sin c}$$

$$= \frac{\cos (b - c) - \cos a}{\sin b \sin c}$$

$$= \frac{- 2 \sin \tfrac{1}{2} (a + b - c) \sin \tfrac{1}{2} (b - c - a)}{\sin b \sin c}, *$$

or,

(H) $$2 \cos^2 \tfrac{1}{2} \alpha = \frac{2 \sin \tfrac{1}{2} (a + b - c) \sin \tfrac{1}{2} (a - b + c)}{\sin b \sin c}.$$

[Since $\sin \tfrac{1}{2}(b - c - a) = - \sin \tfrac{1}{2} (- b + c + a) = \div \sin \tfrac{1}{2}(a - b + c).$]

Substituting from (B) and (C) in (H), we get

$$\cos^2 \tfrac{1}{2} \alpha = \frac{\sin (s - c) \sin (s - b)}{\sin b \sin c},$$

or,

(19) $$\cos \tfrac{1}{2} a = \sqrt{\frac{\sin (s - b) \sin (s - c)}{\sin b \sin c}}.$$

Since $\tan \tfrac{1}{2} \alpha = \dfrac{\sin \tfrac{1}{2} \alpha}{\cos \tfrac{1}{2} \alpha}$, we get from this, by substitution from (18) and (19),

(20) $$\tan \tfrac{1}{2} a = \sqrt{\frac{\sin s \sin (s - a)}{\sin (s - b) \sin (s - c)}}.†$$

* Let

$A = b - c$	$A = b - c$
$B = a$	$B = a$
$A + B = a + b - c$	$A - B = b - c - a$
$\tfrac{1}{2}(A + B) = \tfrac{1}{2}(a + b - c).$	$\tfrac{1}{2}(A - B) = \tfrac{1}{2}(b - c - a).$

Hence, substituting in the formula

$$\cos A - \cos B = - 2 \sin \tfrac{1}{2}(A + B) \sin \tfrac{1}{2}(A - B),$$

we get $\cos (b - c) - \cos a = - 2 \sin \tfrac{1}{2}(a + b - c) \sin \tfrac{1}{2}(b - c - a).$

† In memorizing these formulas it will be found an aid to the memory to note the fact that under each radical

(a) only the sine function occurs;

(b) the denominators of the sine and cosine formulas involve those two sides of the triangle which are not opposite to the angle sought;

(c) in the numerator and denominator of the fraction in the tangent formula, s comes first and then the differences

$$s - a, \; s - b, \; s - c,$$

in cyclical order, s and the first difference occurring also in the numerator of the corresponding sine formula, while the last two differences occur in the numerator of the corresponding cosine formula.

In like manner, we may get

$$(21) \qquad \sin \tfrac{1}{2}\beta = \sqrt{\frac{\sin s \sin (s - b)}{\sin c \sin a}},$$

$$(22) \qquad \cos \tfrac{1}{2}\beta = \sqrt{\frac{\sin (s - c) \sin (s - a)}{\sin c \sin a}},$$

$$(23) \qquad \tan \tfrac{1}{2}\beta = \sqrt{\frac{\sin s \sin (s - b)}{\sin (s - c) \sin (s - a)}}.$$

Also,

$$(24) \qquad \sin \tfrac{1}{2}\gamma = \sqrt{\frac{\sin s \sin (s - c)}{\sin a \sin b}},$$

$$(25) \qquad \cos \tfrac{1}{2}\gamma = \sqrt{\frac{\sin (s - a) \sin (s - b)}{\sin a \sin b}},$$

$$(26) \qquad \tan \tfrac{1}{2}\gamma = \sqrt{\frac{\sin s \sin (s - c)}{\sin (s - a) \sin (s - b)}}.$$

In solving triangles it is sometimes more convenient to use other forms of (20), (23), and (26). Thus, in the right-hand member of (20), multiply both the numerator and denominator of the fraction under the radical by $\sin (s - a)$. This gives

$$\tan \tfrac{1}{2}\alpha = \sqrt{\frac{\sin s \sin^2 (s - a)}{\sin (s - a) \sin (s - b) \sin (s - c)}}$$

$$= \sin (s - a) \sqrt{\frac{\sin s}{\sin (s - a) \sin (s - b) \sin (s - c)}}.$$

Let $\qquad \tan \tfrac{1}{2}d = \sqrt{\dfrac{\sin (s - a) \sin (s - b) \sin (s - c)}{\sin s}};$

then $\qquad \tan \tfrac{1}{2}\alpha = \dfrac{\sin (s - a)}{\tan \tfrac{1}{2}d}.$

Similarly, for $\tan \tfrac{1}{2}\beta$ and $\tan \tfrac{1}{2}\gamma$. Hence

$$(27) \qquad \tan \tfrac{1}{2}d = \sqrt{\frac{\sin (s - a) \sin (s - b) \sin (s - c)}{\sin s}},$$

$$(28) \qquad \tan \tfrac{1}{2}\alpha = \frac{\sin (s - a)}{\tan \tfrac{1}{2}d},$$

$$(29) \qquad \tan \tfrac{1}{2}\beta = \frac{\sin (s - b)}{\tan \tfrac{1}{2}d},$$

$$(30) \qquad \tan \tfrac{1}{2}\gamma = \frac{\sin (s - c)}{\tan \tfrac{1}{2}d}.$$

13. Trigonometric functions of the half sides of a spherical triangle in terms of the supplements of the angles. By making use of the Principle of Duality on page 229, we get at once from formulas (18) to (30), by replacing the supplement of an angle by the opposite side and each side by the supplement of the opposite angle, the following formulas.

Denote half the sum of the angles α, β, γ by the Greek letter σ ("sigma"); that is, let

$$\sigma = \tfrac{1}{2}(\alpha + \beta + \gamma)$$
$$= \tfrac{1}{2}(180° - A + 180° - B + 180° - C)$$
$$= 270° - \tfrac{1}{2}(A + B + C).$$

Then we have

$$(31) \qquad \sin \tfrac{1}{2} a = \sqrt{\frac{\sin \sigma \sin (\sigma - a)}{\sin \beta \sin \gamma}},$$

$$(32) \qquad \cos \tfrac{1}{2} a = \sqrt{\frac{\sin (\sigma - \beta) \sin (\sigma - \gamma)}{\sin \beta \sin \gamma}},$$

$$(33) \qquad \tan \tfrac{1}{2} a = \sqrt{\frac{\sin \sigma \sin (\sigma - a)}{\sin (\sigma - \beta) \sin (\sigma - \gamma)}},$$

$$(34) \qquad \sin \tfrac{1}{2} b = \sqrt{\frac{\sin \sigma \sin (\sigma - \beta)}{\sin \gamma \sin a}},$$

$$(35) \qquad \cos \tfrac{1}{2} b = \sqrt{\frac{\sin (\sigma - \gamma) \sin (\sigma - a)}{\sin \gamma \sin a}},$$

$$(36) \qquad \tan \tfrac{1}{2} b = \sqrt{\frac{\sin \sigma \sin (\sigma - \beta)}{\sin (\sigma - \gamma) \sin (\sigma - a)}},$$

$$(37) \qquad \sin \tfrac{1}{2} c = \sqrt{\frac{\sin \sigma \sin (\sigma - \gamma)}{\sin a \sin \beta}},$$

$$(38) \qquad \cos \tfrac{1}{2} c = \sqrt{\frac{\sin (\sigma - a) \sin (\sigma - \beta)}{\sin a \sin \beta}},$$

$$(39) \qquad \tan \tfrac{1}{2} c = \sqrt{\frac{\sin \sigma \sin (\sigma - \gamma)}{\sin (\sigma - a) \sin (\sigma - \beta)}},$$

$$(40) \qquad \tan \tfrac{1}{2} \delta = \sqrt{\frac{\sin (\sigma - a) \sin (\sigma - \beta) \sin (\sigma - \gamma)}{\sin \sigma}},$$

$$(41) \qquad \tan \tfrac{1}{2} a = \frac{\sin (\sigma - a)}{\tan \tfrac{1}{2} \delta},$$

$$(42) \qquad \tan \tfrac{1}{2} b = \frac{\sin (\sigma - \beta)}{\tan \tfrac{1}{2} \delta},$$

$$(43) \qquad \tan \tfrac{1}{2} c = \frac{\sin (\sigma - \gamma)}{\tan \tfrac{1}{2} \delta}.$$

What we have done amounts to replacing Roman letters and Greek letters in (18) to (30) by the corresponding Greek and Roman letters.

14. Napier's analogies. Dividing (20) by (23), we get

$$\frac{\tan \tfrac{1}{2} \alpha}{\tan \tfrac{1}{2} \beta} = \sqrt{\frac{\sin s \sin (s - a)}{\sin (s - b) \sin (s - c)}} \div \sqrt{\frac{\sin s \sin (s - b)}{\sin (s - c) \sin (s - a)}},$$

or,

$$\frac{\dfrac{\sin \tfrac{1}{2} \alpha}{\cos \tfrac{1}{2} \alpha}}{\dfrac{\sin \tfrac{1}{2} \beta}{\cos \tfrac{1}{2} \beta}} = \sqrt{\frac{\dfrac{\sin s \sin (s - a)}{\sin (s - b) \sin (s - c)}}{\dfrac{\sin s \sin (s - b)}{\sin (s - c) \sin (s - a)}}}.$$

Hence

$$\frac{\sin \tfrac{1}{2} \alpha \cos \tfrac{1}{2} \beta}{\cos \tfrac{1}{2} \alpha \sin \tfrac{1}{2} \beta} = \frac{\sin (s - a)}{\sin (s - b)}.$$

By composition and division, in proportion,

$$\frac{\sin \tfrac{1}{2} \alpha \cos \tfrac{1}{2} \beta + \cos \tfrac{1}{2} \alpha \sin \tfrac{1}{2} \beta}{\sin \tfrac{1}{2} \alpha \cos \tfrac{1}{2} \beta - \cos \tfrac{1}{2} \alpha \sin \tfrac{1}{2} \beta} = \frac{\sin (s - a) + \sin (s - b)}{\sin (s - a) - \sin (s - b)}.$$

From (65), Art. 73, and (66), Art. 74, of the authors' *Plane Trigonometry*, the left-hand member equals

$$\frac{\sin (\tfrac{1}{2} \alpha + \tfrac{1}{2} \beta)}{\sin (\tfrac{1}{2} \alpha - \tfrac{1}{2} \beta)},$$

and by (87) and (88), Art. 80, the right-hand member equals

$$\frac{\sin (s - a) + \sin (s - b)}{\sin (s - a) - \sin (s - b)} = \frac{\tan \tfrac{1}{2} [s - a + (s - b)]}{\tan \tfrac{1}{2} [s - a - (s - b)]} = \frac{\tan \tfrac{1}{2} c}{\tan \tfrac{1}{2} (b - a)}. \quad *$$

Equating these results, we get, noting that $\tan \tfrac{1}{2} (b - a) = - \tan \tfrac{1}{2} (a - b)$,

$$\frac{\sin \tfrac{1}{2} (\alpha + \beta)}{\sin \tfrac{1}{2} (\alpha - \beta)} = - \frac{\tan \tfrac{1}{2} c}{\tan \tfrac{1}{2} (a - b)},$$

or,

$$(44) \qquad \tan \tfrac{1}{2} (a - b) = - \frac{\sin \tfrac{1}{2} (\alpha - \beta)}{\sin \tfrac{1}{2} (\alpha + \beta)} \tan \tfrac{1}{2} c.$$

* For $s - a + s - b = 2s - a - b = a + b + c - a - b = c$, and $s - a - s + b = b - a$.

In the same manner we may get the two similar formulas for $\tan \frac{1}{2}(b - c)$ and $\tan \frac{1}{2}(c - a)$.

Multiplying (20) and (23), we get

$$\tan \tfrac{1}{2}\alpha \tan \tfrac{1}{2}\beta = \sqrt{\frac{\sin s \sin (s - a)}{\sin (s - b) \sin (s - c)}} \sqrt{\frac{\sin s \sin (s - b)}{\sin (s - c) \sin (s - a)}},$$

or,

$$\frac{\sin \tfrac{1}{2}\alpha \sin \tfrac{1}{2}\beta}{\cos \tfrac{1}{2}\alpha \cos \tfrac{1}{2}\beta} = \frac{\sin s}{\sin (s - c)}.$$

By composition and division, in proportion,

$$\frac{\cos \tfrac{1}{2}\alpha \cos \tfrac{1}{2}\beta - \sin \tfrac{1}{2}\alpha \sin \tfrac{1}{2}\beta}{\cos \tfrac{1}{2}\alpha \cos \tfrac{1}{2}\beta + \sin \tfrac{1}{2}\alpha \sin \tfrac{1}{2}\beta} = \frac{\sin (s - c) - \sin s}{\sin (s - c) + \sin s}.$$

From (67), Art. 73, and (68), Art. 74, of the authors' *Plane Trigonometry*, the left-hand member equals

$$\frac{\cos \left(\tfrac{1}{2}\alpha + \tfrac{1}{2}\beta\right)}{\cos \left(\tfrac{1}{2}\alpha - \tfrac{1}{2}\beta\right)};$$

and by (88) and (87), Art. 80, the right-hand member equals

$$\frac{\sin (s - c) - \sin s}{\sin (s - c) + \sin s} = \frac{\tan \tfrac{1}{2}(s - c - s)}{\tan \tfrac{1}{2}(s - c + s)} = \frac{\tan \tfrac{1}{2}(-c)}{\tan \tfrac{1}{2}(a + b)}. \quad *$$

Equating these results, we get, noting that $\tan \frac{1}{2}(-c) = -\tan \frac{1}{2}c$,

$$\frac{\cos \tfrac{1}{2}(\alpha + \beta)}{\cos \tfrac{1}{2}(\alpha - \beta)} = -\frac{\tan \tfrac{1}{2}c}{\tan \tfrac{1}{2}(a + b)},$$

or,

(45) $$\tan \tfrac{1}{2}(a + b) = -\frac{\cos \tfrac{1}{2}(\alpha - \beta)}{\cos \tfrac{1}{2}(\alpha + \beta)} \tan \tfrac{1}{2}c.$$

In the same manner we may get the two similar formulas for $\tan \frac{1}{2}(b + c)$ and $\tan \frac{1}{2}(c + a)$.

By making use of the Principle of Duality on page 229, we get at once, from formulas (44) and (45),

(46) $$\tan \tfrac{1}{2}(a - \beta) = -\frac{\sin \tfrac{1}{2}(a - b)}{\sin \tfrac{1}{2}(a + b)} \tan \tfrac{1}{2}\gamma,$$

(47) $$\tan \tfrac{1}{2}(a + \beta) = -\frac{\cos \tfrac{1}{2}(a - b)}{\cos \tfrac{1}{2}(a + b)} \tan \tfrac{1}{2}\gamma.$$

---

* For $s - c - s = -c$, and $s - c + s = 2s - c = a + b + c - c = a + b$.

By changing the letters in cyclic order at once we may write down the corresponding formulas for $\tan \frac{1}{2}(\beta - \gamma)$, $\tan \frac{1}{2}(\gamma - \alpha)$, $\tan \frac{1}{2}(\beta + \gamma)$, and $\tan \frac{1}{2}(\gamma + \alpha)$.

The relations derived in this section are known as *Napier's analogies*.

Since $\cos \frac{1}{2}(a-b)$ and $\tan \frac{1}{2}\gamma \,(=\tan \frac{1}{2}(180° - C)=\tan(90°-\frac{1}{2}C)$ $= \cot \frac{1}{2} C)$ are always positive, it follows from (47) that $\cos \frac{1}{2}(a+b)$ and $\tan \frac{1}{2}(\alpha+\beta)$ always have opposite signs; or, since $\tan \frac{1}{2}(\alpha+\beta)$ $=\tan \frac{1}{2}(180° - A + 180° - B) = \tan \frac{1}{2}[360° - (A+B)] = \tan[180° - \frac{1}{2}(A+B)] = -\tan \frac{1}{2}(A+B)$, we may say that $\cos \frac{1}{2}(a+b)$ and $\tan \frac{1}{2}(A+B)$ always have the same sign. Hence we have the

Theorem. *In a spherical triangle the sum of any two sides is less than, greater than, or equal to 180°, according as the sum of the corresponding opposite angles is less than, greater than, or equal to 180°.*

15. Solution of oblique spherical triangles. We shall now take up the numerical solution of oblique spherical triangles. There are three cases to consider with two subdivisions under each case.

CASE I.   (*a*) *Given the three sides.*
            (*b*) *Given the three angles.*

CASE II.   (*a*) *Given two sides and their included angle.*
            (*b*) *Given two angles and their included side.*

CASE III.   (*a*) *Given two sides and the angle opposite one of them.*
            (*b*) *Given two angles and the side opposite one of them.*

16. Case I. (*a*) Given the three sides. *Use formulas from page 232, namely,*

$$(27) \qquad \tan \tfrac{1}{2} d = \sqrt{\frac{\sin(s-a)\,\sin(s-b)\,\sin(s-c)}{\sin s}},$$

$$(28) \qquad \tan \tfrac{1}{2}\alpha = \frac{\sin(s-a)}{\tan \frac{1}{2} d},$$

$$(29) \qquad \tan \tfrac{1}{2}\beta = \frac{\sin(s-b)}{\tan \frac{1}{2} d},$$

$$(30) \qquad \tan \tfrac{1}{2}\gamma = \frac{\sin(s-c)}{\tan \frac{1}{2} d},$$

to find α, β, γ, *and therefore A, B, C, and check by the law of sines,*

$$\frac{\sin a}{\sin A} = \frac{\sin b}{\sin B} = \frac{\sin c}{\sin C}.$$

EXAMPLE. Given $a = 60°$, $b = 137° 20'$, $c = 116°$; find A, B, C.

Solution.

$a =\ 60°$	*To find log tan $\frac{1}{2} d$ use* **(27)**
$b = 137° 20'$	$\log \sin (s - a) =\ 9.9971$
$c = 116°$	$\log \sin (s - b) =\ 9.5199$
$2 s = 313° 20'$	$\log \sin (s - c) =\ \underline{9.8140}$
$s = 156° 40'$.	29.3310
$s - a = 96° 40'$.	$\log \sin s =\ 9.5978$
$s - b = 19° 20'$.	$2\ \boxed{19.7332}$
$s - c = 40° 40'$.	$\log \tan \frac{1}{2} d =\ 9.8666$

To find A use **(28)**

$\log \sin (s - a) = 9.9971$

$\log \tan \frac{1}{2} d = \underline{9.8666}$

$\log \tan \frac{1}{2} \alpha = 0.1305$

$\frac{1}{2} \alpha = 53° 29'$.

$\alpha = 106° 58'$.

$\therefore A = 180° - 106° 58'$

$= 73° 2'$.

To find B use **(29)**

$\log \sin (s - b) = 9.5199$

$\log \tan \frac{1}{2} d = \underline{9.8666}$

$\log \tan \frac{1}{2} \beta = 9.6533$

$\frac{1}{2} \beta = 24° 14'$.

$\beta = 48° 28'$.

$\therefore B = 180° - 48° 28'$

$= 131° 32'$.

To find C use **(30)**

$\log \sin (s - c) = 9.8140$

$\log \tan \frac{1}{2} d = \underline{9.8666}$

$\log \tan \frac{1}{2} \gamma = 9.9474$

$\frac{1}{2} \gamma = 41° 32'$.

$\gamma = 83° 4'$.

$\therefore C = 180° - 83° 4'$

$= 96° 56'$.

Check.

$\log \sin a = 9.9375$	$\log \sin b = 9.8311$	$\log \sin c = 9.9537$
$\log \sin A = \underline{9.9807}$	$\log \sin B = \underline{9.8743}$	$\log \sin C = \underline{9.9969}$
9.9568	9.9568	9.9568

This checks up more closely than is to be expected in general. There may be a variation of at most two units in the last figure when the work is accurate.

PROBLEMS

Solve the following oblique spherical triangles.

No.	GIVEN PARTS			REQUIRED PARTS		
1	$a = 150° 20'$	$b = 43° 3'$	$c = 129° 8'$	$A = 140° 20'$	$B = 61° 40'$	$C = 89° 24'$
2	$a = 62° 20'$	$b = 54° 10'$	$c = 97° 50'$			
3	$a = 46° 30'$	$b = 62° 40'$	$c = 83° 20'$	$A = 43° 58'$	$B = 58° 14'$	$C = 108° 6'$
4	$a = 58° 13'$	$b = 80° 24'$	$c = 96° 15'$			
5	$a = 146° 24'$	$b = 126° 32'$	$c = 69° 4'$	$A = 145° 46'$	$B = 125° 12'$	$C = 108° 12'$
6	$a = 110° 40'$	$b = 45° 18'$	$c = 74° 36'$			
7	$a = 153° 38'$	$b = 40° 0'$	$c = 118° 20'$	$A = 160° 14'$	$B = 29° 20'$	$C = 42° 6'$
8	$a = 115° 12'$	$b = 52° 52'$	$c = 133° 15'$			

17. Case I. (b) Given the three angles. *To find a, b, c, use formulas from pages 233 and 234, namely,* *

$$(40) \qquad \tan \tfrac{1}{2} \delta = \sqrt{\frac{\sin (\sigma - \alpha) \sin (\sigma - \beta) \sin (\sigma - \gamma)}{\sin \sigma}},$$

* These formulas may be written down at once from those used in Case I, (a), p. 236, by replacing the Roman or Greek letters by the corresponding Greek or Roman letters.

$$(41) \qquad \tan \tfrac{1}{2} a = \frac{\sin (\sigma - \alpha)}{\tan \tfrac{1}{2} \delta},$$

$$(42) \qquad \tan \tfrac{1}{2} b = \frac{\sin (\sigma - \beta)}{\tan \tfrac{1}{2} \delta},$$

$$(43) \qquad \tan \tfrac{1}{2} c = \frac{\sin (\sigma - \gamma)}{\tan \tfrac{1}{2} \delta};$$

and check by the law of sines, $\dfrac{\sin a}{\sin A} = \dfrac{\sin b}{\sin B} = \dfrac{\sin c}{\sin C}.$

EXAMPLE. Given $A = 70°$, $B = 131° 10'$, $C = 94° 50'$; find a, b, c.

Solution. Here we use the supplements of the angles.

$\alpha = 180° - A = 110°$	*To find log tan $\tfrac{1}{2}$ δ use* **(40)**
$\beta = 180° - B = 48° 50'$	$\log \sin (\sigma - \alpha) = 9.3179$
$\gamma = 180° - C = \underline{85° 10'}$	$\log \sin (\sigma - \beta) = 9.9810$
$2 \sigma = 244°$	$\log \sin (\sigma - \gamma) = \underline{9.7778}$
	29.0767
$\sigma = 122°.$	
$\sigma - \alpha = 12°.$	$\log \sin \sigma = 9.9284$
$\sigma - \beta = 73° 10'.$	$2 \,\boxed{19.1483}$
$\sigma - \gamma = 36° 50'.$	$\log \tan \tfrac{1}{2} \delta = 9.5742$

To find a use **(41)**	*To find b use* **(42)**	*To find c use* **(43)**
$\log \sin (\sigma - \alpha) = 9.3179$	$\log \sin (\sigma - \beta) = 9.9810$	$\log \sin (\sigma - \gamma) = 9.7778$
$\log \tan \tfrac{1}{2} \delta = \underline{9.5742}$	$\log \tan \tfrac{1}{2} \delta = \underline{9.5742}$	$\log \tan \tfrac{1}{2} \delta = \underline{9.5742}$
$\log \tan \tfrac{1}{2} a = 9.7437$	$\log \tan \tfrac{1}{2} b = 0.4068$	$\log \tan \tfrac{1}{2} c = 0.2036$
$\tfrac{1}{2} a = 29°.$	$\tfrac{1}{2} b = 68° 36'.$	$\tfrac{1}{2} c = 57° 58'.$
$\therefore a = 58°.$	$b = 137° 12'.$	$c = 115° 56'.$

Check. $\log \sin a = 9.9284$ $\quad \log \sin b = 9.8321$ $\quad \log \sin c = 9.9539$

$\log \sin A = \underline{9.9730}$ $\quad \log \sin B = \underline{9.8767}$ $\quad \log \sin C = \underline{9.9985}$

$9.9554 \qquad\qquad\quad 9.9554 \qquad\qquad\quad 9.9554$

PROBLEMS

Solve the following oblique spherical triangles:

No.	GIVEN PARTS			REQUIRED PARTS		
1	$A = 116° 45'$	$B = 63° 15'$	$C = 91° 7'$	$a = 120° 56'$	$b = 59° 4'$	$c = 106° 10'$
2	$A = 91° 15'$	$B = 86° 40'$	$C = 71° 40'$			
3	$A = 132° 14'$	$B = 110° 11'$	$C = 99° 42'$	$a = 131° 35'$	$b = 108° 30'$	$c = 84° 47'$
4	$A = 139° 5'$	$B = 23° 46'$	$C = 38° 12'$			
5	$A = 20° 10'$	$B = 55° 53'$	$C = 114° 20'$	$a = 20° 17'$	$b = 56° 20'$	$c = 66° 21'$
6	$A = 28° 20'$	$B = 92° 16'$	$C = 84° 50'$			
7	$A = 100°$	$B = 100°$	$C = 50°$	$a = 112° 14'$	$b = 112° 14'$	$c = 46° 4'$
8	$A = 59° 4'$	$B = 94° 25'$	$C = 123° 10'$			
9	$A = 59° 18'$	$B = 108°$	$C = 76° 22'$	$a = 61° 44'$	$b = 103° 4'$	$c = 84° 32'$
10	$A = 75° 13'$	$B = 81° 52'$	$C = 60° 12'$			

18. Case II. (*a*) **Given two sides and their included angle, as** *a, b, C.* *Use formulas on page 235, namely,*

$$(46) \qquad \tan \tfrac{1}{2}(\alpha - \beta) = - \frac{\sin \tfrac{1}{2}(a - b)}{\sin \tfrac{1}{2}(a + b)} \tan \tfrac{1}{2} \gamma,$$

$$(47) \qquad \tan \tfrac{1}{2}(\alpha + \beta) = - \frac{\cos \tfrac{1}{2}(a - b)}{\cos \tfrac{1}{2}(a + b)} \tan \tfrac{1}{2} \gamma,$$

to find α *and* β *and therefore A and B; and from page 234 use* (**44**) *solved for* $\tan \tfrac{1}{2} c$, *namely,*

$$(44) \qquad \tan \tfrac{1}{2} c = - \frac{\sin \tfrac{1}{2}(\alpha + \beta) \tan \tfrac{1}{2}(a - b)}{\sin \tfrac{1}{2}(\alpha - \beta)},$$

to find c. Check by the law of sines.

EXAMPLE 1. Given $a = 64° 24'$, $b = 42° 30'$, $C = 58° 40'$; find A, B, c.
Solution. $\gamma = 180° - C = 121° 20'$. $\therefore \tfrac{1}{2} \gamma = 60° 40'$.

$a = 64° 24'$	$a = 64° 24'$
$b = 42° 30'$	$b = 42° 30'$
$a + b = 106° 54'$	$a - b = 21° 54'$
$\therefore \tfrac{1}{2}(a + b) = 53° 27'$.	$\therefore \tfrac{1}{2}(a - b) = 10° 57'$.

To find $\tfrac{1}{2}(\alpha - \beta)$ *use* (46)

log sin $\tfrac{1}{2}(a - b) = 9.2786$
log tan $\tfrac{1}{2} \gamma = 0.2503$
$\phantom{log tan \tfrac{1}{2} \gamma = }9.5289$
log sin $\tfrac{1}{2}(a + b) = 9.9049$
log tan $\tfrac{1}{2}(\alpha - \beta) = 9.6240$ (*n*)
$\therefore \tfrac{1}{2}(\alpha - \beta) = -22° 49'$.*

To find $\tfrac{1}{2}(\alpha + \beta)$ *use* (47)

log cos $\tfrac{1}{2}(a - b) = 9.9920$
log tan $\tfrac{1}{2} \gamma = 0.2503$
$\phantom{log tan \tfrac{1}{2} \gamma = }10.2423$
log cos $\tfrac{1}{2}(a + b) = 9.7749$
log tan $\tfrac{1}{2}(\alpha + \beta) = 0.4674$ (*n*)
$180° - \tfrac{1}{2}(\alpha + \beta) = 71° 11'$.†
$\therefore \tfrac{1}{2}(\alpha + \beta) = 108° 49'$.

To find A and B

	$\tfrac{1}{2}(\alpha + \beta) =$	$108° 49'$
	$\tfrac{1}{2}(\alpha - \beta) = -$	$22° 49'$
Adding,	$\alpha =$	$86°$
Subtracting,	$\beta = 131° 38'$.	

$\therefore A = 180° - \alpha = 94°$.
$B = 180° - \beta = 48° 22'$.

To find c use (44)

log sin $\tfrac{1}{2}(\alpha + \beta) = 9.9761$
log tan $\tfrac{1}{2}(a - b) = 9.2867$
$\phantom{log tan \tfrac{1}{2}(a - b) = }19.2628$
log sin $\tfrac{1}{2}(\alpha - \beta) = 9.5886$ (*n*)
log tan $\tfrac{1}{2} c = 9.6742$‡
$\tfrac{1}{2} c = 25° 17'$.
$\therefore c = 50° 34'$.

Check. log sin $a = 9.9551$ log sin $b = 9.8297$ log sin $c = 9.8878$
 log sin $A = 9.9989$ log sin $B = 9.8735$ log sin $C = 9.9315$
9.9562 $\cdot$ 9.9562 9.9563

* Since $\tan \tfrac{1}{2}(\alpha - \beta)$ is negative, $\tfrac{1}{2}(\alpha - \beta)$ may be in the second or fourth quadrant. But $a > b$; therefore $A > B$ and $\alpha < \beta$, since α and β are the supplements of A and B. Hence $\tfrac{1}{2}(\alpha - \beta)$ must be a negative angle numerically less than 90°.

† Here $\tfrac{1}{2}(\alpha + \beta)$ must be a positive angle less than 180°. Since $\tan \tfrac{1}{2}(\alpha + \beta)$ is negative, $\tfrac{1}{2}(\alpha + \beta)$ must lie in the second quadrant, and we get its supplement from the table.

‡ $\tan \tfrac{1}{2} c$ is positive, since $\sin \tfrac{1}{2}(\alpha - \beta)$ is negative and there is a minus sign before the fraction.

If c only is wanted, we may find it from the law of cosines, (14), p. 228, without previously determining A and B. But this formula is not well adapted to logarithmic calculations. Another method is illustrated below, which depends on the solution of right spherical triangles, and hence requires only those formulas which follow from applying *Napier's rules of circular parts*, p. 218.

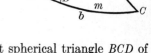

Through B draw an arc of a great circle perpendicular to AC, intersecting AC (or AC produced) at D. Let

$$BD = p, \quad CD = m, \quad AD = n.$$

Applying Rule I, p. 218, to the right spherical triangle BCD of the figure, we have

$$\cos C = \tan m \cot a,$$

or,

(A) $\qquad\qquad \tan m = \tan a \cos C.$

Applying Rule II, p. 218, to BCD,

$$\cos a = \cos m \cos p,$$

or,

(B) $\qquad\qquad \cos p = \cos a \sec m.$

Applying the same rule to ABD,

$$\cos c = \cos n \cos p,$$

or,

(C) $\qquad\qquad \cos p = \cos c \sec n.$

Equating (B) and (C),

$$\cos c \sec n = \cos a \sec m,$$

or, $\qquad\qquad \cos c = \cos a \sec m \cos n.$

But $n = b - m$; therefore

(D) $\qquad\qquad \cos c = \cos a \sec m \cos (b - m).$

Now c may be computed from (A) and (D), namely,

(48) $\qquad\qquad \tan m = \tan a \cos C,$

(49) $\qquad\qquad \cos c = \dfrac{\cos a \cos (b - m)}{\cos m}.$

EXAMPLE 2. Given $a = 98°$, $b = 80°$, $C = 110°$; find c.

Solution. Apply the method just explained.

To find b − m use (**48**)

log tan a = 0.8522 (*n*)

log cos C = 9.5341 (*n*)

log tan m = 0.3863

$m = 67°\,40'.$

$\therefore b - m = 12°\,20'.$

To find c use (**49**)

log cos a = 9.1436 (*n*)

log cos $(b - m)$ = 9.9899

19.1335

log cos m = 9.5798

log cos c = 9.5537 (*n*)

$180° - c = 69°\,2'.$

$c = 110°\,58'.$

PROBLEMS

Solve the following oblique spherical triangles:

No.	Given Parts	Required Parts
1	$a = 37°\,14'$ $b = 121°\,28'$ $C = 161°\,22'$	$A = 26°\,59'$ $B = 39°\,45'$ $c = 154°\,47'$
2	$a = 98°\,10'$ $c = 61°\,20'$ $B = 111°\,11'$	
3	$b = 152°\,44'$ $c = 88°\,12'$ $A = 78°\,16'$	$B = 153°\,17'$ $C = 78°\,44'$ $a = 86°\,15'$
4	$a = 93°\,20'$ $b = 56°\,30'$ $C = 74°\,40'$	
5	$c = 40°\,20'$ $a = 100°\,30'$ $B = 46°\,40'$	$A = 131°\,29'$ $C = 29°\,33'$ $b = 72°\,40'$
6	$b = 121°\,20'$ $c = 72°\,42'$ $A = 51°\,12'$	
7	$a = 128°\,42'$ $c = 107°\,33'$ $B = 55°\,48'$	$A = 125°\,42'$ $C = 82°\,48'$ $b = 52°\,38'$
8	$a = 84°\,23'$ $b = 124°\,48'$ $C = 62°$	
9	$a = 102°\,50'$ $b = 65°\,10'$ $C = 98°\,30'$	$A = 98°\,19'$ $B = 67°\,4'$ $c = 102°\,57'$
10	$b = 136°\,19'$ $c = 115°\,20'$ $A = 70°\,12'$	

19. Case II. (*b*) **Given two angles and their included side, as**
A, B, c. *Use the formulas* * *on pages 234, 235, namely,*

$$(44) \qquad \tan \tfrac{1}{2}(a - b) = -\frac{\sin \tfrac{1}{2}(\alpha - \beta)}{\sin \tfrac{1}{2}(\alpha + \beta)} \tan \tfrac{1}{2} c,$$

$$(45) \qquad \tan \tfrac{1}{2}(a + b) = -\frac{\cos \tfrac{1}{2}(\alpha - \beta)}{\cos \tfrac{1}{2}(\alpha + \beta)} \tan \tfrac{1}{2} c,$$

to find a and b; and from page 235, use (**46**) *solved for* $\tan \tfrac{1}{2} \gamma$, *namely,*

$$(46) \qquad \tan \tfrac{1}{2} \gamma = -\frac{\sin \tfrac{1}{2} (a + b) \tan \tfrac{1}{2}(\alpha - \beta)}{\sin \tfrac{1}{2} (a - b)},$$

to find γ *and therefore C. Check by the law of sines.*

EXAMPLE 1. Given $c = 116°$, $A = 70°$, $B = 131°\,20'$; find a, b, C.

Solution. $\alpha = 180° - A = 110°$, and $\beta = 180° - B = 48°\,40'.$

$\alpha = 110°$

$\beta = \underline{48°\,40'}$

$\alpha + \beta = 158°\,40'$

$\therefore \tfrac{1}{2}(\alpha + \beta) = 79°\,20'.$

$\alpha = 110°$

$\beta = \underline{48°\,40'}$

$\alpha - \beta = 61°\,20'$

$\therefore \tfrac{1}{2}(\alpha - \beta) = 30°\,40'.$

$c = 116°.$

$\therefore \tfrac{1}{2} c = 58°.$

* Same as those used in Case II, (*a*), p. 239, with Greek and Roman letters interchanged.

To find $\frac{1}{2}(a - b)$ use **(44)**

$\log \sin \frac{1}{2}(\alpha - \beta) = 9.7076$
$\log \tan \frac{1}{2} c = \underline{0.2042}$
$\phantom{\log \tan \frac{1}{2} c = } 9.9118$
$\log \sin \frac{1}{2}(\alpha + \beta) = \underline{9.9924}$
$\log \tan \frac{1}{2}(a - b) = 9.9194 \ (n)$
$\therefore \frac{1}{2}(a - b) = -39° \ 43'.{}^*$

To find $\frac{1}{2}(a + b)$ use **(45)**

$\log \cos \frac{1}{2}(\alpha - \beta) = 9.9346$
$\log \tan \frac{1}{2} c = \underline{0.2042}$
$\phantom{\log \tan \frac{1}{2} c = } 10.1388$
$\log \cos \frac{1}{2}(\alpha + \beta) = \underline{9.2674}$
$\log \tan \frac{1}{2}(a + b) = 0.8714 \ (n)$
$180° - \frac{1}{2}(a + b) = 82° \ 21'.$
$\therefore \frac{1}{2}(a + b) = 97° \ 39'.$

To find a and b

$\phantom{\text{Adding,}} \frac{1}{2}(a + b) = 97° \ 39'$
$\phantom{\text{Adding,}} \frac{1}{2}(a - b) = -39° \ 43'$
Adding, $\phantom{\frac{1}{2}(a - b) =} a = 57° \ 56'$
Subtracting, $ b = 137° \ 22'.$

To find C use **(46)**

$\log \sin \frac{1}{2}(a + b) = 9.9961$
$\log \tan \frac{1}{2}(\alpha - \beta) = \underline{9.7730}$
$\phantom{\log \tan \frac{1}{2}(\alpha - \beta) = } 19.7691$
$\log \sin \frac{1}{2}(a - b) = 9.8055 \ (n)$
$\log \tan \frac{1}{2} \gamma = 9.9636$
$\frac{1}{2} \gamma = 42° \ 36'.$
$\gamma = 85° \ 12'.$
$\therefore C = 180° - \gamma = 94° \ 48'.$

Check. $\log \sin a = 9.9281$ $\log \sin b = 9.8308$ $\log \sin c = 9.9537$
$\log \sin A = \underline{9.9730}$ $\log \sin B = \underline{9.8756}$ $\log \sin C = \underline{9.9985}$
9.9551 9.9552 9.9552

If C only is wanted, we can calculate it without previously determining a and b, by dividing the given triangle into two right spherical triangles, as was illustrated on page 240.

Through B draw an arc of a great circle perpendicular to AC, intersecting AC (or AC produced) at D. Let $BD = p$, angle $ABD = x$, angle $CBD = y$. Applying Rule I of Napier's rules, p. 218, to the right spherical triangle ABD of the figure, we have
$$\cos c = \cot x \cot A,$$
or,

(A) $\cot x = \tan A \cos c.$

Applying Rule II, p. 218, to ABD, we have
$$\cos A = \cos p \sin x,$$
or,
(B) $\cos p = \cos A \csc x.$

Applying the same rule to CBD,
$$\cos C = \cos p \sin y,$$
or,
(C) $\cos p = \cos C \csc y.$

* Since $A < B$ it follows that $a < b$, and $\frac{1}{2}(a - b)$ is negative.

Equating (B) and (C),

$\cos C \csc y = \cos A \csc x$, or, $\cos C = \cos A \csc x \sin y$.

But $y = B - x$; therefore

(D) $\cos C = \cos A \csc x \sin (B - x)$.

Now C may be computed from (A) and (D), namely,

(50) $\cot x = \tan A \cos c$.

(51) $$\cos C = \frac{\cos A \sin (B - x)}{\sin x}.$$

EXAMPLE 2. Given $A = 35° 46'$, $B = 115° 9'$, $c = 51° 2'$; find C.

Solution. Apply the method just explained.

To find $B - x$ use (50)	To find C use (51)
log tan A = 9.8575	log cos A = 9.9093
log cos c = 9.7986	log sin $(B - x)$ = 9.8811
log cot x = 9.6561	19.7904
$x = 65° 38'$.	log sin x = 9.9595
$\therefore B - x = 49° 31'$.	log cos C = 9.8309
	$C = 47° 21'$.

PROBLEMS

Solve the following oblique spherical triangles:

No.	GIVEN PARTS			REQUIRED PARTS		
1	$A = 60°$	$B = 87°$	$c = 48°$	$a = 50° 33'$	$b = 62° 55'$	$C = 56° 28'$
2	$B = 97° 40'$	$C = 67° 30'$	$a = 61° 20'$			
3	$C = 110°$	$A = 94°$	$b = 44°$	$a = 114° 10'$	$c = 120° 46'$	$B = 49° 34'$
4	$C = 71° 10'$	$B = 43° 40'$	$a = 49° 45'$			
5	$A = 108° 12'$	$B = 145° 46'$	$c = 126° 32'$	$a = 69° 5'$	$b = 146° 25'$	$C = 125° 12'$
6	$B = 135°$	$C = 50°$	$a = 70° 20'$			
7	$A = 31° 40'$	$C = 122° 20'$	$b = 40° 40'$	$a = 34° 3'$	$c = 64° 19'$	$B = 37° 40'$
8	$A = 78° 30'$	$B = 41° 15'$	$c = 108° 11'$			
9	$A = 130° 36'$	$B = 30° 26'$	$c = 40° 35'$	$a = 71° 15'$	$b = 39° 10'$	$C = 31° 26'$
10	$A = 121° 15'$	$C = 81°$	$b = 52°$			

20. Case III. (*a*) **Given two sides and the angle opposite one of them, as a, b, B (ambiguous case).*** *From the law of sines, p. 226, we get*

(11) $$\sin A = \frac{\sin a \sin B}{\sin b},$$

* As in the corresponding case in the solution of plane oblique triangles (see the authors' *Plane Trigonometry*, Art. 43), there may be *two solutions*, *one solution*, or *no solution*, depending on the given data.

which gives A.* To find C we use, from page 235, formula (**46**) *solved for* $\tan \frac{1}{2} \gamma$, *namely,*

$$(\textbf{46}) \qquad \tan \tfrac{1}{2} \gamma = - \frac{\sin \frac{1}{2}(a+b) \, \tan \frac{1}{2}(\alpha - \beta)}{\sin \frac{1}{2}(a-b)}.$$

To find c, solve (**44**), *p. 234, for* $\tan \frac{1}{2} c$, *namely,*

$$(\textbf{44}) \qquad \tan \tfrac{1}{2} c = - \frac{\sin \frac{1}{2}(\alpha + \beta) \, \tan \frac{1}{2}(a - b)}{\sin \frac{1}{2}(\alpha - \beta)}.$$

Check by the law of sines.

EXAMPLE. Given $a = 58°$, $b = 137° \, 20'$, $B = 131° \, 20'$; find A, C, c.

Solution.

To find A use (**11**)

$\log \sin a =$	9.9284
$\log \sin B =$	9.8756
	19.8040
$\log \sin b =$	9.8311
$\log \sin A =$	9.9729

$\therefore A_1 = 69° \, 58'$,

or, $A_2 = 180° - A_1 = 110° \, 2'$.

$a = 58°$ $a = 58°$
$b = 137° \, 20'$ $b = \underline{137° \, 20'}$
$a + b = 195° \, 20'$ $a - b = -79° \, 20'$
$\frac{1}{2}(a+b) = 97° \, 40'$. $\frac{1}{2}(a-b) = -39° \, 40'$.
$\beta = 180° - B = 48° \, 40'$.

Since $a < b$ and both A_1 and A_2 are less than B, it follows that we have *two solutions.*

First solution. $\alpha_1 = 180° - A_1 = 110° \, 2'$.

$\alpha_1 =$	$110° \, 2'$
$\beta =$	$48° \, 40'$
$\alpha_1 + \beta =$	$158° \, 42'$
$\frac{1}{2}(\alpha_1 + \beta) =$	$79° \, 21'$.

$\alpha_1 =$	$110° \, 2'$
$\beta =$	$48° \, 40'$
$\alpha_1 - \beta =$	$61° \, 22'$
$\frac{1}{2}(\alpha_1 - \beta) =$	$30° \, 41'$.

To find C_1 use (**46**)

$\log \sin \frac{1}{2}(a+b) =$	9.9961
$\log \tan \frac{1}{2}(\alpha_1 - \beta) =$	9.7733
	19.7694
$\log \sin \frac{1}{2}(a-b) =$	$9.8050 \, (n)$
$\log \tan \frac{1}{2} \gamma_1 =$	9.9644
$\frac{1}{2} \gamma_1 =$	$42° \, 39'$.
$\gamma_1 =$	$85° \, 18'$.

$\therefore C_1 = 180° - \gamma_1 = 94° \, 42'$.

To find c_1 use (**44**)

$\log \sin \frac{1}{2}(\alpha_1 + \beta) =$	9.9924
$\log \tan \frac{1}{2}(a - b) =$	$9.9187 \, (n)$
	19.9111
$\log \sin \frac{1}{2}(\alpha_1 - \beta) =$	9.7078
$\log \tan \frac{1}{2} c_1 =$	10.2033
$\frac{1}{2} c_1 =$	$57° \, 57'$.

$\therefore c_1 = 115° \, 54'$.

---

* Since the angle A is here determined from its sine, it is necessary to consider both of the values found. If $a > b$, then $A > B$; and if $a < b$, then $A < B$. Hence *only those values of A should be retained which are greater or less than B according as a is greater or less than b.*

If log sin A = a positive number, there will be no solution.

Check.   log sin $a = 9.9284$ log sin $b = 9.8311$ log sin $c_1 = 9.9541$
            log sin $A_1 = \underline{9.9729}$ log sin $B = \underline{9.8756}$ log sin $C_1 = \underline{9.9985}$
            9.9555 9.9555 9.9556

Second solution. $\alpha_2 = 180° - A_2 = 69° 58'.$

$$\alpha_2 = 69° 58'$$
$$\beta = 48° 40'$$
$$\overline{\alpha_2 + \beta = 118° 38'}$$
$$\tfrac{1}{2}(\alpha_2 + \beta) = 59° 19'.$$

$$\alpha_2 = 69° 58'$$
$$\beta = 48° 40'$$
$$\overline{\alpha_2 - \beta = 21° 18'}$$
$$\tfrac{1}{2}(\alpha_2 - \beta) = 10° 39'.$$

To find C_2 use **(46)**

log sin $\tfrac{1}{2}(a + b) = 9.9961$
log tan $\tfrac{1}{2}(\alpha_2 - \beta) = \underline{9.2743}$
19.2704
log sin $\tfrac{1}{2}(a - b) = 9.8050$ (n)
log tan $\tfrac{1}{2}\gamma_2 = 9.4654$

$$\tfrac{1}{2}\gamma_2 = 16° 17'.$$
$$\gamma_2 = 32° 34'.$$
$$\therefore C_2 = 180° - \gamma_2 = 147° 26'.$$

To find c_1 use **(44)**

log sin $\tfrac{1}{2}(\alpha_2 + \beta) = 9.9345$
log tan $\tfrac{1}{2}(a - b) = \underline{9.9187}$ (n)
19.8532
log sin $\tfrac{1}{2}(\alpha_2 - \beta) = \underline{9.2667}$
log tan $\tfrac{1}{2}c_2 = 10.5865$

$$\tfrac{1}{2}c_2 = 75° 28'.$$
$$\therefore c_2 = 150° 56'.$$

Check.   log sin $a = 9.9284$ log sin $b = 9.8311$ log sin $c_2 = 9.6865$
            log sin $A_2 = \underline{9.9729}$ log sin $B = \underline{9.8756}$ log sin $C_2 = \underline{9.7310}$
            9.9555 9.9555 9.9555

If the side c or the angle C is wanted without first calculating the value of A, we may resolve the given triangle into two right triangles and then apply Napier's rules, as was illustrated under Cases II, (a), and II, (b), pp. 240, 241.

PROBLEMS

Solve the following oblique spherical triangles :

No.	Given Parts	Required Parts
1	$a = 68°53'$ $b = 56°50'$ $B = 45°15'$	$A_1 = 52°20'$ $C_1 = 124°42'$ $c_1 = 104°19'$; or $A_2 = 127°40'$ $C_2 = 15°21'$ $c_2 = 18°10'$
2	$a = 43°20'$ $b = 48°30'$ $A = 58°40'$	
3	$b = 99°40'$ $c = 64°20'$ $B = 95°40'$	$C = 65°30'$ $A = 97°20'$ $a = 100°45'$
4	$a = 56°40'$ $b = 30°50'$ $A = 103°40'$	
5	$a = 30°53'$ $b = 31°9'$ $A = 87°34'$	Impossible
6	$a = 115°20'$ $c = 146°20'$ $C = 141°10'$	
7	$a = 55°$ $c = 138°10'$ $A = 42°30'$	$C = 146°38'$ $B = 55°1'$ $b = 96°34'$
8	$b = 108°30'$ $c = 40°50'$ $C = 39°50'$	
9	$a = 73°50'$ $b = 120°54'$ $A = 88°53'$	$B = 116°43'$ $c = 120°57'$ $C = 116°47'$
10	$a = 162°20'$ $b = 15°40'$ $B = 125°$	

21. Case III. (*b*) **Given two angles and the side opposite one of them, as** *A, B, b* **(ambiguous case).***

From the law of sines, p. 226, we get

$$(11) \qquad \sin a = \frac{\sin A \sin b}{\sin B},$$

which gives a.† To find c we use, from page 234, the formula ‡ (44) solved for $\tan \frac{1}{2} c$, *namely,*

$$(44) \qquad \tan \tfrac{1}{2} c = -\frac{\sin \tfrac{1}{2}(\alpha + \beta)\, \tan \tfrac{1}{2}(a - b)}{\sin \tfrac{1}{2}(\alpha - \beta)}.$$

To find C, solve (46), *page 235, for* $\tan \frac{1}{2} \gamma$, *namely,*

$$(46) \qquad \tan \tfrac{1}{2} \gamma = -\frac{\sin \tfrac{1}{2}(a + b)\, \tan \tfrac{1}{2}(\alpha - \beta)}{\sin \tfrac{1}{2}(a - b)}.$$

Check by the law of sines.

EXAMPLE. Given $A = 110°$, $B = 131° \, 20'$, $b = 137° \, 20'$; find a, c, C.

Solution. $\alpha = 180° - A = 70°$, and $\beta = 180° - B = 48° \, 40'$.

To find a use (11)

log sin A =	9.9730
log sin b =	9.8311
	19.8041
log sin B =	9.8756
log sin a =	9.9285

$$\therefore a_1 = 58° \, 1',$$

or, $\qquad a_2 = 180° - a_1 = 121° \, 59'.$

$\alpha =$	$70°$	$\alpha = 70°$	
$\beta =$	$48° \, 40'$	$\beta = 48° \, 40'$	
$\alpha + \beta =$	$118° \, 40'$	$\alpha - \beta = 21° \, 20'$	

$\tfrac{1}{2}(\alpha + \beta) = 59° \, 20'.$ $\tfrac{1}{2}(\alpha - \beta) = 10° \, 40'.$

Since $A < B$ and both a_1 and a_2 are less than b, it follows that we have *two solutions.*

First solution.

$a_1 =$	$58° \, 1'$
$b =$	$137° \, 20'$
$a_1 + b =$	$195° \, 21'$

$\tfrac{1}{2}(a_1 + b) = 97° \, 41'.$

$a_1 =$	$58° \, 1'$
$b =$	$137° \, 20'$
$a_1 - b =$	$- 79° \, 19'$

$\tfrac{1}{2}(a_1 - b) = - 39° \, 40'.$

---

* Just as in Case III, (*a*), we may have *two solutions, one solution,* or *no solution,* depending on the given data.

† Since the side is here determined from its sine, it is necessary to examine both of the values found. If $A > B$ then $a > b$; and if $A < B$ then $a < b$. Hence *only those values of a should be retained which are greater or less than b according as A is greater or less than B.*

If log sin a = a positive number, there will be no solution.

‡ Same as those used in Case III, (*a*), p. 243, when the Greek and Roman letters **are** interchanged.

To find c_1 use (44)	*To find C_1 use* (46)

To find c_1 use (44)

$\log \sin \frac{1}{2}(\alpha + \beta) = \quad 9.9346$
$\log \tan \frac{1}{2}(a_1 - b) = \quad \underline{9.9187}\ (n)$
$\qquad\qquad\qquad\qquad 19.8533$
$\log \sin \frac{1}{2}(\alpha - \beta) = \quad \underline{9.2674}$
$\log \tan \frac{1}{2}\,c_1 = 10.5859$

$\qquad \frac{1}{2}\,c_1 = 75°\,27'.$

$\qquad \therefore c_1 = 150°\,54'.$

To find C_1 use (46)

$\log \sin \frac{1}{2}(a_1 + b) = \quad 9.9961$
$\log \tan \frac{1}{2}(\alpha - \beta) = \quad \underline{9.2750}$
$\qquad\qquad\qquad\qquad 19.2711$
$\log \sin \frac{1}{2}(a_1 - b) = \quad \underline{9.8050}\ (n)$
$\log \tan \frac{1}{2}\,\gamma_1 = \quad 9.4661$

$\qquad \frac{1}{2}\,\gamma_1 = 16°\,18'.$

$\qquad \gamma_1 = 32°\,36'.$

$\therefore C_1 = 180° - \gamma_1 = 147°\,24'.$

Check. $\log \sin a_1 = 9.9285 \qquad \log \sin b = 9.8311 \qquad \log \sin c_1 = 9.6869$
$\qquad\quad \log \sin A = \underline{9.9730} \qquad \log \sin B = \underline{9.8756} \qquad \log \sin C_1 = \underline{9.7314}$
$\qquad\qquad\qquad\ 9.9555 \qquad\qquad\qquad\ 9.9555 \qquad\qquad\qquad\ 9.9555$

Second solution. This gives $c_2 = 64°\,8'$, and $C_2 = 85°\,18'$.
Remembering that $a_2 = 121°\,59'$, we may now check the second solution.

Check. $\log \sin a_2 = 9.9285 \qquad \log \sin b = 9.8311 \qquad \log \sin c_2 = 9.9542$
$\qquad\quad \log \sin A = \underline{9.9730} \qquad \log \sin B = \underline{9.8756} \qquad \log \sin C_2 = \underline{9.9985}$
$\qquad\qquad\qquad\ 9.9555 \qquad\qquad\qquad\ 9.9555 \qquad\qquad\qquad\ 9.9557$

Hence the two solutions are

$$a_1 = 58°\,1', \qquad c_1 = 150°\,54', \qquad C_1 = 147°\,24',$$
and
$$a_2 = 121°\,59', \qquad c_2 = 64°\,8', \qquad C_2 = 85°\,18'.$$

If the angle C or the side c is wanted without first computing a, we may resolve the given triangle into two right triangles and then apply Napier's rules, as was illustrated under Cases II, (*a*), and II, (*b*), pp. 240, 241.

PROBLEMS

Solve the following oblique spherical triangles:

No.	Given Parts	Required Parts
1	$A = 110°\,10'$ $B = 133°\,18'$ $a = 147°\,6'$	$b = 155°\,5'$ $\quad c = 33°\,2'$ $\qquad C = 70°\,21'$
2	$B = 116°$ $\qquad C = 80°$ $\qquad c = 84°$	
3	$A = 132°$ $\qquad B = 140°$ $\qquad b = 127°$	$a_1 = 67°\,24'$ $C_1 = 164°\,6'$ $\quad c_1 = 160°\,6'$
		$a_2 = 112°\,36'$ $C_2 = 128°\,21'$ $c_2 = 103°\,2'$
4	$A = 61°\,40'$ $\quad C = 140°\,20'$ $\quad c = 150°\,20'$	
5	$A = 113°\,39'$ $B = 123°\,40'$ $a = 65°\,40'$	$b = 124°\,7'$ $\quad c = 159°\,50'$ $C = 159°\,44'$
6	$A = 133°\,50'$ $B = 66°\,30'$ $\quad a = 81°\,10'$	
7	$B = 24°\,33'$ $\quad C = 38°$ $\qquad b = 65°\,20'$	Impossible
8	$A = 108°\,40'$ $C = 134°\,20'$ $a = 145°\,36'$	
9	$A = 100°\,2'$ $\quad B = 98°\,30'$ $\quad a = 95°\,21'$	$b = 90°$ $\qquad c = 147°\,42'$ $C = 148°\,6'$
10	$B = 73°$ $\qquad C = 81°\,20'$ $\quad b = 122°\,40'$	

22. Length of an arc of a circle in linear units. From geometry we know that *the length of an arc of a circle is to the circumference of the circle as the number of degrees in the arc is to 360.* That is,

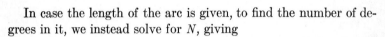

$$L : 2\,\pi R = N : 360,$$

or,

$$(52) \qquad L = \frac{\pi RN}{180},$$

where L = length of arc,

N = number of degrees in arc,

R = length of radius.

In case the length of the arc is given, to find the number of degrees in it, we instead solve for N, giving

$$(53) \qquad\qquad N = \frac{180\,L}{\pi R}.$$

Considering the earth as a sphere, *an arc of one minute* on a great circle is called *a geographical mile* or *a nautical mile.** Hence there are 60 nautical miles in an arc of 1 degree, and $360 \times 60 = 21{,}600$ nautical miles in the circumference of a great circle of the earth. If we assume the radius of the earth to be 3960 statute miles, the length of a nautical mile ($= 1$ min. $= \frac{1}{60}$ of a degree) in statute miles will be, from (52),

$$L = \frac{3.1416 \times 3960 \times \frac{1}{60}}{180} = 1.15 \text{ mi.}$$

EXAMPLE 1. Find the length of an arc of 22° 30′ in a circle of radius 4 in.

Solution. Here $N = 22° \, 30′ = 22.5°$, and $R = 4$ in.

Substituting in (52), $L = \dfrac{3.1416 \times 4 \times 22.5}{180} = 1.57$ in. *Ans.*

EXAMPLE 2. A ship has sailed on a great circle for $5\frac{1}{2}$ hr. at the rate of 12 statute miles an hour. How many degrees are there in the arc passed over?

Solution. Here $L = 5\frac{1}{2} \times 12 = 66$ mi., and $R = 3960$ mi.

Substituting in (53), $N = \dfrac{180 \times 66}{3.1416 \times 3960} = 0.955° = 57.3′.$ *Ans.*

---

* In connection with a ship's rate of sailing, a *nautical mile* is also called a *knot.*

23. Area of a spherical triangle. From spherical geometry we know that *the area of a spherical triangle is to the area of the surface of the sphere as the number of degrees in its spherical excess* * *is to 720.* That is,

$$\text{Area of triangle} : 4\,\pi R^2 = E : 720,$$

or,

(54)   **Area of a spherical triangle** $= \dfrac{\pi R^2 E}{180}.$

In case the three angles of the triangle are not given, we should first find them by solving the triangle. Or, if the three sides of the triangle are given, we may find E directly by Lhuilier's formula,† namely,

(55) $\tan \frac{1}{4} E = \sqrt{\tan \frac{1}{2}\,s \, \tan \frac{1}{2}(s - a)\,\tan \frac{1}{2}(s - b)\,\tan \frac{1}{2}(s - c)},$

where a, b, c denote the sides and $s = \frac{1}{2}(a + b + c)$.

The area of a spherical polygon will evidently be the sum of the areas of the spherical triangles formed by drawing arcs of great circles as diagonals of the polygon.

EXAMPLE. The angles of a spherical triangle on a sphere of 25-inch radius are $A = 74° 40'$, $B = 67° 30'$, $C = 49° 50'$. Find the area of the triangle.

Solution. Here $E = (A + B + C) - 180° = 12°$.

Substituting in (54), $\text{Area} = \dfrac{3.1416 \times (25)^2 \times 12}{180} = 130.9$ sq. in. *Ans.*

PROBLEMS

1. Find the length of an arc of $65°$ in a circle whose radius is 1.5 ft.
                                                    Ans. 1.702 ft.

2. Find the length of an arc of $75° 30'$ in a circle whose radius is 10 yd.

3. How many degrees are there in a circular arc 30 in. long, if the radius is 6 in.?   *Ans.* $286° 36'$.

4. A ship sailed over an arc of $5°$ on a great circle of the earth each day. At what rate was the ship sailing?

5. Find in inches the perimeter of a spherical triangle of sides $48°$, $126°$, $80°$ on a sphere of radius 50 in.   *Ans.* 221.56 in.

---

* The spherical excess (usually denoted by E) of a spherical triangle is the excess of the sum of the angles of the triangle over 180°. Thus, if A, B, and C are the angles of a spherical triangle,

$$E = A + B + C - 180°.$$

† Derived in more advanced treatises.

6. Find the area of a spherical triangle whose angles are 63°, 84° 21′, and 79°, if the radius of the sphere is 10 in.

7. The sides of a spherical triangle are 6.47 in., 8.39 in., and 9.43 in. If the radius of the sphere is 25 in., find the area of the triangle.

Ans. 26.9 sq. in.

8. Considering the earth as a sphere of radius 3963 mi., find the area of a triangle on the surface of the earth whose sides are 47° 15′, 88°, and 101° 30′.

9. In a spherical triangle, $A = 75° 16′$, $B = 39° 20′$, and $c = 26$ ft. If the radius of the sphere is 14 ft., find the area of the triangle.

Ans. 158.45 sq. ft.

10. A steamboat traveling at the rate of 15 knots per hour skirts the entire shore line of an island having the approximate shape of an equilateral triangle in 20 hr. Find the approximate area of the island.

Find the areas of the spherical triangles having the following given parts. The radius of the sphere is R.

11. $a = 128° 43′$, $b = 107° 14′$, $c = 88° 38′$.   *Ans.* 2.8624 R^2.

12. $a = 43° 30′$, $b = 72° 24′$, $c = 87° 50′$; $R = 10$ in.

13. $A = 74° 40′$, $B = 67° 30′$, $C = 49° 50′$; $R = 100$ yd.

Ans. 2094 sq. yd.

14. $A = 127° 23′$, $B = 131° 50′$, $C = 100° 53′$; $R = 6$ ft.

15. $a = 64° 20′$, $b = 42° 30′$, $C = 50° 40′$; $R = 12$ ft. *Ans.* 46.74 sq. ft.

16. $a = 43° 40′$, $b = 47° 10′$, $A = 58° 20′$; $R = 50$ rd.

17. $a = 116° 20′$, $A = 160° 42′$, $C = 171° 27′$.   *Ans.* 5.421 R^2.

18. $b = 67° 16′$, $A = 84° 56′$, $C = 96° 19′$; $R = 20$ ft.

CHAPTER III

APPLICATIONS OF SPHERICAL TRIGONOMETRY TO THE CELESTIAL AND TERRESTRIAL SPHERES

24. Geographical terms. In what follows we shall assume the earth to be a sphere of radius 3960 statute miles.

The *meridian* of a place on the earth is that great circle of the earth which passes through the place and the north and south

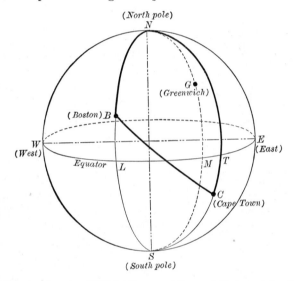

poles. In the figure, *NGS* is the meridian of Greenwich, *NBS* the meridian of Boston, and *NCS* the meridian of Cape Town.

The *latitude* of a place is the arc of the meridian of the place extending from the equator to the place. Latitude is measured north or south of the equator from 0° to 90°. Thus, in the figure, the arc *LB* measures the north latitude of Boston, and the arc *TC* measures the south latitude of Cape Town.

The *longitude* of a place is the arc of the equator extending from the zero meridian * to the meridian of the place. Longitude

---

* As in this case, the zero meridian, or reference meridian, is usually the meridian passing through Greenwich, near London. The meridians of Washington and Paris are also used as reference meridians.

is measured east or west from the Greenwich meridian from 0° to 180°. Thus, in the figure, the arc MT measures the east longitude of Cape Town, while the arc ML measures the west longitude of Boston. Since the arcs MT and ML are the measures of the angles MNT and MNL respectively, it is evident that we can also define the longitude of a place as the angle between the reference meridian and the meridian of the place. Thus, in the figure, the angle MNT is the east longitude of Cape Town, while the angle MNL is the west longitude of Boston.

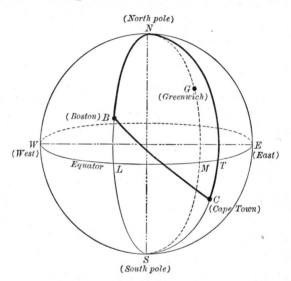

The *bearing* of one place from a second place is the angle between the arc of a great circle drawn from the second place to the first place, and the meridian of the second place. Thus, in the figure, the bearing of Cape Town from Boston is measured by the angle CBN or the angle CBL, while the bearing of Boston from Cape Town is measured by the angle NCB or the angle SCB.*

25. Distance between two points on the surface of the earth. Since we know from geometry that *the shortest distance on the surface of a sphere between any two points on that surface is the arc, not greater than a semicircumference, of the great circle that joins them*, it is evident that the shortest distance between two places on the earth is measured in the same way. Thus, in the figure, the shortest

---

* The *bearing* or *course* of a ship at any point is the angle the path of the ship makes with the meridian at that point.

distance between Boston and Cape Town is measured on the arc BC of a great circle. We observe that this arc BC is one side of a spherical triangle of which the two other sides are the arcs BN and CN. Since

arc $BN = 90° -$ arc $LB = 90° -$ north latitude of Boston,

arc $CN = 90° +$ arc $TC = 90° +$ south latitude of Cape Town,

and angle $BNC = $ angle $MNL + $ angle MNT

$\qquad\qquad = $ west longitude of Boston

$\qquad\qquad\quad + $ east longitude of Cape Town

$\qquad\qquad = $ difference in longitude of Boston and Cape Town,

it is evident that if we know the latitudes and longitudes of Boston and Cape Town, we have all the data necessary for determining two sides and the included angle of the triangle BNC. The third side BC, which is the shortest distance between Boston and Cape Town, may then be found as in Case II, (*a*), p. 239.

In what follows, north latitude will be given the sign $+$ and south latitude the sign $-$.

DIRECTIONS FOR FINDING THE SHORTEST DISTANCE BETWEEN TWO POINTS ON THE EARTH AND THE BEARING OF EACH FROM THE OTHER, THE LATITUDE AND LONGITUDE OF EACH POINT BEING GIVEN

First step. *Subtract the latitude of each place from* 90°.* *The results will be two sides of a spherical triangle.*

Second step. *Find the difference of longitude of the two places by subtracting the lesser longitude from the greater if both are E. or both are W., but add the two if one is E. and the other is W. This gives the included angle of the triangle.*†

Third step. *Solving the triangle by Case II, (a), p. 239, the third side gives the shortest distance between the two points in degrees of arc,*‡ *and the angles give the bearings.*

---

* Note that this is *algebraic* subtraction. Thus, if the two latitudes were 25° N. and 42° S., we would get as the two sides of the triangle,

$$90° - 25° = 65° \quad \text{and} \quad 90° - (-42°) = 90° + 42° = 132°.$$

† If the difference of longitude found is greater than 180°, we should subtract it from 360° and use the remainder as the included angle.

‡ The number of minutes in this arc will be the distance between the two places in geographical (nautical) miles. The distance between the two places in statute miles is given by the formula

$$L = \frac{3.1416 \times 3960 \times N}{180},$$

where $N = $ the number of degrees in the arc.

EXAMPLE. Find the shortest distance along the earth's surface between Boston (lat. 42° 21′ N., long. 71° 4′ W.) and Cape Town (lat. 33° 56′ S., long. 18° 29′ E.), and the bearing of each city from the other.

Solution. Draw a spherical triangle in agreement with the figure on page 252.

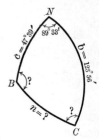

First step.
$$c = 90° - 42° 21' = 47° 39',$$
$$b = 90° - (- 33° 56') = 123° 56'.$$

Second step.
$$N = 71° 4' + 18° 29' = 89° 33' = \text{difference in long.}$$

Third step.
Solving the triangle by Case II, (a), p. 239, we get
$$n = 68° 15' = 68.25° = 4095 \text{ nautical miles,}$$
$$C = 52° 44' = \text{bearing of Boston from Cape Town,}$$
and $B = 116° 42' = \text{bearing of Cape Town from Boston.}$

Hence a ship sailing from Boston to Cape Town on the arc of a great circle *sets out from Boston* on a course S. 63° 18′ E. and *approaches Cape Town* on a course S. 52° 44′ E.*

PROBLEMS

1. Find the shortest distance in nautical miles between New York (lat. 40° 43′ N., long. 74° W.) and Cape Town (lat. 33° 56′ S., long. 18° 29′ E.). Also find the bearing of each from the other.   *Ans.* 6784 nautical miles.
Bearing of New York from Cape Town, N. 55° 22′ W.
Bearing of Cape Town from New York, S. 64° 16′ E.

2. Find the shortest distance in nautical miles between Boston (lat. 42° 21′ N., long. 71° 4′ W.) and Liverpool (lat. 53° 24′ N., long. 3° 4′ W.). Also find the bearing of each from the other.

Find the shortest distance in nautical miles between the following places:

3. Boston (lat. 42° 21′ N., long. 71° 4′ W.) and San Diego (lat. 32° 43′ N., long. 117° 10′ W.).   *Ans.* 2239 nautical miles.

4. New York (lat. 40° 43′ N., long. 74° W.) and San Francisco (lat. 37° 48′ N., long. 122° 28′ W.).

5. San Francisco (lat. 37° 48′ N., long. 122° 28′ W.) and Batavia (lat. 6° 9′ S., long. 106° 53′ E.).   *Ans.* 7516 nautical miles.

6. Seattle (lat. 47° 36′ N., long. 122° 20′ W.) and Bombay (lat. 18° 54′ N., long. 72° 49′ E.).

7. San Francisco (lat. 37° 48′ N., long. 122° 28′ W.) and Valparaiso (lat. 33° 2′ S., long. 71° 41′ W.).   *Ans.* 5109 nautical miles.

8. Chicago (lat. 41° 50′ N., long. 87° 35′ W.) and Manila (lat. 14° 36′ N., long. 121° 5′ E.).

* A ship that sails on a great circle (except on the equator or a meridian) must be continually changing her course. If the ship in the above example keeps constantly on the course S. 63° 18′ E., she will never reach Cape Town.

9. Find the shortest distance in statute miles (taking the diameter of the earth as 7912 mi.) between Boston (lat. 42° 21′ N., long. 71° 4′ W.) and Greenwich (lat. 51° 29′ N.) and the bearing of each place from the other. *Ans.* Distance = 3275 mi.

N. 53° 7′ E. = bearing of Greenwich from Boston.
S. 71° 39′ W. = bearing of Boston from Greenwich.

10. From a point whose latitude is 17° N. and longitude 130° W. a ship sailed on an arc of a great circle over a distance of 4150 statute miles, starting S. 54° 20′ W. Find its latitude and longitude, if the length of 1° is 69⅙ statute miles.

26. Astronomical problems. One of the most important applications of spherical trigonometry is to astronomy. In fact, trigonometry was first developed by astronomers, and for centuries was studied only in connection with astronomy. We shall take up the study of a few simple problems in astronomy.

27. The celestial sphere. When there are no clouds to obstruct the view, the sky appears like a great hemispherical vault, with the observer at the center. The stars seem to glide upon the inner surface of this sphere from east to west, their paths being circles in parallel planes which are perpendicular to the polar axis of the earth, and have their centers in that axis produced. Each star makes a complete revolution, called its diurnal (daily) motion, in 23 hr. 56 min., ordinary clock time. We cannot estimate the distance of the surface of this sphere from us, further than to perceive that it must be very far away indeed, because it lies beyond even the remotest terrestrial objects. To an observer the stars all seem to be at the same enormous distance from him, since his eyes can judge their *directions only* and not their *distances*. We therefore regard this imaginary sphere on which all the heavenly bodies seem to be projected as having a radius of unlimited length. This sphere is called the *celestial sphere*. The earth is conceived of as lying at its center.

The figure on the following page represents the celestial sphere, with the earth at the center showing as a mere dot.

The *zenith* of an observer is the point on the celestial sphere directly overhead. A plumb line held by the observer and extended upwards will pierce the celestial sphere at his zenith (*Z* in figure).

The *nadir* is the point on the celestial sphere which is diametrically opposite to the zenith (*Z′* in the figure).

The *horizon* of an observer is the great circle on the celestial sphere having the observer's zenith for a pole; hence every point on the horizon ($SWNE$ in the figure) will be 90° from the zenith and from the nadir.

Every great circle passing through the zenith will be perpendicular to the horizon ; such circles are called *vertical circles* (as $ZMHZ'$ and $ZQSP'Z'$ in the figure).

The *celestial equator* is the great circle in which the plane of the earth's equator cuts the celestial sphere ($EQWQ'$ in the figure).

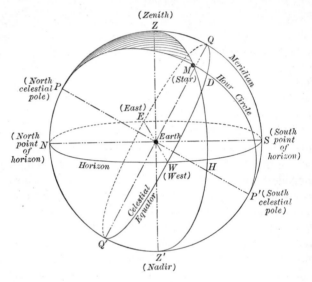

The *poles* of the celestial equator are the points (P and P' in the figure) where the earth's axis, if produced, would pierce the celestial sphere. The Pole Star is near the north celestial pole, being about $1\frac{1}{4}°$ from it. Every point on the celestial equator is 90° from each of the celestial poles.

All points on the earth's surface have the same celestial equator and poles.

The geographical meridian of a place on the earth was defined as that great circle of the earth which passes through the place and the north and south poles. The *celestial meridian* of a point on the earth's surface is the great circle in which the plane of the point's geographical meridian cuts the celestial sphere ($ZQSP'Z'Q'NP$ in the figure). It is evidently that vertical circle of an observer which passes through the north and south points of his horizon. All points on the surface of the earth which do not lie on the same north-and-south line have different celestial meridians.

The *hour circle* of a heavenly body is that great circle of the celestial sphere whose plane passes through the body and through the north and south celestial poles. In the figure, $PMDP'$ is the hour circle of the star M. The hour circles of all the heavenly bodies are continually changing with respect to any observer.

The spherical triangle PZM, having the north pole, the zenith, and a heavenly body at its three vertices, is a very important triangle in astronomy. It is called the *astronomical triangle*.

The *altitude* of a heavenly body is its angular distance above the horizon measured on a vertical circle from 0° to 90°.* Thus the altitude of the sun M is the arc HM. The distance of a heavenly body from the zenith is called its *zenith distance* (ZM in the figure), and it is evidently the complement of its altitude. The altitude of the zenith is 90°. The altitude of the sun at sunrise or sunset is zero (see the figure).

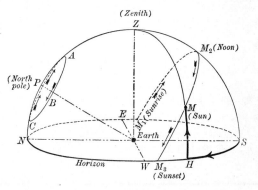

The *declination* of a heavenly body is its angular distance north or south of the celestial equator measured on the hour circle of the body from 0° to 90°.† Thus, in the figure on the following page, the arc DM is a measure of the north declination of the star M. *North declination* is always considered *positive* and *south declination negative*. Hence the declination of the north pole is $+$ 90°, while that of the south pole is $-$ 90°.

The *hour angle* of a heavenly body is the angle between the meridian of the observer and the hour circle of the star measured *westward* from the meridian from 0° to 360°. Thus, in the figure, the hour angle of the star M is the angle QPD (measured by the arc QD). This angle is commonly used as a measure of time, hence the name *hour angle*. Thus the star M makes a complete circuit in 24 hours; that is, the hour angle QPD continually increases at the uniform rate of 360° in 24 hours, or 15° an hour. For this reason

---

* At sea the altitude is usually measured by the sextant, while on land a surveyor's transit is used.

† The declinations of the sun, moon, planets, and some of the fixed stars, for any time of the year, are given in the *Nautical Almanac* or *American Ephemeris*, published by the United States government.

the hour angle of a heavenly body is usually reckoned in hours from 0 to 24, one hour being equal to 15°. When the star is at M_1

(on the observer's meridian) its hour angle is zero. Then the hour angle increases until it becomes the angle M_1PM (when the star is at M). When the star sets on the western horizon its hour angle becomes M_1PM_2. Twelve hours after the star is at M_1 it will be at M_3, when its hour angle will be 180° (= 12 hours). Continuing on its circuit, the star rises at M_4 and finally reaches

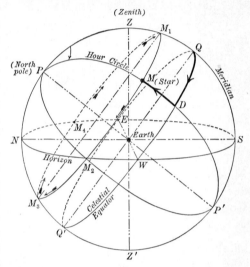

M_1, when its hour angle has become 360° (= 24 hours), or 0° again.

28. Relation between the latitude of the observer and the altitude of the celestial pole. In the figure below, let O be the position of the observer at some place in the northern hemisphere. Then the angle QCO, measured in degrees, determines the latitude

at O. The angles ZCP and QCO are complementary. Hence, in the figures of Art. 27, the arc ZP is the complement of the latitude, and the arc NP equals the latitude. That is, the *latitude of a place and the altitude of the celestial pole are equal.*

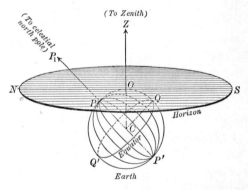

29. To determine the time of day. A very simple relation exists between the hour angle of the sun and the time of day at any place. The sun appears to move from east to west at the uniform rate of 15° per hour, and when the sun is on the meridian of a place it is apparent noon at that place. Comparing,

Hour Angle of Sun	Time of Day
0°	Noon
15°	1 P.M.
30°	2 P.M.
45°	3 P.M.
90°	6 P.M.
180°	Midnight
195°	1 A.M.
210°	2 A.M.
270°	6 A.M.
300°	8 A.M.
360°	Noon

The hour angle of the sun M is the angle at P in the astronomical (spherical) triangle PZM. We may find this hour angle (time of day) by solving the astronomical triangle for the angle at P, provided we know three elements of the triangle.

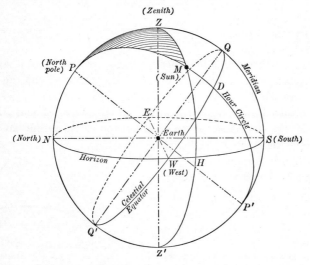

$DM =$ declination of sun, and is found from the Nautical Almanac.

∴ side $PM = 90° - DM = co$-declination of sun.

$HM =$ altitude of sun, and is found by measuring the angular distance of the sun above the horizon with a sextant or transit.

∴ side $MZ = 90° - HM = co$-altitude of sun.

$NP =$ altitude of the celestial pole
    $=$ latitude of the observer (Art. 28).

∴ side $PZ = 90° - NP = co$-latitude of observer.

Hence we have

DIRECTIONS FOR DETERMINING THE TIME OF DAY AT A PLACE WHOSE LATITUDE IS KNOWN, WHEN THE DECLINATION AND ALTITUDE OF THE SUN AT THAT TIME AND PLACE ARE KNOWN

First step. *Take for the three sides of a spherical triangle*
the co-altitude of the sun,
the co-declination of the sun,
the co-latitude of the place.

Second step. *Solve this spherical triangle for the angle opposite the first-mentioned side. This will give the* **hour angle in degrees** *of the sun, if the observation is made in the afternoon. If the observation is made in the forenoon, the hour angle will be* **360° — the angle found.**

Third step. *When the observation is made in the afternoon the time of day will be*

$$\frac{hour\ angle}{15}\ \text{P.M.}$$

When the observation is made in the forenoon the time of day will be

$$\left(\frac{hour\ angle}{15} - 12\right) \text{A.M.}$$

EXAMPLE. In New York (lat. 40° 43′ N.) the sun's altitude is observed to be 30° 40′. Given that the sun's declination is 10° N. and that the observation is made in the afternoon, what is the time of day?

Solution. *First step.* Draw the triangle.

Side a = co-alt. = 90° − 30° 40′ = 59° 20′.

Side b = co-dec. = 90° − 10° = 80°.

Side c = co-lat. = 90° − 40° 43′ = 49° 17′.

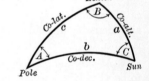

Second step. As we have three sides given, the solution of this triangle comes under Case I, (*a*), p. 236. But as we only want the angle A (hour angle), some labor may be saved by using one of the formulas (**18**), (**19**), (**20**), pp. 230, 231. Let us use (**18**).

$$
\begin{array}{l}
a = 59°\ 20' \\
b = 80° \\
c = \underline{49°\ 17'} \\
2\,s = 188°\ 37' \\[4pt]
s = 94°\ 19'. \\
s - a = 34°\ 59'.
\end{array}
\qquad
\sin \tfrac{1}{2}\alpha = \sqrt{\frac{\sin s \sin (s - a)}{\sin b \sin c}},
$$

$$\log \sin \tfrac{1}{2}\alpha = \tfrac{1}{2}[\log \sin s + \log \sin (s - a) - \{\log \sin b + \log \sin c\}].$$

$$\log \sin s = 9.9988$$
$$\log \sin (s - a) = 9.7584$$
$$\log \text{numerator} = 19.7572$$
$$\log \text{denominator} = 19.8731$$
$$9.8841$$

$$\log \sin b = 9.9934$$
$$\log \sin c = 9.8797$$
$$\log \text{denominator} = 19.8731$$

$$2 | 19.8841$$
$$\log \sin \tfrac{1}{2}\,\alpha = 9.9421$$
$$\tfrac{1}{2}\,\alpha = 61° 4'.$$
$$\alpha = 122° 8'.$$

$$\therefore A = 180° - \alpha = 57° 52' = \text{hour angle of sun.}$$

Third step. Time of day $= \dfrac{\text{hour angle}}{15}$ P.M. $= 3$ hr. 51 min. P.M. *Ans.*

PROBLEMS

1. In Chicago (lat. 41° 50′ N.) the sun's altitude at a forenoon observation is 23° 27′. If the sun's declination is 14° 52′ N., what is the time of day? *Ans.* 7 hr. 13 min. A.M.

2. The latitude of New York is 40° 43′ N. A forenoon observation on the sun gives 30° 40′ as the altitude. If the sun's declination is 10° S., what is the time of day?

3. In Washington (lat. 38° 55′ N.) the sun's altitude at an afternoon observation is 60° 20′ when its declination is 20° 32′. Find the time of day. *Ans.* 1 hr. 48 min. P.M.

4. A government surveyor observes the sun's altitude to be 21°. If the latitude of his station is 27° N. and the declination of the sun 16° N., what is the time of day if the observation is made in the afternoon?

5. In London (lat. 51° 31′ N.) at an afternoon observation the sun's altitude is 15° 40′. Find the time of day, given that the sun's declination is 12° S. *Ans.* 2 hr. 59 min. P.M.

6. At a certain place in latitude 40° N. the altitude of the sun was found to be 41°. If the declination at the time of observation was 20° N., and the observation was made in the morning, how long did it take the sun to reach the meridian?

7. The captain of a steamship observes that the altitude of the sun is 26° 30′. If he is in latitude 45° 30′ N. and the declination of the sun is 18° N., what is the time of day if the observation is made in the afternoon? *Ans.* 4 hr. 41 min. P.M.

30. To find the time of sunrise or sunset. If the latitude of the place and the declination of the sun are known, we have a special case of the preceding problem; for at sunrise or sunset the sun is on the horizon and its altitude is zero. Hence the co-altitude, which is one side of the astronomical triangle, will be 90°, and the triangle will be a quadrantal triangle (p. 223). The triangle may then be solved by the method of the last section or as a quadrantal triangle.

PROBLEMS

1. Find the time of sunrise and of sunset in New York (lat. 40° 43′ N.) when the declination of the sun is 18° 30′ N.   *Ans.* 4 hr. 55 min. A.M.;
7 hr. 7 min. P.M.

2. At what hour will the sun rise in Panama (lat. 8° 57′ N.) if its declination at sunrise is 23° 2′ S.?

3. What is the time of sunset in San Francisco (lat. 37° 48′ N.) when the sun's declination is 8° 25′ N.?   *Ans.* 5 hr. 33 min. P.M.

4. Find the time of sunrise and of sunset in Chicago (lat. 41° 50′ N.) on June 21 if the declination of the sun on that date is 23° 30′ N.

About the first of April the declination of the sun is 4° 30′ N. Find the time of sunrise on that date at the following places:

5. London (lat. 51° 31′ N.).   *Ans.* 5 hr. 37 min. A.M.

6. New York (lat. 40° 43′ N.).

7. New Orleans (lat. 29° 58′ N.).   *Ans.* 5 hr. 50 min. A.M.

8. Sidney (lat. 33° 52′ S.).

31. To determine the latitude of a place when the altitude, declination, and hour angle of some celestial body are known. Referring to the astronomical (spherical) triangle PZM, we see that side MZ

$= 90° - HM$ (alt.)

$=$ co-altitude,

the altitude of the star being found by measurement. Also,

side PM

$= 90° - DM$ (dec.)

$=$ co-declination,

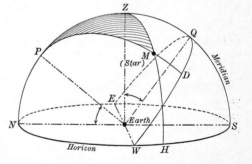

the declination of the star being found from the Nautical Almanac.

Angle $ZPM =$ hour angle, which is given. This hour angle will be the local time when the observation is made on the sun. We then have two sides and the angle opposite one of them given in the spherical triangle PZM. Solving this for the side PZ, by Case III, (a), p. 243, we get

$$latitude\ of\ observer = NP = 90° - PZ.$$

EXAMPLE. The declination of a star is 69° 42′ N., and its hour angle is 60° 44′. What is the north latitude of the place if the altitude of the star is observed to be 49° 40′?

Solution. Referring to the above figure, we have, in this example,

$$side\ MZ = \text{co-alt.} = 90° - 49° 40' = 40° 20',$$
$$side\ PM = \text{co-dec.} = 90° - 69° 42' = 20° 18',$$
$$angle\ ZPM = hour\ angle = 60° 44'.$$

Solving for the side PZ by Case III, (a), p. 243, we get side $PZ = 47° 9' = $ co-lat.
∴ $90° - 47° 9' = 42° 51' = $ north latitude of place. *Ans.*

PROBLEMS

In the following problems the altitude of some heavenly body not on the observer's celestial meridian has been measured. The hour angle and declination are known for the same instant. Find the latitude of the observer in each case.

HEMISPHERE	ALTITUDE	DECLINATION	HOUR ANGLE	LATITUDE
1. Northern	23° 27′	N. 14° 52′	71° 38′	*Ans.* 41° 50′ N.
2. Northern	20°	S. 8°	65°	
3. Northern	52°	N. 19°	2 hr.	48° 16′ N.
4. Northern	27° 23′	N. 8° 27′	3 hr.	
5. Northern	64° 42′	N. 24° 20′	345°	3° 34′ N. or 46° 36′ N.
6. Northern	25°	0°	21 hr.	
7. Northern	9° 26′	0°	72° 22′	57° 14′ N.
8. Southern	38°	S. 12°	52°	
9. Southern	46° 18′	S. 15° 23′	326°	49° 14′ S.
10. Southern	57° 36′	0°	2 hr.	
11. Northern	0°	N. 11° 14′	68° 54′	No solution
12. Northern	39°	N. 10°	50°	

MISCELLANEOUS PROBLEMS

1. A flier starts directly east from Sandy Hook (lat. 40° 28′ N., long. 74° 1′ W.) and flies along an arc of a great circle. Find his latitude and longitude at the end of 8 hr. if he averages 100.4 mi. an hour.

         Ans. Lat. 39° 16′ N., long. 57° 23′ W.

2. The distance between Paris (lat. 48° 50′ N.) and Berlin (lat. 52° 30′ N.) is 472 geographical miles, measured on the arc of a great circle. What time is it at Berlin when it is noon at Paris?

3. What will be the altitude of the sun at 9 A.M. in Mexico City (lat. 19° 25′ N.) if its declination at that time is 8° 23′ N.?   *Ans.* 37° 41′.

4. Find the length of the longest day of the year in Chicago (lat. 41° 50′ N.) if the sun's declination is 23° 30′ N.

5. Find the altitude of the sun at 6 hr. A.M. at Munich (lat. 48° 9′ N.) on the longest day of the year.   *Ans.* 17° 15′.

6. The continent of Asia has nearly the shape of an equilateral triangle. Assuming each side to be 4800 geographical miles and the radius of the earth to be 3440 geographical miles, find the area of Asia.

7. Find the time of day when the sun bears due east and due west on the longest day of the year at Leningrad (lat. 59° 56′ N.).

         Ans. 6 hr. 58 min. A.M., 5 hr. 2 min. P.M.

8. Find the latitude of the place at which the sun rises exactly in the northeast on the longest day of the year.

9. Find the latitude of the place at which the sun sets at 10 hr. P.M. on the longest day of the year.   *Ans.* 63° 23′ N. or S.

10. Given the latitude of the place of observation 52° 30′ N., the declination of a star 38°, its hour angle 28° 17′. Find the altitude of the star.

11. Given the latitude of the place of observation 51° 32′ N., the altitude of the sun west of the meridian 35° 15′, its declination 21° 27′ N. Find the local time.   *Ans.* 3 hr. 59 min. P.M.

CHAPTER IV

RECAPITULATION OF FORMULAS

SPHERICAL TRIGONOMETRY

Right spherical triangles, pp. 211–224.

(1)	$\cos c = \cos a \cos b.$
(2)	$\sin a = \sin c \sin A.$
(3)	$\sin b = \sin c \sin B.$
(4)	$\cos A = \cos a \sin B.$
(5)	$\cos B = \cos b \sin A.$
(6)	$\cos A = \tan b \cot c.$
(7)	$\cos B = \tan a \cot c.$
(8)	$\sin b = \tan a \cot A.$
(9)	$\sin a = \tan b \cot B.$
(10)	$\cos c = \cot A \cot B.$

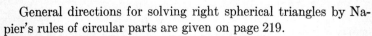

General directions for solving right spherical triangles by Napier's rules of circular parts are given on page 219.

Spherical isosceles and quadrantal triangles are discussed on page 223.

Relations between the sides and angles of oblique spherical triangles, pp. 225–247.

$$\alpha = 180° - A, \quad \beta = 180° - B, \quad \gamma = 180° - C.$$
$$s = \tfrac{1}{2}(a + b + c), \quad \sigma = \tfrac{1}{2}(\alpha + \beta + \gamma).$$

Law of sines, p. 225.

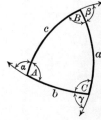

(11)
$$\frac{\sin a}{\sin A} = \frac{\sin b}{\sin B} = \frac{\sin c}{\sin C},$$

or,
$$\frac{\sin a}{\sin \alpha} = \frac{\sin b}{\sin \beta} = \frac{\sin c}{\sin \gamma}.$$

Law of cosines for the sides, p. 228.

(12) $\cos a = \cos b \cos c - \sin b \sin c \cos \alpha.$

Law of cosines for the angles, p. 228.

(15) $\cos \alpha = \cos \beta \cos \gamma - \sin \beta \sin \gamma \cos a.$

Functions of $\frac{1}{2}\alpha$, $\frac{1}{2}\beta$, $\frac{1}{2}\gamma$ in terms of the sides, pp. 230–232.

(18) $\sin \frac{1}{2}\alpha = \sqrt{\dfrac{\sin s \sin (s - a)}{\sin b \sin c}}.$

(19) $\cos \frac{1}{2}\alpha = \sqrt{\dfrac{\sin (s - b) \sin (s - c)}{\sin b \sin c}}.$

(20) $\tan \frac{1}{2}\alpha = \sqrt{\dfrac{\sin s \sin (s - a)}{\sin (s - b) \sin (s - c)}}.$

(27) $\tan \frac{1}{2}d = \sqrt{\dfrac{\sin (s - a) \sin (s - b) \sin (s - c)}{\sin s}}.$

(28) $\tan \frac{1}{2}\alpha = \dfrac{\sin (s - a)}{\tan \frac{1}{2}d}.$

(29) $\tan \frac{1}{2}\beta = \dfrac{\sin (s - b)}{\tan \frac{1}{2}d}.$

(30) $\tan \frac{1}{2}\gamma = \dfrac{\sin (s - c)}{\tan \frac{1}{2}d}.$

Functions of the half sides in terms of α, β, γ, p. 233.

(31) $\sin \frac{1}{2}a = \sqrt{\dfrac{\sin \sigma \sin (\sigma - \alpha)}{\sin \beta \sin \gamma}}.$

(32) $\cos \frac{1}{2}a = \sqrt{\dfrac{\sin (\sigma - \beta) \sin (\sigma - \gamma)}{\sin \beta \sin \gamma}}.$

(33) $\tan \frac{1}{2}a = \sqrt{\dfrac{\sin \sigma \sin (\sigma - \alpha)}{\sin (\sigma - \beta) \sin (\sigma - \gamma)}}.$

(40) $\tan \frac{1}{2}\delta = \sqrt{\dfrac{\sin (\sigma - \alpha) \sin (\sigma - \beta) \sin (\sigma - \gamma)}{\sin \sigma}}.$

(41) $\tan \frac{1}{2}a = \dfrac{\sin (\sigma - \alpha)}{\tan \frac{1}{2}\delta}.$

(42) $\tan \frac{1}{2}b = \dfrac{\sin (\sigma - \beta)}{\tan \frac{1}{2}\delta}.$

(43) $\tan \frac{1}{2}c = \dfrac{\sin (\sigma - \gamma)}{\tan \frac{1}{2}\delta}.$

Napier's analogies, p. 234.

$$(44) \qquad \tan \tfrac{1}{2}(a - b) = - \frac{\sin \tfrac{1}{2}(\alpha - \beta)}{\sin \tfrac{1}{2}(\alpha + \beta)} \tan \tfrac{1}{2} c.$$

$$(45) \qquad \tan \tfrac{1}{2}(a + b) = - \frac{\cos \tfrac{1}{2}(\alpha - \beta)}{\cos \tfrac{1}{2}(\alpha + \beta)} \tan \tfrac{1}{2} c.$$

$$(46) \qquad \tan \tfrac{1}{2}(\alpha - \beta) = - \frac{\sin \tfrac{1}{2}(a - b)}{\sin \tfrac{1}{2}(a + b)} \tan \tfrac{1}{2} \gamma.$$

$$(47) \qquad \tan \tfrac{1}{2}(\alpha + \beta) = - \frac{\cos \tfrac{1}{2}(a - b)}{\cos \tfrac{1}{2}(a + b)} \tan \tfrac{1}{2} \gamma.$$

General directions for the solution of oblique spherical triangles, pp. 236–247.

CASE I.   (a) *Given the three sides, p. 236.*
(b) *Given the three angles, p. 237.*

CASE II.   (a) *Given two sides and their included angle, p. 239.*
(b) *Given two angles and their included side, p. 241.*

CASE III.   (a) *Given two sides and the angle opposite one of them, p. 243.*
(b) *Given two angles and the side opposite one of them, p. 246.*

Length of an arc of a circle in linear units, p. 248.

$$(52) \qquad L = \frac{\pi R N}{180},$$

$N =$ number of degrees in angle.

Area of a spherical triangle, p. 249.

$$(54) \qquad \text{Area} = \frac{\pi R^2 E}{180},$$

$$E = (A + B + C) - 180°.$$

$$(55) \quad \tan \tfrac{1}{4} E = \sqrt{\tan \tfrac{1}{2} s \tan \tfrac{1}{2}(s - a) \tan \tfrac{1}{2}(s - b) \tan \tfrac{1}{2}(s - c)}.$$

INDEX

FOUR-PLACE TABLES

FOUR-PLACE TABLES

BY WILLIAM ANTHONY GRANVILLE, Ph.D., LL.D.
FORMERLY PRESIDENT OF GETTYSBURG COLLEGE

REVISED BY

PERCEY F. SMITH, Ph.D.
Professor of Mathematics in Yale University

AND

JAMES S. MIKESH, B.A.
Master in Mathematics in Lawrenceville School

GINN AND COMPANY

BOSTON · NEW YORK · CHICAGO · LONDON · ATLANTA · DALLAS · COLUMBUS · SAN FRANCISCO

𝕿𝖍𝖊 𝕬𝖙𝖍𝖊𝖓𝖆𝖚𝖒 𝕻𝖗𝖊𝖘𝖘
GINN AND COMPANY · PRO-
PRIETORS · BOSTON · U.S.A.

CONTENTS

TABLE I

TABLE II

TABLE III

TABLE IV

TABLE V

LOGARITHMS

Definition of a logarithm. *The exponent of the power to which a given number, called the base, must be raised to equal a second number is called the logarithm of the second number.*

Thus if $$b^x = N,$$

then $x = $ *the logarithm of N to the base b.* This statement is written in the abbreviated form $$x = \log_b N.$$

For example, the following relations in exponential form, namely,

$$3^2 = 9, \quad 2^5 = 32, \quad (\tfrac{1}{2})^3 = \tfrac{1}{8},$$

are written, respectively, in logarithmic form

$$2 = \log_3 9, \quad 5 = \log_2 32, \quad 3 = \log_{\frac{1}{2}} \tfrac{1}{8}.$$

Common logarithms. Characteristic and mantissa. In common logarithms the base is 10, and it is the one most convenient to use with our decimal system of numbers. In writing a logarithm, when the base is omitted the base 10 is understood. Thus $\log_{10} 100 = 2$ is written $\log 100 = 2$, etc.

Since, for example, $\log 100 = 2$ and $\log 1000 = 3$, if we assume that as a number increases its logarithm also increases, we see that a number between 100 and 1000 has a logarithm between 2 and 3. In fact, the logarithm of any number not an integral power of 10 consists, in general, of a *whole-number* part and a *decimal* part.

The whole-number part of a logarithm is called the *characteristic* of the logarithm.

The decimal part of a logarithm is called the *mantissa* of the logarithm.

Thus, if $\log 357 = 2.5527$, 2 is the characteristic and .5527 is the mantissa.

Rules for determining the characteristic.

1. *The characteristic for a number greater than unity is positive, and one less than the number of digits in the number to the left of the decimal point.*

2. *The characteristic for a number less than unity is negative, and is one greater numerically than the number of zeros between the decimal point and the first significant figure of the number.*

Thus the characteristics of the logarithms of the numbers 27,683, 456.2, 9.67, 26, 0.04, 0.0000612 are, respectively, 4, 2, 0, 1, − 2, − 5.

Mantissa and the decimal point. *Numbers with the same significant figures (and which therefore differ only in the position of the decimal point) have the same mantissa.*

TABLE I

FOUR–PLACE LOGARITHMS OF NUMBERS

This table gives the mantissas of the common logarithms (base 10) of the natural numbers (integers) from 1 to 2009, calculated to four places of decimals.

Use of the table. The following examples illustrate the use of Table I:

EXAMPLE 1. Find the logarithm of 1387.

Solution. From Rule 1 for characteristics, we see that the characteristic is 3. On page 2, Table I, we find 138 in column headed **No.** The required mantissa will be found in the same horizontal row with 138 and in the vertical column which has 7 at the top. This gives the mantissa .1421.

Hence $\qquad$ log 1387 = 3.1421. *Ans.*

EXAMPLE 2. Find log 0.02864.

Solution. In this case we see that the characteristic is − 2. Since the mantissa of 2864 is not found in our table, we use the method of *interpolation*.

From the table (p. 4) we have $\qquad$ log 0.02870 = $\overline{2}$.4579
and $\qquad\qquad\qquad\qquad\qquad$ log 0.02860 = $\overline{2}$.4564
Subtracting, we have the differences $\qquad$ 10 and 15

that is, a difference of 10 (hundred thousandths) in the number produces a difference of 15 (ten thousandths) in the mantissa. Since 0.02864 exceeds 0.02860 by 4 (hundred thousandths), the corresponding increase in the mantissa is $0.4 \times 15 = 6$ (hundred thousandths). This increase we add to the mantissa .4564. Hence $\qquad$ log 0.02864 = $\overline{2}$.4564 + .0006 = $\overline{2}$.4570. *Ans.*

EXAMPLE 3. Find the number whose logarithm is 2.1892.

Solution. On page 3, Table I, we find this mantissa, .1892 exactly, in the same horizontal row with 154 in the **No.** column and in the vertical column with 6 at the top. Hence the first four significant figures of the required number are 1546. Since the characteristic is 2, we place the decimal point so that there will be three digits to the left of the decimal point. Hence the number is 154.6. *Ans.*

EXAMPLE 4. Find x, if log x = 4.8409.

Solution. The given mantissa, .8409, is found to lie between the mantissas .8407 and .8414 on page 4, Table I. The first three significant figures of the number corresponding to the smaller one, that is, to .8407, are 693. The tabular difference between .8407 and .8414 is 7, and the difference between .8407 and the given mantissa .8409 is 2. To find the fourth significant figure of the required number x, we use interpolation; that is, we express $\frac{2}{7}$ to the nearest tenth, as .3, and annex the 3 as the fourth significant figure of x. We place the decimal point according to Rule 1. Hence

$$x = 69{,}330. \ \textit{Ans.}$$

A logarithm found from this table by interpolation may be in error by one unit in the last decimal place.

No.	0	1	2	3	4	5	6	7	8	9
100	0000	0004	0009	0013	0017	0022	0026	0030	0035	0039
101	0043	0048	0052	0056	0060	0065	0069	0073	0077	0082
102	0086	0090	0095	0099	0103	0107	0111	0116	0120	0124
103	0128	0133	0137	0141	0145	0149	0154	0158	0162	0166
104	0170	0175	0179	0183	0187	0191	0195	0199	0204	0208
105	0212	0216	0220	0224	0228	0233	0237	0241	0245	0249
106	0253	0257	0261	0265	0269	0273	0278	0282	0286	0290
107	0294	0298	0302	0306	0310	0314	0318	0322	0326	0330
108	0334	0338	0342	0346	0350	0354	0358	0362	0366	0370
109	0374	0378	0382	0386	0390	0394	0398	0402	0406	0410
110	0414	0418	0422	0426	0430	0434	0438	0441	0445	0449
111	0453	0457	0461	0465	0469	0473	0477	0481	0484	0488
112	0492	0496	0500	0504	0508	0512	0515	0519	0523	0527
113	0531	0535	0538	0542	0546	0550	0554	0558	0561	0565
114	0569	0573	0577	0580	0584	0588	0592	0596	0599	0603
115	0607	0611	0615	0618	0622	0626	0630	0633	0637	0641
116	0645	0648	0652	0656	0660	0663	0667	0671	0674	0678
117	0682	0686	0689	0693	0697	0700	0704	0708	0711	0715
118	0719	0722	0726	0730	0734	0737	0741	0745	0748	0752
119	0755	0759	0763	0766	0770	0774	0777	0781	0785	0788
120	0792	0795	0799	0803	0806	0810	0813	0817	0821	0824
121	0828	0831	0835	0839	0842	0846	0849	0853	0856	0860
122	0864	0867	0871	0874	0878	0881	0885	0888	0892	0896
123	0899	0903	0906	0910	0913	0917	0920	0924	0927	0931
124	0934	0938	0941	0945	0948	0952	0955	0959	0962	0966
125	0969	0973	0976	0980	0983	0986	0990	0993	0997	1000
126	1004	1007	1011	1014	1017	1021	1024	1028	1031	1035
127	1038	1041	1045	1048	1052	1055	1059	1062	1065	1069
128	1072	1075	1079	1082	1086	1089	1093	1096	1099	1103
129	1106	1109	1113	1116	1119	1123	1126	1129	1133	1136
130	1139	1143	1146	1149	1153	1156	1159	1163	1166	1169
131	1173	1176	1179	1183	1186	1189	1193	1196	1199	1202
132	1206	1209	1212	1216	1219	1222	1225	1229	1232	1235
133	1239	1242	1245	1248	1252	1255	1258	1261	1265	1268
134	1271	1274	1278	1281	1284	1287	1290	1294	1297	1300
135	1303	1307	1310	1313	1316	1319	1323	1326	1329	1332
136	1335	1339	1342	1345	1348	1351	1355	1358	1361	1364
137	1367	1370	1374	1377	1380	1383	1386	1389	1392	1396
138	1399	1402	1405	1408	1411	1414	1418	1421	1424	1427
139	1430	1433	1436	1440	1443	1446	1449	1452	1455	1458
140	1461	1464	1467	1471	1474	1477	1480	1483	1486	1489
141	1492	1495	1498	1501	1504	1508	1511	1514	1517	1520
142	1523	1526	1529	1532	1535	1538	1541	1544	1547	1550
143	1553	1556	1559	1562	1565	1569	1572	1575	1578	1581
144	1584	1587	1590	1593	1596	1599	1602	1605	1608	1611
145	1614	1617	1620	1623	1626	1629	1632	1635	1638	1641
146	1644	1647	1649	1652	1655	1658	1661	1664	1667	1670
147	1673	1676	1679	1682	1685	1688	1691	1694	1697	1700
148	1703	1706	1708	1711	1714	1717	1720	1723	1726	1729
149	1732	1735	1738	1741	1744	1746	1749	1752	1755	1758
150	1761	1764	1767	1770	1772	1775	1778	1781	1784	1787
No.	0	1	2	3	4	5	6	7	8	9

Prop. Parts

Extra digit — Difference

Extra digit	5	4	3	2
1	0.5	0.4	0.3	0.2
2	1.0	0.8	0.6	0.4
3	1.5	1.2	0.9	0.6
4	2.0	1.6	1.2	0.8
5	2.5	2.0	1.5	1.0
6	3.0	2.4	1.8	1.2
7	3.5	2.8	2.1	1.4
8	4.0	3.2	2.4	1.6
9	4.5	3.6	2.7	1.8

TABLE I. LOGARITHMS OF NUMBERS   3

No.	0	1	2	3	4	5	6	7	8	9
150	1761	1764	1767	1770	1772	1775	1778	1781	1784	1787
151	1790	1793	1796	1798	1801	1804	1807	1810	1813	1816
152	1818	1821	1824	1827	1830	1833	1836	1838	1841	1844
153	1847	1850	1853	1855	1858	1861	1864	1867	1870	1872
154	1875	1878	1881	1884	1886	1889	1892	1895	1898	1901
155	1903	1906	1909	1912	1915	1917	1920	1923	1926	1928
156	1931	1934	1937	1940	1942	1945	1948	1951	1953	1956
157	1959	1962	1965	1967	1970	1973	1976	1978	1981	1984
158	1987	1989	1992	1995	1998	2000	2003	2006	2009	2011
159	2014	2017	2019	2022	2025	2028	2030	2033	2036	2038
160	2041	2044	2047	2049	2052	2055	2057	2060	2063	2066
161	2068	2071	2074	2076	2079	2082	2084	2087	2090	2092
162	2095	2098	2101	2103	2106	2109	2111	2114	2117	2119
163	2122	2125	2127	2130	2133	2135	2138	2140	2143	2146
164	2148	2151	2154	2156	2159	2162	2164	2167	2170	2172
165	2175	2177	2180	2183	2185	2188	2191	2193	2196	2198
166	2201	2204	2206	2209	2212	2214	2217	2219	2222	2225
167	2227	2230	2232	2235	2238	2240	2243	2245	2248	2251
168	2253	2256	2258	2261	2263	2266	2269	2271	2274	2276
169	2279	2281	2284	2287	2289	2292	2294	2297	2299	2302
170	2304	2307	2310	2312	2315	2317	2320	2322	2325	2327
171	2330	2333	2335	2338	2340	2343	2345	2348	2350	2353
172	2355	2358	2360	2363	2365	2368	2370	2373	2375	2378
173	2380	2383	2385	2388	2390	2393	2395	2398	2400	2403
174	2405	2408	2410	2413	2415	2418	2420	2423	2425	2428
175	2430	2433	2435	2438	2440	2443	2445	2448	2450	2453
176	2455	2458	2460	2463	2465	2467	2470	2472	2475	2477
177	2480	2482	2485	2487	2490	2492	2494	2497	2499	2502
178	2504	2507	2509	2512	2514	2516	2519	2521	2524	2526
179	2529	2531	2533	2536	2538	2541	2543	2545	2548	2550
180	2553	2555	2558	2560	2562	2565	2567	2570	2572	2574
181	2577	2579	2582	2584	2586	2589	2591	2594	2596	2598
182	2601	2603	2605	2608	2610	2613	2615	2617	2620	2622
183	2625	2627	2629	2632	2634	2636	2639	2641	2643	2646
184	2648	2651	2653	2655	2658	2660	2662	2665	2667	2669
185	2672	2674	2676	2679	2681	2683	2686	2688	2690	2693
186	2695	2697	2700	2702	2704	2707	2709	2711	2714	2716
187	2718	2721	2723	2725	2728	2730	2732	2735	2737	2739
188	2742	2744	2746	2749	2751	2753	2755	2758	2760	2762
189	2765	2767	2769	2772	2774	2776	2778	2781	2783	2785
190	2788	2790	2792	2794	2797	2799	2801	2804	2806	2808
191	2810	2813	2815	2817	2819	2822	2824	2826	2828	2831
192	2833	2835	2838	2840	2842	2844	2847	2849	2851	2853
193	2856	2858	2860	2862	2865	2867	2869	2871	2874	2876
194	2878	2880	2883	2885	2887	2889	2891	2894	2896	2898
195	2900	2903	2905	2907	2909	2911	2914	2916	2918	2920
196	2923	2925	2927	2929	2931	2934	2936	2938	2940	2942
197	2945	2947	2949	2951	2953	2956	2958	2960	2962	2964
198	2967	2969	2971	2973	2975	2978	2980	2982	2984	2986
199	2989	2991	2993	2995	2997	2999	3002	3004	3006	3008
200	3010	3012	3015	3017	3019	3021	3023	3025	3028	3030
No.	0	1	2	3	4	5	6	7	8	9

Prop. Parts

Extra digit | Difference

	3
1	0.3
2	0.6
3	0.9
4	1.2
5	1.5
6	1.8
7	2.1
8	2.4
9	2.7

	2
1	0.2
2	0.4
3	0.6
4	0.8
5	1.0
6	1.2
7	1.4
8	1.6
9	1.8

No.	0	1	2	3	4	5	6	7	8	9
20	3010	3032	3054	3075	3096	3118	3139	3160	3181	3201
21	3222	3243	3263	3284	3304	3324	3345	3365	3385	3404
22	3424	3444	3464	3483	3502	3522	3541	3560	3579	3598
23	3617	3636	3655	3674	3692	3711	3729	3747	3766	3784
24	3802	3820	3838	3856	3874	3892	3909	3927	3945	3962
25	3979	3997	4014	4031	4048	4065	4082	4099	4116	4133
26	4150	4166	4183	4200	4216	4232	4249	4265	4281	4298
27	4314	4330	4346	4362	4378	4393	4409	4425	4440	4456
28	4472	4487	4502	4518	4533	4548	4564	4579	4594	4609
29	4624	4639	4654	4669	4683	4698	4713	4728	4742	4757
30	4771	4786	4800	4814	4829	4843	4857	4871	4886	4900
31	4914	4928	4942	4955	4969	4983	4997	5011	5024	5038
32	5051	5065	5079	5092	5105	5119	5132	5145	5159	5172
33	5185	5198	5211	5224	5237	5250	5263	5276	5289	5302
34	5315	5328	5340	5353	5366	5378	5391	5403	5416	5428
35	5441	5453	5465	5478	5490	5502	5514	5527	5539	5551
36	5563	5575	5587	5599	5611	5623	5635	5647	5658	5670
37	5682	5694	5705	5717	5729	5740	5752	5763	5775	5786
38	5798	5809	5821	5832	5843	5855	5866	5877	5888	5900
39	5911	5922	5933	5944	5955	5966	5977	5988	5999	6010
40	6021	6031	6042	6053	6064	6075	6085	6096	6107	6117
41	6128	6138	6149	6160	6170	6180	6191	6201	6212	6222
42	6232	6243	6253	6263	6274	6284	6294	6304	6314	6325
43	6335	6345	6355	6365	6375	6385	6395	6405	6415	6425
44	6435	6444	6454	6464	6474	6484	6493	6503	6513	6522
45	6532	6542	6551	6561	6571	6580	6590	6599	6609	6618
46	6628	6637	6646	6656	6665	6675	6684	6693	6702	6712
47	6721	6730	6739	6749	6758	6767	6776	6785	6794	6803
48	6812	6821	6830	6839	6848	6857	6866	6875	6884	6893
49	6902	6911	6920	6928	6937	6946	6955	6964	6972	6981
50	6990	6998	7007	7016	7024	7033	7042	7050	7059	7067
51	7076	7084	7093	7101	7110	7118	7126	7135	7143	7152
52	7160	7168	7177	7185	7193	7202	7210	7218	7226	7235
53	7243	7251	7259	7267	7275	7284	7292	7300	7308	7316
54	7324	7332	7340	7348	7356	7364	7372	7380	7388	7396
55	7404	7412	7419	7427	7435	7443	7451	7459	7466	7474
56	7482	7490	7497	7505	7513	7520	7528	7536	7543	7551
57	7559	7566	7574	7582	7589	7597	7604	7612	7619	7627
58	7634	7642	7649	7657	7664	7672	7679	7686	7694	7701
59	7709	7716	7723	7731	7738	7745	7752	7760	7767	7774
60	7782	7789	7796	7803	7810	7818	7825	7832	7839	7846
61	7853	7860	7868	7875	7882	7889	7896	7903	7910	7917
62	7924	7931	7938	7945	7952	7959	7966	7973	7980	7987
63	7993	8000	8007	8014	8021	8028	8035	8041	8048	8055
64	8062	8069	8075	8082	8089	8096	8102	8109	8116	8122
65	8129	8136	8142	8149	8156	8162	8169	8176	8182	8189
66	8195	8202	8209	8215	8222	8228	8235	8241	8248	8254
67	8261	8267	8274	8280	8287	8293	8299	8306	8312	8319
68	8325	8331	8338	8344	8351	8357	8363	8370	8376	8382
69	8388	8395	8401	8407	8414	8420	8426	8432	8439	8445
70	8451	8457	8463	8470	8476	8482	8488	8494	8500	8506
No.	0	1	2	3	4	5	6	7	8	9

Prop. Parts

Extra digit / Difference

Extra digit	22	21
1	2.2	2.1
2	4.4	4.2
3	6.6	6.3
4	8.8	8.4
5	11.0	10.5
6	13.2	12.6
7	15.4	14.7
8	17.6	16.8
9	19.8	18.9

Extra digit	20	19
1	2.0	1.9
2	4.0	3.8
3	6.0	5.7
4	8.0	7.6
5	10.0	9.5
6	12.0	11.4
7	14.0	13.3
8	16.0	15.2
9	18.0	17.1

Extra digit	18	17
1	1.8	1.7
2	3.6	3.4
3	5.4	5.1
4	7.2	6.8
5	9.0	8.5
6	10.8	10.2
7	12.6	11.9
8	14.4	13.6
9	16.2	15.3

Extra digit	16	15
1	1.6	1.5
2	3.2	3.0
3	4.8	4.5
4	6.4	6.0
5	8.0	7.5
6	9.6	9.0
7	11.2	10.5
8	12.8	12.0
9	14.4	13.5

Extra digit	14	13
1	1.4	1.3
2	2.8	2.6
3	4.2	3.9
4	5.6	5.2
5	7.0	6.5
6	8.4	7.8
7	9.8	9.1
8	11.2	10.4
9	12.6	11.7

Extra digit	12	11
1	1.2	1.1
2	2.4	2.2
3	3.6	3.3
4	4.8	4.4
5	6.0	5.5
6	7.2	6.6
7	8.4	7.7
8	9.6	8.8
9	10.8	9.9

TABLE I. LOGARITHMS OF NUMBERS 5

No.	0	1	2	3	4	5	6	7	8	9
70	8451	8457	8463	8470	8476	8482	8488	8494	8500	8506
71	8513	8519	8525	8531	8537	8543	8549	8555	8561	8567
72	8573	8579	8585	8591	8597	8603	8609	8615	8621	8627
73	8633	8639	8645	8651	8657	8663	8669	8675	8681	8686
74	8692	8698	8704	8710	8716	8722	8727	8733	8739	8745
75	8751	8756	8762	8768	8774	8779	8785	8791	8797	8802
76	8808	8814	8820	8825	8831	8837	8842	8848	8854	8859
77	8865	8871	8876	8882	8887	8893	8899	8904	8910	8915
78	8921	8927	8932	8938	8943	8949	8954	8960	8965	8971
79	8976	8982	8987	8993	8998	9004	9009	9015	9020	9025
80	9031	9036	9042	9047	9053	9058	9063	9069	9074	9079
81	9085	9090	9096	9101	9106	9112	9117	9122	9128	9133
82	9138	9143	9149	9154	9159	9165	9170	9175	9180	9186
83	9191	9196	9201	9206	9212	9217	9222	9227	9232	9238
84	9243	9248	9253	9258	9263	9269	9274	9279	9284	9289
85	9294	9299	9304	9309	9315	9320	9325	9330	9335	9340
86	9345	9350	9355	9360	9365	9370	9375	9380	9385	9390
87	9395	9400	9405	9410	9415	9420	9425	9430	9435	9440
88	9445	9450	9455	9460	9465	9469	9474	9479	9484	9489
89	9494	9499	9504	9509	9513	9518	9523	9528	9533	9538
90	9542	9547	9552	9557	9562	9566	9571	9576	9581	9586
91	9590	9595	9600	9605	9609	9614	9619	9624	9628	9633
92	9638	9643	9647	9652	9657	9661	9666	9671	9675	9680
93	9685	9689	9694	9699	9703	9708	9713	9717	9722	9727
94	9731	9736	9741	9745	9750	9754	9759	9763	9768	9773
95	9777	9782	9786	9791	9795	9800	9805	9809	9814	9818
96	9823	9827	9832	9836	9841	9845	9850	9854	9859	9863
97	9868	9872	9877	9881	9886	9890	9894	9899	9903	9908
98	9912	9917	9921	9926	9930	9934	9939	9943	9948	9952
99	9956	9961	9965	9969	9974	9978	9983	9987	9991	9996
100	0000	0004	0009	0013	0017	0022	0026	0030	0035	0039
No.	0	1	2	3	4	5	6	7	8	9

Prop. Parts

Ex. dig. — Difference

Ex. dig.	10	9
1	1.0	0.9
2	2.0	1.8
3	3.0	2.7
4	4.0	3.3
5	5.0	4.5
6	6.0	5.4
7	7.0	6.3
8	8.0	7.2
9	9.0	8.1

Ex. dig.	8	7
1	0.8	0.7
2	1.6	1.4
3	2.4	2.1
4	3.2	2.8
5	4.0	3.5
6	4.8	4.2
7	5.6	4.9
8	6.4	5.6
9	7.2	6.3

Ex. dig.	6	5
1	0.6	0.5
2	1.2	1.0
3	1.8	1.5
4	2.4	2.0
5	3.0	2.5
6	3.6	3.0
7	4.2	3.5
8	4.8	4.0
9	5.4	4.5

Ex. dig.	4
1	0.4
2	0.8
3	1.2
4	1.6
5	2.0
6	2.4
7	2.8
8	3.2
9	3.6

RULES FOR FINDING THE LOGARITHMS OF THE TRIGONOMETRIC FUNCTIONS OF ANGLES NEAR 0° AND 90°

The derivation of the following rules will be found in Art. 90 of the authors' *Plane Trigonometry.**

If the angle is given in degrees, minutes, and seconds, it should first be reduced to degrees and the decimal part of a degree. For this purpose use the conversion table on page 17.

Rule I. *To find the logarithms of the functions of an angle near 0°.*

$$\log \sin x° = \bar{2}.2419 + \log x.$$
$$\log \tan x° = \bar{2}.2419 + \log x.$$
$$\log \cot x° = 1.7581 - \log x.$$

log cos x° is found from the tables in the usual way.

Rule II. *To find the logarithms of the functions of an angle near 90°.*

$$\log \cos x° = \bar{2}.2419 + \log (90 - x).$$
$$\log \cot x° = \bar{2}.2419 + \log (90 - x).$$
$$\log \tan x° = 1.7581 - \log (90 - x).$$

log sin x° is found from the tables in the usual way.

These rules will give results accurate to four decimal places for all angles between 0° and 1.1° and between 88.9° and 90°.

---

* Plane Trigonometry by Granville, Smith, and Mikesh (Ginn and Company).

TABLE II

FOUR-PLACE LOGARITHMS OF TRIGONOMETRIC FUNCTIONS, THE ANGLE BEING EXPRESSED IN DEGREES AND MINUTES

This table gives the common logarithms (base 10) of the sines, cosines, tangents, and cotangents of all angles from 0° to 5° and from 85° to 90° for each minute; and from 5° to 85° at intervals of 10 minutes, all calculated to four places of decimals. In order to avoid the printing of negative characteristics, the number 10 has been added to every logarithm in the first, second, and fourth columns (those having **log sin**, **log tan**, and **log cos** at the top). Hence in writing down any logarithm taken from these three columns − 10 should be written after it.

Use of the table. The following examples illustrate the use of Table II:

EXAMPLE 1. Find log sin 23° 16′.

Solution. The exact angle 23° 16′ is not found in Table II; hence we interpolate as follows, using page 14.

$$\begin{array}{ll} \log \sin 23° 30′ = 9.6007 - 10 \\ \log \sin 23° 20′ = 9.5978 - 10 \\ \hline 10′ 29 \end{array}$$

Since an increase of 10′ produces an increase of 29 (ten thousandths) in the mantissa, an increase of 6′ will produce an increase of $0.6 \times 29 = 17.4$, that is, 17.

Hence
$$\begin{aligned} \log \sin 23° 16′ &= 9.5978 - 10 + 0.0017 \\ &= 9.5995 - 10. \ Ans. \end{aligned}$$

EXAMPLE 2. Given log cos $x = 9.3705 - 10$, find x.

Solution. We do not find 9.3705 exactly in the table. But on page 13, in the column having **log cos** at the bottom, we find the next smaller logarithm to be 9.3682, which corresponds to the angle 76° 30′. The corresponding tabular difference for 1′ is 5.2. Hence

$$\begin{array}{ll} \log \cos x = 9.3705 - 10 \\ \log \cos 76° 30′ = 9.3682 - 10 \\ \hline \text{excess} = 23 \end{array}$$

Tab. diff. 1′	Excess	Corr.
5.2	23.0	4
	208	
	22	

Since the function involved is the cosine, we subtract this correction, giving

$$x = 76° 30′ - 4′ = 76° 26′. \ Ans.$$

A logarithm found from this table by interpolation may be in error by one unit in the last decimal place, except for angles between 0° and 18′ or between 89° 42′ and 90°, when the error may be larger. In the latter cases the table refers the student to the formulas on page 6 for more accurate results.

7

TABLE II. LOGARITHMIC SINES

0°

Angle	log sin	diff.1′	log tan	com. diff.1′	log cot	log cos	
0° 0′	——		——		——	10.0000	90° 00′
0° 1′	6.4637		6.4637		3.5363	10.0000	89° 59′
0° 2′	6.7648		6.7648		3.2352	10.0000	89° 58′
0° 3′	6.9408		6.9408		3.0592	10.0000	89° 57′
0° 4′	7.0658		7.0658		2.9342	10.0000	89° 56′
0° 5′	7.1627		7.1627		2.8373	10.0000	89° 55′
0° 6′	7.2419		7.2419		2.7581	10.0000	89° 54′
0° 7′	7.3088		7.3088		2.6912	10.0000	89° 53′
0° 8′	7.3668		7.3668		2.6332	10.0000	89° 52′
0° 9′	7.4180		7.4180		2.5820	10.0000	89° 51′
0° 10′	7.4637		7.4637		2.5363	10.0000	89° 50′
0° 11′	7.5051		7.5051		2.4949	10.0000	89° 49′
0° 12′	7.5429		7.5429		2.4571	10.0000	89° 48′
0° 13′	7.5777		7.5777		2.4223	10.0000	89° 47′
0° 14′	7.6099		7.6099		2.3901	10.0000	89° 46′
0° 15′	7.6398		7.6398		2.3602	10.0000	89° 45′
0° 16′	7.6678		7.6678		2.3322	10.0000	89° 44′
0° 17′	7.6942		7.6942		2.3058	10.0000	89° 43′
0° 18′	7.7190		7.7190		2.2810	10.0000	89° 42′
0° 19′	7.7425	235	7.7425	235	2.2575	10.0000	89° 41′
0° 20′	7.7648	223	7.7648	223	2.2352	10.0000	89° 40′
0° 21′	7.7859	211	7.7860	212	2.2140	10.0000	89° 39′
0° 22′	7.8061	202	7.8062	202	2.1938	10.0000	89° 38′
0° 23′	7.8255	194	7.8255	193	2.1745	10.0000	89° 37′
0° 24′	7.8439	184	7.8439	184	2.1561	10.0000	89° 36′
C° 25′	7.8617	178	7.8617	178	2.1383	10.0000	89° 35′
0° 26′	7.8787	170	7.8787	170	2.1213	10.0000	89° 34′
0° 27′	7.8951	164	7.8951	164	2.1049	10.0000	89° 33′
0° 28′	7.9109	158	7.9109	158	2.0891	10.0000	89° 32′
0° 29′	7.9261	152	7.9261	152	2.0739	10.0000	89° 31′
0° 30′	7.9408	147	7.9409	148	2.0591	10.0000	89° 30′
0° 31′	7.9551	143	7.9551	142	2.0449	10.0000	89° 29′
0° 32′	7.9689	138	7.9689	138	2.0311	10.0000	89° 28′
0° 33′	7.9822	133	7.9823	134	2.0177	10.0000	89° 27′
0° 34′	7.9952	130	7.9952	129	2.0048	10.0000	89° 26′
0° 35′	8.0078	126	8.0078	126	1.9922	10.0000	89° 25′
0° 36′	8.0200	122	8.0200	122	1.9800	10.0000	89° 24′
0° 37′	8.0319	119	8.0319	119	1.9681	10.0000	89° 23′
0° 38′	8.0435	116	8.0435	116	1.9565	10.0000	89° 22′
0° 39′	8.0548	113	8.0548	113	1.9452	10.0000	89° 21′
0° 40′	8.0658	110	8.0658	110	1.9342	10.0000	89° 20′
0° 41′	8.0765	107	8.0765	107	1.9235	10.0000	89° 19′
0° 42′	8.0870	105	8.0870	105	1.9130	10.0000	89° 18′
0° 43′	8.0972	102	8.0972	102	1.9028	10.0000	89° 17′
0° 44′	8.1072	100	8.1072	100	1.8928	10.0000	89° 16′
0° 45′	8.1169	97	8.1170	98	1.8830	10.0000	89° 15′
0° 46′	8.1265	96	8.1265	95	1.8735	10.0000	89° 14′
0° 47′	8.1358	93	8.1359	94	1.8641	10.0000	89° 13′
0° 48′	8.1450	92	8.1450	91	1.8550	10.0000	89° 12′
0° 49′	8.1539	89	8.1540	90	1.8460	10.0000	89° 11′
0° 50′	8.1627	88	8.1627	87	1.8373	10.0000	89° 10′
0° 51′	8.1713	86	8.1713	86	1.8287	10.0000	89° 9′
0° 52′	8.1797	84	8.1798	85	1.8202	10.0000	89° 8′
0° 53′	8.1880	83	8.1880	82	1.8120	10.0000	89° 7′
0° 54′	8.1961	81	8.1962	82	1.8038	9.9999	89° 6′
0° 55′	8.2041	80	8.2041	79	1.7959	9.9999	89° 5′
0° 56′	8.2119	78	8.2120	79	1.7880	9.9999	39° 4′
0° 57′	8.2196	77	8.2196	76	1.7804	9.9999	89° 3′
0° 58′	8.2271	75	8.2272	76	1.7728	9.9999	89° 2′
0° 59′	8.2346	75	8.2346	74	1.7654	9.9999	89° 1′
0° 60′	8.2419	73	8.2419	73	1.7581	9.9999	89° 0′
	log cos	diff.1′	log cot	com. diff.1′	log tan	log sin	Angle

Note in diff columns: *Ordinary interpolation here will in general give inaccurate results. Instead use formulas on p. 6.*

89°

1°							
Angle	log sin	diff. 1′	log tan	com. diff. 1′	log cot	log cos	
1° 0′	8.2419		8.2419		1.7581	9.9999	88° 60′
1° 1′	8.2490	71	8.2491	72	1.7509	9.9999	88° 59′
1° 2′	8.2561	71	8.2562	71	1.7438	9.9999	88° 58′
1° 3′	8.2630	69	8.2631	69	1.7369	9.9999	88° 57′
1° 4′	8.2699	69	8.2700	69	1.7300	9.9999	88° 56′
1° 5′	8.2766	67	8.2767	67	1.7233	9.9999	88° 55′
1° 6′	8.2832	66	8.2833	66	1.7167	9.9999	88° 54′
1° 7′	8.2898	66	8.2899	66	1.7101	9.9999	88° 53′
1° 8′	8.2962	64	8.2963	64	1.7037	9.9999	88° 52′
1° 9′	8.3025	63	8.3026	63	1.6974	9.9999	88° 51′
1° 10′	8.3088	63	8.3089	63	1.6911	9.9999	88° 50′
1° 11′	8.3150	62	8.3150	61	1.6850	9.9999	88° 49′
1° 12′	8.3210	60	8.3211	61	1.6789	9.9999	88° 48′
1° 13′	8.3270	60	8.3271	60	1.6729	9.9999	88° 47′
1° 14′	8.3329	59	8.3330	59	1.6670	9.9999	88° 46′
1° 15′	8.3388	59	8.3389	59	1.6611	9.9999	88° 45′
1° 16′	8.3445	57	8.3446	57	1.6554	9.9999	88° 44′
1° 17′	8.3502	57	8.3503	56	1.6497	9.9999	88° 43′
1° 18′	8.3558	56	8.3559	56	1.6441	9.9999	88° 42′
1° 19′	8.3613	55	8.3614	55	1.6386	9.9999	88° 41′
1° 20′	8.3668	55	8.3669	55	1.6331	9.9999	88° 40′
1° 21′	8.3722	54	8.3723	54	1.6277	9.9999	88° 39′
1° 22′	8.3775	53	8.3776	53	1.6224	9.9999	88° 38′
1° 23′	8.3828	53	8.3829	53	1.6171	9.9999	88° 37′
1° 24′	8.3880	52	8.3881	52	1.6119	9.9999	88° 36′
1° 25′	8.3931	51	8.3932	51	1.6068	9.9999	88° 35′
1° 26′	8.3982	51	8.3983	51	1.6017	9.9999	88° 34′
1° 27′	8.4032	50	8.4033	50	1.5967	9.9999	88° 33′
1° 28′	8.4082	50	8.4083	50	1.5917	9.9999	88° 32′
1° 29′	8.4131	49	8.4132	49	1.5868	9.9999	88° 31′
1° 30′	8.4179	49	8.4181	49	1.5819	9.9999	88° 30′
1° 31′	8.4227	48	8.4229	48	1.5771	9.9998	88° 29′
1° 32′	8.4275	48	8.4276	47	1.5724	9.9998	88° 28′
1° 33′	8.4322	47	8.4323	47	1.5677	9.9998	88° 27′
1° 34′	8.4368	46	8.4370	47	1.5630	9.9998	88° 26′
1° 35′	8.4414	46	8.4416	46	1.5584	9.9998	88° 25′
1° 36′	8.4459	45	8.4461	45	1.5539	9.9998	88° 24′
1° 37′	8.4504	45	8.4506	45	1.5494	9.9998	88° 23′
1° 38′	8.4549	45	8.4551	45	1.5449	9.9998	88° 22′
1° 39′	8.4593	44	8.4595	44	1.5405	9.9998	88° 21′
1° 40′	8.4637	44	8.4638	43	1.5362	9.9998	88° 20′
1° 41′	8.4680	43	8.4682	44	1.5318	9.9998	88° 19′
1° 42′	8.4723	43	8.4725	43	1.5275	9.9998	88° 18′
1° 43′	8.4765	42	8.4767	42	1.5233	9.9998	88° 17′
1° 44′	8.4807	42	8.4809	42	1.5191	9.9998	88° 16′
1° 45′	8.4848	41	8.4851	42	1.5149	9.9998	88° 15′
1° 46′	8.4890	42	8.4892	41	1.5108	9.9998	88° 14′
1° 47′	8.4930	40	8.4933	41	1.5067	9.9998	88° 13′
1° 48′	8.4971	41	8.4973	40	1.5027	9.9998	88° 12′
1° 49′	8.5011	40	8.5013	40	1.4987	9.9998	88° 11′
1° 50′	8.5050	39	8.5053	40	1.4947	9.9998	88° 10′
1° 51′	8.5090	40	8.5092	39	1.4908	9.9998	88° 9′
1° 52′	8.5129	39	8.5131	39	1.4869	9.9998	88° 8′
1° 53′	8.5167	38	8.5170	39	1.4830	9.9998	88° 7′
1° 54′	8.5206	39	8.5208	38	1.4792	9.9998	88° 6′
1° 55′	8.5243	37	8.5246	38	1.4754	9.9998	88° 5′
1° 56′	8.5281	38	8.5283	37	1.4717	9.9998	88° 4′
1° 57′	8.5318	37	8.5321	38	1.4679	9.9997	88° 3′
1° 58′	8.5355	37	8.5358	37	1.4642	9.9997	88° 2′
1° 59′	8.5392	37	8.5394	36	1.4606	9.9997	88° 1′
1° 60′	8.5428	36	8.5431	37	1.4569	9.9997	88° 0′
	log cos	diff. 1′	log cot	com. diff. 1′	log tan	log sin	Angle

| 88° | | | | | | | |

2°

Angle	log sin	diff.1′	log tan	com. diff.1′	log cot	log cos	
2° 0′	8.5428		8.5431		1.4569	9.9997	87° 60′
2° 1′	8.5464	36	8.5467	36	1.4533	9.9997	87° 59′
2° 2′	8.5500	36	8.5503	36	1.4497	9.9997	87° 58′
2° 3′	8.5535	35	8.5538	35	1.4462	9.9997	87° 57′
2° 4′	8.5571	36	8.5573	35	1.4427	9.9997	87° 56′
2° 5′	8.5605	34	8.5608	35	1.4392	9.9997	87° 55′
2° 6′	8.5640	35	8.5643	35	1.4357	9.9997	87° 54′
2° 7′	8.5674	34	8.5677	34	1.4323	9.9997	87° 53′
2° 8′	8.5708	34	8.5711	34	1.4289	9.9997	87° 52′
2° 9′	8.5742	34	8.5745	34	1.4255	9.9997	87° 51′
2° 10′	8.5776	34	8.5779	34	1.4221	9.9997	87° 50′
2° 11′	8.5809	33	8.5812	33	1.4188	9.9997	87° 49′
2° 12′	8.5842	33	8.5845	33	1.4155	9.9997	87° 48′
2° 13′	8.5875	33	8.5878	33	1.4122	9.9997	87° 47′
2° 14′	8.5907	32	8.5911	33	1.4089	9.9997	87° 46′
2° 15′	8.5939	32	8.5943	32	1.4057	9.9997	87° 45′
2° 16′	8.5972	33	8.5975	32	1.4025	9.9997	87° 44′
2° 17′	8.6003	31	8.6007	32	1.3993	9.9997	87° 43′
2° 18′	8.6035	32	8.6038	31	1.3962	9.9997	87° 42′
2° 19′	8.6066	31	8.6070	32	1.3930	9.9996	87° 41′
2° 20′	8.6097	31	8.6101	31	1.3899	9.9996	87° 40′
2° 21′	8.6128	31	8.6132	31	1.3868	9.9996	87° 39′
2° 22′	8.6159	30	8.6163	30	1.3837	9.9996	87° 38′
2° 23′	8.6189	31	8.6193	30	1.3807	9.9996	87° 37′
2° 24′	8.6220	30	8.6223	31	1.3777	9.9996	87° 36′
2° 25′	8.6250	29	8.6254	29	1.3746	9.9996	87° 35′
2° 26′	8.6279	30	8.6283	30	1.3717	9.9996	87° 34′
2° 27′	8.6309	30	8.6313	30	1.3687	9.9996	87° 33′
2° 28′	8.6339	29	8.6343	29	1.3657	9.9996	87° 32′
2° 29′	8.6368	29	8.6372	29	1.3628	9.9996	87° 31′
2° 30′	8.6397	29	8.6401	29	1.3599	9.9996	87° 30′
2° 31′	8.6426	28	8.6430	29	1.3570	9.9996	87° 29′
2° 32′	8.6454	29	8.6459	28	1.3541	9.9996	87° 28′
2° 33′	8.6483	28	8.6487	28	1.3513	9.9996	87° 27′
2° 34′	8.6511	28	8.6515	28	1.3485	9.9996	87° 26′
2° 35′	8.6539	28	8.6544	29	1.3456	9.9996	87° 25′
2° 36′	8.6567	28	8.6571	27	1.3429	9.9996	87° 24′
2° 37′	8.6595	27	8.6599	28	1.3401	9.9995	87° 23′
2° 38′	8.6622	28	8.6627	28	1.3373	9.9995	87° 22′
2° 39′	8.6650	27	8.6654	27	1.3346	9.9995	87° 21′
2° 40′	8.6677	27	8.6682	28	1.3318	9.9995	87° 20′
2° 41′	8.6704	27	8.6709	27	1.3291	9.9995	87° 19′
2° 42′	8.6731	27	8.6736	27	1.3264	9.9995	87° 18′
2° 43′	8.6758	26	8.6762	26	1.3238	9.9995	87° 17′
2° 44′	8.6784	26	8.6789	27	1.3211	9.9995	87° 16′
2° 45′	8.6810	26	8.6815	26	1.3185	9.9995	87° 15′
2° 46′	8.6837	27	8.6842	27	1.3158	9.9995	87° 14′
2° 47′	8.6863	26	8.6868	26	1.3132	9.9995	87° 13′
2° 48′	8.6889	26	8.6894	26	1.3106	9.9995	87° 12′
2° 49′	8.6914	25	8.6920	26	1.3080	9.9995	87° 11′
2° 50′	8.6940	26	8.6945	25	1.3055	9.9995	87° 10′
2° 51′	8.6965	25	8.6971	26	1.3029	9.9995	87° 9′
2° 52′	8.6991	26	8.6996	25	1.3004	9.9995	87° 8′
2° 53′	8.7016	25	8.7021	25	1.2979	9.9995	87° 7′
2° 54′	8.7041	25	8.7046	25	1.2954	9.9994	87° 6′
2° 55′	8.7066	25	8.7071	25	1.2929	9.9994	87° 5′
2° 56′	8.7090	24	8.7096	25	1.2904	9.9994	87° 4′
2° 57′	8.7115	25	8.7121	25	1.2879	9.9994	87° 3′
2° 58′	8.7140	25	8.7145	24	1.2855	9.9994	87° 2′
2° 59′	8.7164	24	8.7170	25	1.2830	9.9994	87° 1′
2° 60′	8.7188	24	8.7194	24	1.2806	9.9994	87° 0′
	log cos	diff.1′	log cot	com. diff.1′	log tan	log sin	Angle

87°

3°							
Angle	log sin	diff.1′	log tan	com. diff.1′	log cot	log cos	
3° 0′	8.7188	24	8.7194	24	1.2806	9.9994	**86° 60′**
3° 1′	8.7212	24	8.7218	24	1.2782	9.9994	86° 59′
3° 2′	8.7236	24	8.7242	24	1.2758	9.9994	86° 58′
3° 3′	8.7260	24	8.7266	24	1.2734	9.9994	86° 57′
3° 4′	8.7283	23	8.7290	24	1.2710	9.9994	86° 56′
3° 5′	8.7307	24	8.7313	23	1.2687	9.9994	86° 55′
3° 6′	8.7330	23	8.7337	24	1.2663	9.9994	86° 54′
3° 7′	8.7354	24	8.7360	23	1.2640	9.9994	86° 53′
3° 8′	8.7377	23	8.7383	23	1.2617	9.9994	86° 52′
3° 9′	8.7400	23	8.7406	23	1.2594	9.9993	86° 51′
3° 10′	8.7423	23	8.7429	23	1.2571	9.9993	**86° 50′**
3° 11′	8.7445	22	8.7452	23	1.2548	9.9993	86° 49′
3° 12′	8.7468	23	8.7475	23	1.2525	9.9993	86° 48′
3° 13′	8.7491	23	8.7497	22	1.2503	9.9993	86° 47′
3° 14′	8.7513	22	8.7520	23	1.2480	9.9993	86° 46′
3° 15′	8.7535	22	8.7542	22	1.2458	9.9993	86° 45′
3° 16′	8.7557	22	8.7565	23	1.2435	9.9993	86° 44′
3° 17′	8.7580	23	8.7587	22	1.2413	9.9993	86° 43′
3° 18′	8.7602	22	8.7609	22	1.2391	9.9993	86° 42′
3° 19′	8.7623	21	8.7631	22	1.2369	9.9993	86° 41′
3° 20′	8.7645	22	8.7652	22	1.2348	9.9993	**86° 40′**
3° 21′	8.7667	22	8.7674	22	1.2326	9.9993	86° 39′
3° 22′	8.7688	21	8.7696	22	1.2304	9.9993	86° 38′
3° 23′	8.7710	22	8.7717	21	1.2283	9.9992	86° 37′
3° 24′	8.7731	21	8.7739	22	1.2261	9.9992	86° 36′
3° 25′	8.7752	21	8.7760	21	1.2240	9.9992	86° 35′
3° 26′	8.7773	21	8.7781	21	1.2219	9.9992	86° 34′
3° 27′	8.7794	21	8.7802	21	1.2198	9.9992	86° 33′
3° 28′	8.7815	21	8.7823	21	1.2177	9.9992	86° 32′
3° 29′	8.7836	21	8.7844	21	1.2156	9.9992	86° 31′
3° 30′	8.7857	20	8.7865	21	1.2135	9.9992	**86° 30′**
3° 31′	8.7877	21	8.7886	20	1.2114	9.9992	86° 29′
3° 32′	8.7898	20	8.7906	21	1.2094	9.9992	86° 28′
3° 33′	8.7918	21	8.7927	20	1.2073	9.9992	86° 27′
3° 34′	8.7939	20	8.7947	20	1.2053	9.9992	86° 26′
3° 35′	8.7959	20	8.7967	20	1.2033	9.9992	86° 25′
3° 36′	8.7979	20	8.7988	21	1.2012	9.9991	86° 24′
3° 37′	8.7999	20	8.8008	20	1.1992	9.9991	86° 23′
3° 38′	8.8019	20	8.8028	20	1.1972	9.9991	86° 22′
3° 39′	8.8039	20	8.8048	20	1.1952	9.9991	86° 21′
3° 40′	8.8059	19	8.8067	20	1.1933	9.9991	**86° 20′**
3° 41′	8.8078	20	8.8087	20	1.1913	9.9991	86° 19′
3° 42′	8.8098	19	8.8107	19	1.1893	9.9991	86° 18′
3° 43′	8.8117	20	8.8126	20	1.1874	9.9991	86° 17′
3° 44′	8.8137	19	8.8146	19	1.1854	9.9991	86° 16′
3° 45′	8.8156	19	8.8165	20	1.1835	9.9991	86° 15′
3° 46′	8.8175	19	8.8185	19	1.1815	9.9991	86° 14′
3° 47′	8.8194	19	8.8204	19	1.1796	9.9991	86° 13′
3° 48′	8.8213	19	8.8223	19	1.1777	9.9990	86° 12′
3° 49′	8.8232	19	8.8242	19	1.1758	9.9990	86° 11′
3° 50′	8.8251	19	8.8261	19	1.1739	9.9990	**86° 10′**
3° 51′	8.8270	19	8.8280	19	1.1720	9.9990	86° 9′
3° 52′	8.8289	18	8.8299	18	1.1701	9.9990	86° 8′
3° 53′	8.8307	19	8.8317	19	1.1683	9.9990	86° 7′
3° 54′	8.8326	19	8.8336	19	1.1664	9.9990	86° 6′
3° 55′	8.8345	18	8.8355	18	1.1645	9.9990	86° 5′
3° 56′	8.8363	18	8.8373	19	1.1627	9.9990	86° 4′
3° 57′	8.8381	19	8.8392	18	1.1608	9.9990	86° 3′
3° 58′	8.8400	18	8.8410	18	1.1590	9.9990	86° 2′
3° 59′	8.8418	18	8.8428	18	1.1572	9.9990	86° 1′
3° 60′	8.8436		8.8446		1.1554	9.9989	**86° 0′**
	log cos	diff.1′	log cot	com. diff.1′	log tan	log sin	Angle
86°							

4°							
Angle	log sin	diff.1′	log tan	com.diff.1′	log cot	log cos	
4° 0′	8.8436		8.8446		1.1554	9.9989	**85° 60′**
4° 1′	8.8454	18	8.8465	19	1.1535	9.9989	85° 59′
4° 2′	8.8472	18	8.8483	18	1.1517	9.9989	85° 58′
4° 3′	8.8490	18	8.8501	18	1.1499	9.9989	85° 57′
4° 4′	8.8508	18	8.8518	17	1.1482	9.9989	85° 56′
4° 5′	8.8525	17	8.8536	18	1.1464	9.9989	85° 55′
4° 6′	8.8543	18	8.8554	18	1.1446	9.9989	85° 54′
4° 7′	8.8560	17	8.8572	18	1.1428	9.9989	85° 53′
4° 8′	8.8578	18	8.8589	17	1.1411	9.9989	85° 52′
4° 9′	8.8595	17	8.8607	18	1.1393	9.9989	85° 51′
4° 10′	8.8613	18	8.8624	17	1.1376	9.9989	**85° 50′**
4° 11′	8.8630	17	8.8642	18	1.1358	9.9988	85° 49′
4° 12′	8.8647	17	8.8659	17	1.1341	9.9988	85° 48′
4° 13′	8.8665	18	8.8676	17	1.1324	9.9988	85° 47′
4° 14′	8.8682	17	8.8694	18	1.1306	9.9988	85° 46′
4° 15′	8.8699	17	8.8711	17	1.1289	9.9988	85° 45′
4° 16′	8.8716	17	8.8728	17	1.1272	9.9988	85° 44′
4° 17′	8.8733	17	8.8745	17	1.1255	9.9988	85° 43′
4° 18′	8.8749	16	8.8762	17	1.1238	9.9988	85° 42′
4° 19′	8.8766	17	8.8778	16	1.1222	9.9988	85° 41′
4° 20′	8.8783	17	8.8795	17	1.1205	9.9988	**85° 40′**
4° 21′	8.8799	16	8.8812	17	1.1188	9.9987	85° 39′
4° 22′	8.8816	17	8.8829	17	1.1171	9.9987	85° 38′
4° 23′	8.8833	17	8.8845	16	1.1155	9.9987	85° 37′
4° 24′	8.8849	16	8.8862	17	1.1138	9.9987	85° 36′
4° 25′	8.8865	16	8.8878	16	1.1122	9.9987	85° 35′
4° 26′	8.8882	17	8.8895	17	1.1105	9.9987	85° 34′
4° 27′	8.8898	16	8.8911	16	1.1089	9.9987	85° 33′
4° 28′	8.8914	16	8.8927	16	1.1073	9.9987	85° 32′
4° 29′	8.8930	16	8.8944	17	1.1056	9.9987	85° 31′
4° 30′	8.8946	16	8.8960	16	1.1040	9.9987	**85° 30′**
4° 31′	8.8962	16	8.8976	16	1.1024	9.9986	85° 29′
4° 32′	8.8978	16	8.8992	16	1.1008	9.9986	85° 28′
4° 33′	8.8994	16	8.9008	16	1.0992	9.9986	85° 27′
4° 34′	8.9010	16	8.9024	16	1.0976	9.9986	85° 26′
4° 35′	8.9026	16	8.9040	16	1.0960	9.9986	85° 25′
4° 36′	8.9042	16	8.9056	16	1.0944	9.9986	85° 24′
4° 37′	8.9057	15	8.9071	15	1.0929	9.9986	85° 23′
4° 38′	8.9073	16	8.9087	16	1.0913	9.9986	85° 22′
4° 39′	8.9089	16	8.9103	16	1.0897	9.9986	85° 21′
4° 40′	8.9104	15	8.9118	15	1.0882	9.9986	**85° 20′**
4° 41′	8.9119	15	8.9134	16	1.0866	9.9985	85° 19′
4° 42′	8.9135	16	8.9150	16	1.0850	9.9985	85° 18′
4° 43′	8.9150	15	8.9165	15	1.0835	9.9985	85° 17′
4° 44′	8.9166	16	8.9180	15	1.0820	9.9985	85° 16′
4° 45′	8.9181	15	8.9196	16	1.0804	9.9985	85° 15′
4° 46′	8.9196	15	8.9211	15	1.0789	9.9985	85° 14′
4° 47′	8.9211	15	8.9226	15	1.0774	9.9985	85° 13′
4° 48′	8.9226	15	8.9241	15	1.0759	9.9985	85° 12′
4° 49′	8.9241	15	8.9256	15	1.0744	9.9985	85° 11′
4° 50′	8.9256	15	8.9272	16	1.0728	9.9985	**85° 10′**
4° 51′	8.9271	15	8.9287	15	1.0713	9.9984	85° 9′
4° 52′	8.9286	15	8.9302	15	1.0698	9.9984	85° 8′
4° 53′	8.9301	15	8.9316	14	1.0684	9.9984	85° 7′
4° 54′	8.9315	14	8.9331	15	1.0669	9.9984	85° 6′
4° 55′	8.9330	15	8.9346	15	1.0654	9.9984	85° 5′
4° 56′	8.9345	15	8.9361	15	1.0639	9.9984	85° 4′
4° 57′	8.9359	14	8.9376	15	1.0624	9.9984	85° 3′
4° 58′	8.9374	15	8.9390	14	1.0610	9.9984	85° 2′
4° 59′	8.9388	15	8.9405	15	1.0595	9.9984	85° 1′
4° 60′	8.9403	15	8.9420	15	1.0580	9.9983	**85° 0′**
	log cos	diff.1′	log cot	com.diff.1′	log tan	log sin	Angle

85°

5°–15°

Angle	log sin	diff.1′	log tan	com. diff.1′	log cot	log cos	diff.1′	Angle
5° 0′	8.9403		8.9420		1.0580	9.9983		85° 0′
		14.2		14.3			.1	
5° 10′	8.9545		8.9563		1.0437	9.9982		84° 50′
		13.7		13.8			.1	
5° 20′	8.9682		8.9701		1.0299	9.9981		84° 40′
		13.4		13.5			.1	
5° 30′	8.9816		8.9836		1.0164	9.9980		84° 30′
		12.9		13.0			.1	
5° 40′	8.9945		8.9966		1.0034	9.9979		84° 20′
		12.5		12.7			.2	
5° 50′	9.0070		9.0093		0.9907	9.9977		84° 10′
		12.2		12.3			.1	
6° 0′	9.0192		9.0216		0.9784	9.9976		84° 0′
		11.9		12.0			.1	
6° 10′	9.0311		9.0336		0.9664	9.9975		83° 50′
		11.5		11.7			.2	
6° 20′	9.0426		9.0453		0.9547	9.9973		83° 40′
		11.3		11.4			.1	
6° 30′	9.0539		9.0567		0.9433	9.9972		83° 30′
		10.9		11.1			.1	
6° 40′	9.0648		9.0678		0.9322	9.9971		83° 20′
		10.7		10.8			.2	
6° 50′	9.0755		9.0786		0.9214	9.9969		83° 10′
		10.4		10.5			.1	
7° 0′	9.0859		9.0891		0.9109	9.9968		83° 0′
		10.2		10.4			.2	
7° 10′	9.0961		9.0995		0.9005	9.9966		82° 50′
		9.9		10.1			.2	
7° 20′	9.1060		9.1096		0.8904	9.9964		82° 40′
		9.7		9.8			.1	
7° 30′	9.1157		9.1194		0.8806	9.9963		82° 30′
		9.5		9.7			.2	
7° 40′	9.1252		9.1291		0.8709	9.9961		82° 20′
		9.3		9.4			.2	
7° 50′	9.1345		9.1385		0.8615	9.9959		82° 10′
		9.1		9.3			.1	
8° 0′	9.1436		9.1478		0.8522	9.9958		82° 0′
		8.9		9.1			.2	
8° 10′	9.1525		9.1569		0.8431	9.9956		81° 50′
		8.7		8.9			.2	
8° 20′	9.1612		9.1658		0.8342	9.9954		81° 40′
		8.5		8.7			.2	
8° 30′	9.1697		9.1745		0.8255	9.9952		81° 30′
		8.4		8.6			.2	
8° 40′	9.1781		9.1831		0.8169	9.9950		81° 20′
		8.2		8.4			.2	
8° 50′	9.1863		9.1915		0.8085	9.9948		81° 10′
		8.0		8.2			.2	
9° 0′	9.1943		9.1997		0.8003	9.9946		81° 0′
		7.9		8.1			.2	
9° 10′	9.2022		9.2078		0.7922	9.9944		80° 50′
		7.8		8.0			.2	
9° 20′	9.2100		9.2158		0.7842	9.9942		80° 40′
		7.6		7.8			.2	
9° 30′	9.2176		9.2236		0.7764	9.9940		80° 30′
		7.5		7.7			.2	
9° 40′	9.2251		9.2313		0.7687	9.9938		80° 20′
		7.3		7.6			.2	
9° 50′	9.2324		9.2389		0.7611	9.9936		80° 10′
		7.3		7.4			.2	
10° 0′	9.2397		9.2463		0.7537	9.9934		80° 0′
		7.1		7.3			.3	
10° 10′	9.2468		9.2536		0.7464	9.9931		79° 50′
		7.0		7.3			.2	
10° 20′	9.2538		9.2609		0.7391	9.9929		79° 40′
		6.8		7.1			.2	
10° 30′	9.2606		9.2680		0.7320	9.9927		79° 30′
		6.8		7.0			.3	
10° 40′	9.2674		9.2750		0.7250	9.9924		79° 20′
		6.6		6.9			.2	
10° 50′	9.2740		9.2819		0.7181	9.9922		79° 10′
		6.6		6.8			.3	
11° 0′	9.2806		9.2887		0.7113	9.9919		79° 0′
		6.4		6.6			.2	
11° 10′	9.2870		9.2953		0.7047	9.9917		78° 50′
		6.4		6.7			.3	
11° 20′	9.2934		9.3020		0.6980	9.9914		78° 40′
		6.3		6.5			.2	
11° 30′	9.2997		9.3085		0.6915	9.9912		78° 30′
		6.1		6.4			.3	
11° 40′	9.3058		9.3149		0.6851	9.9909		78° 20′
		6.1		6.3			.2	
11° 50′	9.3119		9.3212		0.6788	9.9907		78° 10′
		6.0		6.3			.3	
12° 0′	9.3179		9.3275		0.6725	9.9904		78° 0′
		5.9		6.1			.3	
12° 10′	9.3238		9.3336		0.6664	9.9901		77° 50′
		5.8		6.1			.2	
12° 20′	9.3296		9.3397		0.6603	9.9899		77° 40′
		5.7		6.1			.3	
12° 30′	9.3353		9.3458		0.6542	9.9896		77° 30′
		5.7		5.9			.3	
12° 40′	9.3410		9.3517		0.6483	9.9893		77° 20′
		5.6		5.9			.3	
12° 50′	9.3466		9.3576		0.6424	9.9890		77° 10′
		5.5		5.8			.3	
13° 0′	9.3521		9.3634		0.6366	9.9887		77° 0′
		5.4		5.7			.3	
13° 10′	9.3575		9.3691		0.6309	9.9884		76° 50′
		5.4		5.7			.3	
13° 20′	9.3629		9.3748		0.6252	9.9881		76° 40′
		5.3		5.6			.3	
13° 30′	9.3682		9.3804		0.6196	9.9878		76° 30′
		5.2		5.5			.3	
13° 40′	9.3734		9.3859		0.6141	9.9875		76° 20′
		5.2		5.5			.3	
13° 50′	9.3786		9.3914		0.6086	9.9872		76° 10′
		5.1		5.4			.3	
14° 0′	9.3837		9.3968		0.6032	9.9869		76° 0′
		5.0		5.3			.3	
14° 10′	9.3887		9.4021		0.5979	9.9866		75° 50′
		5.0		5.3			.3	
14° 20′	9.3937		9.4074		0.5926	9.9863		75° 40′
		4.9		5.3			.4	
14° 30′	9.3986		9.4127		0.5873	9.9859		75° 30′
		4.9		5.1			.3	
14° 40′	9.4035		9.4178		0.5822	9.9856		75° 20′
		4.8		5.2			.3	
14° 50′	9.4083		9.4230		0.5770	9.9853		75° 10′
		4.7		5.1			.4	
15° 0′	9.4130		9.4281		0.5719	9.9849		75° 0′
	log cos	diff.1′	log cot	com. diff.1′	log tan	log sin	diff.1′	Angle

75°–85°

15°–25°

Angle	log sin	diff.1′	log tan	com. diff.1′	log cot	log cos	diff.1′	Angle
15° 0′	9.4130		9.4281		0.5719	9.9849		75° 0′
15° 10′	9.4177	4.7	9.4331	5.0	0.5669	9.9846	.3	74° 50′
15° 20′	9.4223	4.6	9.4381	5.0	0.5619	9.9843	.3	74° 40′
15° 30′	9.4269	4.6	9.4430	4.9	0.5570	9.9839	.4	74° 30′
15° 40′	9.4314	4.5	9.4479	4.9	0.5521	9.9836	.3	74° 20′
15° 50′	9.4359	4.5	9.4527	4.8	0.5473	9.9832	.4	74° 10′
16° 0′	9.4403	4.4	9.4575	4.8	0.5425	9.9828	.4	74° 0′
16° 10′	9.4447	4.4	9.4622	4.7	0.5378	9.9825	.3	73° 50′
16° 20′	9.4491	4.4	9.4669	4.7	0.5331	9.9821	.4	73° 40′
16° 30′	9.4533	4.2	9.4716	4.7	0.5284	9.9817	.4	73° 30′
16° 40′	9.4576	4.3	9.4762	4.6	0.5238	9.9814	.3	73° 20′
16° 50′	9.4618	4.2	9.4808	4.6	0.5192	9.9810	.4	73° 10′
17° 0′	9.4659	4.1	9.4853	4.5	0.5147	9.9806	.4	73° 0′
17° 10′	9.4700	4.1	9.4898	4.5	0.5102	9.9802	.4	72° 50′
17° 20′	9.4741	4.1	9.4943	4.5	0.5057	9.9798	.4	72° 40′
17° 30′	9.4781	4.0	9.4987	4.4	0.5013	9.9794	.4	72° 30′
17° 40′	9.4821	4.0	9.5031	4.4	0.4969	9.9790	.4	72° 20′
17° 50′	9.4861	4.0	9.5075	4.4	0.4925	9.9786	.4	72° 10′
18° 0′	9.4900	3.9	9.5118	4.3	0.4882	9.9782	.4	72° 0′
18° 10′	9.4939	3.9	9.5161	4.3	0.4839	9.9778	.4	71° 50′
18° 20′	9.4977	3.8	9.5203	4.2	0.4797	9.9774	.4	71° 40′
18° 30′	9.5015	3.8	9.5245	4.2	0.4755	9.9770	.4	71° 30′
18° 40′	9.5052	3.7	9.5287	4.2	0.4713	9.9765	.5	71° 20′
18° 50′	9.5090	3.8	9.5329	4.2	0.4671	9.9761	.4	71° 10′
19° 0′	9.5126	3.6	9.5370	4.1	0.4630	9.9757	.4	71° 0′
19° 10′	9.5163	3.7	9.5411	4.1	0.4589	9.9752	.5	70° 50′
19° 20′	9.5199	3.6	9.5451	4.0	0.4549	9.9748	.4	70° 40′
19° 30′	9.5235	3.6	9.5491	4.0	0.4509	9.9743	.5	70° 30′
19° 40′	9.5270	3.5	9.5531	4.0	0.4469	9.9739	.4	70° 20′
19° 50′	9.5306	3.6	9.5571	4.0	0.4429	9.9734	.5	70° 10′
20° 0′	9.5341	3.5	9.5611	4.0	0.4389	9.9730	.4	70° 0′
20° 10′	9.5375	3.4	9.5650	3.9	0.4350	9.9725	.5	69° 50′
20° 20′	9.5409	3.4	9.5689	3.9	0.4311	9.9721	.4	69° 40′
20° 30′	9.5443	3.4	9.5727	3.8	0.4273	9.9716	.5	69° 30′
20° 40′	9.5477	3.4	9.5766	3.9	0.4234	9.9711	.5	69° 20′
20° 50′	9.5510	3.3	9.5804	3.8	0.4196	9.9706	.5	69° 10′
21° 0′	9.5543	3.3	9.5842	3.8	0.4158	9.9702	.4	69° 0′
21° 10′	9.5576	3.3	9.5879	3.7	0.4121	9.9697	.5	68° 50′
21° 20′	9.5609	3.3	9.5917	3.8	0.4083	9.9692	.5	68° 40′
21° 30′	9.5641	3.2	9.5954	3.7	0.4046	9.9687	.5	68° 30′
21° 40′	9.5673	3.2	9.5991	3.7	0.4009	9.9682	.5	68° 20′
21° 50′	9.5704	3.1	9.6028	3.7	0.3972	9.9677	.5	68° 10′
22° 0′	9.5736	3.2	9.6064	3.6	0.3936	9.9672	.5	68° 0′
22° 10′	9.5767	3.1	9.6100	3.6	0.3900	9.9667	.6	67° 50′
22° 20′	9.5798	3.1	9.6136	3.6	0.3864	9.9661	.5	67° 40′
22° 30′	9.5828	3.0	9.6172	3.6	0.3828	9.9656	.5	67° 30′
22° 40′	9.5859	3.1	9.6208	3.6	0.3792	9.9651	.5	67° 20′
22° 50′	9.5889	3.0	9.6243	3.5	0.3757	9.9646	.6	67° 10′
23° 0′	9.5919	3.0	9.6279	3.6	0.3721	9.9640	.5	67° 0′
23° 10′	9.5948	2.9	9.6314	3.5	0.3686	9.9635	.6	66° 50′
23° 20′	9.5978	3.0	9.6348	3.4	0.3652	9.9629	.5	66° 40′
23° 30′	9.6007	2.9	9.6383	3.5	0.3617	9.9624	.6	66° 30′
23° 40′	9.6036	2.9	9.6417	3.4	0.3583	9.9618	.5	66° 20′
23° 50′	9.6065	2.9	9.6452	3.5	0.3548	9.9613	.6	66° 10′
24° 0′	9.6093	2.8	9.6486	3.4	0.3514	9.9607	.6	66° 0′
24° 10′	9.6121	2.8	9.6520	3.4	0.3480	9.9602	.5	65° 50′
24° 20′	9.6149	2.8	9.6553	3.3	0.3447	9.9596	.6	65° 40′
24° 30′	9.6177	2.8	9.6587	3.4	0.3413	9.9590	.6	65° 30′
24° 40′	9.6205	2.8	9.6620	3.3	0.3380	9.9584	.6	65° 20′
24° 50′	9.6232	2.7	9.6654	3.4	0.3346	9.9579	.5	65° 10′
25° 0′	9.6259	2.7	9.6687	3.3	0.3313	9.9573	.6	65° 0′
	log cos	diff.1′	log cot	com. diff.1′	log tan	log sin	diff.1′	Angle

65°–75°

25°–35°

Angle	log sin	diff.1'	log tan	com. diff.1'	log cot	log cos	diff.1'	Angle
25° 0'	9.6259		9.6687		0.3313	9.9573		65° 0'
		2.7		3.3			.6	
25° 10'	9.6286		9.6720		0.3280	9.9567		64° 50'
		2.7		3.2			.6	
25° 20'	9.6313		9.6752		0.3248	9.9561		64° 40'
		2.7		3.3			.6	
25° 30'	9.6340		9.6785		0.3215	9.9555		64° 30'
		2.6		3.2			.6	
25° 40'	9.6366		9.6817		0.3183	9.9549		64° 20'
		2.6		3.3			.6	
25° 50'	9.6392		9.6850		0.3150	9.9543		64° 10'
		2.6		3.2			.6	
26° 0'	9.6418		9.6882		0.3118	9.9537		64° 0'
		2.6		3.2			.7	
26° 10'	9.6444		9.6914		0.3086	9.9530		63° 50'
		2.6		3.2			.6	
26° 20'	9.6470		9.6946		0.3054	9.9524		63° 40'
		2.6		3.2			.6	
26° 30'	9.6495		9.6977		0.3023	9.9518		63° 30'
		2.5		3.1			.6	
26° 40'	9.6521		9.7009		0.2991	9.9512		63° 20'
		2.6		3.2			.6	
26° 50'	9.6546		9.7040		0.2960	9.9505		63° 10'
		2.5		3.1			.7	
27° 0'	9.6570		9.7072		0.2928	9.9499		63° 0'
		2.4		3.2			.6	
27° 10'	9.6595		9.7103		0.2897	9.9492		62° 50'
		2.5		3.1			.7	
27° 20'	9.6620		9.7134		0.2866	9.9486		62° 40'
		2.5		3.1			.6	
27° 30'	9.6644		9.7165		0.2835	9.9479		62° 30'
		2.4		3.1			.7	
27° 40'	9.6668		9.7196		0.2804	9.9473		62° 20'
		2.4		3.1			.6	
27° 50'	9.6692		9.7226		0.2774	9.9466		62° 10'
		2.4		3.0			.7	
28° 0'	9.6716		9.7257		0.2743	9.9459		62° 0'
		2.4		3.1			.7	
28° 10'	9.6740		9.7287		0.2713	9.9453		61° 50'
		2.3		3.0			.6	
28° 20'	9.6763		9.7317		0.2683	9.9446		61° 40'
		2.4		3.0			.7	
28° 30'	9.6787		9.7348		0.2652	9.9439		61° 30'
		2.3		3.1			.7	
28° 40'	9.6810		9.7378		0.2622	9.9432		61° 20'
		2.3		3.0			.7	
28° 50'	9.6833		9.7408		0.2592	9.9425		61° 10'
		2.3		3.0			.7	
29° 0'	9.6856		9.7438		0.2562	9.9418		61° 0'
		2.2		3.0			.7	
29° 10'	9.6878		9.7467		0.2533	9.9411		60° 50'
		2.3		2.9			.7	
29° 20'	9.6901		9.7497		0.2503	9.9404		60° 40'
		2.2		3.0			.7	
29° 30'	9.6923		9.7526		0.2474	9.9397		60° 30'
		2.3		2.9			.7	
29° 40'	9.6946		9.7556		0.2444	9.9390		60° 20'
		2.2		3.0			.7	
29° 50'	9.6968		9.7585		0.2415	9.9383		60° 10'
		2.2		2.9			.8	
30° 0'	9.6990		9.7614		0.2386	9.9375		60° 0'
		2.2		2.9			.7	
30° 10'	9.7012		9.7644		0.2356	9.9368		59° 50'
		2.1		2.9			.7	
30° 20'	9.7033		9.7673		0.2327	9.9361		59° 40'
		2.2		2.8			.8	
30° 30'	9.7055		9.7701		0.2299	9.9353		59° 30'
		2.1		2.9			.7	
30° 40'	9.7076		9.7730		0.2270	9.9346		59° 20'
		2.1		2.9			.8	
30° 50'	9.7097		9.7759		0.2241	9.9338		59° 10'
		2.1		2.9			.7	
31° 0'	9.7118		9.7788		0.2212	9.9331		59° 0'
		2.1		2.8			.8	
31° 10'	9.7139		9.7816		0.2184	9.9323		58° 50'
		2.1		2.9			.8	
31° 20'	9.7160		9.7845		0.2155	9.9315		58° 40'
		2.1		2.8			.7	
31° 30'	9.7181		9.7873		0.2127	9.9308		58° 30'
		2.0		2.9			.8	
31° 40'	9.7201		9.7902		0.2098	9.9300		58° 20'
		2.1		2.8			.8	
31° 50'	9.7222		9.7930		0.2070	9.9292		58° 10'
		2.0		2.8			.8	
32° 0'	9.7242		9.7958		0.2042	9.9284		58° 0'
		2.0		2.8			.8	
32° 10'	9.7262		9.7986		0.2014	9.9276		57° 50'
		2.0		2.8			.8	
32° 20'	9.7282		9.8014		0.1986	9.9268		57° 40'
		2.0		2.8			.8	
32° 30'	9.7302		9.8042		0.1958	9.9260		57° 30'
		2.0		2.8			.8	
32° 40'	9.7322		9.8070		0.1930	9.9252		57° 20'
		2.0		2.7			.8	
32° 50'	9.7342		9.8097		0.1903	9.9244		57° 10'
		1.9		2.8			.8	
33° 0'	9.7361		9.8125		0.1875	9.9236		57° 0'
		1.9		2.8			.8	
33° 10'	9.7380		9.8153		0.1847	9.9228		56° 50'
		2.0		2.7			.9	
33° 20'	9.7400		9.8180		0.1820	9.9219		56° 40'
		1.9		2.8			.8	
33° 30'	9.7419		9.8208		0.1792	9.9211		56° 30'
		1.9		2.7			.8	
33° 40'	9.7438		9.8235		0.1765	9.9203		56° 20'
		1.9		2.8			.9	
33° 50'	9.7457		9.8263		0.1737	9.9194		56° 10'
		1.9		2.7			.8	
34° 0'	9.7476		9.8290		0.1710	9.9186		56° 0'
		1.8		2.7			.9	
34° 10'	9.7494		9.8317		0.1683	9.9177		55° 50'
		1.9		2.7			.8	
34° 20'	9.7513		9.8344		0.1656	9.9169		55° 40'
		1.8		2.7			.9	
34° 30'	9.7531		9.8371		0.1629	9.9160		55° 30'
		1.9		2.7			.9	
34° 40'	9.7550		9.8398		0.1602	9.9151		55° 20'
		1.8		2.7			.9	
34° 50'	9.7568		9.8425		0.1575	9.9142		55° 10'
		1.8		2.7			.8	
35° 0'	9.7586		9.8452		0.1548	9.9134		55° 0'
	log cos	diff.1'	log cot	com. diff.1'	log tan	log sin	diff.1'	Angle

55°–65°

35°–45°

Angle	log sin	diff. 1′	log tan	com. diff. 1′	log cot	log cos	diff. 1′	Angle
35° 0′	9.7586		9.8452		0.1548	9.9134		55° 0′
		1.8		2.7			.9	
35° 10′	9.7604		9.8479		0.1521	9.9125		54° 50′
		1.8		2.7			.9	
35° 20′	9.7622		9.8506		0.1494	9.9116		54° 40′
		1.8		2.7			.9	
35° 30′	9.7640		9.8533		0.1467	9.9107		54° 30′
		1.7		2.6			.9	
35° 40′	9.7657		9.8559		0.1441	9.9098		54° 20′
		1.8		2.7			.9	
35° 50′	9.7675		9.8586		0.1414	9.9089		54° 10′
		1.7		2.7			.9	
36° 0′	9.7692		9.8613		0.1387	9.9080		54° 0′
		1.8		2.6			1.0	
36° 10′	9.7710		9.8639		0.1361	9.9070		53° 50′
		1.7		2.7			.9	
36° 20′	9.7727		9.8666		0.1334	9.9061		53° 40′
		1.7		2.6			.9	
36° 30′	9.7744		9.8692		0.1308	9.9052		53° 30′
		1.7		2.6			1.0	
36° 40′	9.7761		9.8718		0.1282	9.9042		53° 20′
		1.7		2.7			.9	
36° 50′	9.7778		9.8745		0.1255	9.9033		53° 10′
		1.7		2.6			1.0	
37° 0′	9.7795		9.8771		0.1229	9.9023		53° 0′
		1.6		2.6			.9	
37° 10′	9.7811		9.8797		0.1203	9.9014		52° 50′
		1.7		2.7			1.0	
37° 20′	9.7828		9.8824		0.1176	9.9004		52° 40′
		1.6		2.6			.9	
37° 30′	9.7844		9.8850		0.1150	9.8995		52° 30′
		1.7		2.3			1.0	
37° 40′	9.7861		9.8876		0.1124	9.8985		52° 20′
		1.6		2.6			1.0	
37° 50′	9.7877		9.8902		0.1098	9.8975		52° 10′
		1.6		2.6			1.0	
38° 0′	9.7893		9.8928		0.1072	9.8965		52° 0′
		1.7		2.6			1.0	
38° 10′	9.7910		9.8954		0.1046	9.8955		51° 50′
		1.6		2.6			1.0	
38° 20′	9.7926		9.8980		0.1020	9.8945		51° 40′
		1.5		2.6			1.0	
38° 30′	9.7941		9.9006		0.0994	9.8935		51° 30′
		1.6		2.6			1.0	
38° 40′	9.7957		9.9032		0.0968	9.8925		51° 20′
		1.6		2.6			1.0	
38° 50′	9.7973		9.9058		0.0942	9.8915		51° 10′
		1.6		2.6			1.0	
39° 0′	9.7989		9.9084		0.0916	9.8905		51° 0′
		1.5		2.6			1.0	
39° 10′	9.8004		9.9110		0.0890	9.8895		50° 50′
		1.6		2.5			1.1	
39° 20′	9.8020		9.9135		0.0865	9.8884		50° 40′
		1.5		2.6			1.0	
39° 30′	9.8035		9.9161		0.0839	9.8874		50° 30′
		1.5		2.6			1.0	
39° 40′	9.8050		9.9187		0.0813	9.8864		50° 20′
		1.6		2.5			1.1	
39° 50′	9.8066		9.9212		0.0788	9.8853		50° 10′
		1.5		2.6			1.0	
40° 0′	9.8081		9.9238		0.0762	9.8843		50° 0′
		1.5		2.6			1.1	
40° 10′	9.8096		9.9264		0.0736	9.8832		49° 50′
		1.5		2.5			1.1	
40° 20′	9.8111		9.9289		0.0711	9.8821		49° 40′
		1.4		2.6			1.1	
40° 30′	9.8125		9.9315		0.0685	9.8810		49° 30′
		1.5		2.6			1.0	
40° 40′	9.8140		9.9341		0.0659	9.8800		49° 20′
		1.5		2.5			1.1	
40° 50′	9.8155		9.9366		0.0634	9.8789		49° 10′
		1.4		2.6			1.1	
41° 0′	9.8169		9.9392		0.0608	9.8778		49° 0′
		1.5		2.5			1.1	
41° 10′	9.8184		9.9417		0.0583	9.8767		48° 50′
		1.4		2.6			1.1	
41° 20′	9.8198		9.9443		0.0557	9.8756		48° 40′
		1.5		2.5			1.1	
41° 30′	9.8213		9.9468		0.0532	9.8745		48° 30′
		1.4		2.6			1.2	
41° 40′	9.8227		9.9494		0.0506	9.8733		48° 20′
		1.4		2.5			1.1	
41° 50′	9.8241		9.9519		0.0481	9.8722		48° 10′
		1.4		2.5			1.1	
42° 0′	9.8255		9.9544		0.0456	9.8711		48° 0′
		1.4		2.6			1.2	
42° 10′	9.8269		9.9570		0.0430	9.8699		47° 50′
		1.4		2.5			1.1	
42° 20′	9.8283		9.9595		0.0405	9.8688		47° 40′
		1.4		2.6			1.2	
42° 30′	9.8297		9.9621		0.0379	9.8676		47° 30′
		1.4		2.5			1.1	
42° 40′	9.8311		9.9646		0.0354	9.8665		47° 20′
		1.3		2.5			1.2	
42° 50′	9.8324		9.9671		0.0329	9.8653		47° 10′
		1.4		2.6			1.2	
43° 0′	9.8338		9.9697		0.0303	9.8641		47° 0′
		1.3		2.5			1.2	
43° 10′	9.8351		9.9722		0.0278	9.8629		46° 50′
		1.4		2.5			1.1	
43° 20′	9.8365		9.9747		0.0253	9.8618		46° 40′
		1.3		2.5			1.2	
43° 30′	9.8378		9.9772		0.0228	9.8606		46° 30′
		1.3		2.6			1.2	
43° 40′	9.8391		9.9798		0.0202	9.8594		46° 20′
		1.4		2.5			1.2	
43° 50′	9.8405		9.9823		0.0177	9.8582		46° 10′
		1.3		2.5			1.3	
44° 0′	9.8418		9.9848		0.0152	9.8569		46° 0′
		1.3		2.6			1.2	
44° 10′	9.8431		9.9874		0.0126	9.8557		45° 50′
		1.3		2.5			1.2	
44° 20′	9.8444		9.9899		0.0101	9.8545		45° 40′
		1.3		2.5			1.3	
44° 30′	9.8457		9.9924		0.0076	9.8532		45° 30′
		1.2		2.5			1.2	
44° 40′	9.8469		9.9949		0.0051	9.8520		45° 20′
		1.3		2.6			1.3	
44° 50′	9.8482		9.9975		0.0025	9.8507		45° 10′
		1.3		2.5			1.2	
45° 0′	9.8495		0.0000		0.0000	9.8495		45° 0′
	log cos	diff. 1′	log cot	com. diff. 1′	log tan	log sin	diff. 1′	Angle

45°–55°

To change from Minutes and Seconds into the Decimal Parts of a Degree or into Radians

From seconds	From minutes	From degrees into radians
1″=0.00028°=0.0000048 Rad.	1′=0.017°=0.00029 Rad.	1°=0.01745 Rad.
2″=0.00056°=0.0000097 "	2′=0.033°=0.00058 "	2°=0.03491 "
3″=0.00083°=0.0000145 "	3′=0.050°=0.00087 "	3°=0.05236 "
4″=0.00111°=0.0000194 "	4′=0.067°=0.00116 "	4°=0.06981 "
5″=0.00139°=0.0000242 "	5′=0.083°=0.00145 "	5°=0.08727 "
6″=0.00167°=0.0000291 "	6′=0.100°=0.00175 "	6°=0.10472 "
7″=0.00194°=0.0000339 "	7′=0.117°=0.00204 "	7°=0.12217 "
8″=0.00222°=0.0000388 "	8′=0.133°=0.00233 "	8°=0.13963 "
9″=0.00250°=0.0000436 "	9′=0.150°=0.00262 "	9°=0.15708 "
10″=0.00278°=0.0000485 "	10′=0.167°=0.00291 "	10°=0.17453 "
20″=0.00556°=0.0000970 "	20′=0.333°=0.00582 "	20°=0.34907 "
30″=0.00833°=0.0001454 "	30′=0.500°=0.00873 "	30°=0.52360 "
40″=0.01111°=0.0001939 "	40′=0.667°=0.01164 "	40°=0.69813 "
50″=0.01389°=0.0002424 "	50′=0.833°=0.01454 "	50°=0.87266 "

To change from Decimal Parts of a Degree into Minutes and Seconds

0.0000° = 0.000′ = 0″	0.20° = 12.0′ = 12′	0.60° = 36.0′ = 36′
0.0001° = 0.006′ = 0.36″	0.21° = 12.6′ = 12′ 36″	0.61° = 36.6′ = 36′ 36″
0.0002° = 0.012′ = 0.72″	0.22° = 13.2′ = 13′ 12″	0.62° = 37.2′ = 37′ 12″
0.0003° = 0.018′ = 1.08″	0.23° = 13.8′ = 13′ 48″	0.63° = 37.8′ = 37′ 48″
0.0004° = 0.024′ = 1.44″	0.24° = 14.4′ = 14′ 24″	0.64° = 38.4′ = 38′ 24″
0.0005° = 0.030′ = 1.80″	0.25° = 15.0′ = 15′	0.65° = 39.0′ = 39′
0.0006° = 0.036′ = 2.16″	0.26° = 15.6′ = 15′ 36″	0.66° = 39.6′ = 39′ 36″
0.0007° = 0.042′ = 2.52″	0.27° = 16.2′ = 16′ 12″	0.67° = 40.2′ = 40′ 12″
0.0008° = 0.048′ = 2.88″	0.28° = 16.8′ = 16′ 48″	0.68° = 40.8′ = 40′ 48″
0.0009° = 0.054′ = 3.24″	0.29° = 17.4′ = 17′ 24″	0.69° = 41.4′ = 41′ 24″
0.0010° = 0.060′ = 3.60″	0.30° = 18.0′ = 18′	0.70° = 42.0′ = 42′
0.001° = 0.06′ = 3.6″	0.31° = 18.6′ = 18′ 36″	0.71° = 42.6′ = 42′ 36″
0.002° = 0.12′ = 7.2″	0.32° = 19.2′ = 19′ 12″	0.72° = 43.2′ = 43′ 12″
0.003° = 0.18′ = 10.8″	0.33° = 19.8′ = 19′ 48″	0.73° = 43.8′ = 43′ 48″
0.004° = 0.24′ = 14.4″	0.34° = 20.4′ = 20′ 24″	0.74° = 44.4′ = 44′ 24″
0.005° = 0.30′ = 18.0″	0.35° = 21.0′ = 21′	0.75° = 45.0′ = 45′
0.006° = 0.36′ = 21.6″	0.36° = 21.6′ = 21′ 36″	0.76° = 45.6′ = 45′ 36″
0.007° = 0.42′ = 25.2″	0.37° = 22.2′ = 22′ 12″	0.77° = 46.2′ = 46′ 12″
0.008° = 0.48′ = 28.8″	0.38° = 22.8′ = 22′ 48″	0.78° = 46.8′ = 46′ 48″
0.009° = 0.54′ = 32.4″	0.39° = 23.4′ = 23′ 24″	0.79° = 47.4′ = 47′ 24″
0.010° = 0.60′ = 36.0″	0.40° = 24.0′ = 24′	0.80° = 48.0′ = 48′
0.01° = 0.6′ = 36″	0.41° = 24.6′ = 24′ 36″	0.81° = 48.6′ = 48′ 36″
0.02° = 1.2′ = 1′ 12″	0.42° = 25.2′ = 25′ 12″	0.82° = 49.2′ = 49′ 12″
0.03° = 1.8′ = 1′ 48″	0.43° = 25.8′ = 25′ 48″	0.83° = 49.8′ = 49′ 48″
0.04° = 2.4′ = 2′ 24″	0.44° = 26.4′ = 26′ 24″	0.84° = 50.4′ = 50′ 24″
0.05° = 3.0′ = 3′	0.45° = 27.0′ = 27′	0.85° = 51.0′ = 51′
0.06° = 3.6′ = 3′ 36″	0.46° = 27.6′ = 27′ 36″	0.86° = 51.6′ = 51′ 36″
0.07° = 4.2′ = 4′ 12″	0.47° = 28.2′ = 28′ 12″	0.87° = 52.2′ = 52′ 12″
0.08° = 4.8′ = 4′ 48″	0.48° = 28.8′ = 28′ 48″	0.88° = 52.8′ = 52′ 48″
0.09° = 5.4′ = 5′ 24″	0.49° = 29.4′ = 29′ 24″	0.89° = 53.4′ = 53′ 24″
0.10° = 6.0′ = 6′	0.50° = 30.0′ = 30′	0.90° = 54.0′ = 54′
0.11° = 6.6′ = 6′ 36″	0.51° = 30.6′ = 30′ 36″	0.91° = 54.6′ = 54′ 36″
0.12° = 7.2′ = 7′ 12″	0.52° = 31.2′ = 31′ 12″	0.92° = 55.2′ = 55′ 12″
0.13° = 7.8′ = 7′ 48″	0.53° = 31.8′ = 31′ 48″	0.93° = 55.8′ = 55′ 48″
0.14° = 8.4′ = 8′ 24″	0.54° = 32.4′ = 32′ 24″	0.94° = 56.4′ = 56′ 24″
0.15° = 9.0′ = 9′	0.55° = 33.0′ = 33′	0.95° = 57.0′ = 57′
0.16° = 9.6′ = 9′ 36″	0.56° = 33.6′ = 33′ 36″	0.96° = 57.6′ = 57′ 36″
0.17° = 10.2′ = 10′ 12″	0.57° = 34.2′ = 34′ 12″	0.97° = 58.2′ = 58′ 12″
0.18° = 10.8′ = 10′ 48″	0.58° = 34.8′ = 34′ 48″	0.98° = 58.8′ = 58′ 48″
0.19° = 11.4′ = 11′ 24″	0.59° = 35.4′ = 35′ 24″	0.99° = 59.4′ = 59′ 24″
0.20° = 12.0′ = 12′	0.60° = 36.0′ = 36′	1.00° = 60.0′ = 60′

USE OF TABLE III

The following examples illustrate the use of this table:

EXAMPLE 1. Find log sin 27.4°.

Solution. On page 34, Table III, we find the angle 27.4° exactly. Hence we get at once

$$\log \sin 27.4° = 9.6629 - 10. \ Ans.$$

EXAMPLE 2. Find log cot 3.17°.

Solution. On page 26 we find the angle 3.17° exactly; hence we get immediately from the table

$$\log \cot 3.17° = 1.2566. \ Ans.$$

EXAMPLE 3. Find log tan 61.87°.

Solution. The exact angle is not found in our tables. From page 34,

$$\log \tan 61.8° = 10.2707 - 10$$

and we interpolate for the extra digit 7 of the given angle. The tabular difference between log tan 61.8° and log tan 61.9° is 18. In the Prop. Parts column under 18 and opposite the extra digit 7 we find the proportional part 12.6 (= 13).

Then

$$\log \tan 61.80° = 0.2707$$
$$\underline{\hspace{2cm} 13 \text{ Prop. Part.}}$$
$$\log \tan 61.87° = 0.2720. \ Ans.$$

EXAMPLE 4. Given log tan $x = 9.5364 - 10$; find the angle x.

Solution. We do not find 9.5364 exactly in the table. But we locate it on page 32 between 9.5345 and 9.5370. Except for the last digit the required angle will be the smaller of the two corresponding angles, that is, 18.9°.

Then

$$\log \tan 18.9° = 9.5345 - 10$$
$$\log \tan x = \underline{9.5364 - 10}$$
$$\text{difference} = \quad 19$$

The corresponding tabular difference being 25, we find in the Prop. Parts column that 20 is the proportional part under 25 which is nearest 19. To the left of 20 is the last (extra) digit 8 of the required angle. Hence

$$x = 18.98°. \ Ans.$$

EXAMPLE 5. Given log cos $x = 8.6820 - 10$; find x.

Solution. On page 25 we locate 8.6820 between 8.6810 and 8.6826. Except for the last digit, the required angle must be the smaller of the two corresponding angles, that is, 87.24°. Then

$$\log \cos 87.24° = 8.6826 - 10$$
$$\log \cos x = \underline{8.6820 \hspace{1.2cm}}$$
$$\text{difference} = \quad 6$$

The corresponding tabular difference being 16, we find in the Prop. Parts column that 6.4 is the proportional part under 16 which is nearest 6. To the left of 6.4 is the last (extra) digit of the required angle. Hence

$$x = 87.244°. \ Ans.$$

18

TABLE III

FOUR-PLACE LOGARITHMS OF TRIGONOMETRIC FUNC-TIONS, THE ANGLE BEING EXPRESSED IN DEGREES AND THE DECIMAL PART OF A DEGREE

This table gives the common logarithms (base 10) of the sines, cosines, tangents, and cotangents of all angles from 0° to 5°, and from 85° to 90° for every hundredth part of a degree, and from 5° to 85° for every tenth of a degree, all calculated to four places of decimals. In order to avoid the printing of negative characteristics, the number 10 has been added to every logarithm in the first, second, and fourth columns (those having **log sin**, **log tan**, and **log cos** at the top). Hence in writing down any logarithm taken from these three columns − 10 should be written after it. Logarithms taken from the third column (having **log cot** at the top) should be used as printed.

A logarithm found from this table by interpolation may be in error by one unit in the last decimal place, except for angles between 0° and 0.3° or between 89.7° and 90°, when the error may be larger. In the latter cases the table refers the student to the formulas on page 6 for more accurate results.

0°

Angle	log sin	diff.	log tan	com. diff.	log cot	log cos		Prop. Parts
0.00°	——		——		——	10.0000	**90.00°**	Extra digit
0.01°	6.2419		6.2419		3.7581	10.0000	89.99°	
0.02°	6.5429		6.5429		3.4571	10.0000	89.98°	Difference
0.03°	6.7190		6.7190		3.2810	10.0000	89.97°	
0.04°	6.8439		6.8439		3.1561	10.0000	89.96°	
0.05°	6.9408		6.9408		3.0592	10.0000	89.95°	
0.06°	7.0200		7.0200		2.9800	10.0000	89.94°	

	79	78	77
1	7.9	7.8	7.7
2	15.8	15.6	15.4
3	23.7	23.4	23.1
4	31.6	31.2	30.8
5	39.5	39.0	38.5
6	47.4	46.8	46.2
7	55.3	54.6	53.9
8	63.2	62.4	61.6
9	71.1	70.2	69.3

Angle	log sin	log tan	log cot	log cos	
0.07°	7.0870	7.0870	2.9130	10.0000	89.93°
0.08°	7.1450	7.1450	2.8550	10.0000	89.92°
0.09°	7.1961	7.1961	2.8039	10.0000	89.91°
0.10°	7.2419	7.2419	2.7581	10.0000	**89.90°**
0.11°	7.2833	7.2833	2.7167	10.0000	89.89°
0.12°	7.3211	7.3211	2.6789	10.0000	89.88°
0.13°	7.3558	7.3558	2.6442	10.0000	89.87°

	76	75	74
1	7.6	7.5	7.4
2	15.2	15.0	14.8
3	22.8	22.5	22.2
4	30.4	30.0	29.6
5	38.0	37.5	37.0
6	45.6	45.0	44.4
7	53.2	52.5	51.8
8	60.8	60.0	59.2
9	68.4	67.5	66.6

Angle	log sin	log tan	log cot	log cos	
0.14°	7.3880	7.3880	2.6120	10.0000	89.86°
0.15°	7.4180	7.4180	2.5820	10.0000	89.85°
0.16°	7.4460	7.4460	2.5540	10.0000	89.84°
0.17°	7.4723	7.4723	2.5277	10.0000	89.83°
0.18°	7.4971	7.4972	2.5028	10.0000	89.82°
0.19°	7.5206	7.5206	2.4794	10.0000	89.81°
0.20°	7.5429	7.5429	2.4571	10.0000	**89.80°**
0.21°	7.5641	7.5641	2.4359	10.0000	89.79°
0.22°	7.5843	7.5843	2.4157	10.0000	89.78°
0.23°	7.6036	7.6036	2.3964	10.0000	89.77°

	73	72	71
1	7.3	7.2	7.1
2	14.6	14.4	14.2
3	21.9	21.6	21.3
4	29.2	28.8	28.4
5	36.5	36.0	35.5
6	43.8	43.2	42.6
7	51.1	50.4	49.7
8	58.4	57.6	56.8
9	65.7	64.8	63.9

Angle	log sin	log tan	log cot	log cos	
0.24°	7.6221	7.6221	2.3779	10.0000	89.76°
0.25°	7.6398	7.6398	2.3602	10.0000	89.75°
0.26°	7.6568	7.6569	2.3431	10.0000	89.74°
0.27°	7.6732	7.6732	2.3268	10.0000	89.73°
0.28°	7.6890	7.6890	2.3110	10.0000	89.72°
0.29°	7.7043	7.7043	2.2957	10.0000	89.71°
0.30°	7.7190	7.7190	2.2810	10.0000	**89.70°**

	69	68	67
1	6.9	6.8	6.7
2	13.8	13.6	13.4
3	20.7	20.4	20.1
4	27.6	27.2	26.8
5	34.5	34.0	33.5
6	41.4	40.8	40.2
7	48.3	47.6	46.9
8	55.2	54.4	53.6
9	62.1	61.2	60.3

Angle	log sin	diff.	log tan	com. diff.	log cot	log cos	
0.31°	7.7332	142	7.7332	142	2.2668	10.0000	89.69°
0.32°	7.7470	138	7.7470	138	2.2530	10.0000	89.68°
0.33°	7.7604	134	7.7604	134	2.2396	10.0000	89.67°
0.34°	7.7734	130	7.7734	130	2.2266	10.0000	89.66°
0.35°	7.7859	125	7.7860	126	2.2140	10.0000	89.65°
0.36°	7.7982	123	7.7982	122	2.2018	10.0000	89.64°
		119		119			

	66	65	64
1	6.6	6.5	6.4
2	13.2	13.0	12.8
3	19.8	19.5	19.2
4	26.4	26.0	25.6
5	33.0	32.5	32.0
6	39.6	39.0	38.4
7	46.2	45.5	44.8
8	52.8	52.0	51.2
9	59.4	58.5	57.6

Angle	log sin	diff.	log tan	com. diff.	log cot	log cos	
0.37°	7.8101	116	7.8101	116	2.1899	10.0000	89.63°
0.38°	7.8217	112	7.8217	112	2.1783	10.0000	89.62°
0.39°	7.8329	110	7.8329	110	2.1671	10.0000	89.61°
0.40°	7.8439	108	7.8439	108	2.1561	10.0000	**89.60°**
0.41°	7.8547	104	7.8547	104	2.1453	10.0000	89.59°
0.42°	7.8651	102	7.8651	103	2.1349	10.0000	89.58°
0.43°	7.8753	100	7.8754	99	2.1246	10.0000	89.57°

	63	62	61
1	6.3	6.2	6.1
2	12.6	12.4	12.2
3	18.9	18.6	18.3
4	25.2	24.8	24.4
5	31.5	31.0	30.5
6	37.8	37.2	36.6
7	44.1	43.4	42.7
8	50.4	49.6	48.8
9	56.7	55.8	54.9

Angle	log sin	diff.	log tan	com. diff.	log cot	log cos	
0.44°	7.8853	98	7.8853	98	2.1147	10.0000	89.56°
0.45°	7.8951	95	7.8951	95	2.1049	10.0000	89.55°
0.46°	7.9046	94	7.9046	94	2.0954	10.0000	89.54°
0.47°	7.9140	91	7.9140	91	2.0860	10.0000	89.53°
0.48°	7.9231	90	7.9231	90	2.0769	10.0000	89.52°
0.49°	7.9321	87	7.9321	88	2.0678	10.0000	89.51°
0.50°	7.9408		7.9409		2.0591	10.0000	**89.50°**

Note in first three columns (over diff./log tan/com. diff. area): *Ordinary interpolation here will in general give inaccurate results. Instead use formulas on p. 6.*

	log cos	diff.	log cot	com. diff.	log tan	log sin	Angle	

89°

0°

Angle	log sin	diff.	log tan	com. diff.	log cot	log cos	
0.50°	7.9408		7.9409		2.0591	10.0000	**89.50°**
		86		86			
0.51°	7.9494		7.9495		2.0505	10.0000	89.49°
		85		84			
0.52°	7.9579		7.9579		2.0421	10.0000	89.48°
		82		83			
0.53°	7.9661		7.9662		2.0338	10.0000	89.47°
		82		81			
0.54°	7.9743		7.9743		2.0257	10.0000	89.46°
		79		80			
0.55°	7.9822		7.9823		2.0177	10.0000	89.45°
		79		78			
0.56°	7.9901		7.9901		2.0099	10.0000	89.44°
		76		77			
0.57°	7.9977		7.9978		2.0022	10.0000	89.43°
		76		75			
0.58°	8.0053		8.0053		1.9947	10.0000	89.42°
		74		74			
0.59°	8.0127		8.0127		1.9873	10.0000	89.41°
		73		73			
0.60°	8.0200		8.0200		1.9800	10.0000	**89.40°**
		72		72			
0.61°	8.0272		8.0272		1.9728	10.0000	89.39°
		71		71			
0.62°	8.0343		8.0343		1.9657	10.0000	89.38°
		69		69			
0.63°	8.0412		8.0412		1.9588	10.0000	89.37°
		68		69			
0.64°	8.0480		8.0481		1.9519	10.0000	89.36°
		68		67			
0.65°	8.0548		8.0548		1.9452	10.0000	89.35°
		66		66			
0.66°	8.0614		8.0614		1.9386	10.0000	89.34°
		65		66			
0.67°	8.0679		8.0680		1.9320	10.0000	89.33°
		65		64			
0.68°	8.0744		8.0744		1.9256	10.0000	89.32°
		63		63			
0.69°	8.0807		8.0807		1.9193	10.0000	89.31°
		63		63			
0.70°	8.0870		8.0870		1.9130	10.0000	**89.30°**
		61		62			
0.71°	8.0931		8.0932		1.9068	10.0000	89.29°
		61		60			
0.72°	8.0992		8.0992		1.9008	10.0000	89.28°
		60		60			
0.73°	8.1052		8.1052		1.8948	10.0000	89.27°
		59		59			
0.74°	8.1111		8.1111		1.8889	10.0000	89.26°
		58		59			
0.75°	8.1169		8.1170		1.8830	10.0000	89.25°
		58		57			
0.76°	8.1227		8.1227		1.8773	10.0000	89.24°
		57		57			
0.77°	8.1284		8.1284		1.8716	10.0000	89.23°
		56		56			
0.78°	8.1340		8.1340		1.8660	10.0000	89.22°
		55		55			
0.79°	8.1395		8.1395		1.8605	10.0000	89.21°
		55		55			
0.80°	8.1450		8.1450		1.8550	10.0000	**89.20°**
		53		54			
0.81°	8.1503		8.1504		1.8496	10.0000	89.19°
		54		53			
0.82°	8.1557		8.1557		1.8443	10.0000	89.18°
		52		53			
0.83°	8.1609		8.1610		1.8390	10.0000	89.17°
		52		52			
0.84°	8.1661		8.1662		1.8338	10.0000	89.16°
		52		51			
0.85°	8.1713		8.1713		1.8287	10.0000	89.15°
		51		51			
0.86°	8.1764		8.1764		1.8236	10.0000	89.14°
		50		50			
0.87°	8.1814		8.1814		1.8186	9.9999	89.13°
		49		50			
0.88°	8.1863		8.1864		1.8136	9.9999	89.12°
		49		49			
0.89°	8.1912		8.1913		1.8087	9.9999	89.11°
		49		49			
0.90°	8.1961		8.1962		1.8038	9.9999	**89.10°**
		48		48			
0.91°	8.2009		8.2010		1.7990	9.9999	89.09°
		47		47			
0.92°	8.2056		8.2057		1.7943	9.9999	89.08°
		47		47			
0.93°	8.2103		8.2104		1.7896	9.9999	89.07°
		47		46			
0.94°	8.2150		8.2150		1.7850	9.9999	89.06°
		46		46			
0.95°	8.2196		8.2196		1.7804	9.9999	89.05°
		45		46			
0.96°	8.2241		8.2242		1.7758	9.9999	89.04°
		45		45			
0.97°	8.2286		8.2287		1.7713	9.9999	89.03°
		45		44			
0.98°	8.2331		8.2331		1.7669	9.9999	89.02°
		44		45			
0.99°	8.2375		8.2376		1.7624	9.9999	89.01°
		44		43			
1.00°	8.2419		8.2419		1.7581	9.9999	**89.00°**
	log cos	diff.	log cot	com. diff.	log tan	log sin	Angle

Prop. Parts

Extra digit — Difference

	60	59	58
1	6.0	5.9	5.8
2	12.0	11.8	11.6
3	18.0	17.7	17.4
4	24.0	23.6	23.2
5	30.0	29.5	29.0
6	36.0	35.4	34.8
7	42.0	41.3	40.6
8	48.0	47.2	46.4
9	54.0	53.1	52.2

	57	56	55
1	5.7	5.6	5.5
2	11.4	11.2	11.0
3	17.1	16.8	16.5
4	22.8	22.4	22.0
5	28.5	28.0	27.5
6	34.2	33.6	33.0
7	39.9	39.2	38.5
8	45.6	44.8	44.0
9	51.3	50.4	49.5

	54	53	52
1	5.4	5.3	5.2
2	10.8	10.6	10.4
3	16.2	15.9	15.6
4	21.6	21.2	20.8
5	27.0	26.5	26.0
6	32.4	31.8	31.2
7	37.8	37.1	36.4
8	43.2	42.4	41.6
9	48.6	47.7	46.8

	51	50	49
1	5.1	5.0	4.9
2	10.2	10.0	9.8
3	15.3	15.0	14.7
4	20.4	20.0	19.6
5	25.5	25.0	24.5
6	30.6	30.0	29.4
7	35.7	35.0	34.3
8	40.8	40.0	39.2
9	45.9	45.0	44.1

	48	47	46
1	4.8	4.7	4.6
2	9.6	9.4	9.2
3	14.4	14.1	13.8
4	19.2	18.8	18.4
5	24.0	23.5	23.0
6	28.8	28.2	27.6
7	33.6	32.9	32.2
8	38.4	37.6	36.8
9	43.2	42.3	41.4

	45	44	43
1	4.5	4.4	4.3
2	9.0	8.8	8.6
3	13.5	13.2	12.9
4	18.0	17.6	17.2
5	22.5	22.0	21.5
6	27.0	26.4	25.8
7	31.5	30.8	30.1
8	36.0	35.2	34.4
9	40.5	39.6	38.7

89°

1°

Angle	log sin	diff.	log tan	com. diff.	log cot	log cos	
1.00°	8.2419	43	8.2419	43	1.7581	9.9999	**89.00°**
1.01°	8.2462	43	8.2462	43	1.7538	9.9999	88.99°
1.02°	8.2505	42	8.2505	43	1.7495	9.9999	88.98°
1.03°	8.2547	42	8.2548	42	1.7452	9.9999	88.97°
1.04°	8.2589	41	8.2590	41	1.7410	9.9999	88.96°
1.05°	8.2630	42	8.2631	41	1.7369	9.9999	88.95°
1.06°	8.2672	40	8.2672	41	1.7328	9.9999	88.94°
1.07°	8.2712	41	8.2713	41	1.7287	9.9999	88.93°
1.08°	8.2753	40	8.2754	40	1.7246	9.9999	88.92°
1.09°	8.2793	39	8.2794	40	1.7206	9.9999	88.91°
1.10°	8.2832	40	8.2833	40	1.7167	9.9999	**88.90°**
1.11°	8.2872	39	8.2873	39	1.7127	9.9999	88.89°
1.12°	8.2911	38	8.2912	38	1.7088	9.9999	88.88°
1.13°	8.2949	39	8.2950	38	1.7050	9.9999	88.87°
1.14°	8.2988	37	8.2988	38	1.7012	9.9999	88.86°
1.15°	8.3025	38	8.3026	38	1.6974	9.9999	88.85°
1.16°	8.3063	37	8.3064	37	1.6936	9.9999	88.84°
1.17°	8.3100	37	8.3101	37	1.6899	9.9999	88.83°
1.18°	8.3137	37	8.3138	37	1.6862	9.9999	88.82°
1.19°	8.3174	36	8.3175	36	1.6825	9.9999	88.81°
1.20°	8.3210	36	8.3211	36	1.6789	9.9999	**88.80°**
1.21°	8.3246	36	8.3247	36	1.6753	9.9999	88.79°
1.22°	8.3282	35	8.3283	35	1.6717	9.9999	88.78°
1.23°	8.3317	36	8.3318	36	1.6682	9.9999	88.77°
1.24°	8.3353	35	8.3354	35	1.6646	9.9999	88.76°
1.25°	8.3388	34	8.3389	34	1.6611	9.9999	88.75°
1.26°	8.3422	34	8.3423	35	1.6577	9.9999	88.74°
1.27°	8.3456	35	8.3458	34	1.6542	9.9999	88.73°
1.28°	8.3491	33	8.3492	33	1.6508	9.9999	88.72°
1.29°	8.3524	34	8.3525	34	1.6475	9.9999	88.71°
1.30°	8.3558	33	8.3559	33	1.6441	9.9999	**88.70°**
1.31°	8.3591	33	8.3592	33	1.6408	9.9999	88.69°
1.32°	8.3624	33	8.3625	33	1.6375	9.9999	88.68°
1.33°	8.3657	32	8.3658	33	1.6342	9.9999	88.67°
1.34°	8.3689	33	8.3691	32	1.6309	9.9999	88.66°
1.35°	8.3722	32	8.3723	32	1.6277	9.9999	88.65°
1.36°	8.3754	32	8.3755	32	1.6245	9.9999	88.64°
1.37°	8.3786	31	8.3787	31	1.6213	9.9999	88.63°
1.38°	8.3817	31	8.3818	32	1.6182	9.9999	88.62°
1.39°	8.3848	32	8.3850	31	1.6150	9.9999	88.61°
1.40°	8.3880	31	8.3881	31	1.6119	9.9999	**88.60°**
1.41°	8.3911	30	8.3912	31	1.6088	9.9999	88.59°
1.42°	8.3941	31	8.3943	30	1.6057	9.9999	88.58°
1.43°	8.3972	30	8.3973	30	1.6027	9.9999	88.57°
1.44°	8.4002	30	8.4003	30	1.5997	9.9999	88.56°
1.45°	8.4032	30	8.4033	30	1.5967	9.9999	88.55°
1.46°	8.4062	29	8.4063	30	1.5937	9.9999	88.54°
1.47°	8.4091	30	8.4093	29	1.5907	9.9999	88.53°
1.48°	8.4121	29	8.4122	30	1.5878	9.9999	88.52°
1.49°	8.4150	29	8.4152	30	1.5848	9.9999	88.51°
1.50°	8.4179		8.4181		1.5819	9.9999	**88.50°**
	log cos	diff.	log cot	com. diff.	log tan	log sin	Angle

88°

Prop. Parts

Extra digit

Difference

	43	42
1	4.3	4.2
2	8.6	8.4
3	12.9	12.6
4	17.2	16.8
5	21.5	21.0
6	25.8	25.2
7	30.1	29.4
8	34.4	33.6
9	38.7	37.8

	41	40
1	4.1	4.0
2	8.2	8.0
3	12.3	12.0
4	16.4	16.0
5	20.5	20.0
6	24.6	24.0
7	28.7	28.0
8	32.8	32.0
9	36.9	36.0

	39	38
1	3.9	3.8
2	7.8	7.6
3	11.7	11.4
4	15.6	15.2
5	19.5	19.0
6	23.4	22.8
7	27.3	26.6
8	31.2	30.4
9	35.1	34.2

	37	36	35
1	3.7	3.6	3.5
2	7.4	7.2	7.0
3	11.1	10.8	10.5
4	14.8	14.4	14.0
5	18.5	18.0	17.5
6	22.2	21.6	21.0
7	25.9	25.2	24.5
8	29.6	28.8	28.0
9	33.3	32.4	31.5

	34	33	32
1	3.4	3.3	3.2
2	6.8	6.6	6.4
3	10.2	9.9	9.6
4	13.6	13.2	12.8
5	17.0	16.5	16.0
6	20.4	19.8	19.2
7	23.8	23.1	22.4
8	27.2	26.4	25.6
9	30.6	29.7	28.8

	31	30	29
1	3.1	3.0	2.9
2	6.2	6.0	5.8
3	9.3	9.0	8.7
4	12.4	12.0	11.6
5	15.5	15.0	14.5
6	18.6	18.0	17.4
7	21.7	21.0	20.3
8	24.8	24.0	23.2
9	27.9	27.0	26.1

1°

Angle	log sin	diff.	log tan	com. diff.	log cot	log cos	
1.50°	8.4179		8.4181		1.5819	9.9999	**88.50°**
1.51°	8.4208	29	8.4210	29	1.5790	9.9998	88.49°
1.52°	8.4237	29	8.4238	28	1.5762	9.9998	88.48°
1.53°	8.4265	28	8.4267	29	1.5733	9.9998	88.47°
		28		28			
1.54°	8.4293		8.4295		1.5705	9.9998	88.46°
1.55°	8.4322	29	8.4323	28	1.5677	9.9998	88.45°
1.56°	8.4349	27	8.4351	28	1.5649	9.9998	88.44°
		28		28			
1.57°	8.4377		8.4379		1.5621	9.9998	88.43°
1.58°	8.4405	28	8.4406	27	1.5594	9.9998	88.42°
1.59°	8.4432	27	8.4434	28	1.5566	9.9998	88.41°
1.60°	8.4459	27	8.4461	27	1.5539	9.9998	**88.40°**
1.61°	8.4486	27	8.4488	27	1.5512	9.9998	88.39°
1.62°	8.4513	27	8.4515	27	1.5485	9.9998	88.38°
1.63°	8.4540	27	8.4542	27	1.5458	9.9998	88.37°
		27		26			
1.64°	8.4567		8.4568		1.5432	9.9998	88.36°
1.65°	8.4593	26	8.4595	27	1.5405	9.9998	88.35°
1.66°	8.4619	26	8.4621	26	1.5379	9.9998	88.34°
		26		26			
1.67°	8.4645		8.4647		1.5353	9.9998	88.33°
1.68°	8.4671	26	8.4673	26	1.5327	9.9998	88.32°
1.69°	8.4697	26	8.4699	26	1.5301	9.9998	88.31°
1.70°	8.4723	26	8.4725	26	1.5275	9.9998	**88.30°**
1.71°	8.4748	25	8.4750	25	1.5250	9.9998	88.29°
1.72°	8.4773	25	8.4775	25	1.5225	9.9998	88.28°
1.73°	8.4799	26	8.4801	26	1.5199	9.9998	88.27°
		25		25			
1.74°	8.4824		8.4826		1.5174	9.9998	88.26°
1.75°	8.4848	24	8.4851	25	1.5149	9.9998	88.25°
1.76°	8.4873	25	8.4875	24	1.5125	9.9998	88.24°
		25		25			
1.77°	8.4898		8.4900		1.5100	9.9998	88.23°
1.78°	8.4922	24	8.4924	24	1.5076	9.9998	88.22°
1.79°	8.4947	25	8.4949	25	1.5051	9.9998	88.21°
1.80°	8.4971	24	8.4973	24	1.5027	9.9998	**88.20°**
1.81°	8.4995	24	8.4997	24	1.5003	9.9998	88.19°
1.82°	8.5019	24	8.5021	24	1.4979	9.9998	88.18°
1.83°	8.5043	24	8.5045	24	1.4955	9.9998	88.17°
		23		23			
1.84°	8.5066		8.5068		1.4932	9.9998	88.16°
1.85°	8.5090	24	8.5092	24	1.4908	9.9998	88.15°
1.86°	8.5113	23	8.5115	23	1.4885	9.9998	88.14°
		23		24			
1.87°	8.5136		8.5139		1.4861	9.9999	88.13°
1.88°	8.5160	24	8.5162	23	1.4838	9.9998	88.12°
1.89°	8.5183	23	8.5185	23	1.4815	9.9998	88.11°
1.90°	8.5206	23	8.5208	23	1.4792	9.9998	**88.10°**
1.91°	8.5228	22	8.5231	23	1.4769	9.9998	88.09°
1.92°	8.5251	23	8.5253	22	1.4747	9.9998	88.08°
1.93°	8.5274	23	8.5276	23	1.4724	9.9998	88.07°
		22		22			
1.94°	8.5296		8.5298		1.4702	9.9998	88.06°
1.95°	8.5318	22	8.5321	23	1.4679	9.9997	88.05°
1.96°	8.5340	22	8.5343	22	1.4657	9.9997	88.04°
		23		22			
1.97°	8.5363		8.5365		1.4635	9.9997	88.03°
1.98°	8.5385	22	8.5387	22	1.4613	9.9997	88.02°
1.99°	8.5406	21	8.5409	22	1.4591	9.9997	88.01°
2.00°	8.5428	22	8.5431	22	1.4569	9.9997	**88.00°**
	log cos	diff.	log cot	com. diff.	log tan	log sin	Angle

Prop. Parts

Extra digit

Difference

	29	28
1	2.9	2.8
2	5.8	5.6
3	8.7	8.4
4	11.6	11.2
5	14.5	14.0
6	17.4	16.8
7	20.3	19.6
8	23.2	22.4
9	26.1	25.2

	27	26
1	2.7	2.6
2	5.4	5.2
3	8.1	7.8
4	10.8	10.4
5	13.5	13.0
6	16.2	15.6
7	18.9	18.2
8	21.6	20.8
9	24.3	23.4

	25	24
1	2.5	2.4
2	5.0	4.8
3	7.5	7.2
4	10.0	9.6
5	12.5	12.0
6	15.0	14.4
7	17.5	16.8
8	20.0	19.2
9	22.5	21.6

	23	22
1	2.3	2.2
2	4.6	4.4
3	6.9	6.6
4	9.2	8.8
5	11.5	11.0
6	13.8	13.2
7	16.1	15.4
8	18.4	17.6
9	20.7	19.8

	21	
1	2.1	
2	4.2	
3	6.3	
4	8.4	
5	10.5	
6	12.6	
7	14.7	
8	16.8	
9	18.9	

88°

2°

Angle	log sin	diff.	log tan	com. diff.	log cot	log cos	
2.00°	8.5428		8.5431		1.4569	9.9997	**88.00°**
		22		22			
2.01°	8.5450		8.5453		1.4547	9.9997	87.99°
		21		21			
2.02°	8.5471		8.5474		1.4526	9.9997	87.98°
		22		22			
2.03°	8.5493		8.5496		1.4504	9.9997	87.97°
		21		21			
2.04°	8.5514		8.5517		1.4483	9.9997	87.96°
		21		21			
2.05°	8.5535		8.5538		1.4462	9.9997	87.95°
		22		21			
2.06°	8.5557		8.5559		1.4441	9.9997	87.94°
		21		21			
2.07°	8.5578		8.5580		1.4420	9.9997	87.93°
		20		21			
2.08°	8.5598		8.5601		1.4399	9.9997	87.92°
		21		21			
2.09°	8.5619		8.5622		1.4378	9.9997	87.91°
		21		21			
2.10°	8.5640		8.5643		1.4357	9.9997	**87.90°**
		21		21			
2.11°	8.5661		8.5664		1.4336	9.9997	87.89°
		20		20			
2.12°	8.5681		8.5684		1.4316	9.9997	87.88°
		21		21			
2.13°	8.5702		8.5705		1.4295	9.9997	87.87°
		20		20			
2.14°	8.5722		8.5725		1.4275	9.9997	87.86°
		20		20			
2.15°	8.5742		8.5745		1.4255	9.9997	87.85°
		20		20			
2.16°	8.5762		8.5765		1.4235	9.9997	87.84°
		20		20			
2.17°	8.5782		8.5785		1.4215	9.9997	87.83°
		20		20			
2.18°	8.5802		8.5805		1.4195	9.9997	87.82°
		20		20			
2.19°	8.5822		8.5825		1.4175	9.9997	87.81°
		20		20			
2.20°	8.5842		8.5845		1.4155	9.9997	**87.80°**
		20		20			
2.21°	8.5862		8.5865		1.4135	9.9997	87.79°
		19		19			
2.22°	8.5881		8.5884		1.4116	9.9997	87.78°
		20		20			
2.23°	8.5901		8.5904		1.4096	9.9997	87.77°
		19		19			
2.24°	8.5920		8.5923		1.4077	9.9997	87.76°
		19		20			
2.25°	8.5939		8.5943		1.4057	9.9997	87.75°
		20		19			
2.26°	8.5959		8.5962		1.4038	9.9997	87.74°
		19		19			
2.27°	8.5978		8.5981		1.4019	9.9997	87.73°
		19		19			
2.28°	8.5997		8.6000		1.4000	9.9997	87.72°
		19		19			
2.29°	8.6016		8.6019		1.3981	9.9997	87.71°
		19		19			
2.30°	8.6035		8.6038		1.3962	9.9996	**87.70°**
		19		19			
2.31°	8.6054		8.6057		1.3943	9.9996	87.69°
		18		19			
2.32°	8.6072		8.6076		1.3924	9.9996	87.68°
		19		19			
2.33°	8.6091		8.6095		1.3905	9.9996	87.67°
		19		18			
2.34°	8.6110		8.6113		1.3887	9.9996	87.66°
		18		19			
2.35°	8.6128		8.6132		1.3868	9.9996	87.65°
		19		18			
2.36°	8.6147		8.6150		1.3850	9.9996	87.64°
		18		19			
2.37°	8.6165		8.6169		1.3831	9.9996	87.63°
		18		18			
2.38°	8.6183		8.6187		1.3813	9.9996	87.62°
		18		18			
2.39°	8.6201		8.6205		1.3795	9.9996	87.61°
		19		18			
2.40°	8.6220		8.6223		1.3777	9.9996	**87.60°**
		18		19			
2.41°	8.6238		8.6242		1.3758	9.9996	87.59°
		18		18			
2.42°	8.6256		8.6260		1.3740	9.9996	87.58°
		18		17			
2.43°	8.6274		8.6277		1.3723	9.9996	87.57°
		17		18			
2.44°	8.6291		8.6295		1.3705	9.9996	87.56°
		18		18			
2.45°	8.6309		8.6313		1.3687	9.9996	87.55°
		18		18			
2.46°	8.6327		8.6331		1.3669	9.9996	87.54°
		17		17			
2.47°	8.6344		8.6348		1.3652	9.9996	87.53°
		18		18			
2.48°	8.6362		8.6366		1.3634	9.9996	87.52°
		17		18			
2.49°	8.6379		8.6384		1.3616	9.9996	87.51°
		18		17			
2.50°	8.6397		8.6401		1.3599	9.9996	**87.50°**
	log cos	diff.	log cot	com. diff.	log tan	log sin	Angle

Prop. Parts

Extra digit — Difference

	22		**21**		**20**		**19**		**18**		**17**
1	2.2	1	2.1	1	2.0	1	1.9	1	1.8	1	1.7
2	4.4	2	4.2	2	4.0	2	3.8	2	3.6	2	3.4
3	6.6	3	6.3	3	6.0	3	5.7	3	5.4	3	5.1
4	8.8	4	8.4	4	8.0	4	7.6	4	7.2	4	6.8
5	11.0	5	10.5	5	10.0	5	9.5	5	9.0	5	8.5
6	13.2	6	12.6	6	12.0	6	11.4	6	10.8	6	10.2
7	15.4	7	14.7	7	14.0	7	13.3	7	12.6	7	11.9
8	17.6	8	16.8	8	16.0	8	15.2	8	14.4	8	13.6
9	19.8	9	18.9	9	18.0	9	17.1	9	16.2	9	15.3

87°

2°

Angle	log sin	diff.	log tan	com. diff.	log cot	log cos		Prop. Parts	
2.50°	8.6397		8.6401		1.3599	9.9996	**87.50°**		
2.51°	8.6414	17	8.6418	17	1.3582	9.9996	87.49°		
2.52°	8.6431	17	8.6436	18	1.3564	9.9996	87.48°		
2.53°	8.6449	18	8.6453	17	1.3547	9.9996	87.47°		
2.54°	8.6466	17	8.6470	17	1.3530	9.9996	87.46°		
2.55°	8.6483	17	8.6487	17	1.3513	9.9996	87.45°		
2.56°	8.6500	17	8.6504	17	1.3496	9.9996	87.44°		**18**
2.57°	8.6517	17	8.6521	17	1.3479	9.9996	87.43°	1	1.8
2.58°	8.6534	17	8.6538	17	1.3462	9.9996	87.42°	2	3.6
2.59°	8.6550	16	8.6555	17	1.3445	9.9996	87.41°	3	5.4
2.60°	8.6567	17	8.6571	16	1.3429	9.9996	**87.40°**	4	7.2
2.61°	8.6584	17	8.6588	17	1.3412	9.9995	87.39°	5	9.0
2.62°	8.6600	16	8.6605	17	1.3395	9.9995	87.38°	6	10.8
2.63°	8.6617	17	8.6621	16	1.3379	9.9995	87.37°	7	12.6
2.64°	8.6633	16	8.6638	17	1.3362	9.9995	87.36°	8	14.4
2.65°	8.6650	17	8.6654	16	1.3346	9.9995	87.35°	9	16.2
2.66°	8.6666	16	8.6671	17	1.3329	9.9995	87.34°		
2.67°	8.6682	16	8.6687	16	1.3313	9.9995	87.33°		**17**
2.68°	8.6699	17	8.6703	16	1.3297	9.9995	87.32°	1	1.7
2.69°	8.6715	16	8.6719	16	1.3281	9.9995	87.31°	2	3.4
2.70°	8.6731	16	8.6736	17	1.3264	9.9995	**87.30°**	3	5.1
2.71°	8.6747	16	8.6752	16	1.3248	9.9995	87.29°	4	6.8
2.72°	8.6763	16	8.6768	16	1.3232	9.9995	87.28°	5	8.5
2.73°	8.6779	16	8.6784	16	1.3216	9.9995	87.27°	6	10.2
2.74°	8.6795	16	8.6800	16	1.3200	9.9995	87.26°	7	11.9
2.75°	8.6810	15	8.6815	15	1.3185	9.9995	87.25°	8	13.6
2.76°	8.6826	16	8.6831	16	1.3169	9.9995	87.24°	9	15.3
2.77°	8.6842	16	8.6847	16	1.3153	9.9995	87.23°		**16**
2.78°	8.6858	16	8.6863	16	1.3137	9.9995	87.22°	1	1.6
2.79°	8.6873	15	8.6878	15	1.3122	9.9995	87.21°	2	3.2
2.80°	8.6889	16	8.6894	16	1.3106	9.9995	**87.20°**	3	4.8
2.81°	8.6904	15	8.6909	15	1.3091	9.9995	87.19°	4	6.4
2.82°	8.6920	16	8.6925	16	1.3075	9.9995	87.18°	5	8.0
2.83°	8.6935	15	8.6940	15	1.3060	9.9995	87.17°	6	9.6
2.84°	8.6950	15	8.6956	16	1.3044	9.9995	87.16°	7	11.2
2.85°	8.6965	15	8.6971	15	1.3029	9.9995	87.15°	8	12.8
2.86°	8.6981	16	8.6986	15	1.3014	9.9995	87.14°	9	14.4
2.87°	8.6996	15	8.7001	15	1.2999	9.9995	87.13°		
2.88°	8.7011	15	8.7016	15	1.2984	9.9995	87.12°		**15**
2.89°	8.7026	15	8.7031	15	1.2969	9.9994	87.11°	1	1.5
2.90°	8.7041	15	8.7046	15	1.2954	9.9994	**87.10°**	2	3.0
2.91°	8.7056	15	8.7061	15	1.2939	9.9994	87.09°	3	4.5
2.92°	8.7071	15	8.7076	15	1.2924	9.9994	87.08°	4	6.0
2.93°	8.7086	14	8.7091	15	1.2909	9.9994	87.07°	5	7.5
2.94°	8.7100	15	8.7106	15	1.2894	9.9994	87.06°	6	9.0
2.95°	8.7115	15	8.7121	15	1.2879	9.9994	87.05°	7	10.5
2.96°	8.7130	14	8.7136	14	1.2864	9.9994	87.04°	8	12.0
2.97°	8.7144	15	8.7150	15	1.2850	9.9994	87.03°	9	13.5
2.98°	8.7159	15	8.7165	14	1.2835	9.9994	87.02°		
2.99°	8.7174	14	8.7179	15	1.2821	9.9994	87.01°		**14**
3.00°	8.7188		8.7194		1.2806	9.9994	**87.00°**	1	1.4
								2	2.8
								3	4.2
								4	5.6
								5	7.0
								6	8.4
								7	9.8
								8	11.2
								9	12.6
	log cos	diff.	log cot	com. diff.	log tan	log sin	Angle		

87°

3°

Angle	log sin	diff.	log tan	com. diff.	log cot	log cos	
3.00°	8.7188		8.7194		1.2806	9.9994	**87.00°**
		14		14			
3.01°	8.7202		8.7208		1.2792	9.9994	86.99°
		15		15			
3.02°	8.7217		8.7223		1.2777	9.9994	86.98°
		14		14			
3.03°	8.7231		8.7237		1.2763	9.9994	86.97°
		14		15			
3.04°	8.7245		8.7252		1.2748	9.9994	86.96°
		15		14			
3.05°	8.7260		8.7266		1.2734	9.9994	86.95°
		14		14			
3.06°	8.7274		8.7280		1.2720	9.9994	86.94°
		14		14			
3.07°	8.7288		8.7294		1.2706	9.9994	86.93°
		14		14			
3.08°	8.7302		8.7308		1.2692	9.9994	86.92°
		14		15			
3.09°	8.7316		8.7323		1.2677	9.9994	86.91°
		14		14			
3.10°	8.7330		8.7337		1.2663	9.9994	**86.90°**
		14		14			
3.11°	8.7344		8.7351		1.2649	9.9994	86.89°
		14		14			
3.12°	8.7358		8.7365		1.2635	9.9994	86.88°
		14		14			
3.13°	8.7372		8.7379		1.2621	9.9994	86.87°
		14		13			
3.14°	8.7386		8.7392		1.2608	9.9993	86.86°
		14		14			
3.15°	8.7400		8.7406		1.2594	9.9993	86.85°
		13		14			
3.16°	8.7413		8.7420		1.2580	9.9993	86.84°
		14		14			
3.17°	8.7427		8.7434		1.2566	9.9993	86.83°
		14		14			
3.18°	8.7441		8.7448		1.2552	9.9993	86.82°
		13		13			
3.19°	8.7454		8.7461		1.2539	9.9993	86.81°
		14		14			
3.20°	8.7468		8.7475		1.2525	9.9993	**86.80°**
		14		13			
3.21°	8.7482		8.7488		1.2512	9.9993	86.79°
		13		14			
3.22°	8.7495		8.7502		1.2498	9.9993	86.78°
		13		13			
3.23°	8.7508		8.7515		1.2485	9.9993	86.77°
		14		14			
3.24°	8.7522		8.7529		1.2471	9.9993	86.76°
		13		13			
3.25°	8.7535		8.7542		1.2458	9.9993	86.75°
		14		14			
3.26°	8.7549		8.7556		1.2444	9.9993	86.74°
		13		13			
3.27°	8.7562		8.7569		1.2431	9.9993	86.73°
		13		13			
3.28°	8.7575		8.7582		1.2418	9.9993	86.72°
		13		14			
3.29°	8.7588		8.7596		1.2404	9.9993	86.71°
		14		13			
3.30°	8.7602		8.7609		1.2391	9.9993	**86.70°**
		13		13			
3.31°	8.7615		8.7622		1.2378	9.9993	86.69°
		13		13			
3.32°	8.7628		8.7635		1.2365	9.9993	86.68°
		13		13			
3.33°	8.7641		8.7648		1.2352	9.9993	86.67°
		13		13			
3.34°	8.7654		8.7661		1.2339	9.9993	86.66°
		13		13			
3.35°	8.7667		8.7674		1.2326	9.9993	86.65°
		13		13			
3.36°	8.7680		8.7687		1.2313	9.9993	86.64°
		13		13			
3.37°	8.7693		8.7700		1.2300	9.9992	86.63°
		12		13			
3.38°	8.7705		8.7713		1.2287	9.9992	86.62°
		13		13			
3.39°	8.7718		8.7726		1.2274	9.9992	86.61°
		13		13			
3.40°	8.7731		8.7739		1.2261	9.9992	**86.60°**
		13		12			
3.41°	8.7744		8.7751		1.2249	9.9992	86.59°
		12		13			
3.42°	8.7756		8.7764		1.2236	9.9992	86.58°
		13		13			
3.43°	8.7769		8.7777		1.2223	9.9992	86.57°
		13		13			
3.44°	8.7782		8.7790		1.2210	9.9992	86.56°
		12		12			
3.45°	8.7794		8.7802		1.2198	9.9992	86.55°
		13		13			
3.46°	8.7807		8.7815		1.2185	9.9992	86.54°
		12		12			
3.47°	8.7819		8.7827		1.2173	9.9992	86.53°
		13		13			
3.48°	8.7832		8.7840		1.2160	9.9992	86.52°
		12		12			
3.49°	8.7844		8.7852		1.2148	9.9992	86.51°
		13		13			
3.50°	8.7857		8.7865		1.2135	9.9992	**86.50°**
	log cos	diff.	log cot	com. diff.	log tan	log sin	Angle

Prop. Parts (Extra digit / Difference)

15		14		13		12	
1	1.5	1	1.4	1	1.3	1	1.2
2	3.0	2	2.8	2	2.6	2	2.4
3	4.5	3	4.2	3	3.9	3	3.6
4	6.0	4	5.6	4	5.2	4	4.8
5	7.5	5	7.0	5	6.5	5	6.0
6	9.0	6	8.4	6	7.8	6	7.2
7	10.5	7	9.8	7	9.1	7	8.4
8	12.0	8	11.2	8	10.4	8	9.6
9	13.5	9	12.6	9	11.7	9	10.8

86°

3°

Angle	log sin	diff.	log tan	com. diff.	log cot	log cos		Prop. Parts	
3.50°	8.7857		8.7865		1.2135	9.9992	**86.50°**	Extra digit	Difference
3.51°	8.7869	12	8.7877	12	1.2123	9.9992	86.49°		
3.52°	8.7881	12	8.7890	13	1.2110	9.9992	86.48°		
3.53°	8.7894	13	8.7902	12	1.2098	9.9992	86.47°		
3.54°	8.7906	12	8.7914	12	1.2086	9.9992	86.46°		
3.55°	8.7918	12	8.7927	13	1.2073	9.9992	86.45°		
3.56°	8.7930	12	8.7939	12	1.2061	9.9992	86.44°		**13**
3.57°	8.7943	13	8.7951	12	1.2049	9.9992	86.43°	1	1.3
3.58°	8.7955	12	8.7963	12	1.2037	9.9992	86.42°	2	2.6
3.59°	8.7967	12	8.7975	12	1.2025	9.9991	86.41°	3	3.9
		12		13				4	5.2
3.60°	8.7979	12	8.7988	12	1.2012	9.9991	**86.40°**	5	6.5
3.61°	8.7991		8.8000		1.2000	9.9991	86.39°	6	7.8
3.62°	8.8003	12	8.8012	12	1.1988	9.9991	86.38°	7	9.1
3.63°	8.8015	12	8.8024	12	1.1976	9.9991	86.37°	8	10.4
		12		12				9	11.7
3.64°	8.8027	12	8.8036	12	1.1964	9.9991	86.36°		
3.65°	8.8039	12	8.8048	12	1.1952	9.9991	86.35°		
3.66°	8.8051	11	8.8059	11	1.1941	9.9991	86.34°		
3.67°	8.8062	12	8.8071	12	1.1929	9.9991	86.33°		**12**
3.68°	8.8074	12	8.8083	12	1.1917	9.9991	86.32°	1	1.2
3.69°	8.8086	12	8.8095	12	1.1905	9.9991	86.31°	2	2.4
		12		12				3	3.6
3.70°	8.8098	11	8.8107	12	1.1893	9.9991	**86.30°**	4	4.8
3.71°	8.8109		8.8119		1.1881	9.9991	86.29°	5	6.0
3.72°	8.8121	12	8.8130	11	1.1870	9.9991	86.28°	6	7.2
3.73°	8.8133	12	8.8142	12	1.1858	9.9991	86.27°	7	8.4
		11		12				8	9.6
3.74°	8.8144	12	8.8154	11	1.1846	9.9991	86.26°	9	10.8
3.75°	8.8156	12	8.8165	12	1.1835	9.9991	86.25°		
3.76°	8.8168	11	8.8177	11	1.1823	9.9991	86.24°		
3.77°	8.8179	12	8.8188	12	1.1812	9.9991	86.23°		
3.78°	8.8191	11	8.8200	12	1.1800	9.9991	86.22°		**11**
3.79°	8.8202	11	8.8212	11	1.1788	9.9990	86.21°	1	1.1
		11		11				2	2.2
3.80°	8.8213	12	8.8223	11	1.1777	9.9990	**86.20°**	3	3.3
3.81°	8.8225		8.8234		1.1766	9.9990	86.19°	4	4.4
3.82°	8.8236	11	8.8246	12	1.1754	9.9990	86.18°	5	5.5
3.83°	8.8248	12	8.8257	11	1.1743	9.9990	86.17°	6	6.6
		11		12				7	7.7
3.84°	8.8259	11	8.8269	11	1.1731	9.9990	86.16°	8	8.8
3.85°	8.8270	11	8.8280	11	1.1720	9.9990	86.15°	9	9.9
3.86°	8.8281	12	8.8291	11	1.1709	9.9990	86.14°		
3.87°	8.8293	11	8.8302	11	1.1698	9.9990	86.13°		
3.88°	8.8304	11	8.8314	12	1.1686	9.9990	86.12°		
3.89°	8.8315	11	8.8325	11	1.1675	9.9990	86.11°		**10**
		11		11				1	1.0
3.90°	8.8326	11	8.8336	11	1.1664	9.9990	**86.10°**	2	2.0
3.91°	8.8337		8.8347		1.1653	9.9990	86.09°	3	3.0
3.92°	8.8348	11	8.8358	11	1.1642	9.9990	86.08°	4	4.0
3.93°	8.8359	11	8.8370	12	1.1630	9.9990	86.07°	5	5.0
		11		11				6	6.0
3.94°	8.8370	11	8.8381	11	1.1619	9.9990	86.06°	7	7.0
3.95°	8.8381	11	8.8392	11	1.1608	9.9990	86.05°	8	8.0
3.96°	8.8392	11	8.8403	11	1.1597	9.9990	86.04°	9	9.0
3.97°	8.8403	11	8.8414	11	1.1586	9.9990	86.03°		
3.98°	8.8414	11	8.8425	11	1.1575	9.9990	86.02°		
3.99°	8.8425	11	8.8436	11	1.1564	9.9989	86.01°		
4.00°	8.8436	11	8.8446	10	1.1554	9.9989	**86.00°**		
	log cos	diff.	log cot	com. diff.	log tan	log sin	Angle		

86°

4°

Angle	log sin	diff.	log tan	com. diff.	log cot	log cos	
4.00°	8.8436	11	8.8446	11	1.1554	9.9989	**86.00°**
4.01°	8.8447	10	8.8457	11	1.1543	9.9989	85.99°
4.02°	8.8457	11	8.8468	11	1.1532	9.9989	85.98°
4.03°	8.8468	11	8.8479	11	1.1521	9.9989	85.97°
4.04°	8.8479	11	8.8490	11	1.1510	9.9989	85.96°
4.05°	8.8490	10	8.8501	10	1.1499	9.9989	85.95°
4.06°	8.8500	11	8.8511	11	1.1489	9.9989	85.94°
4.07°	8.8511	11	8.8522	11	1.1478	9.9989	85.93°
4.08°	8.8522	10	8.8533	10	1.1467	9.9989	85.92°
4.09°	8.8532	11	8.8543	11	1.1457	9.9989	85.91°
4.10°	8.8543	10	8.8554	11	1.1446	9.9989	**85.90°**
4.11°	8.8553	11	8.8565	10	1.1435	9.9989	85.89°
4.12°	8.8564	11	8.8575	11	1.1425	9.9989	85.88°
4.13°	8.8575	10	8.8586	10	1.1414	9.9989	85.87°
4.14°	8.8585	10	8.8596	11	1.1404	9.9989	85.86°
4.15°	8.8595	11	8.8607	10	1.1393	9.9989	85.85°
4.16°	8.8606	10	8.8617	11	1.1383	9.9989	85.84°
4.17°	8.8616	11	8.8628	10	1.1372	9.9988	85.83°
4.18°	8.8627	10	8.8638	11	1.1362	9.9988	85.82°
4.19°	8.8637	10	8.8649	10	1.1351	9.9988	85.81°
4.20°	8.8647	11	8.8659	10	1.1341	9.9988	**85.80°**
4.21°	8.8658	10	8.8669	11	1.1331	9.9988	85.79°
4.22°	8.8668	10	8.8680	10	1.1320	9.9988	85.78°
4.23°	8.8678	10	8.8690	10	1.1310	9.9988	85.77°
4.24°	8.8688	11	8.8700	11	1.1300	9.9988	85.76°
4.25°	8.8699	10	8.8711	10	1.1289	9.9988	85.75°
4.26°	8.8709	10	8.8721	10	1.1279	9.9988	85.74°
4.27°	8.8719	10	8.8731	10	1.1269	9.9988	85.73°
4.28°	8.8729	10	8.8741	10	1.1259	9.9988	85.72°
4.29°	8.8739	10	8.8751	11	1.1249	9.9988	85.71°
4.30°	8.8749	10	8.8762	10	1.1238	9.9988	**85.70°**
4.31°	8.8759	10	8.8772	10	1.1228	9.9988	85.69°
4.32°	8.8769	11	8.8782	10	1.1218	9.9988	85.68°
4.33°	8.8780	10	8.8792	10	1.1208	9.9988	85.67°
4.34°	8.8790	9	8.8802	10	1.1198	9.9988	85.66°
4.35°	8.8799	10	8.8812	10	1.1188	9.9987	85.65°
4.36°	8.8809	10	8.8822	10	1.1178	9.9987	85.64°
4.37°	8.8819	10	8.8832	10	1.1168	9.9987	85.63°
4.38°	8.8829	10	8.8842	10	1.1158	9.9987	85.62°
4.39°	8.8839	10	8.8852	10	1.1148	9.9987	85.61°
4.40°	8.8849	10	8.8862	10	1.1138	9.9987	**85.60°**
4.41°	8.8859	10	8.8872	10	1.1128	9.9987	85.59°
4.42°	8.8869	9	8.8882	9	1.1118	9.9987	85.58°
4.43°	8.8878	10	8.8891	10	1.1109	9.9987	85.57°
4.44°	8.8888	10	8.8901	10	1.1099	9.9987	85.56°
4.45°	8.8898	10	8.8911	10	1.1089	9.9987	85.55°
4.46°	8.8908	9	8.8921	10	1.1079	9.9987	85.54°
4.47°	8.8917	10	8.8931	9	1.1069	9.9987	85.53°
4.48°	8.8927	10	8.8940	10	1.1060	9.9987	85.52°
4.49°	8.8937	9	8.8950	10	1.1050	9.9987	85.51°
4.50°	8.8946		8.8960		1.1040	9.9987	**85.50°**
	log cos	diff.	log cot	com. diff.	log tan	log sin	Angle

Prop. Parts

Extra digit	Difference
	11
1	1.1
2	2.2
3	3.3
4	4.4
5	5.5
6	6.6
7	7.7
8	8.8
9	9.9
	10
1	1.0
2	2.0
3	3.0
4	4.0
5	5.0
6	6.0
7	7.0
8	8.0
9	9.0
	9
1	0.9
2	1.8
3	2.7
4	3.6
5	4.5
6	5.4
7	6.3
8	7.2
9	8.1

85°

4°

Angle	log sin	diff.	log tan	com. diff.	log cot	log cos	Angle
4.50°	8.8946	10	8.8960	10	1.1040	9.9987	**85.50°**
4.51°	8.8956	10	8.8970	9	1.1030	9.9987	85.49°
4.52°	8.8966	9	8.8979	10	1.1021	9.9986	85.48°
4.53°	8.8975	10	8.8989	9	1.1011	9.9986	85.47°
4.54°	8.8985	9	8.8998	10	1.1002	9.9986	85.46°
4.55°	8.8994	10	8.9008	10	1.0992	9.9986	85.45°
4.56°	8.9004	9	8.9018	9	1.0982	9.9986	85.44°
4.57°	8.9013	10	8.9027	10	1.0973	9.9986	85.43°
4.58°	8.9023	9	8.9037	9	1.0963	9.9986	85.42°
4.59°	8.9032	10	8.9046	10	1.0954	9.9986	85.41°
4.60°	8.9042	9	8.9056	9	1.0944	9.9986	**85.40°**
4.61°	8.9051	9	8.9065	10	1.0935	9.9986	85.39°
4.62°	8.9060	10	8.9075	9	1.0925	9.9986	85.38°
4.63°	8.9070	9	8.9084	9	1.0916	9.9986	85.37°
4.64°	8.9079	10	8.9093	10	1.0907	9.9986	85.36°
4.65°	8.9089	9	8.9103	9	1.0897	9.9986	85.35°
4.66°	8.9098	9	8.9112	10	1.0888	9.9986	85.34°
4.67°	8.9107	9	8.9122	9	1.0878	9.9986	85.33°
4.68°	8.9116	10	8.9131	9	1.0869	9.9985	85.32°
4.69°	8.9126	9	8.9140	10	1.0860	9.9985	85.31°
4.70°	8.9135	9	8.9150	9	1.0850	9.9985	**85.30°**
4.71°	8.9144	9	8.9159	9	1.0841	9.9985	85.29°
4.72°	8.9153	9	8.9168	9	1.0832	9.9985	85.28°
4.73°	8.9162	10	8.9177	9	1.0823	9.9985	85.27°
4.74°	8.9172	9	8.9186	10	1.0814	9.9985	85.26°
4.75°	8.9181	9	8.9196	9	1.0804	9.9985	85.25°
4.76°	8.9190	9	8.9205	9	1.0795	9.9985	85.24°
4.77°	8.9199	9	8.9214	9	1.0786	9.9985	85.23°
4.78°	8.9208	9	8.9223	9	1.0777	9.9985	85.22°
4.79°	8.9217	9	8.9232	9	1.0768	9.9985	85.21°
4.80°	8.9226	9	8.9241	9	1.0759	9.9985	**85.20°**
4.81°	8.9235	9	8.9250	10	1.0750	9.9985	85.19°
4.82°	8.9244	9	8.9260	9	1.0740	9.9985	85.18°
4.83°	8.9253	9	8.9269	9	1.0731	9.9985	85.17°
4.84°	8.9262	9	8.9278	9	1.0722	9.9984	85.16°
4.85°	8.9271	9	8.9287	9	1.0713	9.9984	85.15°
4.86°	8.9280	9	8.9296	9	1.0704	9.9984	85.14°
4.87°	8.9289	9	8.9305	8	1.0695	9.9984	85.13°
4.88°	8.9298	9	8.9313	9	1.0687	9.9984	85.12°
4.89°	8.9307	8	8.9322	9	1.0678	9.9984	85.11°
4.90°	8.9315	9	8.9331	9	1.0669	9.9984	**85.10°**
4.91°	8.9324	9	8.9340	9	1.0660	9.9984	85.09°
4.92°	8.9333	9	8.9349	9	1.0651	9.9984	85.08°
4.93°	8.9342	9	8.9358	9	1.0642	9.9984	85.07°
4.94°	8.9351	8	8.9367	9	1.0633	9.9984	85.06°
4.95°	8.9359	9	8.9376	8	1.0624	9.9984	85.05°
4.96°	8.9368	9	8.9384	9	1.0616	9.9984	85.04°
4.97°	8.9377	9	8.9393	9	1.0607	9.9984	85.03°
4.98°	8.9386	8	8.9402	9	1.0598	9.9984	85.02°
4.99°	8.9394	9	8.9411	9	1.0589	9.9984	85.01°
5.00°	8.9403		8.9420		1.0580	9.9983	**85.00°**
	log cos	diff.	log cot	com. diff.	log tan	log sin	Angle

Prop. Parts

Extra digit / Difference

	10
1	1.0
2	2.0
3	3.0
4	4.0
5	5.0
6	6.0
7	7.0
8	8.0
9	9.0

	9
1	0.9
2	1.8
3	2.7
4	3.6
5	4.5
6	5.4
7	6.3
8	7.2
9	8.1

	8
1	0.8
2	1.6
3	2.4
4	3.2
5	4.0
6	4.8
7	5.6
8	6.4
9	7.2

85°

5°–10°

Angle	log sin	diff.	log tan	com. diff.	log cot	log cos	diff.	
5.0°	8.9403	86	8.9420	86	1.0580	9.9983	0	**85.0°**
5.1°	8.9489	84	8.9506	85	1.0494	9.9983	1	84.9°
5.2°	8.9573	82	8.9591	83	1.0409	9.9982	1	84.8°
5.3°	8.9655	81	8.9674	82	1.0326	9.9981	0	84.7°
5.4°	8.9736	80	8.9756	80	1.0244	9.9981	1	84.6°
5.5°	8.9816	78	8.9836	79	1.0164	9.9980	1	84.5°
5.6°	8.9894	76	8.9915	77	1.0085	9.9979	1	84.4°
5.7°	8.9970	76	8.9992	76	1.0008	9.9978	0	84.3°
5.8°	9.0046	74	9.0068	75	0.9932	9.9978	1	84.2°
5.9°	9.0120	72	9.0143	73	0.9857	9.9977	1	84.1°
6.0°	9.0192	72	9.0216	73	0.9784	9.9976	1	**84.0°**
6.1°	9.0264	70	9.0289	71	0.9711	9.9975	0	83.9°
6.2°	9.0334	69	9.0360	70	0.9640	9.9975	1	83.8°
6.3°	9.0403	69	9.0430	69	0.9570	9.9974	1	83.7°
6.4°	9.0472	67	9.0499	68	0.9501	9.9973	1	83.6°
6.5°	9.0539	66	9.0567	66	0.9433	9.9972	1	83.5°
6.6°	9.0605	65	9.0633	66	0.9367	9.9971	1	83.4°
6.7°	9.0670	64	9.0699	65	0.9301	9.9970	1	83.3°
6.8°	9.0734	63	9.0764	64	0.9236	9.9969	0	83.2°
6.9°	9.0797	62	9.0828	63	0.9172	9.9968	0	83.1°
7.0°	9.0859	61	9.0891	63	0.9109	9.9968		**83.0°**
7.1°	9.0920	61	9.0954	61	0.9046	9.9967	1	82.9°
7.2°	9.0981	59	9.1015	61	0.8985	9.9966	1	82.8°
7.3°	9.1040	59	9.1076	59	0.8924	9.9965	1	82.7°
7.4°	9.1099	58	9.1135	59	0.8865	9.9964	1	82.6°
7.5°	9.1157	57	9.1194	58	0.8806	9.9963	1	82.5°
7.6°	9.1214	57	9.1252	58	0.8748	9.9962	1	82.4°
7.7°	9.1271	55	9.1310	57	0.8690	9.9961	1	82.3°
7.8°	9.1326	55	9.1367	56	0.8633	9.9960	1	82.2°
7.9°	9.1381	55	9.1423	55	0.8577	9.9959	1	82.1°
8.0°	9.1436	53	9.1478	55	0.8522	9.9958	2	**82.0°**
8.1°	9.1489	53	9.1533	54	0.8467	9.9956	1	81.9°
8.2°	9.1542	52	9.1587	53	0.8413	9.9955	1	81.8°
8.3°	9.1594	52	9.1640	53	0.8360	9.9954	1	81.7°
8.4°	9.1646	51	9.1693	52	0.8307	9.9953	1	81.6°
8.5°	9.1697	50	9.1745	52	0.8255	9.9952	1	81.5°
8.6°	9.1747	50	9.1797	51	0.8203	9.9951	1	81.4°
8.7°	9.1797	50	9.1848	50	0.8152	9.9950	1	81.3°
8.8°	9.1847	48	9.1898	50	0.8102	9.9949	2	81.2°
8.9°	9.1895	48	9.1948	49	0.8052	9.9947	1	81.1°
9.0°	9.1943	48	9.1997	49	0.8003	9.9946	1	**81.0°**
9.1°	9.1991	47	9.2046	48	0.7954	9.9945	1	80.9°
9.2°	9.2038	47	9.2094	48	0.7906	9.9944	1	80.8°
9.3°	9.2085	46	9.2142	47	0.7858	9.9943	2	80.7°
9.4°	9.2131	45	9.2189	47	0.7811	9.9941	1	80.6°
9.5°	9.2176	45	9.2236	46	0.7764	9.9940	1	80.5°
9.6°	9.2221	45	9.2282	46	0.7718	9.9939	2	80.4°
9.7°	9.2266	44	9.2328	46	0.7672	9.9937	1	80.3°
9.8°	9.2310	43	9.2374	45	0.7626	9.9936	1	80.2°
9.9°	9.2353	44	9.2419	44	0.7581	9.9935	1	80.1°
10.0°	9.2397		9.2463		0.7537	9.9934		**80.0°**
	log cos	diff.	log cot	com. diff.	log tan	log sin	diff.	Angle

Prop. Parts

Extra digit — Difference

	62	61	60
1	6.2	6.1	6.0
2	12.4	12.2	12.0
3	18.6	18.3	18.0
4	24.8	24.4	24.0
5	31.0	30.5	30.0
6	37.2	36.6	36.0
7	43.4	42.7	42.0
8	49.6	48.8	48.0
9	55.8	54.9	54.0

	59	58	57
1	5.9	5.8	5.7
2	11.8	11.6	11.4
3	17.7	17.4	17.1
4	23.6	23.2	22.8
5	29.5	29.0	28.5
6	35.4	34.8	34.2
7	41.3	40.6	39.9
8	47.2	46.4	45.6
9	53.1	52.2	51.3

	56	55	54
1	5.6	5.5	5.4
2	11.2	11.0	10.8
3	16.8	16.5	16.2
4	22.4	22.0	21.6
5	28.0	27.5	27.0
6	33.6	33.0	32.4
7	39.2	,38.5	37.8
8	44.8	44.0	43.2
9	50.4	49.5	48.6

	53	52	51
1	5.3	5.2	5.1
2	10.6	10.4	10.2
3	15.9	15.6	15.3
4	21.2	20.8	20.4
5	26.5	26.0	25.5
6	31.8	31.2	30.6
7	37.1	36.4	35.7
8	42.4	41.6	40.8
9	47.7	46.8	45.9

	50	49	48
1	5.0	4.9	4.8
2	10.0	9.8	9.6
3	15.0	14.7	14.4
4	20.0	19.6	19.2
5	25.0	24.5	24.0
6	30.0	29.4	28.8
7	35.0	34.3	33.6
8	40.0	39.2	38.4
9	45.0	44.1	43.2

	47	46	45
1	4.7	4.6	4.5
2	9.4	9.2	9.0
3	14.1	13.8	13.5
4	18.8	18.4	18.0
5	23.5	23.0	22.5
6	28.2	27.6	27.0
7	32.9	32.2	31.5
8	37.6	36.8	36.0
9	42.3	41.4	40.5

80°–85°

10°–15°

Angle	log sin	diff.	log tan	com. diff.	log cot	log cos	diff.		Prop. Parts
10.0°	9.2397	42	9.2463	44	0.7537	9.9934	2	**80.0°**	Extra digit
10.1°	9.2439	43	9.2507	44	0.7493	9.9932	1	79.9°	
10.2°	9.2482	42	9.2551	43	0.7449	9.9931	1	79.8°	Difference
10.3°	9.2524	41	9.2594	43	0.7406	9.9929	2	79.7°	
10.4°	9.2565	41	9.2637	43	0.7363	9.9928	1	79.6°	
10.5°	9.2606	41	9.2680	43	0.7320	9.9927	1	79.5°	
10.6°	9.2647	40	2.2722	42	0.7278	9.9925	2	79.4°	
10.7°	9.2687	40	9.2764	42	0.7236	9.9924	1	79.3°	
10.8°	9.2727	40	9.2805	41	0.7195	9.9922	2	79.2°	
10.9°	9.2767	39	9.2846	41	0.7154	9.9921	1	79.1°	
11.0°	9.2806	39	9.2887	41	0.7113	9.9919	2	**79.0°**	
11.1°	9.2845	38	9.2927	40	0.7073	9.9918	1	78.9°	
11.2°	9.2883	38	9.2967	40	0.7033	9.9916	2	78.8°	
11.3°	9.2921	38	9.3006	39	0.6994	9.9915	1	78.7°	
11.4°	9.2959	38	9.3046	40	0.6954	9.9913	2	78.6°	
11.5°	9.2997	37	9.3085	39	0.6915	9.9912	1	78.5°	
11.6°	9.3034	36	9.3123	38	0.6877	9.9910	2	78.4°	
11.7°	9.3070	37	9.3162	39	0.6838	9.9909	1	78.3°	
11.8°	9.3107	36	9.3200	38	0.6800	9.9907	2	78.2°	
11.9°	9.3143	36	9.3237	37	0.6763	9.9906	1	78.1°	
12.0°	9.3179	35	9.3275	38	0.6725	9.9904	2	**78.0°**	
12.1°	9.3214	36	9.3312	37	0.6688	9.9902	1	77.9°	
12.2°	9.3250	34	9.3349	37	0.6651	9.9901	2	77.8°	
12.3°	9.3284	35	9.3385	36	0.6615	9.9899	2	77.7°	
12.4°	9.3319	34	9.3422	37	0.6578	9.9897	1	77.6°	
12.5°	9.3353	34	9.3458	36	0.6542	9.9896	2	77.5°	
12.6°	9.3387	34	9.3493	35	0.6507	9.9894	2	77.4°	
12.7°	9.3421	34	9.3529	36	0.6471	9.9892	1	77.3°	
12.8°	9.3455	34	9.3564	35	0.6436	9.9891	2	77.2°	
12.9°	9.3488	33	9.3599	35	0.6401	9.9889	2	77.1°	
13.0°	9.3521	33	9.3634	35	0.6366	9.9887	2	**77.0°**	
13.1°	9.3554	33	9.3668	34	0.6332	9.9885	1	76.9°	
13.2°	9.3586	32	9.3702	34	0.6298	9.9884	2	76.8°	
13.3°	9.3618	32	9.3736	34	0.6264	9.9882	2	76.7°	
13.4°	9.3650	32	9.3770	34	0.6230	9.9880	2	76.6°	
13.5°	9.3682	32	9.3804	34	0.6196	9.9878	2	76.5°	
13.6°	9.3713	31	9.3837	33	0.6163	9.9876	1	76.4°	
13.7°	9.3745	32	9.3870	33	0.6130	9.9875	2	76.3°	
13.8°	9.3775	30	9.3903	33	0.6097	9.9873	2	76.2°	
13.9°	9.3806	31	9.3935	32	0.6065	9.9871	2	76.1°	
14.0°	9.3837	31	9.3968	33	0.6032	9.9869	2	**76.0°**	
14.1°	9.3867	30	9.4000	32	0.6000	9.9867	2	75.9°	
14.2°	9.3897	30	9.4032	32	0.5968	9.9865	2	75.8°	
14.3°	9.3927	30	9.4064	32	0.5936	9.9863	2	75.7°	
14.4°	9.3957	30	9.4095	31	0.5905	9.9861	2	75.6°	
14.5°	9.3986	29	9.4127	32	0.5873	9.9859	2	75.5°	
14.6°	9.4015	29	9.4158	31	0.5842	9.9857	2	75.4°	
14.7°	9.4044	29	9.4189	31	0.5811	9.9855	2	75.3°	
14.8°	9.4073	29	9.4220	31	0.5780	9.9853	2	75.2°	
14.9°	9.4102	29	9.4250	30	0.5750	9.9851	2	75.1°	
15.0°	9.4130	28	9.4281	31	0.5719	9.9849		**75.0°**	
	log cos	diff.	log cot	com. diff.	log tan	log sin	diff.	Angle	

Prop. Parts — Difference

	44	43	42
1	4.4	4.3	4.2
2	8.8	8.6	8.4
3	13.2	12.9	12.6
4	17.6	17.2	16.8
5	22.0	21.5	21.0
6	26.4	25.8	25.2
7	30.8	30.1	29.4
8	35.2	34.5	33.6
9	39.6	38.8	37.8

	41	40	39
1	4.1	4.0	3.9
2	8.2	8.0	7.8
3	12.3	12.0	11.7
4	16.4	16.0	15.6
5	20.5	20.0	19.5
6	24.6	24.0	23.4
7	28.7	28.0	27.3
8	32.8	32.0	31.2
9	36.9	36.0	35.1

	38	37	36
1	3.8	3.7	3.6
2	7.6	7.4	7.2
3	11.4	11.1	10.8
4	15.2	14.8	14.4
5	19.0	18.5	18.0
6	22.8	22.2	21.6
7	26.6	25.9	25.2
8	30.4	29.6	28.8
9	34.2	33.3	32.4

	35	34	33
1	3.5	3.4	3.3
2	7.0	6.8	6.6
3	10.5	10.2	9.9
4	14.0	13.6	13.2
5	17.5	17.0	16.5
6	21.0	20.4	19.8
7	24.5	23.8	23.1
8	28.0	27.2	26.4
9	31.5	30.6	29.7

	32	31	30
1	3.2	3.1	3.0
2	6.4	6.2	6.0
3	9.6	9.3	9.0
4	12.8	12.4	12.0
5	16.0	15.5	15.0
6	19.2	18.6	18.0
7	22.4	21.7	21.0
8	25.6	24.8	24.0
9	28.8	27.9	27.0

	29	28	2
1	2.9	2.8	0.2
2	5.8	5.6	0.4
3	8.7	8.4	0.6
4	11.6	11.2	0.8
5	14.5	14.0	1.0
6	17.4	16.8	1.2
7	20.3	19.6	1.4
8	23.2	22.4	1.6
9	26.1	25.2	1.8

75°–80°

15°–20°

Angle	log sin	diff.	log tan	com. diff.	log cot	log cos	diff.	
15.0°	9.4130	28	9.4281	30	0.5719	9.9849	2	**75.0°**
15.1°	9.4158	28	9.4311	30	0.5689	9.9847	2	74.9°
15.2°	9.4186	28	9.4341	30	0.5659	9.9845	2	74.8°
15.3°	9.4214	28	9.4371	29	0.5629	9.9843	2	74.7°
15.4°	9.4242	27	9.4400	30	0.5600	9.9841	2	74.6°
15.5°	9.4269	27	9.4430	29	0.5570	9.9839	2	74.5°
15.6°	9.4296	27	9.4459	29	0.5541	9.9837	2	74.4°
15.7°	9.4323	27	9.4488	29	0.5512	9.9835	2	74.3°
15.8°	9.4350	27	9.4517	29	0.5483	9.9833	2	74.2°
15.9°	9.4377	26	9.4546	29	0.5454	9.9831	3	74.1°
16.0°	9.4403	27	9.4575	28	0.5425	9.9828	2	**74.0°**
16.1°	9.4430	26	9.4603	29	0.5397	9.9826	2	73.9°
16.2°	9.4456	26	9.4632	28	0.5368	9.9824	2	73.8°
16.3°	9.4482	26	9.4660	28	0.5340	9.9822	2	73.7°
16.4°	9.4508	25	9.4688	28	0.5312	9.9820	3	73.6°
16.5°	9.4533	26	9.4716	28	0.5284	9.9817	2	73.5°
16.6°	9.4559	25	9.4744	27	0.5256	9.9815	2	73.4°
16.7°	9.4584	25	9.4771	28	0.5229	9.9813	2	73.3°
16.8°	9.4609	25	9.4799	27	0.5201	9.9811	3	73.2°
16.9°	9.4634	25	9.4826	27	0.5174	9.9808	2	73.1°
17.0°	9.4659	25	9.4853	27	0.5147	9.9806	2	**73.0°**
17.1°	9.4684	25	9.4880	27	0.5120	9.9804	3	72.9°
17.2°	9.4709	24	9.4907	27	0.5093	9.9801	2	72.8°
17.3°	9.4733	24	9.4934	27	0.5066	9.9799	2	72.7°
17.4°	9.4757	24	9.4961	26	0.5039	9.9797	3	72.6°
17.5°	9.4781	24	9.4987	27	0.5013	9.9794	2	72.5°
17.6°	9.4805	24	9.5014	26	0.4986	9.9792	3	72.4°
17.7°	9.4829	24	9.5040	26	0.4960	9.9789	2	72.3°
17.8°	9.4853	23	9.5066	26	0.4934	9.9787	2	72.2°
17.9°	9.4876	24	9.5092	26	0.4908	9.9785	3	72.1°
18.0°	9.4900	23	9.5118	25	0.4882	9.9782	2	**72.0°**
18.1°	9.4923	23	9.5143	26	0.4857	9.9780	3	71.9°
18.2°	9.4946	23	9.5169	26	0.4831	9.9777	2	71.8°
18.3°	9.4969	23	9.5195	25	0.4805	9.9775	3	71.7°
18.4°	9.4992	23	9.5220	25	0.4780	9.9772	2	71.6°
18.5°	9.5015	22	9.5245	25	0.4755	9.9770	3	71.5°
18.6°	9.5037	23	9.5270	25	0.4730	9.9767	3	71.4°
18.7°	9.5060	22	9.5295	25	0.4705	9.9764	2	71.3°
18.8°	9.5082	22	9.5320	25	0.4680	9.9762	3	71.2°
18.9°	9.5104	22	9.5345	25	0.4655	9.9759	2	71.1°
19.0°	9.5126	22	9.5370	24	0.4630	9.9757	3	**71.0°**
19.1°	9.5148	22	9.5394	25	0.4606	9.9754	3	70.9°
19.2°	9.5170	22	9.5419	24	0.4581	9.9751	3	70.8°
19.3°	9.5192	21	9.5443	24	0.4557	9.9749	3	70.7°
19.4°	9.5213	22	9.5467	24	0.4533	9.9746	3	70.6°
19.5°	9.5235	21	9.5491	25	0.4509	9.9743	2	70.5°
19.6°	9.5256	22	9.5516	23	0.4484	9.9741	3	70.4°
19.7°	9.5278	21	9.5539	24	0.4461	9.9738	3	70.3°
19.8°	9.5299	21	9.5563	24	0.4437	9.9735	2	70.2°
19.9°	9.5320	21	9.5587	24	0.4413	9.9733	3	70.1°
20.0°	9.5341		9.5611		0.4389	9.9730		**70.0°**
	log cos	diff.	log cot	com. diff.	log tan	log sin	diff.	Angle

Prop. Parts

Extra digit — Difference

	30	29
1	3.0	2.9
2	6.0	5.8
3	9.0	8.7
4	12.0	11.6
5	15.0	14.5
6	18.0	17.4
7	21.0	20.3
8	24.0	23.2
9	27.0	26.1

	28	27
1	2.8	2.7
2	5.6	5.4
3	8.4	8.1
4	11.2	10.8
5	14.0	13.5
6	16.8	16.2
7	19.6	18.9
8	22.4	21.6
9	25.2	24.3

	26	25
1	2.6	2.5
2	5.2	5.0
3	7.8	7.5
4	10.4	10.0
5	13.0	12.5
6	15.6	15.0
7	18.2	17.5
8	20.8	20.0
9	23.4	22.5

	24	23
1	2.4	2.3
2	4.8	4.6
3	7.2	6.9
4	9.6	9.2
5	12.0	11.5
6	14.4	13.8
7	16.8	16.1
8	19.2	18.4
9	21.6	20.7

	22	21
1	2.2	2.1
2	4.4	4.2
3	6.6	6.3
4	8.8	8.4
5	11.0	10.5
6	13.2	12.6
7	15.4	14.7
8	17.6	16.8
9	19.8	18.9

70°–75°

20°–25°

Angle	log sin	diff.	log tan	com. diff.	log cot	log cos	diff.	Angle
20.0°	9.5341	20	9.5611	23	0.4389	9.9730	3	70.0°
20.1°	9.5361	21	9.5634	24	0.4366	9.9727	3	69.9°
20.2°	9.5382	20	9.5658	23	0.4342	9.9724	3	69.8°
20.3°	9.5402	21	9.5681	23	0.4319	9.9722	2	69.7°
20.4°	9.5423	20	9.5704	23	0.4296	9.9719	3	69.6°
20.5°	9.5443	20	9.5727	23	0.4273	9.9716	3	69.5°
20.6°	9.5463	21	9.5750	23	0.4250	9.9713	3	69.4°
20.7°	9.5484	20	9.5773	23	0.4227	9.9710	3	69.3°
20.8°	9.5504	19	9.5796	23	0.4204	9.9707	3	69.2°
20.9°	9.5523	20	9.5819	23	0.4181	9.9704	2	69.1°
21.0°	9.5543	20	9.5842	22	0.4158	9.9702	3	69.0°
21.1°	9.5563	20	9.5864	23	0.4136	9.9699	3	68.9°
21.2°	9.5583	19	9.5887	22	0.4113	9.9696	3	68.8°
21.3°	9.5602	19	9.5909	23	0.4091	9.9693	3	68.7°
21.4°	9.5621	20	9.5932	22	0.4068	9.9690	3	68.6°
21.5°	9.5641	19	9.5954	22	0.4046	9.9687	3	68.5°
21.6°	9.5660	19	9.5976	22	0.4024	9.9684	3	68.4°
21.7°	9.5679	19	9.5998	22	0.4002	9.9681	3	68.3°
21.8°	9.5698	19	9.6020	22	0.3980	9.9678	3	68.2°
21.9°	9.5717	19	9.6042	22	0.3958	9.9675	3	68.1°
22.0°	9.5736	18	9.6064	22	0.3936	9.9672	3	68.0°
22.1°	9.5754	19	9.6086	22	0.3914	9.9669	3	67.9°
22.2°	9.5773	19	9.6108	21	0.3892	9.9666	4	67.8°
22.3°	9.5792	18	9.6129	22	0.3871	9.9662	3	67.7°
22.4°	9.5810	18	9.6151	21	0.3849	9.9659	3	67.6°
22.5°	9.5828	19	9.6172	22	0.3828	9.9656	3	67.5°
22.6°	9.5847	18	9.6194	21	0.3806	9.9653	3	67.4°
22.7°	9.5865	18	9.6215	21	0.3785	9.9650	3	67.3°
22.8°	9.5883	18	9.6236	21	0.3764	9.9647	4	67.2°
22.9°	9.5901	18	9.6257	22	0.3743	9.9643	3	67.1°
23.0°	9.5919	18	9.6279	21	0.3721	9.9640	3	67.0°
23.1°	9.5937	17	9.6300	21	0.3700	9.9637	3	66.9°
23.2°	9.5954	18	9.6321	20	0.3679	9.9634	3	66.8°
23.3°	9.5972	18	9.6341	21	0.3659	9.9631	4	66.7°
23.4°	9.5990	17	9.6362	21	0.3638	9.9627	3	66.6°
23.5°	9.6007	17	9.6383	21	0.3617	9.9624	3	66.5°
23.6°	9.6024	18	9.6404	20	0.3596	9.9621	4	66.4°
23.7°	9.6042	17	9.6424	21	0.3576	9.9617	3	66.3°
23.8°	9.6059	17	9.6445	20	0.3555	9.9614	3	66.2°
23.9°	9.6076	17	9.6465	21	0.3535	9.9611	4	66.1°
24.0°	9.6093	17	9.6486	20	0.3514	9.9607	3	66.0°
24.1°	9.6110	17	9.6506	21	0.3494	9.9604	3	65.9°
24.2°	9.6127	17	9.6527	20	0.3473	9.9601	4	65.8°
24.3°	9.6144	17	9.6547	20	0.3453	9.9597	3	65.7°
24.4°	9.6161	16	9.6567	20	0.3433	9.9594	4	65.6°
24.5°	9.6177	17	9.6587	20	0.3413	9.9590	3	65.5°
24.6°	9.6194	16	9.6607	20	0.3393	9.9587	4	65.4°
24.7°	9.6210	17	9.6627	20	0.3373	9.9583	3	65.3°
24.8°	9.6227	16	9.6647	20	0.3353	9.9580	4	65.2°
24.9°	9.6243	16	9.6667	20	0.3333	9.9576	3	65.1°
25.0°	9.6259		9.6687		0.3313	9.9573		65.0°
	log cos	diff.	log cot	com. diff.	log tan	log sin	diff.	Angle

Prop. Parts

Extra digit — Difference

	23	22
1	2.3	2.2
2	4.6	4.4
3	6.9	6.6
4	9.2	8.8
5	11.5	11.0
6	13.8	13.2
7	16.1	15.4
8	18.4	17.6
9	20.7	19.8

	21	20
1	2.1	2.0
2	4.2	4.0
3	6.3	6.0
4	8.4	8.0
5	10.5	10.0
6	12.6	12.0
7	14.7	14.0
8	16.8	16.0
9	18.9	18.0

	19	18
1	1.9	1.8
2	3.8	3.6
3	5.7	5.4
4	7.6	7.2
5	9.5	9.0
6	11.4	10.8
7	13.3	12.6
8	15.2	14.4
9	17.1	16.2

	17	16
1	1.7	1.6
2	3.4	3.2
3	5.1	4.8
4	6.8	6.4
5	8.5	8.0
6	10.2	9.6
7	11.9	11.2
8	13.6	12.8
9	15.3	14.4

	2
1	0.2
2	0.4
3	0.6
4	0.8
5	1.0
6	1.2
7	1.4
8	1.6
9	1.8

	3	4
1	0.3	0.4
2	0.6	0.8
3	0.9	1.2
4	1.2	1.6
5	1.5	2.0
6	1.8	2.4
7	2.1	2.8
8	2.4	3.2
9	2.7	3.6

25°–30°

Angle	log sin	diff.	log tan	com. diff.	log cot	log cos	diff.	Angle
25.0°	9.6259	17	9.6687	19	0.3313	9.9573	4	**65.0°**
25.1°	9.6276	16	9.6706	20	0.3294	9.9569	3	64.9°
25.2°	9.6292	16	9.6726	20	0.3274	9.9566	4	64.8°
25.3°	9.6308	16	9.6746	19	0.3254	9.9562	4	64.7°
25.4°	9.6324	16	9.6765	20	0.3235	9.9558	3	64.6°
25.5°	9.6340	16	9.6785	19	0.3215	9.9555	4	64.5°
25.6°	9.6356	15	9.6804	20	0.3196	9.9551	3	64.4°
25.7°	9.6371	16	9.6824	19	0.3176	9.9548	4	64.3°
25.8°	9.6387	16	9.6843	20	0.3157	9.9544	4	64.2°
25.9°	9.6403	15	9.6863	19	0.3137	9.9540	3	64.1°
26.0°	9.6418	16	9.6882	19	0.3118	9.9537	4	**64.0°**
26.1°	9.6434	15	9.6901	19	0.3099	9.9533	4	63.9°
26.2°	9.6449	16	9.6920	19	0.3080	9.9529	4	63.8°
26.3°	9.6465	15	9.6939	19	0.3061	9.9525	3	63.7°
26.4°	9.6480	15	9.6958	19	0.3042	9.9522	4	63.6°
26.5°	9.6495	15	9.6977	19	0.3023	9.9518	4	63.5°
26.6°	9.6510	16	9.6996	19	0.3004	9.9514	4	63.4°
26.7°	9.6526	15	9.7015	19	0.2985	9.9510	4	63.3°
26.8°	9.6541	15	9.7034	19	0.2966	9.9506	3	63.2°
26.9°	9.6556	14	9.7053	19	0.2947	9.9503	4	63.1°
27.0°	9.6570	15	9.7072	18	0.2928	9.9499	4	**63.0°**
27.1°	9.6585	15	9.7090	19	0.2910	9.9495	4	62.9°
27.2°	9.6600	15	9.7109	19	0.2891	9.9491	4	62.8°
27.3°	9.6615	14	9.7128	18	0.2872	9.9487	4	62.7°
27.4°	9.6629	15	9.7146	19	0.2854	9.9483	4	62.6°
27.5°	9.6644	15	9.7165	18	0.2835	9.9479	4	62.5°
27.6°	9.6659	14	9.7183	19	0.2817	9.9475	4	62.4°
27.7°	9.6673	14	9.7202	18	0.2798	9.9471	4	62.3°
27.8°	9.6687	15	9.7220	18	0.2780	9.9467	4	62.2°
27.9°	9.6702	14	9.7238	19	0.2762	9.9463	4	62.1°
28.0°	9.6716	14	9.7257	18	0.2743	9.9459	4	**62.0°**
28.1°	9.6730	14	9.7275	18	0.2725	9.9455	4	61.9°
28.2°	9.6744	15	9.7293	18	0.2707	9.9451	4	61.8°
28.3°	9.6759	14	9.7311	18	0.2689	9.9447	4	61.7°
28.4°	9.6773	14	9.7330	18	0.2670	9.9443	4	61.6°
28.5°	9.6787	14	9.7348	18	0.2652	9.9439	4	61.5°
28.6°	9.6801	13	9.7366	18	0.2634	9.9435	4	61.4°
28.7°	9.6814	14	9.7384	18	0.2616	9.9431	4	61.3°
28.8°	9.6828	14	9.7402	18	0.2598	9.9427	5	61.2°
28.9°	9.6842	14	9.7420	18	0.2580	9.9422	4	61.1°
29.0°	9.6856	13	9.7438	17	0.2562	9.9418	4	**61.0°**
29.1°	9.6869	14	9.7455	18	0.2545	9.9414	4	60.9°
29.2°	9.6883	13	9.7473	18	0.2527	9.9410	4	60.8°
29.3°	9.6896	14	9.7491	18	0.2509	9.9406	5	60.7°
29.4°	9.6910	13	9.7509	17	0.2491	9.9401	4	60.6°
29.5°	9.6923	14	9.7526	18	0.2474	9.9397	4	60.5°
29.6°	9.6937	13	9.7544	18	0.2456	9.9393	5	60.4°
29.7°	9.6950	13	9.7562	17	0.2438	9.9388	4	60.3°
29.8°	9.6963	14	9.7579	18	0.2421	9.9384	4	60.2°
29.9°	9.6977	13	9.7597	17	0.2403	9.9380	5	60.1°
30.0°	9.6990		9.7614		0.2386	9.9375		**60.0°**
	log cos	diff.	log cot	com. diff.	log tan	log sin	diff.	Angle

Prop. Parts

Extra digit — Difference

	20	19
1	2.0	1.9
2	4.0	3.8
3	6.0	5.7
4	8.0	7.6
5	10.0	9.5
6	12.0	11.4
7	14.0	13.3
8	16.0	15.2
9	18.0	17.1

	18	17
1	1.8	1.7
2	3.6	3.4
3	5.4	5.1
4	7.2	6.8
5	9.0	8.5
6	10.8	10.2
7	12.6	11.9
8	14.4	13.6
9	16.2	15.3

	16	15
1	1.6	1.5
2	3.2	3.0
3	4.8	4.5
4	6.4	6.0
5	8.0	7.5
6	9.6	9.0
7	11.2	10.5
8	12.8	12.0
9	14.4	13.5

	14	13
1	1.4	1.3
2	2.8	2.6
3	4.2	3.9
4	5.6	5.2
5	7.0	6.5
6	8.4	7.8
7	9.8	9.1
8	11.2	10.4
9	12.6	11.7

	3	4
1	0.3	0.4
2	0.6	0.8
3	0.9	1.2
4	1.2	1.6
5	1.5	2.0
6	1.8	2.4
7	2.1	2.8
8	2.4	3.2
9	2.7	3.6

30°–35°

Angle	log sin	diff.	log tan	com. diff.	log cot	log cos	diff.	
30.0°	9.6990	13	9.7614	18	0.2386	9.9375	4	**60.0°**
30.1°	9.7003	13	9.7632	17	0.2368	9.9371	4	59.9°
30.2°	9.7016	13	9.7649	18	0.2351	9.9367	4	59.8°
30.3°	9.7029	13	9.7667	17	0.2333	9.9362	5	59.7°
30.4°	9.7042	13	9.7684	17	0.2316	9.9358	4	59.6°
30.5°	9.7055	13	9.7701	18	0.2299	9.9353	5	59.5°
30.6°	9.7068	12	9.7719	17	0.2281	9.9349	4	59.4°
30.7°	9.7080	13	9.7736	17	0.2264	9.9344	5	59.3°
30.8°	9.7093	13	9.7753	18	0.2247	9.9340	4	59.2°
30.9°	9.7106	12	9.7771	17	0.2229	9.9335	5	59.1°
31.0°	9.7118	13	9.7788	17	0.2212	9.9331	5	**59.0°**
31.1°	9.7131	13	9.7805	17	0.2195	9.9326	5	58.9°
31.2°	9.7144	12	9.7822	17	0.2178	9.9322	4	58.8°
31.3°	9.7156	12	9.7839	17	0.2161	9.9317	5	58.7°
31.4°	9.7168	13	9.7856	17	0.2144	9.9312	5	58.6°
31.5°	9.7181	12	9.7873	17	0.2127	9.9308	4	58.5°
31.6°	9.7193	12	9.7890	17	0.2110	9.9303	5	58.4°
31.7°	9.7205	13	9.7907	17	0.2093	9.9298	5	58.3°
31.8°	9.7218	12	9.7924	17	0.2076	9.9294	4	58.2°
31.9°	9.7230	12	9.7941	17	0.2059	9.9289	5	58.1°
32.0°	9.7242	12	9.7958	17	0.2042	9.9284	5	**58.0°**
32.1°	9.7254	12	9.7975	17	0.2025	9.9279	5	57.9°
32.2°	9.7266	12	9.7992	16	0.2008	9.9275	4	57.8°
32.3°	9.7278	12	9.8008	17	0.1992	9.9270	5	57.7°
32.4°	9.7290	12	9.8025	17	0.1975	9.9265	5	57.6°
32.5°	9.7302	12	9.8042	17	0.1958	9.9260	5	57.5°
32.6°	9.7314	12	9.8059	16	0.1941	9.9255	5	57.4°
32.7°	9.7326	12	9.8075	17	0.1925	9.9251	4	57.3°
32.8°	9.7338	11	9.8092	17	0.1908	9.9246	5	57.2°
32.9°	9.7349	12	9.8109	16	0.1891	9.9241	5	57.1°
33.0°	9.7361	12	9.8125	17	0.1875	9.9236	5	**57.0°**
33.1°	9.7373	11	9.8142	16	0.1858	9.9231	5	56.9°
33.2°	9.7384	12	9.8158	17	0.1842	9.9226	5	56.8°
33.3°	9.7396	11	9.8175	16	0.1825	9.9221	5	56.7°
33.4°	9.7407	12	9.8191	17	0.1809	9.9216	5	56.6°
33.5°	9.7419	11	9.8208	16	0.1792	9.9211	5	56.5°
33.6°	9.7430	12	9.8224	17	0.1776	9.9206	5	56.4°
33.7°	9.7442	11	9.8241	16	0.1759	9.9201	5	56.3°
33.8°	9.7453	11	9.8257	17	0.1743	9.9196	5	56.2°
33.9°	9.7464	12	9.8274	16	0.1726	9.9191	5	56.1°
34.0°	9.7476	11	9.8290	16	0.1710	9.9186	5	**56.0°**
34.1°	9.7487	11	9.8306	17	0.1694	9.9181	6	55.9°
34.2°	9.7498	11	9.8323	16	0.1677	9.9175	5	55.8°
34.3°	9.7509	11	9.8339	16	0.1661	9.9170	5	55.7°
34.4°	9.7520	11	9.8355	16	0.1645	9.9165	5	55.6°
34.5°	9.7531	11	9.8371	17	0.1629	9.9160	5	55.5°
34.6°	9.7542	11	9.8388	16	0.1612	9.9155	6	55.4°
34.7°	9.7553	11	9.8404	16	0.1596	9.9149	5	55.3°
34.8°	9.7564	11	9.8420	16	0.1580	9.9144	5	55.2°
34.9°	9.7575	11	9.8436	16	0.1564	9.9139	5	55.1°
35.0°	9.7586		9.8452		0.1548	9.9134		**55.0°**

| | log cos | diff. | log cot | com. diff. | log tan | log sin | diff. | Angle |

Prop. Parts

Extra digit — Difference

	18	17
1	1.8	1.7
2	3.6	3.4
3	5.4	5.1
4	7.2	6.8
5	9.0	8.5
6	10.8	10.2
7	12.6	11.9
8	14.4	13.6
9	16.2	15.3

	16
1	1.6
2	3.2
3	4.8
4	6.4
5	8.0
6	9.6
7	11.2
8	12.8
9	14.4

	13	12
1	1.3	1.2
2	2.6	2.4
3	3.9	3.6
4	5.2	4.8
5	6.5	6.0
6	7.8	7.2
7	9.1	8.4
8	10.4	9.6
9	11.7	10.8

	11
1	1.1
2	2.2
3	3.3
4	4.4
5	5.5
6	6.6
7	7.7
8	8.8
9	9.9

	5	6
1	0.5	0.6
2	1.0	1.2
3	1.5	1.8
4	2.0	2.4
5	2.5	3.0
6	3.0	3.6
7	3.5	4.2
8	4.0	4.8
9	4.5	5.4

55°–60°

35°–40°

Angle	log sin	diff.	log tan	com. diff.	log cot	log cos	diff.	
35.0°	9.7586	11	9.8452	16	0.1548	9.9134	6	**55.0°**
35.1°	9.7597	10	9.8468	16	0.1532	9.9128	5	54.9°
35.2°	9.7607	11	9.8484	17	0.1516	9.9123	5	54.8°
35.3°	9.7618	11	9.8501	16	0.1499	9.9118	6	54.7°
35.4°	9.7629	11	9.8517	16	0.1483	9.9112	5	54.6°
35.5°	9.7640	10	9.8533	16	0.1467	9.9107	6	54.5°
35.6°	9.7650	11	9.8549	16	0.1451	9.9101	5	54.4°
35.7°	9.7661	10	9.8565	16	0.1435	9.9096	5	54.3°
35.8°	9.7671	11	9.8581	16	0.1419	9.9091	6	54.2°
35.9°	9.7682	10	9.8597	16	0.1403	9.9085	5	54.1°
36.0°	9.7692	11	9.8613	16	0.1387	9.9080	6	**54.0°**
36.1°	9.7703	10	9.8629	15	0.1371	9.9074	5	53.9°
36.2°	9.7713	10	9.8644	16	0.1356	9.9069	6	53.8°
36.3°	9.7723	11	9.8660	16	0.1340	9.9063	6	53.7°
36.4°	9.7734	10	9.8676	16	0.1324	9.9057	5	53.6°
36.5°	9.7744	10	9.8692	16	0.1308	9.9052	6	53.5°
36.6°	9.7754	10	9.8708	16	0.1292	9.9046	5	53.4°
36.7°	9.7764	10	9.8724	16	0.1276	9.9041	6	53.3°
36.8°	9.7774	11	9.8740	15	0.1260	9.9035	6	53.2°
36.9°	9.7785	10	9.8755	16	0.1245	9.9029	6	53.1°
37.0°	9.7795	10	9.8771	16	0.1229	9.9023	5	**53.0°**
37.1°	9.7805	10	9.8787	16	0.1213	9.9018	6	52.9°
37.2°	9.7815	10	9.8803	15	0.1197	9.9012	6	52.8°
37.3°	9.7825	10	9.8818	16	0.1182	9.9006	6	52.7°
37.4°	9.7835	9	9.8834	16	0.1166	9.9000	5	52.6°
37.5°	9.7844	10	9.8850	15	0.1150	9.8995	6	52.5°
37.6°	9.7854	10	9.8865	16	0.1135	9.8989	6	52.4°
37.7°	9.7864	10	9.8881	16	0.1119	9.8983	6	52.3°
37.8°	9.7874	10	9.8897	15	0.1103	9.8977	6	52.2°
37.9°	9.7884	9	9.8912	16	0.1088	9.8971	6	52.1°
38.0°	9.7893	10	9.8928	16	0.1072	9.8965	6	**52.0°**
38.1°	9.7903	10	9.8944	15	0.1056	9.8959	6	51.9°
38.2°	9.7913	9	9.8959	16	0.1041	9.8953	6	51.8°
38.3°	9.7922	10	9.8975	15	0.1025	9.8947	6	51.7°
38.4°	9.7932	9	9.8990	16	0.1010	9.8941	6	51.6°
38.5°	9.7941	10	9.9006	16	0.0994	9.8935	6	51.5°
38.6°	9.7951	9	9.9022	15	0.0978	9.8929	6	51.4°
38.7°	9.7960	10	9.9037	16	0.0963	9.8923	6	51.3°
38.8°	9.7970	9	9.9053	15	0.0947	9.8917	6	51.2°
38.9°	9.7979	10	9.9068	16	0.0932	9.8911	6	51.1°
39.0°	9.7989	9	9.9084	15	0.0916	9.8905	6	**51.0°**
39.1°	9.7998	9	9.9099	16	0.0901	9.8899	6	50.9°
39.2°	9.8007	10	9.9115	15	0.0885	9.8893	6	50.8°
39.3°	9.8017	9	9.9130	16	0.0870	9.8887	7	50.7°
39.4°	9.8026	9	9.9146	15	0.0854	9.8880	6	50.6°
39.5°	9.8035	9	9.9161	15	0.0839	9.8874	6	50.5°
39.6°	9.8044	9	9.9176	16	0.0824	9.8868	6	50.4°
39.7°	9.8053	10	9.9192	15	0.0808	9.8862	7	50.3°
39.8°	9.8063	9	9.9207	16	0.0793	9.8855	6	50.2°
39.9°	9.8072	9	9.9223	15	0.0777	9.8849	6	50.1°
40.0°	9.8081		9.9238	15	0.0762	9.8843	6	**50.0°**
	log cos	diff.	log cot	com. diff.	log tan	log sin	diff.	Angle

Prop. Parts — Difference

	17	16
1	1.7	1.6
2	3.4	3.2
3	5.1	4.8
4	6.8	6.4
5	8.5	8.0
6	10.2	9.6
7	11.9	11.2
8	13.6	12.8
9	15.3	14.4

	15
1	1.5
2	3.0
3	4.5
4	6.0
5	7.5
6	9.0
7	10.5
8	12.0
9	13.5

	11	10
1	1.1	1.0
2	2.2	2.0
3	3.3	3.0
4	4.4	4.0
5	5.5	5.0
6	6.6	6.0
7	7.7	7.0
8	8.8	8.0
9	9.9	9.0

	9
1	0.9
2	1.8
3	2.7
4	3.6
5	4.5
6	5.4
7	6.3
8	7.2
9	8.1

	5	6
1	0.5	0.6
2	1.0	1.2
3	1.5	1.8
4	2.0	2.4
5	2.5	3.0
6	3.0	3.6
7	3.5	4.2
8	4.0	4.8
9	4.5	5.4

50°–55°

40°–45°

Angle	log sin	diff.	log tan	com. diff.	log cot	log cos	diff.	Angle
40.0°	9.8081	9	9.9238	16	0.0762	9.8843	7	**50.0°**
40.1°	9.8090	9	9.9254	15	0.0746	9.8836	6	49.9°
40.2°	9.8099	9	9.9269	15	0.0731	9.8830	7	49.8°
40.3°	9.8108	9	9.9284	16	0.0716	9.8823	6	49.7°
40.4°	9.8117	8	9.9300	15	0.0700	9.8817	7	49.6°
40.5°	9.8125	9	9.9315	15	0.0685	9.8810	6	49.5°
40.6°	9.8134	9	9.9330	16	0.0670	9.8804	7	49.4°
40.7°	9.8143	9	9.9346	15	0.0654	9.8797	6	49.3°
40.8°	9.8152	9	9.9361	15	0.0639	9.8791	7	49.2°
40.9°	9.8161	8	9.9376	16	0.0624	9.8784	6	49.1°
41.0°	9.8169	9	9.9392	15	0.0608	9.8778	7	**49.0°**
41.1°	9.8178	9	9.9407	15	0.0593	9.8771	6	48.9°
41.2°	9.8187	8	9.9422	16	0.0578	9.8765	7	48.8°
41.3°	9.8195	9	9.9438	15	0.0562	9.8758	7	48.7°
41.4°	9.8204	9	9.9453	15	0.0547	9.8751	6	48.6°
41.5°	9.8213	8	9.9468	15	0.0532	9.8745	7	48.5°
41.6°	9.8221	9	9.9483	16	0.0517	9.8738	7	48.4°
41.7°	9.8230	8	9.9499	15	0.0501	9.8731	7	48.3°
41.8°	9.8238	9	9.9514	15	0.0486	9.8724	6	48.2°
41.9°	9.8247	8	9.9529	15	0.0471	9.8718	7	48.1°
42.0°	9.8255	9	9.9544	16	0.0456	9.8711	7	**48.0°**
42.1°	9.8264	8	9.9560	15	0.0440	9.8704	7	47.9°
42.2°	9.8272	8	9.9575	15	0.0425	9.8697	7	47.8°
42.3°	9.8280	9	9.9590	15	0.0410	9.8690	7	47.7°
42.4°	9.8289	8	9.9605	16	0.0395	9.8683	7	47.6°
42.5°	9.8297	8	9.9621	15	0.0379	9.8676	7	47.5°
42.6°	9.8305	8	9.9636	15	0.0364	9.8669	7	47.4°
42.7°	9.8313	9	9.9651	15	0.0349	9.8662	7	47.3°
42.8°	9.8322	8	9.9666	15	0.0334	9.8655	7	47.2°
42.9°	9.8330	8	9.9681	16	0.0319	9.8648	7	47.1°
43.0°	9.8338	8	9.9697	15	0.0303	9.8641	7	**47.0°**
43.1°	9.8346	8	9.9712	15	0.0288	9.8634	7	46.9°
43.2°	9.8354	8	9.9727	15	0.0273	9.8627	7	46.8°
43.3°	9.8362	8	9.9742	15	0.0258	9.8620	7	46.7°
43.4°	9.8370	8	9.9757	15	0.0243	9.8613	7	46.6°
43.5°	9.8378	8	9.9772	16	0.0228	9.8606	8	46.5°
43.6°	9.8386	8	9.9788	15	0.0212	9.8598	7	46.4°
43.7°	9.8394	8	9.9803	15	0.0197	9.8591	7	46.3°
43.8°	9.8402	8	9.9818	15	0.0182	9.8584	7	46.2°
43.9°	9.8410	8	9.9833	15	0.0167	9.8577	8	46.1°
44.0°	9.8418	8	9.9848	16	0.0152	9.8569	7	**46.0°**
44.1°	9.8426	7	9.9864	15	0.0136	9.8562	7	45.9°
44.2°	9.8433	8	9.9879	15	0.0121	9.8555	8	45.8°
44.3°	9.8441	8	9.9894	15	0.0106	9.8547	7	45.7°
44.4°	9.8449	8	9.9909	15	0.0091	9.8540	8	45.6°
44.5°	9.8457	7	9.9924	15	0.0076	9.8532	7	45.5°
44.6°	9.8464	8	9.9939	16	0.0061	9.8525	8	45.4°
44.7°	9.8472	8	9.9955	15	0.0045	9.8517	7	45.3°
44.8°	9.8480	7	9.9970	15	0.0030	9.8510	8	45.2°
44.9°	9.8487	8	9.9985	15	0.0015	9.8502	7	45.1°
45.0°	9.8495		10.0000		0.0000	9.8495		**45.0°**
	log cos	diff.	log cot	com. diff.	log tan	log sin	diff.	Angle

Prop. Parts

Extra digit — Difference

16		15		9		8		7		6	
1	1.6	1	1.5	1	0.9	1	0.8	1	0.7	1	0.6
2	3.2	2	3.0	2	1.8	2	1.6	2	1.4	2	1.2
3	4.8	3	4.5	3	2.7	3	2.4	3	2.1	3	1.8
4	6.4	4	6.0	4	3.6	4	3.2	4	2.8	4	2.4
5	8.0	5	7.5	5	4.5	5	4.0	5	3.5	5	3.0
6	9.6	6	9.0	6	5.4	6	4.8	6	4.2	6	3.6
7	11.2	7	10.5	7	6.3	7	5.6	7	4.9	7	4.2
8	12.8	8	12.0	8	7.2	8	6.4	8	5.6	8	4.8
9	14.4	9	13.5	9	8.1	9	7.2	9	6.3	9	5.4

45°–50°

USE OF TABLES IV AND V

EXAMPLE 1. Find sin 28° 40'.

Solution. On page 40, in the column headed **Ang. deg.**, we find 28°. Proceeding to the right into the column headed **40'**, we find the number 0.4797.
Hence
$$\sin 28° 40' = 0.4797. \; Ans.$$

EXAMPLE 2. Find sin 62° 46'.

Solution. The angle 62° 46' is not found exactly in the table. We must therefore use the process of *interpolation* as follows. On page 41 we find
$$\sin 62° 50' = 0.8897$$
and
$$\sin 62° 40' = 0.8884.$$

We see that an increase of 10' in the angle produces an increase of 0.0013 in the sine. If we assume that the increase in the sine is proportional to the increase in the angle, the increase in the sine corresponding to an increase of 6' is $0.6 \times 0.0013 = 0.00078$. This number is now "rounded off" to the accuracy of our table, that is, to four decimal places. Thus, we round off 0.00078 to 0.0008. Hence
$$\sin 62° 46' = 0.8884 + 0.0008 = 0.8892. \; Ans.$$

We must note at this point, however, that the increase in the sine of an angle is not exactly proportional to the increase in the angle. But since the change is small, our interpolation is sufficiently accurate.

EXAMPLE 3. Given sin $A = 0.8150$, find A.

Solution. On page 41 we find that 0.8150 lies between 0.8141 and 0.8158.
Also,
$$\sin 54° 40' = 0.8158$$
$$\underline{\sin 54° 30' = 0.8141}$$
$$10' \quad 0.0017$$

An increase of 0.0017 in the sine produces an increase of 10' in the angle. Hence an increase of $0.8150 - 0.8141$ or 0.0009 in the sine will produce an increase of $\frac{9}{17}$ of $10' = 5.3'$. A four-place table, however, gives the corresponding accuracy in the angle to the nearest minute only. Hence
$$A = 54° 30' + 5' = 54° 35'. \; Ans.$$

EXAMPLE 4. Given cos $A = 0.3362$, find A.

Solution. On page 40 we find
$$\cos 70° 30' = 0.3338$$
$$\underline{\cos 70° 20' = 0.3365}$$
$$10' \quad 0.0027$$

A decrease of 0.0027 in the cosine produces an increase of 10' in the angle. Hence the proportional part $\frac{3}{27}$ of 10', or 1', is added to the smaller angle.
Hence
$$A = 70° 21'. \; Ans.$$

Table V is used in a manner similar to that shown in the examples above, which illustrate the use of Table IV.

38

TABLES IV AND V *

In Table IV are given the natural values of the sine and cosine of angles from 0° to 90° at an interval of 10'. In Table V are given the natural values of the tangent and cotangent of angles from 0° to 90° at an interval of 10'.

Interpolation must be used for an acute angle not given exactly. The value found by interpolation may be in error by one in the last decimal place. In Table V, however, the error may be greater for the tangent of an angle exceeding 82°, or the cotangent of an angle less than 7°.

The values of the sine in Table IV show four significant figures for angles greater than 5° 44'. For angles less than 1° 31' the formula

(1) $\sin x° = $ **value of $x°$ in radians**

may be used to obtain four significant figures. For this purpose the equivalents

1 minute = 0.000290888 radian,

1 degree = 0.0174533 radian

are given. (See also page 17.) For angles from 1° 31' to 5° 44', inclusive, find the logarithm from Table II and the corresponding number by Table I.

The values of the cosine show four significant figures for angles less than 84° 16'. For angles exceeding 88° 29' find the value of the sine of the complementary angle by (1) above. For angles from 84° 16' to 88° 29', inclusive, use Tables II and I.

The values of the tangent in Table V show four significant figures for angles greater than 5° 42'. For angles less than 1° 11', the formula

(2) $\tan x° = $ **value of $x°$ in radians**

may be used to obtain four significant figures. For angles from 1° 11' to 5° 42', inclusive, use Tables II and I.

The values of the cotangent show four significant figures for angles less than 84° 18'. For angles exceeding 88° 49' find the value of the tangent of the complementary angle by (2). For angles from 84° 18' to 88° 49', inclusive, use Tables II and I.

* See Arts. 38 and 39 in *Plane Trigonometry* by Granville, Smith, and Mikesh (Ginn and Company).

Ang., deg.	Sine							
	0′	10′	20′	30′	40′	50′	60′	
0	0.0000	0.0029	0.0058	0.0087	0.0116	0.0145	0.0175	89
1	0.0175	0.0204	0.0233	0.0262	0.0291	0.0320	0.0349	88
2	0.0349	0.0378	0.0407	0.0436	0.0465	0.0494	0.0523	87
3	0.0523	0.0552	0.0581	0.0610	0.0640	0.0669	0.0698	86
4	0.0698	0.0727	0.0756	0.0785	0.0814	0.0843	0.0872	85
5	0.0872	0.0901	0.0929	0.0958	0.0987	0.1016	0.1045	84
6	0.1045	0.1074	0.1103	0.1132	0.1161	0.1190	0.1219	83
7	0.1219	0.1248	0.1276	0.1305	0.1334	0.1363	0.1392	82
8	0.1392	0.1421	0.1449	0.1478	0.1507	0.1536	0.1564	81
9	0.1564	0.1593	0.1622	0.1650	0.1679	0.1708	0.1736	80
10	0.1736	0.1765	0.1794	0.1822	0.1851	0.1880	0.1908	79
11	0.1908	0.1937	0.1965	0.1994	0.2022	0.2051	0.2079	78
12	0.2079	0.2108	0.2136	0.2164	0.2193	0.2221	0.2250	77
13	0.2250	0.2278	0.2306	0.2334	0.2363	0.2391	0.2419	76
14	0.2419	0.2447	0.2476	0.2504	0.2532	0.2560	0.2588	75
15	0.2588	0.2616	0.2644	0.2672	0.2700	0.2728	0.2756	74
16	0.2756	0.2784	0.2812	0.2840	0.2868	0.2896	0.2924	73
17	0.2924	0.2952	0.2979	0.3007	0.3035	0.3062	0.3090	72
18	0.3090	0.3118	0.3145	0.3173	0.3201	0.3228	0.3256	71
19	0.3256	0.3283	0.3311	0.3338	0.3365	0.3393	0.3420	70
20	0.3420	0.3448	0.3475	0.3502	0.3529	0.3557	0.3584	69
21	0.3584	0.3611	0.3638	0.3665	0.3692	0.3719	0.3746	68
22	0.3746	0.3773	0.3800	0.3827	0.3854	0.3881	0.3907	67
23	0.3907	0.3934	0.3961	0.3987	0.4014	0.4041	0.4067	66
24	0.4067	0.4094	0.4120	0.4147	0.4173	0.4200	0.4226	65
25	0.4226	0.4253	0.4279	0.4305	0.4331	0.4358	0.4384	64
26	0.4384	0.4410	0.4436	0.4462	0.4488	0.4514	0.4540	63
27	0.4540	0.4566	0.4592	0.4617	0.4643	0.4669	0.4695	62
28	0.4695	0.4720	0.4746	0.4772	0.4797	0.4823	0.4848	61
29	0.4848	0.4874	0.4899	0.4924	0.4950	0.4975	0.5000	60
30	0.5000	0.5025	0.5050	0.5075	0.5100	0.5125	0.5150	59
31	0.5150	0.5175	0.5200	0.5225	0.5250	0.5275	0.5299	58
32	0.5299	0.5324	0.5348	0.5373	0.5398	0.5422	0.5446	57
33	0.5446	0.5471	0.5495	0.5519	0.5544	0.5568	0.5592	56
34	0.5592	0.5616	0.5640	0.5664	0.5688	0.5712	0.5736	55
35	0.5736	0.5760	0.5783	0.5807	0.5831	0.5854	0.5878	54
36	0.5878	0.5901	0.5925	0.5948	0.5972	0.5995	0.6018	53
37	0.6018	0.6041	0.6065	0.6088	0.6111	0.6134	0.6157	52
38	0.6157	0.6180	0.6202	0.6225	0.6248	0.6271	0.6293	51
39	0.6293	0.6316	0.6338	0.6361	0.6383	0.6406	0.6428	50
40	0.6428	0.6450	0.6472	0.6494	0.6517	0.6539	0.6561	49
41	0.6561	0.6583	0.6604	0.6626	0.6648	0.6670	0.6691	48
42	0.6691	0.6713	0.6734	0.6756	0.6777	0.6799	0.6820	47
43	0.6820	0.6841	0.6862	0.6884	0.6905	0.6926	0.6947	46
44	0.6947	0.6967	0.6988	0.7009	0.7030	0.7050	0.7071	45
	60′	50′	40′	30′	20′	10′	0′	Ang., deg.
	Cosine							

TABLE IV. NATURAL SINES AND COSINES 41

Ang., deg.	Sine							
	0′	10′	20′	30′	40′	50′	60′	
45	0.7071	0.7092	0.7112	0.7133	0.7153	0.7173	0.7193	44
46	0.7193	0.7214	0.7234	0.7254	0.7274	0.7294	0.7314	43
47	0.7314	0.7333	0.7353	0.7373	0.7392	0.7412	0.7431	42
48	0.7431	0.7451	0.7470	0.7490	0.7509	0.7528	0.7547	41
49	0.7547	0.7566	0.7585	0.7604	0.7623	0.7642	0.7660	40
50	0.7660	0.7679	0.7698	0.7716	0.7735	0.7753	0.7771	39
51	0.7771	0.7790	0.7808	0.7826	0.7844	0.7862	0.7880	38
52	0.7880	0.7898	0.7916	0.7934	0.7951	0.7969	0.7986	37
53	0.7986	0.8004	0.8021	0.8039	0.8056	0.8073	0.8090	36
54	0.8090	0.8107	0.8124	0.8141	0.8158	0.8175	0.8192	35
55	0.8192	0.8208	0.8225	0.8241	0.8258	0.8274	0.8290	34
56	0.8290	0.8307	0.8323	0.8339	0.8355	0.8371	0.8387	33
57	0.8387	0.8403	0.8418	0.8434	0.8450	0.8465	0.8480	32
58	0.8480	0.8496	0.8511	0.8526	0.8542	0.8557	0.8572	31
59	0.8572	0.8587	0.8601	0.8616	0.8631	0.8646	0.8660	30
60	0.8660	0.8675	0.8689	0.8704	0.8718	0.8732	0.8746	29
61	0.8746	0.8760	0.8774	0.8788	0.8802	0.8816	0.8829	28
62	0.8829	0.8843	0.8857	0.8870	0.8884	0.8897	0.8910	27
63	0.8910	0.8923	0.8936	0.8949	0.8962	0.8975	0.8988	26
64	0.8988	0.9001	0.9013	0.9026	0.9038	0.9051	0.9063	25
65	0.9063	0.9075	0.9088	0.9100	0.9112	0.9124	0.9135	24
66	0.9135	0.9147	0.9159	0.9171	0.9182	0.9194	0.9205	23
67	0.9205	0.9216	0.9228	0.9239	0.9250	0.9261	0.9272	22
68	0.9272	0.9283	0.9293	0.9304	0.9315	0.9325	0.9336	21
69	0.9336	0.9346	0.9356	0.9367	0.9377	0.9387	0.9397	20
70	0.9397	0.9407	0.9417	0.9426	0.9436	0.9446	0.9455	19
71	0.9455	0.9465	0.9474	0.9483	0.9492	0.9502	0.9511	18
72	0.9511	0.9520	0.9528	0.9537	0.9546	0.9555	0.9563	17
73	0.9563	0.9572	0.9580	0.9588	0.9596	0.9605	0.9613	16
74	0.9613	0.9621	0.9628	0.9636	0.9644	0.9652	0.9659	15
75	0.9659	0.9667	0.9674	0.9681	0.9689	0.9696	0.9703	14
76	0.9703	0.9710	0.9717	0.9724	0.9730	0.9737	0.9744	13
77	0.9744	0.9750	0.9757	0.9763	0.9769	0.9775	0.9781	12
78	0.9781	0.9787	0.9793	0.9799	0.9805	0.9811	0.9816	11
79	0.9816	0.9822	0.9827	0.9833	0.9838	0.9843	0.9848	10
80	0.9848	0.9853	0.9858	0.9863	0.9868	0.9872	0.9877	9
81	0.9877	0.9881	0.9886	0.9890	0.9894	0.9899	0.9903	8
82	0.9903	0.9907	0.9911	0.9914	0.9918	0.9922	0.9925	7
83	0.9925	0.9929	0.9932	0.9936	0.9939	0.9942	0.9945	6
84	0.9945	0.9948	0.9951	0.9954	0.9957	0.9959	0.9962	5
85	0.9962	0.9964	0.9967	0.9969	0.9971	0.9974	0.9976	4
86	0.9976	0.9978	0.9980	0.9981	0.9983	0.9985	0.9986	3
87	0.9986	0.9988	0.9989	0.9990	0.9992	0.9993	0.9994	2
88	0.9994	0.9995	0.9996	0.9997	0.9997	0.9998	0.9998	1
89	0.9998	0.9999	0.9999	1.0000	1.0000	1.0000	1.0000	0
	60′	50′	40′	30′	20′	10′	0′	Ang., deg.
	Cosine							

Ang., deg.	Tangent							
	0′	10′	20′	30′	40′	50′	60′	
0	0.0000	0.0029	0.0058	0.0087	0.0116	0.0145	0.0175	89
1	0.0175	0.0204	0.0233	0.0262	0.0291	0.0320	0.0349	88
2	0.0349	0.0378	0.0407	0.0437	0.0466	0.0495	0.0524	87
3	0.0524	0.0553	0.0582	0.0612	0.0641	0.0670	0.0699	86
4	0.0699	0.0729	0.0758	0.0787	0.0816	0.0846	0.0875	85
5	0.0875	0.0904	0.0934	0.0963	0.0992	0.1022	0.1051	84
6	0.1051	0.1080	0.1110	0.1139	0.1169	0.1198	0.1228	83
7	0.1228	0.1257	0.1287	0.1317	0.1346	0.1376	0.1405	82
8	0.1405	0.1435	0.1465	0.1495	0.1524	0.1554	0.1584	81
9	0.1584	0.1614	0.1644	0.1673	0.1703	0.1733	0.1763	80
10	0.1763	0.1793	0.1823	0.1853	0.1883	0.1914	0.1944	79
11	0.1944	0.1974	0.2004	0.2035	0.2065	0.2095	0.2126	78
12	0.2126	0.2156	0.2186	0.2217	0.2247	0.2278	0.2309	77
13	0.2309	0.2339	0.2370	0.2401	0.2432	0.2462	0.2493	76
14	0.2493	0.2524	0.2555	0.2586	0.2617	0.2648	0.2679	75
15	0.2679	0.2711	0.2742	0.2773	0.2805	0.2836	0.2867	74
16	0.2867	0.2899	0.2931	0.2962	0.2994	0.3026	0.3057	73
17	0.3057	0.3089	0.3121	0.3153	0.3185	0.3217	0.3249	72
18	0.3249	0.3281	0.3314	0.3346	0.3378	0.3411	0.3443	71
19	0.3443	0.3476	0.3508	0.3541	0.3574	0.3607	0.3640	70
20	0.3640	0.3673	0.3706	0.3739	0.3772	0.3805	0.3839	69
21	0.3839	0.3872	0.3906	0.3939	0.3973	0.4006	0.4040	68
22	0.4040	0.4074	0.4108	0.4142	0.4176	0.4210	0.4245	67
23	0.4245	0.4279	0.4314	0.4348	0.4383	0.4417	0.4452	66
24	0.4452	0.4487	0.4522	0.4557	0.4592	0.4628	0.4663	65
25	0.4663	0.4699	0.4734	0.4770	0.4806	0.4841	0.4877	64
26	0.4877	0.4913	0.4950	0.4986	0.5022	0.5059	0.5095	63
27	0.5095	0.5132	0.5169	0.5206	0.5243	0.5280	0.5317	62
28	0.5317	0.5354	0.5392	0.5430	0.5467	0.5505	0.5543	61
29	0.5543	0.5581	0.5619	0.5658	0.5696	0.5735	0.5774	60
30	0.5774	0.5812	0.5851	0.5890	0.5930	0.5969	0.6009	59
31	0.6009	0.6048	0.6088	0.6128	0.6168	0.6208	0.6249	58
32	0.6249	0.6289	0.6330	0.6371	0.6412	0.6453	0.6494	57
33	0.6494	0.6536	0.6577	0.6619	0.6661	0.6703	0.6745	56
34	0.6745	0.6787	0.6830	0.6873	0.6916	0.6959	0.7002	55
35	0.7002	0.7046	0.7089	0.7133	0.7177	0.7221	0.7265	54
36	0.7265	0.7310	0.7355	0.7400	0.7445	0.7490	0.7536	53
37	0.7536	0.7581	0.7627	0.7673	0.7720	0.7766	0.7813	52
38	0.7813	0.7860	0.7907	0.7954	0.8002	0.8050	0.8098	51
39	0.8098	0.8146	0.8195	0.8243	0.8292	0.8342	0.8391	50
40	0.8391	0.8441	0.8491	0.8541	0.8591	0.8642	0.8693	49
41	0.8693	0.8744	0.8796	0.8847	0.8899	0.8952	0.9004	48
42	0.9004	0.9057	0.9110	0.9163	0.9217	0.9271	0.9325	47
43	0.9325	0.9380	0.9435	0.9490	0.9545	0.9601	0.9657	46
44	0.9657	0.9713	0.9770	0.9827	0.9884	0.9942	1.0000	45
	60′	50′	40′	30′	20′	10′	0′	Ang., deg.
	Cotangent							

TABLE V. NATURAL TANGENTS AND COTANGENTS 43

Ang., deg.	Tangent							
	0′	10′	20′	30′	40′	50′	60′	
45	1.000	1.006	1.012	1.018	1.024	1.030	1.036	44
46	1.036	1.042	1.048	1.054	1.060	1.066	1.072	43
47	1.072	1.079	1.085	1.091	1.098	1.104	1.111	42
48	1.111	1.117	1.124	1.130	1.137	1.144	1.150	41
49	1.150	1.157	1.164	1.171	1.178	1.185	1.192	40
50	1.192	1.199	1.206	1.213	1.220	1.228	1.235	39
51	1.235	1.242	1.250	1.257	1.265	1.272	1.280	38
52	1.280	1.288	1.295	1.303	1.311	1.319	1.327	37
53	1.327	1.335	1.343	1.351	1.360	1.368	1.376	36
54	1.376	1.385	1.393	1.402	1.411	1.419	1.428	35
55	1.428	1.437	1.446	1.455	1.464	1.473	1.483	34
56	1.483	1.492	1.501	1.511	1.520	1.530	1.540	33
57	1.540	1.550	1.560	1.570	1.580	1.590	1.600	32
58	1.600	1.611	1.621	1.632	1.643	1.653	1.664	31
59	1.664	1.675	1.686	1.698	1.709	1.720	1.732	30
60	1.732	1.744	1.756	1.767	1.780	1.792	1.804	29
61	1.804	1.816	1.829	1.842	1.855	1.868	1.881	28
62	1.881	1.894	1.907	1.921	1.935	1.949	1.963	27
63	1.963	1.977	1.991	2.006	2.020	2.035	2.050	26
64	2.050	2.066	2.081	2.097	2.112	2.128	2.145	25
65	2.145	2.161	2.177	2.194	2.211	2.229	2.246	24
66	2.246	2.264	2.282	2.300	2.318	2.337	2.356	23
67	2.356	2.375	2.394	2.414	2.434	2.455	2.475	22
68	2.475	2.496	2.517	2.539	2.560	2.583	2.605	21
69	2.605	2.628	2.651	2.675	2.699	2.723	2.747	20
70	2.747	2.773	2.798	2.824	2.850	2.877	2.904	19
71	2.904	2.932	2.960	2.989	3.018	3.047	3.078	18
72	3.078	3.108	3.140	3.172	3.204	3.237	3.271	17
73	3.271	3.305	3.340	3.376	3.412	3.450	3.487	16
74	3.487	3.526	3.566	3.606	3.647	3.689	3.732	15
75	3.732	3.776	3.821	3.867	3.914	3.962	4.011	14
76	4.011	4.061	4.113	4.165	4.219	4.275	4.331	13
77	4.331	4.390	4.449	4.511	4.574	4.638	4.705	12
78	4.705	4.773	4.843	4.915	4.989	5.066	5.145	11
79	5.145	5.226	5.309	5.396	5.485	5.576	5.671	10
80	5.671	5.769	5.871	5.976	6.084	6.197	6.314	9
81	6.314	6.435	6.561	6.691	6.827	6.968	7.115	8
82*	7.115	7.269	7.429	7.596	7.770	7.953	8.144	7*
83*	8.144	8.345	8.556	8.777	9.010	9.255	9.514	6*
84*	9.514	9.788	10.08	10.39	10.71	11.06	11.43	5*
85*	11.43	11.83	12.25	12.71	13.20	13.73	14.30	4*
86*	14.30	14.92	15.60	16.35	17.17	18.07	19.08	3*
87*	19.08	20.21	21.47	22.90	24.54	26.43	28.64	2*
88*	28.64	31.24	34.37	38.19	42.96	49.10	57.29	1*
89*	57.29	68.75	85.94	114.6	171.9	343.8	∞	0*
	60′	50′	40′	30′	20′	10′	0′	Ang., deg.
	Cotangent							

* Do not interpolate.